Kripke's *Wittgenstein on Rules and Private Language* at 40

Saul Kripke's *Wittgenstein on Rules and Private Language* is one of the most celebrated and important books in philosophy of language and mind of the past forty years. It generated an avalanche of responses from the moment it was published and has revolutionized the way in which we think about meaning, intentionality, and the work of Ludwig Wittgenstein. It introduced a series of questions that had never been raised before concerning, most prominently, the normativity of meaning and the prospects for a reductionist account of meaning. This volume of new essays reassesses the continuing influence of Kripke's book and demonstrates that many of the issues first raised by Kripke, both exegetical and philosophical, remain as thought-provoking and as relevant as they were when he first introduced them.

Claudine Verheggen is Professor of Philosophy at York University, Toronto. She is the coauthor (with Robert Myers) of *Donald Davidson's Triangulation Argument: A Philosophical Inquiry* (2016) and the editor of *Wittgenstein and Davidson on Language, Thought, and Action* (Cambridge University Press, 2017).

Cambridge Philosophical Anniversaries

The volumes in this series reflect on classic philosophy books from the second half of the twentieth century, assessing their achievements, their influence on the field, and their lasting significance.

Titles Published in This Series

Kripke's *Wittgenstein on Rules and Private Language* at 40
Edited by Claudine Verheggen

Kuhn's *The Structure of Scientific Revolutions* at 60
Edited by K. Brad Wray

MacIntyre's *After Virtue* at 40
Edited by Tom Angier

Rawls's *A Theory of Justice* at 50
Edited by Paul Weithman

Cavell's *Must We Mean What We Say?* at 50
Edited by Greg Chase, Juliet Floyd, and Sandra Laugier

This list can also be seen at www.cambridge.org/cpa

Kripke's *Wittgenstein on Rules and Private Language* at 40

Edited by
Claudine Verheggen
York University, Toronto

CAMBRIDGE
UNIVERSITY PRESS

Shaftesbury Road, Cambridge CB2 8EA, United Kingdom

One Liberty Plaza, 20th Floor, New York, NY 10006, USA

477 Williamstown Road, Port Melbourne, VIC 3207, Australia

314–321, 3rd Floor, Plot 3, Splendor Forum, Jasola District Centre, New Delhi – 110025, India

103 Penang Road, #05–06/07, Visioncrest Commercial, Singapore 238467

Cambridge University Press is part of Cambridge University Press & Assessment, a department of the University of Cambridge.

We share the University's mission to contribute to society through the pursuit of education, learning and research at the highest international levels of excellence.

www.cambridge.org
Information on this title: www.cambridge.org/9781009096881

DOI: 10.1017/9781009099103

© Cambridge University Press & Assessment 2024

This publication is in copyright. Subject to statutory exception and to the provisions of relevant collective licensing agreements, no reproduction of any part may take place without the written permission of Cambridge University Press & Assessment.

First published 2024
First paperback edition 2025

A catalogue record for this publication is available from the British Library

ISBN 978-1-009-09821-2 Hardback
ISBN 978-1-009-09688-1 Paperback

Cambridge University Press & Assessment has no responsibility for the persistence or accuracy of URLs for external or third-party internet websites referred to in this publication and does not guarantee that any content on such websites is, or will remain, accurate or appropriate.

In memory of Barry Stroud

Contents

List of Contributors		*page* ix
Acknowledgments		x
	Introduction CLAUDINE VERHEGGEN	1
1	Kripke's Wittgenstein's Skepticism about Rules and Meaning: In Defense of the Standard Interpretation ALEXANDER MILLER	14
2	Putting Wittgenstein Back into Kripkenstein: Meaning Skepticism and Knowing How to Go On HANNAH GINSBORG	35
3	Answering Kripke's Skeptic: Dispositions without 'Dispositionalism' HENRY JACKMAN	55
4	Wittgensteinean Notions of Uniformity and Kripkensteinean Skepticism JAMES R. SHAW	69
5	Wittgenstein's Naturalism and the Skeptical Paradox MARIE McGINN	87
6	Kripke and Wittgenstein on Rules and Meaning GARY EBBS	107
7	Semantic Normativity, Properly So Called DANIEL WHITING	124
8	What Is the Skeptical Problem? Wittgenstein's Response to Kripke CLAUDINE VERHEGGEN	142

9	How Not to Brush Questions under the Rug OLIVIA SULTANESCU	163
10	Quadders and Zombies: A Kripkean Argument against Physicalism ANANDI HATTIANGADI	181
11	Communitarianism, Interpersonalism, and Individualism in Kripke's "Skeptical Solution" CHRISTOPHER CAMPBELL	201
12	"Considered in Isolation" ARIF AHMED	220
13	The Meaning of Meaning Ascriptions: Assertibility Conditions and Meaning Facts JOSÉ L. ZALABARDO	238

Bibliography 259
Index 274

Contributors

ARIF AHMED *University of Cambridge*

CHRISTOPHER CAMPBELL *York University, Toronto*

GARY EBBS *Indiana University Bloomington*

HANNAH GINSBORG *University of California, Berkeley*

ANANDI HATTIANGADI *Stockholm University*

HENRY JACKMAN *York University, Toronto*

MARIE McGINN *University of York, York*

ALEXANDER MILLER *University of Otago*

JAMES R. SHAW *University of Pittsburgh*

OLIVIA SULTANESCU *Concordia University*

CLAUDINE VERHEGGEN *York University, Toronto*

DANIEL WHITING *University of Southampton*

JOSÉ L. ZALABARDO *University College London*

Acknowledgments

I am very grateful to the authors for their contributions to this volume, all of which demonstrate that Kripke, in the spirit of Wittgenstein, continues to provoke new thought-provoking thoughts. I also want to thank the participants in a workshop on Kripke's *Wittgenstein on Rules and Private Language* at 40, which I organized at York University, Toronto, in June 2022, and the Department of Philosophy for sponsoring it. Preparation of the volume was made possible in part by a Research Leader Release from the Faculty of Liberal Arts and Professional Studies at York University and a Small Research Grant from York University. Thanks are also due to my editor, Hilary Gaskin, for first encouraging me to put together this volume for the Cambridge Philosophical Anniversaries series and for her support throughout the whole process. Finally, I am grateful to Nathan Malcomson, Robert Myers, and Olivia Sultanescu for their help with the preparation of the volume.

I dedicate this book to the memory of Barry Stroud, who taught me much about Wittgenstein and philosophy, and who, I think, even though (or perhaps because) he often disagreed with Kripke's interpretation of Wittgenstein, would have found this book congenial, as it fulfills Wittgenstein's (and, I think, Kripke's) goal not to spare people the trouble of thinking but to stimulate them to thoughts of their own. I am sorry that neither he nor Kripke lived to see it.

Introduction

Claudine Verheggen

Four decades ago, a book came out that was going to revolutionize the ways in which we think philosophically about meaning and, more generally, about intentionality, as well as the ways in which we think about the book's inspiration, namely, the later writings of Ludwig Wittgenstein. This book, Saul Kripke's *Wittgenstein on Rules and Private Language* (WRPL hereafter),[1] has caused, and continues to cause, almost as much ink to be spilt as its precursor, *Philosophical Investigations* (PI hereafter), did and continues to do. Indeed, interest in the latter was significantly revived with the publication of the former. The fortieth anniversary of Kripke's book is obviously a reason to celebrate it anew and to reflect on what it has accomplished. The purpose of this volume is to do just that. It is intended to demonstrate that many of the issues first raised by Kripke, both exegetical and philosophical, are alive and well, indeed, that, though they have evolved, they remain as unresolved as they were when Kripke first introduced them.

Kripke presented a highly original way of interpreting Wittgenstein's writings on meaning and rule-following and an utterly new skeptical problem, which he took to be embodied in the rule-following paradox Wittgenstein expresses in section 201 of PI: "this was our paradox: no course of action could be determined by a rule, because every course of action can be made to accord with the rule." Following Wittgenstein, Kripke developed the problem with a mathematical example, but it applies to all linguistic expressions. Briefly put, the problem is this. Suppose that I have so far computed only numbers that are smaller than 57, and suppose that I encounter a "bizarre" skeptic who questions my confidence that the answer to "68 + 57?" should be "125" rather than, say, "5." What makes me so sure, the skeptic asks, that in the past I used '+' to mean plus rather than quus, where quus is defined as a function that yields the sum for arguments less than 57, but yields the value 5

---

[1] The book first appeared in 1982, but an earlier version was published in Block (1981).

otherwise? After all, "in the past, I gave myself only a finite number of examples instantiating this function" (WRPL: 8), all of which are compatible with its being either function that I meant. Similarly, suppose that I encounter a skeptic who questions my confidence that I should apply the word 'table' to the table I see for the first time at the base of the Eiffel Tower. What makes me so sure, the skeptic asks, that in the past I used 'table' to mean table rather than tabair, where 'tabair' is defined as "anything that is a table not found at the base of the Eiffel Tower, or a chair found there?" After all, I presumably did not "think explicitly of the Eiffel Tower when I first 'grasped the concept of' a table, gave myself directions for what I meant by 'table'" (WRPL: 19). Kripke summarized the problem as a two-fold skeptical challenge: first, to give an account of the facts about an individual that constitute her meaning what she does by her expressions; second, to show how these facts justify her in applying the expressions in the way she does. He then argued that this twofold challenge cannot be met, leaving us with the skeptical conclusion that "there can be no such thing as meaning anything by any word" (WRPL: 55). Still, Kripke, allegedly following Wittgenstein, did not leave things at that. Accordingly, his next step was to give the skeptical problem a skeptical solution, on the model of Hume's skeptical solution to his own skeptical doubts about induction. The idea was to concede that the facts the skeptic is seeking could not be found – finding them would be to provide a "straight" solution to the problem – while maintaining that an alternative way of explaining our ascriptions of meaning to language users' utterances could be developed. The key was to replace the "picture of language" based on truth conditions with one based on assertibility conditions (WRPL: 74).

Though Kripke's book importantly contributed to making the remarks surrounding the expression of the paradox, which became known as "the rule-following considerations," the centerpiece of PI, the first wave of reactions to the book was, by and large, intensely antagonistic. For they were focused on Kripke's interpretation of Wittgenstein,[2] and this interpretation was almost unanimously rejected. In particular, most commentators thought that attributing to Wittgenstein a skeptical problem that needs to be solved was a gross misrepresentation of what Wittgenstein was doing. And, in so far as the paradox is uncontestably present in Wittgenstein's book, they maintained that Wittgenstein meant

---

[2] Kripke himself did not contend that his interpretation is accurate, nor did he endorse the views he developed. For these reasons, they are often attributed to "Kripke's Wittgenstein" or "Kripkenstein." I shall stick with "Kripke," simply referring to the author of the book.

to dissolve rather than solve it, that is, that he meant to show that it is based on a mistaken assumption, as his remarks immediately following the expression of the paradox, which they accused Kripke of neglecting, make explicit.

However, very soon, a second wave of reactions was to take over. Wittgenstein was relegated to the background, and philosophers concentrated on the problem Kripke had developed and on its solution. Whether or not it was Wittgenstein's problem, many thought that it was a problem that could not simply be dismissed. Two main foci of interest soon emerged from Kripke's twofold skeptical challenge. On the one hand, much effort was devoted to finding meaning-constituting facts that would satisfy the skeptic. In particular, much effort was devoted to trying to rescue dispositional facts, which, though largely ignored by Wittgenstein, were the main target of Kripke's skeptic. This is to say, more generally, that much effort was devoted to preserving a reductive, naturalistic account of meaning. Of course, those who pursued this task paid no attention to Kripke's own skeptical solution, as it is based on conceding that there are no meaning-constituting facts of the sort sought by the skeptic. On the other hand, much effort was devoted to clarifying the second part of the challenge and to determining the exact threat it poses to dispositionalism, which Kripke had taken to be defeated by it. For, intimately connected with the second part of the challenge, is the question whether meaning is essentially normative. And it was generally thought that a positive answer to this question could not be reconciled with a reductive account of meaning. Alongside these two broad themes, that of reductionism and that of normativity, there was also always the question whether Kripke had succeeded in ruling out the possibility, not just of a private language, but of a solitary one, as most took him to have attempted to do.

The contributions to the present volume could be regarded as part of a third wave of reactions to Kripke's book. This wave is more difficult to characterize than the first two, rough though my description of them might be, for the reactions have become increasingly richer, more varied, and more complex. But there are two elements that strike me as especially significant.

First, though reductionist responses to the skeptical problem continue to be offered, Kripke's book is more and more inspiring philosophers to do constructive work that is non-reductionist and which, therefore, though it does not attempt to give an account of the nature of meaning in terms that do not presuppose it, is still intended to illuminate it philosophically. Relatedly, more philosophers also attempt to shed new light on Kripke's skeptical solution, which was initially rather neglected.

Second, in their endeavor to address Kripke's skeptical problem, more and more philosophers return to Wittgenstein's writings to see if a solution could not be found there, whether or not they think that Kripke's problem was also Wittgenstein's. Indeed, some return to Wittgenstein to get clearer about Kripke's skeptical problem to begin with. Of course, some philosophers continue to argue that Kripke got Wittgenstein wrong in many respects. But even this is a positive stance, as it allows them to appreciate better both Kripke's and Wittgenstein's accomplishments.

All of the above themes are covered in the present volume, which starts with two strikingly different takes on Kripke's skeptical problem. Alexander Miller defends the standard interpretation of the skeptical argument, according to which the epistemological considerations invoked to reach the metaphysical conclusion that there are no meaning-constituting facts are a mere "dramatic device," not essential to reaching this conclusion. Miller defends this interpretation against Hannah Ginsborg's objections to it, as well as against her alternative interpretation, according to which the epistemological considerations constitute an indispensable "sub-argument in an overall argument to a metaphysical conclusion." Thus, he argues, contra Ginsborg, first that the answer the standard interpretation invites, that is, a non-reductionist answer, is not the "too easy" answer that she claims it to be. For, as he sees it, following Crispin Wright, this answer must accommodate "the intuitive first-person epistemology of meaning and intention," as well as "what Wright calls their 'disposition-like theoreticity'." Second, Miller argues, the standard interpretation does not make the argument depend on a "general and objectionable form of verificationism." Third, nothing distinctively philosophical is lost by reading the argument in a way that makes the skeptic dispensable. Miller further argues that the first of these objections applies to Ginsborg's own reading of the argument, and that the standard reading of the argument also better fits Kripke's text. Finally, according to Miller, Ginsborg's answer to her own version of the challenge, an answer which appeals to the notion of "primitive normativity," according to which the present use of an expression can be seen as conforming to a past use independently of what, if anything, was meant by the expression previously, does not succeed. Neither does it succeed in addressing the standard version of the challenge.

Hannah Ginsborg defends a reading of the skeptical problem that is different from the standard reading in three respects. According to the standard reading, first, the skeptical problem should be understood independently of Wittgenstein's remarks on meaning and rule-following. Second (as discussed in Miller's Chapter 1), the problem is fundamentally metaphysical rather than epistemological, arising from the difficulty of providing the skeptic with meaning-constituting facts. Third, "the very first move in the skeptical dialectic," in which a skeptic challenges me to justify the answer I give in response to a mathematical problem, "is not essential to the argument." Against this reading, Ginsborg argues that the skeptical conclusion that there is no such thing as meaning follows from my inability to know, not what I previously meant by an expression, but that the answer I now give is the correct one, in that it conforms to my previous uses. To make her case, Ginsborg appeals to Wittgenstein's discussion of "knowing how to go on," which she takes to be the "inspiration for Kripke's skeptical argument." According to Wittgenstein, she argues, if I do not know that I should say "1002" after "1000" when being ordered "+2," then I do not understand '+2'. Similarly, she continues, the skeptic's first move is to challenge my confidence that my answer is "metalinguistically correct," that is, that I am using '+' correctly given how I used it, or intended to use it, in the past, that I am "going on correctly from previous uses of '+'." If I cannot meet the challenge, I do not understand the expression. And if I do not understand it, I do not mean anything by it. Thus, for Ginsborg, the source of the skeptical problem is essentially epistemological, making her reading "closer to Kripke's own intentions," and yielding a "stronger and more distinctive argument against the possibility of meaning." In particular, it does not face the often-heard objection that the argument rests on an "unargued reductionism." However, according to Ginsborg, I can know how to go on from my previous uses even though I have no knowledge of their meaning. If this is right, she concludes, the skeptic can be answered without providing an account of what meaning consists in.

Henry Jackman considers anew Kripke's criticism of the dispositionalist answer to the skeptic's challenge. He believes that, once properly understood, the answer can address Kripke's objections to dispositionalism. The key is to distinguish the initial "naïve" dispositionalist answer from the dispositionalist view Kripke has in mind. The naïve answer to the skeptic who challenges me to find a fact about me that entitles me to claim that I meant plus rather than quus by '+' in the past is simply that, even if I have never added the numbers I am now asked to add, had I been asked to add them, I would have responded with their sum, and not their quum, which entitles me to say that I did mean plus rather than quus. Kripke's mistake, according to Jackman, is to think of the dispositionalist theory as an atomistic use-based theory, according to which the meanings of particular words are tied to particular dispositions. This is in contrast with the naïve view, which should be seen as a holistic use-based theory, where meaning is understood in terms of, for example, the notion of radical interpretation (familiar from Donald Davidson and

David Lewis). So understood, the naïve view can address Kripke's objection that dispositionalism is incompatible with the fact that we can be disposed to make mistakes, as well as his objection that it cannot make room for the idea that our applications of words are justified, and even what Jackman takes to be Kripke's most serious objection, namely, that it ignores the fact that our dispositions are finite.

James Shaw is among those who do not think that Wittgenstein ever engaged with semantic skepticism. Yet, he thinks that an answer to the skeptic can be extracted from his writings by appealing to "notions of uniformity" such as "regularity, constancy, and (qualitative) sameness," which Wittgenstein employs when he addresses foundational semantic questions, which are, for Wittgenstein, metalinguistic questions such as "how do we use the word 'meaning'?." Focusing on the notion of regularity, which Shaw thinks has a "distinctive power" against Kripke's skeptical considerations, Shaw argues that, for Wittgenstein, "regularity of use is something that sometimes helps 'constitute' the presence of meanings." Thus, using the notion of regularity, we have a straightforward, "naïve" (obviously to be distinguished from Jackman's) reply to the metaphysical side of skepticism (Shaw is not concerned to address the normative side). In a nutshell, I meant addition rather than quaddition by '+' because "addition is the most regular and uniform continuation of the core, good applications" I and other calculators have made. Regularity is one of the factors that influence our meaning-ascriptions, how we use the term 'meaning'. Contra David Lewis, however, who proposed a similar answer, according to Shaw, Wittgenstein's notions of uniformity are just "ordinary, intuitive concepts," which, Shaw thinks, Kripke would approve of. Shaw considers several objections that might be thought to appear in Kripke's text, but he argues that they in fact have no force against the naïve reply, a reply, Shaw concludes, Kripke never considers. Importantly, Shaw stresses that "notions of uniformity plainly state non-semantic facts," as they should, according to Shaw, as "we are supposed to answer the skeptic with non-semantic facts to ground the semantic ones, lest we lapse into a form of semantic primitivism."

Marie McGinn reassesses Kripke's interpretation of Wittgenstein, in particular, of what Kripke takes to be the connection between Wittgenstein's naturalism and the paradox he expresses in section 201 of PI, and of the kind of naturalism Kripke ends up attributing to Wittgenstein. Kripke is right, she thinks, to emphasize what she calls the "methodological" component of Wittgenstein's naturalism, according to which attention must be paid to the circumstances in which ascriptions of meaning to language users' utterances are justified, and the mental states that may accompany their use of expressions are irrelevant to these ascriptions. And Kripke is also right, she thinks, to emphasize what she calls the "ontological" component of Wittgenstein's naturalism, which gives a central place to the "natural history of human beings," in particular, their "agreement in ungrounded ways of acting" which is "sustained by nothing more than natural facts," and the ways in which their language use is woven into other human activities. According to McGinn, however, Kripke is wrong in maintaining that Wittgenstein's naturalism is involved in a skeptical solution to a skeptical problem, leaving no room for norms and being "inevitably" reductionist. Drawing on remarks Wittgenstein makes in *Philosophical Grammar* and *The Blue and Brown Books*, she argues, contra Kripke, that Wittgenstein's naturalism is not a response to the skepticism that may seem to arise from a mentalistic conception of meaning, where meanings, or interpretations, are regarded as intermediaries between signs and their applications. Rather, "a pressure towards the mentalistic conception" should be seen as arising within the naturalistic approach. The search for intermediaries that accompany our use of signs then leads to the paradox, but this in turn is overcome by Wittgenstein's appeal to naturalism, which should be understood as neither reductionist nor problematically quietist, as "no question about the nature of normativity that should be answered ... remains unanswered."

Gary Ebbs focuses on the second part of the skeptical challenge, according to which, to put it in the terms of Kripke's that Ebbs focuses on, any putative candidate for a meaning-constituting fact "must, in some sense, show how I am justified in giving the answer '125' to '68 + 57'. The 'directions' [I previously gave myself], ... that determine what I should do in each instance, must somehow be 'contained' in any candidate for the fact as to what I meant" (WRPL: 11). Ebbs offers an interpretation of this condition that differs from the more widespread interpretation, which construes the condition as implying that meaning is in some sense categorically normative. Ebbs's interpretation helps him to make sense of "Kripke's sketches of our ordinary view of meaning" and to explain why Kripke does not question or revise it despite its skeptical consequences. According to Ebbs, Kripke's condition is to be understood as the following requirement for being warranted in asserting a sentence. One is warranted in asserting a sentence only if the truth-conditions of this sentence are determined by the meanings of the words in it, which are in turn determined by facts that are conceptually prior to and independent of one's assertion of the sentence, and which constitute one's grasp of the truth-conditions of that sentence. This requirement, Ebbs argues, is what entails Kripke's criticisms of all the attempts to answer the skeptic he considers, in particular, his criticism of dispositional accounts of meaning, his criticism of the view that meaning something by a term is a primitive mental state of a special kind, and his criticism of Wittgenstein's descriptions of our meaning-ascribing and rule-following practices. All these responses "fail to show that [Kripke's] requirement is satisfied." Ebbs ends with a Wittgensteinian critique of Kripke's requirement.

Daniel Whiting, too, focuses on the second part of the skeptical challenge, stressing Kripke's description of it as the "fundamental requirement" on a fact as to what I mean, namely, that it "*justify* my future actions, ... make them *inevitable* if I wish to use words with the same meaning with which I used them before" (WRPL: 40). As I indicated earlier, this requirement is supposed to capture the normativity of meaning, the idea that the "relation of meaning and intention to future action is *normative*, not *descriptive*" (WRPL: 37). Whiting's goal is not to assess the claim that semantic skepticism follows from there being no fact that could satisfy this requirement. Nor is it even to defend the claim that meaning is normative. Rather, it is to get clear about what the normativity of meaning amounts to, so as to put us in a better position to evaluate the skeptical argument. Against some recent critics, viz., Alan Millar and Indrek Reiland, Whiting defends the "standard or orthodox" interpretation of the claim that meaning is normative: "If meaning is normative, it is normative in the sense that there are norms of truth governing the applications of expressions (in assertion) that hold in virtue of the meanings of those expressions." That is, norms of meaning are to be understood in terms of norms of truth. Whiting argues that recent attempts at replacing the orthodox interpretation are either "unmotivated" or not "genuine competitors." While doing this, he also makes clear that the orthodox interpretation leaves room for other norms governing the use of expressions, such as norms that concern the doxastic, epistemic, and motivational states of agents. But these norms should be viewed as "explanatorily posterior to the norm of truth."

The next three contributors examine the prospects for a non-reductionist account of meaning. Claudine Verheggen does this by revisiting Wittgenstein's PI in light of Kripke's WRPL. Though she thinks that Kripke's reading of what leads Wittgenstein to the rule-following paradox is faithful to Wittgenstein in many respects, she agrees, contra Kripke, with the most widespread interpretation of PI, according to which Wittgenstein dissolves the skeptical problem embodied in the paradox rather than providing it with a skeptical solution. However, Kripke's writings have suggested to her anew that Wittgenstein, though a non-reductionist, was not a quietist about meaning, that is, did not maintain that nothing philosophically constructive could be said about it. She, in fact, takes "the quietist and Kripke to have much in common."

For, though they both conceive of the skeptical challenge as a meta-semantical challenge, calling for a foundational account of meaning, they both end up with "purely semantic, descriptive remarks about meaning." Of course, the quietist and Kripke follow a different path to reach these remarks. The quietist argues that the skeptical challenge is fundamentally misguided, and hence rejects the skeptical problem and its ensuing skeptical conclusion. Kripke argues that the challenge is legitimate but cannot be met, hence the skeptical problem and conclusion. Verheggen then argues that, failing to share his diagnosis of the paradox with Wittgenstein, Kripke does not recognize that, once the skeptical problem is dissolved, a new meta-semantical challenge arises, which is connected to the essential link Wittgenstein emphasizes between meaning and use, and which is the problem of "reconciling this link with the claim that meaning is objective, and thus presumably, in some sense, independent of use." As a result, she further argues, Kripke does not see that the positive remarks Wittgenstein makes after dismissing the paradox are meant to do some constructive, not just descriptive, work, in response to the problem newly arisen. "In particular, he does not see that the notion of agreement plays an important meta-semantic role in Wittgenstein's remarks, rather than being a brute notion about which nothing can be said."

Olivia Sultanescu, too, advocates non-reductionism as a response to Kripke's skeptic, and she, too, thinks that non-reductionism does not preclude philosophically constructive work about meaning, contra some non-reductionists such as Paul Boghossian and Crispin Wright. Though, they argue, the proponent of non-reductionism can make sense of the idea that an agent has a particular rule in mind, she cannot make sense of the idea that the agent is *following* a rule. As Sultanescu sees it, the pessimism expressed here is in fact aligned with Kripke's diagnosis of the non-reductionist proposal, which, he says, "brushes ... questions under the rug" (WRPL). However, she argues, if non-reductionism is understood properly, it is capable of meeting Kripke's challenge "in all its complexity." Sultanescu's first step is to get clear about why exactly Kripke thinks that the non-reductionist cannot meet the challenge. According to her, the central problem, as Kripke sees it, is that postulating sui generis "primitive" states of meaning leaves the nature of the states "mysterious." What many commentators do not recognize, she continues, is that the problem is not just about the "nature of meaning states" but also about the "nature of meaningful uses," that is, not just about the "internalization of the rule" but also about "its application in a new case." The problem is to reconcile the idea that, when I apply a rule, the application is somehow present in my mind, since "internalizing the rule just is internalizing something that covers indefinitely many cases," with the idea that the relevant application is not yet present in my mind, as I have to apply the rule to a new particular case. In response, Sultanescu argues that the question of what it is to follow a rule in a certain way, what it is to come to apply an expression to a new case, can be answered by providing an inferential justification: "to work out one's response is simply to infer what the rule requires in a particular case and act accordingly." Sultanescu then considers Wright's objection to this "naïve" answer, an objection which concludes that "one cannot be said to be guided by rules – or, more generally, to be acting for reasons – in one's uses of basic expressions." The key element of her reply is that one is led to this conclusion by a conception of guidance that the non-reductionist need not accept. However, the whole range of theoretical options will become visible to the non-reductionist only if she ceases conceiving of herself as merely positing meaning states and allows that she can elucidate meaning by appealing to the notion of meaningful use, thus conducting her inquiry from "inside" meaning and understanding, and not from a point of view that presupposes neither. Then the non-reductionist can argue that "in basic cases, the justification for the application of a rule can only be given from 'inside' a commitment to that rule." Sultanescu ends by suggesting a foundational account of the determination of the contents of thoughts that shows how thoughts stand in internal relations, as they must if the naïve answer is right.

Anandi Hattiangadi defends a version of non-reductionism that she calls "semantic dualism." She acknowledges that her position goes against the conclusion of the skeptical argument. Yet, it is inspired by Kripke's WRPL (together with his *Naming and Necessity*), which, she argues, "contains the resources for a powerful argument against the physicalist thesis that meanings and contents exist but are in some sense 'nothing over and above' the physical," the thesis, that is, that "intentional facts supervene on the physical with metaphysical necessity," where supervenience is weakly understood as this: "for any metaphysically possible world, w, if w is a minimal physical duplicate of the actual world, a, then w is an intentional duplicate of a." As it targets supervenience, the argument is against both reductive and non-reductive forms of physicalism. And it turns on the metaphysical possibility of deviant worlds: "minimal physical duplicates of our world which differ from it in some semantic or intentional respects," thus worlds which contain either quadders, where quadders are minimal physical duplicates of us who mean quaddition rather than addition by '+', or zombies, where zombies are minimal physical duplicates of us who lack intentional states. Hattiangadi argues, against the reductive physicalist, that deviant worlds are conceivable, using "considerations Kripke raises in WRPL concerning the essential natures of meanings and contents." Specifically, she uses two of Kripke's "insights" into this nature. One is that meanings and contents are general, transcending the physical facts about use. The other is that meanings and contents are "weakly normative," essentially giving rise to "standards of use whose normative authority is not absolute or objective, but relative to and dependent on the intentional states of some agent or agents." Exploiting the same insights as well as Kripke's remarks about essence in *Naming and Necessity*, she then argues against the non-reductive physicalist that deviant worlds are not only conceivable but also possible. She ends by indicating how Kripke's two insights might cast doubt on David Lewis's reductive program and Davidson's non-reductive program for naturalizing meaning and intentionality. Hence, she concludes, supervenience is false; dualism is supported, and intentionality is revealed to be no more mysterious from this perspective than from the perspective of physicalism.

The next three contributors reassess Kripke's skeptical solution. Christopher Campbell argues against the received view of the skeptical solution, which has been described as "communitarian." He does so by first distinguishing two questions concerning the sense in which language might be social. First, there is the "constitutive question" (properly construed in terms of Kripke's framework), which asks whether one can "(at least in principle) become a language-user i) on one's own, ii) only through interaction with other individuals, or iii) only in virtue of one's membership in an entire community, where this transcends, in some way, mere individual interaction." He calls the respective answers "constitutive individualism," "constitutive interpersonalism," and "constitutive communitarianism." The second question, that of "agreement of meaning," asks whether the meanings with which one uses one's words "i) (sometimes, often, or always) differ from those with which the people with whom one has interacted use them, or must they coincide either ii) with those, or iii) with those of one's community as a whole?" He calls the respective answers "meaning-individualism," "meaning-interpersonalism," and "meaning-communitarianism." Campbell argues that the skeptical solution may be regarded as giving an interpersonalist, rather than communitarian, answer to the constitutive question. This, he argues, is warranted by a close examination of Kripke's references to "the community." And, he further argues, the skeptical solution is compatible with meaning-individualism. These answers are much in line with a Davidsonian account of meaning, though, he makes clear, whereas Davidson's account is not skeptical, Kripke's skeptical solution does remain skeptical. Campbell ends by suggesting, however, that Wittgenstein's remarks might support a version of constitutive communitarianism, and that it, too, is compatible with meaning-individualism. On this view, Wittgenstein's appeal to the notions of customs, institutions, and practices explains how we acquire "conceptuality in general, or language itself." That is, it explains how we acquire the practice of using words meaningfully, not how our words acquire specific meanings, hence the lack of tension between constitutive communitarianism and meaning-individualism.

Arif Ahmed defends the "fictionalist" reading of Kripke's skeptical solution, according to which, since there are no facts about what anyone means by their words, all meaning-ascriptions are false. But this does not entail communitarianism, Ahmed argues. For false meaning-ascriptions might still be useful, even "when made by, or applied to, or addressed by, an individual 'considered in isolation'." Ahmed argues that the apparent inconsistency between saying that Jones does not mean addition by '+' and saying that "Jones means addition by '+'" can be appropriately asserted can be resolved by acknowledging that sometimes "it is appropriate to assert (and to assert the truth of) things that you know are false." That is, sometimes it is appropriate to assert false things "that have true consequences about what matters to you or your audience at the time." Thus it is appropriate for someone to tell me that Jones means addition by '+' as it follows from this that if I ask Jones "What is 68 + 57?" he will answer "125," which might be useful for me to know. As Ahmed sees it, just as it might be useful to me to be told by a third party that Jones means addition by '+', so my ascribing meanings to the words of a solitaire, such as a congenital Crusoe, might be useful to you. And Crusoe's ascriptions of meaning to his own past self might be useful to his own future self, and to others. So might his ascriptions of meaning to his own present self. Ahmed ends by responding to an objection that has been made by Miller, according to which a solitaire cannot distinguish between what is right and what seems right to him, a distinction which is required for the "propriety of meaning-talk." There is a sense, Ahmed argues, in which the distinction is available to the solitaire, and which is "sufficient to ground the propriety of meaning-talk ... If he can later see his own present self from the perspective of his future self, the seems/is right distinction is perfectly recoverable from Crusoe's situation."

José Zalabardo develops an account of meaning that rejects the skeptical conclusion that there is no fact of the matter as to what one means by an expression. According to his "compatibilist" account, which follows Crispin Wright's, specifying the ground of a sentence – the fact that it has the meaning it has – in terms of its assertibility conditions "is compatible with the idea that there is a state of affairs that the sentence represents as obtaining." This opens the way for being at once an assertibilist and a factualist about meaning. According to Zalabardo, compatibilism faces two challenges. One, which he calls the "problem of harmony," is that of reconciling the claim that the assertibility conditions of a sentence are sufficient for it to have the meaning it has with the claim that the sentence would not have the meaning it has if it did not represent as obtaining the state of affairs it does. The second challenge is that of explaining "how the existence of a state of affairs that a sentence represents does not render an account of its meaning ground in terms of its assertibility conditions redundant," as its existence suggests that a truth conditional ground would be available. Zalabardo proposes to meet these challenges by drawing on the abstractionist model familiar from the philosophy of mathematics, thus defining by abstraction the state of affairs a sentence represents. Zalabardo then argues that, though Kripke is right in maintaining that an explicit definition – an informative specification of what has to be the case in order for this state of affairs to obtain – of the state of affairs represented by "Jones means addition by '+'" cannot be provided, he is wrong in thinking that it follows from this that "Jones means addition by '+'" does not represent a state of affairs.

As may be gathered from these brief summaries of the volume's chapters, little consensus is reached among its contributors. Yet, I believe that the arguments and interpretations presented here all contribute to making progress on the foundational issues Kripke grappled with, and they are all immensely thought-provoking. This is, of course, the result of the many intricate ways in which Kripke's book continues to be thought-provoking. Perhaps this is the mark of a great book and, indeed, the highest achievement to be expected from a great book, in Wittgenstein's words, that it does not "spare other people the trouble of thinking," but that it "stimulate[s] someone to thoughts of his own" (PI: vi).

1 Kripke's Wittgenstein's Skepticism about Rules and Meaning
In Defense of the Standard Interpretation*

Alexander Miller

1 Introduction

It is agreed on all sides that the skeptic who takes center stage in Chapter 2 of Saul Kripke's *Wittgenstein on Rules and Private Language* aims for a metaphysical (as opposed to merely epistemological) conclusion: That there is no fact in virtue of which, for example, I mean *addition* by "+," or, more radically still, that I do not mean *addition* by "+." How, then, to account for the overtly epistemological nature of the arguments that take up the bulk of Chapter 2: The arguments, for example, that question my knowledge that I mean *addition* (and not *quaddition*) by the "+" sign, or my claim that I am justified in responding to the query "68 + 57" with "125" (rather than "5")? In the secondary literature, the most common way of reconciling the epistemological argumentation and metaphysical conclusion of the skeptic's ruminations has been to see the epistemological argumentation as merely a "dramatic device" for developing a fundamentally metaphysical argument: The epistemological challenge – to defend your claim that you know that you mean addition and your claim that you are justified in answering "125" – takes place under conditions in which you are granted ideal epistemological access to all of the sorts of fact capable of constituting your meaning addition by "+." An epistemological argument operating under an assumption of ideal access in this way is effectively a metaphysical argument presented in an epistemological "guise," a "guise" which is, therefore, strictly speaking dispensable. In this chapter, I'll refer to this way of viewing the skeptical argument of Chapter 2 as the "standard

---

* Versions of this chapter were presented at the New Zealand Association of Philosophy conference in Auckland 2019, the Normativity conference at Seoul National University in January 2020, the University of Otago in September 2020, and Victoria University of Wellington in May 2021. For comments and discussion, I'm grateful to the audiences on those occasions and to Rachel Cao, Ramon Das, Florian Demont, Matti Eklund, Hannah Ginsborg, Jinho Kang, Simon Keller, Ed Mares, Charles Pigden, Olivia Sultanescu, and Claudine Verheggen.

interpretation": Variants of it are proposed by, among others, Colin McGinn, Warren Goldfarb, Crispin Wright, and Paul Boghossian. As I will show, the standard interpretation appears to be mandated by a number of passages in Kripke's exegesis of the skeptical argument. Recently, however, the standard interpretation has been challenged in a stimulating and provocative discussion by Hannah Ginsborg. Ginsborg argues that the standard interpretation faces a number of insuperable objections and proposes an alternative interpretation in which the epistemological considerations in Kripke's Chapter 2 amount to more than a mere dispensable device for running a fundamentally metaphysical argument: Rather, according to Ginsborg, they constitute a fundamentally epistemological argument that features as an indispensable sub-argument in an overall argument to a metaphysical conclusion.[1] In this chapter, I will defend the standard interpretation in the face of Ginsborg's attack, and I'll argue that the standard interpretation fits the text of Kripke's Chapter 2 more smoothly than Ginsborg's alternative proposal. Furthermore, in addition to arguing for an unorthodox, more fundamentally epistemological reading of the skeptic's argument, Ginsborg also suggests that the skeptic's argument, construed as she construes it, can be defused via the deployment of a notion of primitive normativity. In Section 10, I will develop some objections to this use of the notion of primitive normativity.

2   The Standard Interpretation

To put the argument in an epistemological guise, we can focus on the justification of semantic judgments about the "+" sign and linguistic responses to particular arithmetical queries involving it.[2] Recall Kripke's famous example in which we are confronted by a skeptic who challenges us to respond to the query "68 + 57 = ?" and in which we are assumed not to have faced arithmetical queries in the past involving numbers greater than 56. When we answer "125," the skeptic replies that in order to be faithful to our past understanding of the "+" sign we ought rather to have answered "5," since by "+" we in fact meant *quaddition* ($\oplus$), where this is defined as follows:

$$x \oplus y = x + y, \text{ if } x, y < 57$$
$$= 5 \quad \text{otherwise.}$$

---

[1] Ginsborg (2018).
[2] In what follows, "Kripke's skeptical argument" and "Kripke's Wittgenstein's skeptical argument" refer to the argument of the skeptic in chapter 2 of Kripke (1982). (As is well known, Kripke himself does not endorse the argument or the solution outlined in chapter 3 [see 1982: 5], so strictly speaking this is inaccurate, but for ease of exposition, I ignore this complication in what follows.)

We now face the challenge of showing the skeptic that we don't mean quaddition, and the skeptic argues that there are no facts about our mental life, behavioral dispositions, or social history that we can cite in order to do this or in order to justify our answer "125" to the initial query. Speaking about this example, Kripke comments:

> We have just summarized the problem in terms of the basis of my present particular response: what tells me that I should say '125' and not '5'? Of course the problem can be put equivalently in terms of the skeptical query regarding my present intent: nothing in my mental history establishes whether I meant plus or quus. So formulated, the problem may appear to be epistemological – how can anyone know which of these I meant? Given, however, that everything in my mental history is compatible both with the conclusion that I meant plus and with the conclusion that I meant quus, it is clear that the skeptical challenge is not really an epistemological one. It purports to show that nothing in my mental history or past behavior – not even what an omniscient God would know – could establish whether I meant plus or quus. But then it appears to follow that there was no *fact* about me that constituted my having meant plus rather than quus. How could there be, if nothing in my internal mental history or external behavior will answer the skeptic who supposes that in fact I meant quus? (Kripke 1982: 21)

We could capture the nerve of the argument here as follows:

(1a) If I mean addition by "+," then unlimited access to the potentially relevant evidence about my mental life, behavioral dispositions, and social history will allow me to justify the claim that I mean *addition* (and not, say, *quaddition*) by "+" and allow me to justify the answer "125" to the query "68 + 57 = ?"

(2a) Unlimited access to the potentially relevant evidence about my mental life, behavioral dispositions, and social history does not allow me to justify the claim that I mean *addition* (and not, say, *quaddition*) by "+" or to justify the answer "125" to the query "68 + 57 = ?"

So,

(3) It is not the case that I mean *addition* by "+."

Here, (1a) and (2a) are framed in terms of what I can and cannot *justify* vis-à-vis what I mean by "+" or how I ought to respond to "68 + 57," but the reference to unlimited access means that this apparently epistemological argument is simply a dramatization of an argument that is fundamentally metaphysical. As Kripke himself puts it:

> Wittgenstein's skeptic argues that he knows of no fact about an individual that could constitute his state of meaning plus rather than quus. ... The skeptic does not argue that our own limitations of access to the facts prevent us from knowing something hidden. He claims that an omniscient being, with access to *all* available facts, still would not find any fact that differentiates between the plus and the quus hypotheses. ... Now the reference, in our exposition, to what an

omniscient being could or would know is merely a dramatic device. When the skeptic denies that even God, who knows all the facts, could know whether I meant plus or quus, he is simply giving colorful expression to his denial that there is any fact of the matter as to which I meant. (Kripke 1982: 39, 40–41)

Thus, the argument from (1a) and (2a) to (3) is effectively a dressed-up version of the following argument, in which there is no mention of justification or knowledge:

(1b) If I mean *addition* by "+," then there is a fact about my mental life, behavioral dispositions, or social history which constitutes my meaning *addition* by "+."

(2b) No fact about my mental life, behavioral dispositions, or social history constitutes my meaning *addition* by "+."

So,

(3) It is not the case that I mean *addition* by "+."

In the argument from (1a) and (2a) to (3), we have an argument in "epistemological guise" for a metaphysical conclusion that we could in principle derive from (1b) and (2b). In particular, the epistemological argumentation surrounding (2a) is simply a dispensable "dramatic device." This is the core of the standard interpretation of the skeptical argument.[3,4]

3   Ginsborg's "Epistemological" Interpretation of the Skeptical Argument

We can work toward outlining Ginsborg's alternative to the standard interpretation by outlining her construal of the famous skeptical argument in the first of Descartes' *Meditations*. According to Ginsborg, this goes as follows, where we take my knowledge that I'm currently sitting by the fire holding a piece of paper as the putative best case of a piece of empirical knowledge:

---

[3] I take Wright (1984a) and Boghossian (1989) to be the paradigm proponents of the standard interpretation, but other examples of philosophers who appear to accept the standard interpretation would include McGinn (1984), Goldfarb (1985), Pettit (1990), Millikan (1990), Wilson (1994), Horwich (1995), and Zalabardo (1997). Note that although Wright and Boghossian agree in their view of the overall structure of the skeptic's argument, they disagree about the nature of the constraints that govern responses to it and over how the skeptical argument can best be answered. However, these differences don't concern us here.

[4] Although the argument from (1a) and (2a) to (3) is formulated in epistemological terms, according to the standard interpretation – and adapting Lewis (1974: 333–334) – it is concerned with how *the facts* about a speaker's mental life, behavioral dispositions, etc. *determine the facts* about what he means by the expressions of his language.

(i) If I don't know that I'm awake (and not dreaming) then I don't know that I'm sitting by the fire holding a piece of paper.

Moreover,

(ii) No evidence that I am in principle capable of obtaining will allow me to justify the claim that I'm awake (and not dreaming).

So,

(iii) I have no justification for the claim that I'm awake (and not dreaming).

So,

(iv) I don't know that I'm awake (and not dreaming).

So,

(v) I don't know that I'm sitting by the fire holding a piece of paper.

So,

(vi) I don't know anything.

Note that the Cartesian skeptic concludes that I don't *know* that I'm sitting by the fire holding a piece of paper, not that it is not the case that I'm sitting by the fire holding a piece of paper.

According to Ginsborg, Kripke's skeptical argument incorporates an analogue of the argument from (i) to (v). This can be set out as follows:

(I) If I don't know that I meant *addition* (and not, say, *quaddition*) by "+," then I don't know that I ought to answer "125" to accord with my previous uses of "+."

Here, the quaddition hypothesis plays the role of the dreaming hypothesis in the *Meditations*, and the claim that I ought to answer "125" is the analogue of the judgment that I'm sitting by the fire, etc.[5] The argument continues:

(II) No evidence that I am in principle capable of obtaining will allow me to justify the claim that I meant *addition* (and not, say, *quaddition*) by "+."

So,

(III) I have no justification for the claim that I meant *addition* by "+."

So,

(IV) I don't know that I meant *addition* by "+."

---

[5] Note, though, that there are dissimilarities between the two. The dreaming hypothesis casts into doubt any belief about the external world (for Descartes operates with the principle that, if I don't know that I am not dreaming that p, I don't know that p), while the *quus* hypothesis doesn't have this generality: It is tailored to the particular use that is at issue in the conversation with the skeptic. (I'm grateful here to Olivia Sultanescu.)

So,

(V) I don't know that I ought to answer "125" to accord with my previous uses of "+."

So far, we have an analogue of the epistemological argument in the first of the *Meditations*, but Ginsborg acknowledges that Kripke's skeptic goes on from this to derive a metaphysical or constitutive conclusion from a claim (VI) about how meaning and knowledge of correct use are related:

(VI) In order to mean something by an expression E, I need to know how I ought to use E to accord with my previous uses.

Given (V) and (VI), we can move to the conclusion,

(VII) I don't mean anything by E.

The argument is still conceived of as an argument for a metaphysical conclusion, but the key respect in which the skeptic's argument, as characterized by Ginsborg, differs from that as characterized by the standard interpretation, is that in Ginsborg's interpretation, the argument contains an indispensable sub-argument (from [I] to [V]) which is a straightforward analogue of the epistemological skeptic's argument in the first *Meditation*.

It might be worthwhile at this point to contrast Ginsborg's epistemological reading of the skeptical argument with instances of the standard interpretation which nevertheless impose epistemological constraints on the selection of putative meaning-constituting facts. Versions of this latter variant of the standard interpretation have been proposed by Crispin Wright (1989b) and José Zalabardo (1997). In Wright's case, the first premise of the argument would be:

(W1) If I mean *addition* by "+," then there is a fact about my mental life, behavioral dispositions, or social history which constitutes my meaning *addition* by "+," *and this fact must be consistent with the non-inferential and first-person authoritative nature of self-knowledge of meaning.*[6]

The argument then proceeds as before: No fact capable of cohering with the intuitive first-person epistemology of meaning can be found, so that the conclusion once again is that I don't mean addition by "+." In Zalabardo's case, the first premise of the argument would be:

(Z1) If I mean *addition* by "+," then there is a fact about my mental life, behavioral dispositions, or social history which constitutes my meaning *addition* by

---

[6] See Section 1.4 for more detail on this.

"+," *with which I can consciously engage in a way capable of justifying my answers to arithmetical queries involving* "+."[7]

And the argument then proceeds as before. In both cases, constraints are imposed which concern epistemological notions like self-knowledge or justification and which serve to narrow down the range of candidate meaning-constituting facts that can be appealed to. But the structure of the argument remains as before. Whereas in Ginsborg's interpretation, the argument as a whole contains a sub-argument ([I] to [V]) with a purely epistemological interim conclusion ([V]), this is not the case in the versions of the skeptical argument proposed by Wright and Zalabardo.[8]

Ginsborg develops three objections to the standard interpretation. She then argues that although her preferred epistemological version of the skeptic's argument avoids the objections to the standard interpretation, it can be resisted using a notion of "primitive normativity." I will defend the standard interpretation against Ginsborg's objections, raise some objections to her epistemological version, and argue that the notion of "primitive normativity" in fact fails to disable it.

4 Ginsborg's Central Objection

Ginsborg argues:

[T]he metaphysical reading allows Kripke's challenge to be too easily answered. It can simply be pointed out that Kripke is operating with an unwarrantedly narrow conception of fact, or that he is refusing to accept that meaning facts could be primitive and irreducible (2018: 153),

and mentions Goldfarb (1985), McGinn (1984), Wright (1989a, 1989b), and Boghossian (1989) as proposing responses along these lines.

Does construing the skeptical argument in the standard metaphysical way make it too easy to respond to? I think not: This would be so only if there were no constraints that the non-reductionist response had to satisfy. On Wright's reading, in particular, there are such constraints: Wright argues that before the non-reductionist response can be deemed acceptable, it has to be squared with the intuitive epistemology of self-ascriptions of meaning and intention, which, according to Wright, is first-person authoritative and non-inferential. For example, I don't

---

[7] On Zalabardo's reading, then, there is an internalist constraint on the selection of candidate meaning-constituting facts (see Zalabardo 1997, sections IV and V).

[8] Ginsborg herself counts both Wright and Zalabardo as proposing versions of the standard interpretation. See Ginsborg (2018: 152) on Wright and Ginsborg (2018: 164 n.30) on Zalabardo.

have to infer that I intend to travel to Moeraki this weekend, and my avowal that I do so intend ordinarily stands as correct by default unless someone produces concrete evidence to the contrary (perhaps evidence that I'm lying, self-deceived, or whatever), and Wright suggests that the intuitive epistemology of self-ascriptions of meaning and understanding is similar.

Ginsborg in fact considers this reply later in her paper and argues that it does not affect her point:

> [W]hen the challenge is framed in this metaphysical way [and subject to epistemological constraints], it is all too easy to respond by appealing to the existence of irreducible meaning facts with just the epistemological properties specified: we can say that it is simply in the nature of meaning facts that they are ... first-personally knowable. (2018: 161)[9]

In response, it can be argued that Ginsborg fails to appreciate the depth of the difficulty that Wright is grappling with: the problem is not simply that of accommodating the intuitive first-person epistemology of meaning and intention but doing so in a way that also accommodates what Wright calls their "disposition-like theoreticity" (Wright 2001a: 87):

> [How] is it possible to be effortlessly, non-inferentially and generally reliably authoritative about psychological states which have no distinctive occurrent phenomenology *and which have to answer, after the fashion of dispositions, to what one says and does in situations so far unconsidered?* (Wright 1989a: 150, emphasis added)

Rule-following, meaning, and understanding are like character traits such as courage insofar as "the proof of the pudding is in subsequent performance" (Wright 1987: 137). The ascription of courage to me at the start of the war will be deemed to have been false if, in the absence of some suitable explanation why not, at the first sign of the enemy I take to my heels. This meshes with the fact that self-ascriptions of courage do not display the intuitive first-person epistemology of meaning and intention, and, indeed, as Wright observes, "the confident self-ascription, without behavioral grounds, of intelligence, courage, patience or endurance is, so far from being authoritative, a mere conceit" (1987: 136). Likewise, though, the ascription to me of understanding "+" to mean addition will be deemed to have been false if, in the absence of some substantial explanation why not, I begin confidently answering "5" to queries when the numbers involved exceed some specific numerical threshold; and the ascription to me of intending to follow the rule for addition of 2 will be

---

[9] Ginsborg also mentions guidance and justification here, but I've dropped this in order to focus on Wright's discussion of first-person authority.

deemed to have been false if, when I reach 1,000, I confidently continue 1,004, 1,008, 1,012 .... So we require a substantive account of *how*, nonetheless, meaning and intention can have the intuitive first person epistemology that they do, one that is non-inferential and first-person authoritative. Providing this would appear to be far from being "all too easy."[10,11]

5 Ginsborg's Second Objection

Ginsborg picks up on a comment Wright makes in explaining why Kripke's Wittgenstein's skeptic is merely an instrument for getting to a metaphysical conclusion:

[T]he overarching thought behind [the skeptical dialectic] is ... that claims of a certain kind cannot be supposed to deal in matters of real fact if someone could know all possible facts which might conceivably constitute the truth of such a claim yet be unable to defeat a skeptic concerning his knowledge of its truth. (Wright 2001a: 82)

She replies:

However, the "overarching thought" might seem questionable to those lacking verificationist sympathies. Why should your inability to justify your belief that you meant addition, even given the knowledge that Kripke's skeptic allows you, entail that your belief lacks factual content? (2018: 154)[12]

---

[10] Wright himself (1989b) develops a "judgement-dependent" account of meaning and intention to explore how a non-reductionist might rise to this challenge. Note too that some quietist non-reductionists (e.g. McDowell) might actually welcome the "all-too-easy" claim, since they think that the question at the heart of the skeptical challenge – "How is meaning possible?" – is not even a genuine question (I'm grateful here to Charles Pigden). Either way, with Wright's anti-realist or McDowell's quietist realist, the "all-too-easy" objection fails to bite.

[11] Another way of putting the point here would be to observe that Ginsborg's second objection works only if Wright fails to get the better of McGinn in his (1989a). Wright criticizes McGinn on grounds of "philosophical stone-kicking" for failing to appreciate that a non-reductionist response to the skeptic's argument has to square the first-person epistemology of meaning with its "disposition-like theoreticity." Note that although Boghossian in his (1989) does not to the same extent emphasize the need to square the first-person epistemology of meaning with its disposition-like theoreticity, he still mentions self-knowledge as a problem the non-reductionist has to contend with and suggests, moreover, that the non-reductionist faces the far from trivial task of according content properties a role in the rationalistic explanation of action in a way that does not imply the essential incompleteness of physics. See Boghossian (1989: 186–187).

[12] Ginsborg goes on immediately after this comment to reiterate her previous point about the reading leaving open the too-readily available non-reductionist response, but my points above about first-person epistemology and disposition-like theoreticity speak to this.

In response, it's not clear to me that anything like a general and objectionable form of verificationism is required to drive the standard reading of Kripke's argument. Wright doesn't need the general idea that if there is a fact of the matter in a particular domain then that fact must be in principle accessible to us if we are granted idealized evidence-acquiring powers. All he needs is the *specific* claim that that is so vis-à-vis facts about meaning (as, arguably, it would be in the case of putatively moral or aesthetic facts). It may be possible to challenge this specific claim in the meaning case, but it doesn't seem to me to depend in any obvious way on any *general* verificationist sympathies.

To put the point another way, the metaphysical reading can proceed via Wright's "overarching thought" only if the relevant facts are guaranteed to be accessible on the basis of unlimited access to the relevant evidence: without this, there will be no license for the move from (2a) to (3) in the "epistemological" variant of the standard interpretation of the skeptical argument as outlined above. In the case of meaning, the idea that there is such a guarantee seems intuitively acceptable: the idea that the truth about meaning might be potentially evidence-transcendent is not an appealing one. The same plausibly holds in the cases of morals and humor, as Wright himself notes:

> [I]t might seem implausible to claim that the sense of humour is a faculty which enables us to track independently constituted comic qualities; but it would ascend to a quite different order of implausibility to add that the obtaining of such qualities may altogether transcend, even in principle, our abilities of recognition. A similar point applies to morals. There are, no doubt, kinds of moral realism which do have the consequence that moral reality may transcend all possibility of detection. But it is surely not essential to any view worth regarding as realist about morals that it incorporate a commitment to that idea. (Wright 1992: 8–9)

However, resistance to the idea that truth is potentially evidence-transcendent in the case of morals and comedy needn't commit us to the idea that truth is essentially epistemically constrained across the board; indeed, Wright thinks that it is a distinct advantage of his brand of pluralism about truth that it is able to accommodate this variability Wright 1992: Chapters 1 and 2).[13] Of course, a consequence of this is that analogues of the strategy adopted in the epistemological variant of the standard interpretation of Kripke's Wittgenstein's skeptical argument will not be available in areas where the idea that truth is epistemically constrained is not attractive; this, however, is something that

---

[13] See Boghossian (2001: 237), where a similar point is made vis a vis epistemic facts.

proponents of the standard interpretation of Kripke's Wittgenstein's skeptical argument can happily accept.[14,15]

6 Ginsborg's Third Objection

Ginsborg writes:

[I]t is hard to believe that, without the skeptic and the quaddition hypothesis, Kripke's challenge would have been able to engage the interest of so many philosophers. Although this is not itself decisive, it seems reasonable to suspect that the skeptical dialectic is not just novel packaging for a familiar product, but corresponds to something philosophically distinctive about Kripke's challenge, something that is lost if we read the challenge in a way which makes the skeptic dispensable. (Ginsborg 2018: 153)

This appears to me to underplay the degree of creativity and ingenuity that can be involved in constructing vivid thought-experiments in order to bring philosophical problems to life, even if the thought-experiments are strictly speaking dispensable and the relevant problems can in principle be formulated without their aid. Philosophy is replete with instances of this: The Cave Dwellers in Book VII of Plato's *Republic*,[16] Putnam's Twin-Earth (Putnam 1975), Burge's Arthritis (Burge 1979), Davidson's Swampman (Davidson 1987), the Beetle-in-the-Box of Wittgenstein's *Philosophical Investigations* §293, Williams's Jim and the Indians (Williams 1973), and the list could go on.

However, it might be objected that these don't appear to be examples of dispensable *epistemological* vehicles usable in the pursuit of *metaphysical* conclusions and that it is examples of this that are required to speak to Ginsborg's worry. I'm not entirely convinced by this objection, but we can reply to it in any event by citing examples of arguments that do use epistemological vehicles to establish metaphysical conclusions in ways that offer structural parallel's with Kripke's Wittgenstein's skeptic's argument as standardly construed.

---

[14] The exception will be philosophers who advocate the idea that truth is globally epistemically constrained. These are few in number: Wright, for example, does not hold this global view of truth as everywhere epistemically constrained (though the view that it is is sometimes erroneously attributed to him (see e.g. Horgan and Timmons (2006: 277 n.15))).

[15] Note that (1a) in §2 is in fact a little weaker than the principle that Wright proposes at (2001a: 82), insofar as (1a) as explicitly formulated concerns only *truth* while the principle in (2001a: 82) concerns *truth-aptitude*. For our present purposes, nothing of importance turns on this.

[16] And the corresponding allegory toward the end of *Phaedo* (at 109b) in which humans are unaware of a purer world above them.

A clear example is provided by Frank Jackson's "Knowledge Argument" against physicalism (Jackson 1982, 1986). In these papers, Jackson uses the example of "Black and White Mary" to argue that there are aspects of reality – in particular, facts about the nature of our experiences of colors – that are not explicable in purely physicalistic terms. Now one could frame the anti-physicalist argument in terms of the determination of facts about the relevant characteristics of color experience by the physical facts, without mentioning Black and White Mary or the knowledge she allegedly acquires on stepping out of her seclusion. The fact that thus stated (i.e. without Black and White Mary) the argument would not have generated such widespread interest does not require that the Knowledge Argument featuring Mary is indispensable. Philosophical creativity is often a matter of taking an argument or set of concerns and bringing it (or them) vividly to life by deploying a compelling but in principle dispensable vehicle for doing so, and there are cases of this in which metaphysical conclusions are pursued via epistemological vehicles. The existence of alternative formulations of the anti-physicalist argument that don't deploy something like Black and White Mary and the associated epistemological claims don't deprive Jackson of the philosophical kudos he deserves for coming up with the compelling formulation of the argument in which she appears.

Other examples of philosophers aiming to establish metaphysical or constitutive conclusions via in principle dispensable epistemological vehicles might include: Thomas Nagel's (1974) anti-physicalist argument in "What is it Like to be a Bat?"; John Searle's (1980) "Chinese Room" argument, attempting to establish that "instantiating a computer program is never by itself a sufficient condition of intentionality" (Searle 1980: 417) and to challenge the thesis that "mental processes are computational processes over formally defined elements" (1980: 422); W. V. Quine's (1960) "gavagai" example and discussion of radical translation, arguing that there are no facts about fine-grained meaning or synonymy (beyond Quine's notions of stimulus-meaning and stimulus-synonymy).

Insofar as Kripke's skeptical challenge and the ensuing dialectic concerning the *quus* hypothesis are examples of a relatively familiar philosophical phenomenon – the bringing to life of metaphysical issues and arguments via vivid, though in principle dispensable, epistemological vehicles – Ginsborg's third objection to the standard interpretation appears to be unconvincing.

Overall, then, the standard construal of the skeptic's argument as fundamentally metaphysical can withstand the three objections which Ginsborg raises against it.

7 An *Ad Hominem* Objection to Ginsborg's "Epistemological" Interpretation

I will argue that if the standard, metaphysical interpretation of Kripke's Wittgenstein's skeptic's argument is susceptible to Ginsborg's main objection, then so is Ginsborg's own, fundamentally epistemological reading of the argument.[17]

Ginsborg herself provides a lucid formulation of this train of thought:

> Now a critic of Kripke who accepted the epistemological-skeptical reading I have offered of the argument might here propose an epistemological variant of the charge of reductionism. Perhaps Kripke is failing to recognize, not just that there can be primitive facts of meaning, but that we have a primitive capacity to know that such facts obtain. In that case you can respond to the skeptic's challenge "How do you know you meant addition?" by saying simply "I just know I meant addition; no explanation or justification necessary." (2018: 158–159)

However, she goes on to argue that it is not compelling:

> [T]he availability of this response, unlike the original charge of reductionism, is not a weakness in Kripke's argument specifically but rather a feature of skeptical arguments generally. We might equally well respond to the external-world skeptic's dreaming or brain-in-a-vat hypothesis by saying "I just know I'm awake now" or "I just know I have a body." To respond this way is not to answer the skeptical challenge but to refuse to take it seriously, and it is no objection to Kripke's skeptical argument that it is open to this kind of rejection. (2018: 159)

It is difficult to know what to make of this passage. It surely cannot just be saying that construed in Ginsborg's preferred epistemological fashion the skeptical argument is prone to an objection (that there is an "all too easy" response to it), but that this is an objection to which all forms of epistemological skeptical argument are prone.[18] Depending on how it goes, this may mean that Kripke's Wittgenstein's skeptic's argument is open to an objection, but an objection to which all arguments of the same sort are susceptible. This seems weak: an objection directed at one argument of a particular type isn't somehow undermined just because it applies to all other arguments of the same type.

---

[17] The argument is only *ad hominem* because – as argued immediately above – Ginsborg's argument that the standard interpretation is susceptible to an "all too easy" non-reductionist response is unsuccessful.

[18] A non-reductionist reply to a metaphysical challenge regarding putative facts of type F cites the existence of an F-type fact in reply. The analogue of this in the case of a fundamentally epistemological challenge to knowledge of F-type facts involves in effect a form of non-inferentialism: the citation of knowledge of F-type states of affairs, viewing this as something we have in virtue of a primitive knowledge-acquiring capacity, with no attempt to confer epistemic authority on F-type judgments by viewing them as inferred from some other, independently secure, pieces of knowledge.

Ginsborg's thought seems to be, rather, that whereas a non-reductionist response to a metaphysical challenge is sometimes legitimate, a non-inferentialist response to an epistemological challenge is always simply "to refuse to take it [the challenge] seriously." On the metaphysical interpretation of Kripke's Wittgenstein's skeptic's argument, then, there is a potentially genuine response ready to hand (non-reductionism), while this is not so on the argument construed as fundamentally epistemological. However, this seems implausible: how plausible is it to see a non-inferentialist response to an epistemological challenge as *always* unacceptable, as not even *potentially* genuine? Indeed, the relevant argument of Wright's here is couched in explicitly epistemological terms. Wright takes the "rules of the game" imposed by the skeptic to require that any response to his questioning of your claim to know that you mean, for example, addition by "+" must proceed by inferring that knowledge from knowledge of states of affairs which can be characterized without recourse to the notion of content, and he writes:

Are not such rules guaranteed to ensure success for a Kripke-style skeptic in any case where a contested subject matter is thought of as known non-inferentially? If the sufficient and adequate ground of my knowledge that P is precisely my non-inferential apprehension of the very fact that P, then it is to be expected that I may fare badly if in discussion with someone who doubts that P I am allowed to proceed only by reference to considerations of a quite different kind, considerations which could in principle at best defeasibly warrant an inference that P. (Wright 2001a: 84)

And again

[I]t cannot always be possible to justify a presumed genre of knowledge "from without" in the way the skeptic is here demanding. At any rate, it is obvious enough that, if we were to allow the propriety quite generally of this skeptical move, the results would be calamitous. Imagine, for example, a skeptic who questions a claim about my former perceptions, say, "Yesterday, I saw it raining." And suppose the ground rules are as for the dialogue with Kripke's skeptic; that is, I am to be permitted to adduce any relevant fact so long as I do not thereby presuppose that there is such a thing as knowledge of what I formerly perceived – since it is of belief in the very existence of that genre of knowledge that the skeptic is demanding justification. So I cannot simply claim to remember what I perceived: my ammunition will be restricted to my present *seeming-memories*, the presently available testimony of others, presently accessible putative traces, like damp ground and meteorological office and newspaper records. It ought to be a straightforward, if tedious, exercise for the skeptic to accommodate all that without granting me the truth of my claim about my perception of yesterday's weather. So I can know "all relevant facts" without knowing anything about what I formerly perceived. So there is no fact of the matter about what I formerly perceived. So, since the arguments will work just as well in the future, when now is "then," there is no fact of the matter about what I presently perceive. So, since the argument applies to all of us, there is no such thing as perceptual knowledge. "There's glory for you!" (Wright 1984a: 110)

Wright is here rejecting any constraint that restricts us, in attempting to defeat the skeptic about meaning, to "considerations which could in principle defeasibly warrant an inference" to a semantic claim; and the rejection of this constraint entails that sometimes, at least, a non-inferentialist reply to an epistemological challenge can be genuine. The challenge – which Wright takes McGinn to shirk, and which he attempts to address in his own judgment-dependent account of meaning and intention – is to see *how* a non-inferentialist response to the skeptical challenge can be developed in a way that accommodates their "disposition-like theoreticity."

Thus, contra Ginsborg, there is no asymmetry of the kind she canvasses between the skeptical argument standardly construed and the skeptical argument construed as she construes it. This completes our *ad hominem* argument against Ginsborg's interpretation of the skeptical argument.

8   Against the Epistemological Interpretation

Thus far, we have concentrated on defending the standard reading of the skeptical argument against Ginsborg's objection. Arguably, a case can be made that certain key passages in Kripke's book fit the standard interpretation much better than Ginsborg's epistemological alternative. These are passages in which Kripke describes the skepticism as metaphysical rather than epistemological. One such key passage is:

[T]he problem may appear to be epistemological – how can anyone know which of these I meant? Given, however, that everything in my mental history is compatible both with the conclusion that I meant plus and with the conclusion that I meant quus, it is clear that the skeptical challenge is not really an epistemological one. It purports to show that nothing in my mental history or past behavior – not even what an omniscient God would know – could establish whether I meant plus or quus. But then it appears to follow that there was no *fact* about me that constituted my having meant plus rather than quus. (1982: 21)

Ginsborg realizes that this passage has to be explained away, and she writes:

When Kripke explicitly describes the skepticism as metaphysical rather than epistemological (1982: 21; see also 38–39), his aim is to distinguish the metaphysical conclusion that there is no fact of your meaning addition from the epistemological conclusion that you do not know that you meant addition, not to distinguish the metaphysical conclusion from the epistemological conclusion that you do not know that "125" conforms to your previous usage. (2018: 159)

So her claim is that in this passage Kripke is distinguishing the metaphysical *conclusion* of the argument from an epistemological *conclusion*, rather than a metaphysical argument from an indispensable epistemological sub-argument (with the conclusion that I don't know that I ought to answer "125" to conform to my previous usage), so that the passage is consistent with the falsity of the standard interpretation and the truth of Ginsborg's alternative reading. However, this is not borne out by a closer look at the relevant passage. Let's look again at the passage, this time focusing on the phrase emphasized in bold:

[T]he problem may appear to be epistemological – how can anyone know which of these I meant? Given, however, that everything in my mental history is compatible both with the conclusion that I meant plus and with the conclusion that I meant quus, it is clear that the skeptical challenge is not really an epistemological one. It purports to show that nothing in my mental history or past behavior – not even what an omniscient God would know – could establish whether I meant plus or quus. **But then it appears to follow that** there was no *fact* about me that constituted my having meant plus rather than quus. (1982: 21, emphasis in bold added)

The emphasis in bold here makes it clear that the reference to the omniscient God appears as a *premise* in the argument to the conclusion that there is no fact of your meaning addition, not in the conclusion, so it can't simply be reiterating the point that the conclusion is metaphysical. This fits the standard interpretation perfectly, since the invocation of the being with omniscient access to all there is to know about your mental history and past behavior connects straightforwardly to premise (2a) (and hence also premise [2b]) in the standard interpretation. Ginsborg thus fails in her attempt to explain away Kripke's remarks in the relevant passage.[19]

---

[19] Ginsborg goes on to reflect on other passages where epistemological considerations are in play, and argues (i) that these can be accommodated in her epistemological interpretation and (ii) that there are problems in attempting to accommodate them in the standard interpretation (in which the selection of a meaning constituting fact is subject to epistemological constraints). I won't engage with (i) as I think my remark immediately above concerning (1982: 21) is enough to justify the standard interpretation over Ginsborg's alternative, and I won't engage with (ii) since at this point Ginsborg simply refers to her central objection to the standard interpretation which has been dealt with in §4. So the appearance of God in Kripke's text suggests that the standard interpretation is on the mark: Ginsborg's attempt to explain it away is unsuccessful. Perhaps one could try to find a role for God, thought of as a being omniscient with respect to all of the relevant evidence, in the purely epistemological argument from (I) to (V), perhaps with respect to premise (II). However, it is far from obvious how this would go – the argument is meant to concern *our* capacity to secure knowledge, not a being with superior cognitive powers to ours – and the fact that there is no role for God to play in the first of Descartes' *Meditations* (other than to contrast with the "evil genius") suggests that this is not a promising line of defense for Ginsborg.

We might even go further than the defense of the standard interpretation mounted thus far and argue that the boot is altogether on the other foot: given that epistemological skepticism has been subjected to a vast battery of responses of one sort or another since the founding of modern epistemology by Descartes in the seventeenth century, Ginsborg's construal of Kripke's Wittgenstein's skeptical argument as fundamentally epistemological leaves it open to this battery of counter-arguments. It could well be, then, that the standard metaphysical interpretation better captures Kripke's remark that the argument that is given by his skeptic is "the most radical and original skeptical problem that philosophy has seen to date" (Kripke 1982: 60). An argument that could potentially be disabled by responses to the skeptical argument of the first *Meditation* would hardly merit the designation "A new form of skepticism."[20,21]

9 Ginsborg's Response to the Skeptical Argument

Although Ginsborg argues that her epistemological reading of Kripke's skeptical argument is better placed than the standard reading to recognize its prima facie force, she nevertheless holds that there is a way to escape its devastating consequences. This involves the notion of what Ginsborg calls "primitive normativity," "the idea that we can make sense of a notion of conformity to previous use that is independent of conformity to previous meaning – and, more generally, of conformity to a rule grasped in one's previous use" (2018: 162).[22] The idea is that a present use of an expression can accord (or fail to accord) with one's previous uses of an expression, in a sense that is independent of any assumptions

---

[20] Indeed, it may well be that these considerations leave Ginsborg's interpretation open to an "all-too-easy" objection of its own: if the argument of the semantic skeptic relies on an notion of justification according to which the mere possibility of doubt undermines knowledge, the argument can be rejected by pointing out how artificial and inflated that notion of justification is. Another question worth asking concerns the relationship between the skeptical argument in Kripke's Wittgenstein and Quine's arguments for the indeterminacy of translation. Kripke himself notes the parallels and contrasts at a number of places (see e.g. Kripke 1982: 14–15, 56–57). Does Ginsborg's epistemological reading of Kripke's Wittgenstein carry over to Quine?

[21] Another question for Ginsborg's interpretation concerns the "skeptical solution" to the skeptical argument that Kripke expounds in Chapter 3. Defenders of the standard interpretation usually take this to involve a kind of non-factualism about ascriptions of meaning, and it is relatively straightforward to see how this might block the skeptical argument as standardly conceived (see Miller 2010a). How exactly, for Ginsborg, does the skeptical solution outlined in chapter 3 of Kripke (1982) connect with the skeptical argument as she understands it? And what becomes of the argument against private (or solitary) language? I'm grateful to Ed Mares for raising these issues.

[22] See also Ginsborg (2010), (2011a), (2011b), (2012), (2020), (2022), and in particular §4 of Ginsborg (2020).

about what anyone understood that expression to mean in the past. In application to the case that takes center stage in Kripke's presentation:

It is possible for you to hold that "125" is the appropriate response to "68 + 57" in the light of your previous history of responding to "+" questions irrespective of what, if anything, you meant when you used the expression previously. So you can concede to the skeptic that you meant quaddition, and hence that, in saying "125," you are failing to accord with what you meant in the past, and still maintain that "125" accords with your previous uses of "+." Regardless of what you meant when you used the "+" sign in the past, the appropriate way to go on from the sequence of your past responses to "+" questions is to respond to "68 + 57" with "125" and not "5." (Ginsborg 2018: 161–162)

Recall that the first premise in the skeptic's argument, as construed by Ginsborg was:

(I) If I don't know that I meant *addition* (and not, say, *quaddition*) by "+," then I don't know that I ought to answer "125" to accord with my previous uses of "+."

Ginsborg uses the notion of primitive normativity to deny this:

Kripke is wrong to assume that, in order to be confident that "125" is "metalinguistically correct"-that it conforms to your previous uses of "+"- you must know that you meant addition rather than quaddition in those previous uses. (2018: 161)

In other words, one could use the notion of primitive normativity to concede that the antecedent of the skeptic's (I) might be true while rejecting the consequent as false.

Ginsborg's idea is that the knowledge of how one ought to use an expression in order to use it meaningfully, is knowledge of how to use it to accord with one's previous uses, where, since the relevant previous uses are to be characterized independently of any assumptions about what you formerly meant, the notion of "accord" in play is primitive, and not a notion of accord with meaning.[23]

I will argue that Ginsborg's response to the skeptical argument, thus read, is unsuccessful because it mischaracterizes the type of knowledge of normative accord that is necessary for one's uses of linguistic expressions to count as meaningful.

In Kripke's example, in order to mean what I do by, for example, "+" I need to know that I ought to respond to the "68 + 57" query with

---

[23] This is especially clear in the discussion of the adult at (2011b: 240): "That an adult counting by twos conceives of herself as following the add-two rule, and takes '42' to accord with that rule, does not exclude her taking '42' to fit the preceding series *simpliciter*, in a way which does not depend on the assumption that she was following the add-two rule rather than a quadd-like variant."

"125" rather than "5" to accord with my previous uses of "+." Note, first, that by "previous usage" here, Ginsborg means "not just your own utterances of and responses to linguistic expressions, but all uses that you have observed, including those of your parents and teachers" (2018: 157). This immediately raises the question whether the kind of knowledge – of how to use expressions in order to accord with past usage – is even possible to the extent required by Ginsborg. For one thing, it would only make sense to ascribe it to a speaker if they knew what their past use, described independently of meaning, actually was. Try it yourself: can you give me such an account of your previous use of "+"? Even in the past 24 hours? A negative answer here is all the more likely given the broadening of the notion to include not only your own uses but also those that you have observed! Indeed, even putting the issue of knowledge of past use to one side, it seems far-fetched even to ascribe to speakers *beliefs* about their past uses of "+." But if speakers don't have beliefs about their past use of a sign, it makes little sense to ascribe to them knowledge of how to use expressions to accord with their – and their parents and teachers – past use. On the other hand, matters stand differently when we lift the restriction prohibiting the use of the notion of meaning in characterizing past usage (or what it is that my current use ought to accord with). I certainly do have a belief (and possibly knowledge) of my past usage of "+": as I used it in the past I meant addition, as, I assume, did my parents and teachers.

A further problem stems from the fact that even competent speakers of the same language are unlikely to have the same history when it comes to past usage of expressions of their language, construed in accordance with Ginsborg's restriction. Take Smith and Jones to be ordinary speakers of English, imagine them in the scenario that takes center stage in Kripke where they face the query "68 + 57 = ?," and consider:

(a) Both Smith and Jones ought to answer "125."
(b) The answer that they each ought to give is determined by what primitively accords with their past use of "+."
(c) Their past use is different: they have different histories of past use of "+."

The third proposition is arguably true, and Ginsborg holds that (a) and (b) are true too, but how is it possible for (a), (b), and (c) to be true simultaneously? How can it be that how they ought to use "+" in the primitive sense is the same, when this is a matter of primitive accord with past use and their histories of past use are different (perhaps even radically different)? The fact that speakers' histories of use – characterized without recourse to the notion of meaning – are different is masked by the fact that in the examples Ginsborg uses to explain the notion of primitive normativity, the uses with which a speaker's current response primitively accords turns out to instantiate the rule grasp of which is eventually attributed to the speaker. For example, in the case discussed in (2011b: 233–235) – that of a child who does not yet mean add 2 by "+2"[24] – it is assumed that the child's previous history of use in expanding the series is

$$2, 4, 6, 8, \ldots, 40$$

that is, de facto in accord with the rule "Add 2!" as ordinarily understood. In a real life case, however, the child's previous use is just as likely to be more like

$$2, 4, 6, 8, 10, 12, 14, 15, 16, \ldots, 40$$

Are we to hold that in this latter case "42" is the continuation of the series that primitively accords with the previous use? This seems unlikely given that we want "42" to be the continuation that primitively accords with the previous use in the former case. On the other hand, though, if the latter case is discounted because it contains a "mistake" – insofar as one element ("15") in the series fails to accord with "Add 2!" as ordinarily understood – we seem to have retreated from primitive normativity back toward to a notion of normative accord with meaning.

Ginsborg's response to the skeptical argument, construed as she construes it, thus faces the following three problems. First, that speakers won't generally be able to remember more than a small fragment of their history of previous uses (when this is characterized without recourse to the notion of meaning). Second, that no two speakers are likely to have the same histories of previous use. Third, that a speaker's history of previous use is likely to contain "mistakes" (by the lights of the understanding of the expression that we want to attribute to them). Clearly, the way out of the impasse is to cut down the multiplicity of histories of previous use by focusing on a history of use in which the relevant expression is used

---

[24] There's no suggestion in Ginsborg's description of the example that the child eventually means anything other than what "+2" means as ordinarily understood (i.e. add 2). Likewise in the example featuring "green" which follows immediately after: the child in the example "is not *yet* obviously in command of colour concepts" and "has not *yet* mastered use of the word 'green'" (Ginsborg 2011b: 235, emphasis added), and there is no suggestion that the concept the child will eventually be deemed to grasp is anything other than the concept *green* or that she will mean anything other than green by "green." (Likewise the adult on (2011b: 240) is assumed to be following the add 2 rule.)

in accord with its meaning, knowledge of which (or at least beliefs about which) will be attributable to the speakers concerned. This, though, is not available to Ginsborg given her requirement that "previous use" be characterized independently of the notion of meaning. So, if we construe the skeptical argument in the epistemological fashion advocated by Ginsborg, her notion of primitive normativity will not be able to yield a plausible response to it. Since the worries I have raised about primitive normativity are not specific to its deployment in responding to the epistemological reading of Kripke's Wittgenstein's skeptic's argument, we can conclude that it cannot be invoked to respond to the skeptical argument when this is interpreted, in the standard way, as fundamentally metaphysical or constitutive.[25]

10 Conclusion

Overall, then, we can conclude that Ginsborg's objections to the standard "metaphysical" interpretation of Kripke's Wittgenstein's skeptic's argument miss their mark, and that the standard interpretation is in fact a much better fit for Kripke's text than Ginsborg's alternative. In addition, matters of interpretation aside, there are problems for Ginsborg's notion of primitive normativity that render it an unlikely candidate for responding to Kripke's skeptic's argument, whether or not that argument is to be conceived of as fundamentally epistemological, or, as I have argued in this chapter, fundamentally metaphysical.

---

[25] For further worries about Ginsborg's reply to Kripke's Wittgenstein, see Miller (2018: Chapter 6, Section 9), Miller (2019), Verheggen (2015), and Sultanescu (2021).

2 Putting Wittgenstein Back into Kripkenstein:
Meaning Skepticism and Knowing How to Go On

Hannah Ginsborg

1 Introduction

Since the publication of *Wittgenstein on Rules and Private Language*, a substantial literature has emerged discussing the skeptical problem that Kripke ascribed to Wittgenstein and its implications for meaning and rule-following. Despite the extent and variety of this literature, there has been considerable convergence, if not on how to address the problem, at least on how it is to be understood. Most commentators agree, first, that although Kripke formulated the problem as an interpretation of Wittgenstein, the problem should be understood in its own right rather than by reference to Wittgenstein's discussion of meaning and rule-following. The proponent of the skeptical argument has come to be labeled "Kripkenstein," a philosopher whose views can be fully understood by reference to Kripke's text, without recourse to Wittgenstein.[1] A second point of agreement is that the problem is fundamentally metaphysical rather than epistemological: it arises from the difficulty, given certain constraints which Kripke specifies, of coming up with an adequate philosophical account of what meaning or grasp of a rule consists in. The skeptical conclusion that there is no such thing as meaning is understood to follow more or less directly from our supposed inability to specify a fact which constitutes a person's meaning something by an expression. A third point of agreement is that the very first move in the skeptical dialectic – in which a skeptic challenges my supposed knowledge that I ought to say "125" in response to "what's 58 + 67?" – is not essential to the argument; all that is needed to establish the skeptical conclusion is to undermine candidate answers to the question of what meaning consists in.[2]

---

[1] The term "Kripkenstein" has been in in use at least since Schiffer (1986) and is now widespread.

[2] Although this third point is often left implicit, it is made very clear by Paul Boghossian, who makes a point of describing the argument without any reference to the skeptic (1989: 515). Gary Ebbs, in this volume, diverges from the consensus regarding the second and third points, since he takes the question of my epistemic warrant for saying "125" to be crucial in motivating the skepticism. But his reading differs sharply from mine, in ways that I do not have space to discuss here.

In this chapter, I offer an alternative reading of the skeptical problem which differs from this consensus on all three points. I think that the skeptical problem is best understood, not in isolation but in light of Wittgenstein's discussion of rule-following, and specifically his discussion of "knowing how to go on." Relatedly, I understand the source of the skeptical problem as essentially epistemological: the skeptical conclusion that there is no such thing as meaning arises from my supposed inability to know, when I respond to "68 + 57?" with "125," that I am going on correctly from previous uses of "+." And, again relatedly, I take the skeptic's challenge to my knowledge of the correctness of "125" to be crucial to the argument.[3] I will argue that this reading, as well as being closer to Kripke's own intentions, yields a stronger and more distinctive argument against the possibility of meaning. Nonetheless, as I will indicate in conclusion, the argument can be answered: not in the usual way, by offering an account of meaning and intentionality that supposedly meets Kripke's constraints, but by showing that such an account is not needed in order to avoid the skeptical conclusion.[4]

2 The Skeptical Argument

I begin by rehearsing the opening phase of the skeptical argument, with a view to considering how it leads to the skeptical conclusion. We assume that I am an apparently competent speaker of English who knows basic arithmetic but who happens never to have added numbers larger than 57. I am now asked, "What is 68 + 57?" and I answer, "125." In so doing, Kripke says, I am confident that "125" is correct "both in the arithmetical sense that 125 is the sum of 68 and 57 and in the metalinguistic sense that 'plus,' as I intended to use that word in the past, denoted a function which, when applied to [68 and 57] ... yields the value 125" (8).[5] I am confident, that is, both that I have calculated correctly, and that I am using the linguistic expression "+" correctly given how I used it, or intended to use it, in the past. At this point, however, I encounter a skeptic who challenges

---

[3] I have argued for the second two points in Ginsborg (2018); the present chapter draws on the connection with Wittgenstein to expand and strengthen that argument. See also Ginsborg (2022) and (In Press).

[4] Note that my aspiration to "put Wittgenstein back into Kripkenstein" extends only to the skeptical argument, and not to the skeptical solution. As I indicate in Section 5, I take Wittgenstein's own answer to the skeptical problem to be quite different from the communitarian solution proposed on his behalf by Kripke.

[5] Unless otherwise specified, page references are to Kripke (1982). Note Kripke's reference to my use of the word *in the past*; unlike most commentators, I take this as indicating that the correctness at issue has an essentially temporal dimension. The significance of this will emerge later.

my confidence in what Kripke calls the "metalinguistic" correctness of my answer. This skeptic raises the possibility that "as I used the term 'plus' in the past, the answer I intended for '68 + 57' should have been '5'" (8). My first reaction is to dismiss this suggestion as insane, but the skeptic goes on to give a reason. He points out that my past uses of "+" are consistent with the hypothesis that I meant, not addition, but quaddition, a function which yields the sum for arguments less than 57, but which otherwise yields the value 5. Unless I can rule out that hypothesis, he says, I have to give up my confidence in the "metalinguistic" correctness of my answer. In fact, unless I can show that I specifically meant addition, I have no reason at all to believe that "125" is correct in this sense, that is, that it conforms to what I meant by "+" when I used it previously. He puts this by saying that my choice of "125" as an answer to the question "what is 68 + 57" is arbitrary, an unjustified "leap in the dark" (10, 15).

After this opening phase, the skeptical dialectic continues in the form of my making various attempts to show that I meant addition, and the skeptic arguing that these attempts are inadequate. In a preamble to this stretch of the dialectic, Kripke describes my task as that of "citing a fact in which my meaning addition consists." Accordingly, I put forward a range of possible facts, most of which correspond to established philosophical accounts of meaning; regarding each of them, the skeptic argues that it fails to meet constraints essential to capturing the idea of meaning, notably the constraint that meaning is normative – at a first approximation, that what I mean by an expression determines, and puts me in a position to recognize, how I ought to use the expression. One immediate upshot of this extended stretch of argument is that I cannot rule out the skeptical hypothesis and, more generally, cannot show that I meant addition in my previous uses of "+." This upshot, at least on the face of it, is epistemological: it amounts to saying that I lack justification both for claiming that I meant addition and that I ought now to say "125." But Kripke makes clear that he takes the argument to yield a metaphysical conclusion as well. The argument establishes not just that I do not know that I meant addition, but that there is no fact of my having meant, or now meaning, addition. This conclusion generalizes to all uses of language: "there can be no fact as to what I mean by 'plus' or any other word at any time" (21). And it applies not just to what an individual means but to meaning generally: "it seems that the entire idea of meaning vanishes into thin air" (22).

How does this metaphysical conclusion follow from the epistemological considerations that precede it? Kripke is not clear on this point, and this may be part of the reason why many readers have discounted the initial, epistemological, phase of the argument. Readers who have attempted to accommodate the argument's epistemological starting point have typically justified the move to the metaphysical conclusion by pointing out that I am an "idealized" subject, in that the skeptic grants me complete cognitive access to my former behavior and conscious mental states. On the assumption that facts about meaning lie in one of those domains, it follows from my not knowing that I mean addition that there is no such thing as my meaning addition. However, this move is successful only if we allow the assumption that facts about meaning are facts about behavior and conscious mental states, and, more specifically, that they are the kinds of facts that are in principle knowable through observation or introspection. The skeptic grants me idealized versions of my ordinary cognitive powers of observation, introspection, and memory: he does not, however, grant me a God-like omniscience about all metaphysically possible aspects of reality. So without further argument to the effect that meaning facts must in principle be facts about observable behavior or introspectible mental contents, the argument, so construed, does not go through. And this is a ground for understanding the argument, in line with most recent interpreters, as fundamentally metaphysical, that is, as turning directly on the difficulty of saying what meaning consists in.

However, if the argument is understood in this latter way, then it is open to an obvious objection, raised by several of Kripke's early commentators under the head of "unargued reductionism."[6] What is to stop us responding to the challenge to "cite the fact" of my meaning addition by saying that it is, simply, the fact that I mean addition? Famously, Kripke characterizes this approach, that of taking meaning facts as "sui generis," as "desperate and mysterious." But it is not clear what is desperate about taking facts about meaning to be primitive, nor why – if it is impossible to reduce meaning facts to facts that are more fundamental – the irreducibility of putative meaning facts should be thought to imply that there are no such facts. Typically, if we find ourselves unable to reduce facts of one kind to facts of a supposedly more fundamental kind, we do not conclude that there simply are no facts of the first kind. It might be replied that, in fact, the true moral of the skeptical argument is not that there are no meaning facts at all, but rather that there are insuperable obstacles in the way of a reductive account of meaning.[7]

---

[6] McGinn (1984: 150–152); for further references, and more discussion, see Ginsborg (2018: 153).

[7] Verheggen (In Press) reads the argument primarily as a challenge to semantic reductionism, although one that, in combination with the claim that primitivism about meaning is unsatisfactory, leads to the "provocative" conclusion that there are no meaning facts. Anandi Hattiangadi (this volume) sees the primary interest of the argument as lying in the challenge it offers to materialist or physicalist views of meaning and intentionality, whether reductive or non-reductive.

But although that is certainly an interesting and significant conclusion, it is considerably less ambitious than the conclusion which the skeptical argument claimed to establish. So, one way or another, we are left with a weaker argument than initially advertised, one which fails to establish the dramatic and seemingly paradoxical conclusion that all language is meaningless.

The reading I propose avoids this objection by taking the argument to turn, not on the metaphysical challenge of saying what meaning consists, but on the epistemological challenge of justifying my confidence in the correctness of "125" as a response to "68+57?" On this reading, the metaphysical conclusion depends on the epistemological considerations raised at the beginning of the argument, but it is arrived at through a different route from that considered above. My failure to know that I meant addition rather than quaddition by "+" is not intended to lead directly to the conclusion that there is no such thing as meaning; rather, it is intended to show that, in the scenario Kripke asks us to imagine, I do not know, or am not warranted in believing, that "125" is correct given my past use of "+." It is this last claim – the claim that "125" is a "leap in the dark" – that, when generalized to all my particular uses of language, yields the conclusion that there is no such thing as meaning. Epistemological considerations are thus central to the argument, but the knowledge that is most crucial is not knowledge of what I mean by a given expression, but rather knowledge of what Kripke labels the "metalinguistic" correctness of my particular uses of expressions: knowledge, in each use, that it conforms to previous uses. To see how the argument works, though, we need to look more closely at this kind of correctness, and to consider why failure to recognize that my uses of language are correct in this sense should lead to the disappearance of meaning. We can do this most effectively by looking at some of the passages in Wittgenstein which, arguably, are the inspiration for Kripke's skeptical argument. I turn to this in the next section (Section 3).

3 Knowing How to Go On

The most important passage for our purposes is *Philosophical Investigations (PI)* §185 where Wittgenstein describes an aberrant pupil who goes on wrongly in developing the sequence 0, 2, 4, 6, 8…. We first encounter this pupil in *PI* §141, where he is learning the basics of the decimal system, first learning to copy sequences of numerals, then learning how to write the numerals 0 through 9 in the correct order, and then (as described in *PI* §143) learning to develop sequences of numerals into the tens and hundreds. Wittgenstein reintroduces him in *PI* §185. He now seems to have got the hang of the decimal system, so we go on to teach him to develop simple arithmetical sequences in response to orders like "+1," "+2," and "+3." For example, when we say "+2" he is to write a segment of the sequence 0, 2, 4, 6, 8.... The pupil appears to have got the hang of this too, because we have tested him on two- and three-digit numbers and he has been successful every time: he has, let us say, responded to the order "+2" by writing out the whole sequence up to 998 and has gone on, as we expect, to write "1000." But now, instead of writing "1002, 1004," he writes "1004, 1008, 1012." When we protest that we told him to add two, and tell him to look at what he wrote earlier (with the implication that he should do the same as he was doing earlier), he is baffled. He insists that what he is doing is correct and that he is going on in the same way as he did earlier. Wittgenstein continues as follows:

– It would now be no use to us to say 'But don't you see...?' – and repeat for him the old explanations and examples. – In such a case, we might perhaps say: this person naturally understands our order, once given our explanations, as *we* would understand the order 'Add 2 up to 1000, 4 up to 2000, 6 up to 3000, and so on.' This case would be like one in which a person naturally reacted to a pointing gesture with the hand by looking in the direction from fingertip to wrist, instead of looking in the direction towards the fingertip.

Although the example is in the first instance about someone else's apparent failure to continue a sequence correctly, and hence to understand an expression (in this case, "add two") that we are trying to teach him, Wittgenstein clearly intends the case to raise a question also about our own knowledge of how to continue the sequence and hence our own understanding of the expression "add two." How do *I* know, when I continue the sequence with "1002, 1004" rather than with "1004, 1008," that it is *I* who am going on correctly, and not the pupil? And if I do not know, then how can I be confident that it is I, and not the pupil, who have arrived at the correct understanding of the expression "add two" as it was used previously? This becomes clear in the next section, §186, where Wittgenstein asks the more general question: "How is it decided what is the right step to take at any particular point?" His interlocutor proposes that "[t]he right step is the one that is in accordance with the order – as it was *meant*." The suggestion is that I can appeal to what I meant in the past to justify my claim that the pupil is going on wrong and that I am going on correctly. But then Wittgenstein asks, rhetorically, "So when you gave the order "+ 2" you meant that he was to write 1002 after 1000 – and did you then also mean that he should write 1868 after 1866, and 100036 after 100034, and so on – an infinite number of such sentences?" My meaning "add two" when I gave the order did not involve my having in mind an explicit instruction to write "1002" after "1000"; what I had in mind was thus seemingly compatible with the thought that the correct thing to write after "1000" was "1004." So I cannot appeal to my past meaning, conceived as a state of mind, to justify the correctness of writing "1002" at this point. I am thus left with the apparently skeptical question: how do I know that I should respond to the instruction "add two," once I have got to 1000, by writing 1002? Or, to quote a related passage from *Remarks on the Foundations of Mathematics* (*RFM*) I §3: "How do I know that in continuing the series +2 I must write '20004, 20006' not '20004, 20008?' (The question 'How do I know this colour is "red"? is similar.)'[8] And the implication is that if I do not know that, then I have failed to understand the expression "+2" or the word "red."

Another way to put this implication is in terms of the notion of "knowing how to go on," which figures in a number of passages in the *Investigations* leading up to the example of the aberrant pupil (*PI* §§151, 154–155, 179, 183–184). As Wittgenstein suggests, the expressions "now I can go on," "now I know how to go on" and "now I understand" are used interchangeably to express our confidence that we have grasped the rule instantiated by a series of examples. We say we have grasped the rule – and, accordingly, understood the expression associated with the rule – when we are confident in our capacity to recognize the correct next step in a sequence. (Here "sequence" and "next step" should be understood in a way that accommodates non-numerical examples: in the case of a child learning the expression "red," the "sequence" would be the uses of "red" she has already observed, and the correct "next step" would be, say, pointing to the strawberry rather than the banana when asked, "Show me the red one.") We take for granted, with respect to our ordinary linguistic expressions, that we know how to go on in their use, which is to say that we can recognize which uses are correct given the uses we have already made or observed. If we lacked this knowledge, then – going by the interchangeability of "now I know how to go on!" and "now I understand!" – we would not understand the expressions. The question invited by the case of the aberrant pupil – how do *I* know that I should write "1002" after "1000"? – in turn raises the possibility

---

[8] Both the turn to the first person and the connection with understanding are explicit in notes taken from lectures Wittgenstein gave in 1939: "We are ... tempted to say, "We can never really know that he will not differ from us when squaring numbers over, say, 1,000,000,000. And that shows that you never know for sure that another person understands." *But the real difficulty is, how do you know that you yourself understand a symbol?* [emphasis mine]" (*Remarks on the Foundations of Mathematics*, 28).

that my confidence in the correctness of "1002" may be no more warranted than the pupil's confidence that he should write "1004." If that is so, then, despite the fact that I do indeed "go on" in my uses of expressions like "add two" and "red," in the sense that I use them, with confidence, in new cases, this "going on" does not reflect any knowledge on my part: to borrow an expression from Kripke, each new use of the expression is an "unjustified leap in the dark." But if I do not know how to go on, then I do not understand the expressions. Wittgenstein, characteristically, does not generalize beyond the particular cases he discusses, but the skeptical threat is clear. If I do not know that "1002" is the correct next step, then not only do I not understand "add two," but nobody ever understands any expression. And, on the plausible assumption that there can be no linguistic meaning without linguistic understanding, it follows that nobody ever means anything by an expression either.

Although Kripke does not cite the passage from §185 or its continuation in §186, it is natural to understand the skeptical dialectic as modeled on the example of the aberrant pupil. I am confident that I should say "125," just as the pupil is confident that he should write "1004." But the skeptic attempts to challenge my confidence, just as we attempt to challenge the confidence of the pupil who says 1004. In raising the possibility that the "metalinguistically correct" response to "68 + 57?" is "5" rather than "125" – he is suggesting that I am in the same situation with respect to "+" as that of the aberrant pupil with respect to "add two." Just as the pupil wrongly takes "1004" to be the correct thing to write after "1000" given what he wrote previously in response to "add two," so I may be wrongly taking "125 to the correct response to "68 + 57?," given my previous responses to "+" questions. And the skeptic uses that possibility to argue that I do not know how to go on in my use of "+," just as we take it that the aberrant pupil does not know how to go on in the sequence "0,2,4,6,8…" and hence in his use of the associated expression "+2." On this way of understanding the skeptical scenario, the initial skeptical challenge is very close to the question implicitly raised by the example of the aberrant pupil (and more explicitly in the passage Kripke quotes from *RFM* I §3): how do *I* know that the right way to go on from "0,2,4,6,8…998" is to write "1000, 1002" and not "1000, 1004"?

Now we saw that Wittgenstein does not explicitly draw the conclusion that, if I do not know the right way to go on, then there is no such thing as understanding, or meaning anything by, a linguistic expression. But we saw that this conclusion in fact seems to follow. So it is natural to read Kripke as attempting to make explicit the damaging consequences for meaning and understanding that appear to be raised by the example of the aberrant pupil. On this reading, Kripke highlights the first-personal implications of Wittgenstein's example by reversing the perspective: rather than my questioning someone else's mastery of an expression, it is my own mastery of an expression which is under scrutiny. He also sharpens the question, and makes clearer its potentially damaging implications, by asking not *how*, but, in a skeptical spirit, *whether* I know the right way to go on. And he goes to great lengths to argue, on behalf of the skeptic, that I do *not* know the right way to go on – that my confidence about the right way to go on does not amount to knowledge. It is in this context that he undertakes his extensive examination of philosophical accounts of meaning. Because he assumes that knowledge of how to go on in one's uses of an expression depends on knowledge of what one meant by the expression in one's previous uses, he takes the skeptic's task to be that of undermining my putative knowledge that I meant addition rather than quaddition in my previous uses. This leads him to the demand that I should "cite a fact" in which my meaning addition consists, and so to the lengthy discussion – nowhere paralleled in Wittgenstein – of the inadequacies of various attempts to account for meaning in more fundamental terms. These differences aside, though, the skeptical problem raised by Kripke parallels – and, I believe, should be understood in terms of – the problem that is implicitly raised by Wittgenstein in the passages under discussion. The question that the skeptic first raises about my entitlement to regard "125" as "metalinguistically correct" is a question about what Wittgenstein calls "knowing how to go on." And it is my failure to answer that question – and not, as such, my failure to provide a reductive account of meaning – that leads to the skeptical threat that there are no such phenomena as understanding or meaning.

One further difference that might obscure the parallel is that, in Kripke's example, the question concerns the conformity of my present use specifically to my own past usage, whereas for Wittgenstein, the question primarily concerns the pupil's conformity, or lack of it, to the usage of his teachers. Even though it is the pupil himself who has been developing the sequence up to 1000, it is part of the background of the example that those uses have been endorsed by his teachers as well, and that he thinks his writing 1004 after 1000 is correct in light of *their* previous use of the expression "+2." The pupil's failure to understand "+2" – which prompts the question whether we ourselves understand "+2" – thus appears initially as a failure to *learn* the use of "+2." The corresponding first-personal question likewise can be framed in terms of learning: am I using "+2" correctly given the examples my teachers showed me, or am I responding arbitrarily to their instruction? But I do not think that this difference is consequential. The primary reason Kripke recasts the example in terms of conformity to my own previous usage, rather than that of my teachers, is to make the point that the problem does not rest on behavioristic assumptions (see at 14). Putting the skeptic's initial question in terms of whether "125" conforms to my own past usage of "+," rather than that of other people I have observed, makes clear that the problem does not rest on my inability to draw inferences about meaning from external behavior. But Kripke could equally well have put it in terms of my conformity to others' use of "+" while allowing me telepathic access to the contents of their minds. Moreover, Kripke himself suggests in a number of contexts that the problem has something to do with learning. He motivates the hypothesis that I meant quaddition by noting that "[in] the past, I gave myself only a finite number of examples [of the function associated with '+']" (8). The talk of "giving myself examples" suggests that, as for Wittgenstein, conformity to past usage is conformity to the usage of a teacher: the difference is just that, for Kripke, the teacher is my own past self. Other formulations make an explicit connection with learning. In connection with the *tabair* example, Kripke says that "I think that I have learned the term 'table' in such a way that it will apply to indefinitely many future items" (19). And in connection with the *duckog* example, he describes the problem as one of how I can extend the term "duck" from ducks seen in Central Park (which is where I learned the term "duck") to ducks not found there (117). So there is no reason to think that Kripke differs from Wittgenstein regarding whether the problem concerns conformity to previous uses in general, or just to my own previous uses.

4   The Idiolect-of-the-Moment Hypothesis and the Importance of Previous Use

The skeptical argument as I have presented it depends on the claim that there cannot be such a thing as anyone's meaning anything by an expression – for example, my meaning addition by "+" – unless we are in a position to know, of each of our uses of the expression, that it conforms to previous uses of the expression, whether our own or those of our teachers. I have motivated this claim in terms of the connection Wittgenstein draws between the idea of understanding and the idea of the correct next step in a sequence of uses. In the case of a child learning the use of an expression, we can say that she has come to understand the expression, and by extension, that she uses it meaningfully, only once she knows how to go on in her use of the expression, where this implies a capacity to recognize her uses as correct in light of the preceding uses.[9] But is this connection sufficient to warrant the claim that the meaning as such depends on knowing how to go on in this sense? Most interpreters of the skeptical argument assume that the crucial constraint on the possibility of meaning – the so-called normativity of meaning – requires that my use of an expression at any one time conform, not to previous uses of the expression, but to what I mean by the expression at the time of the use. Although, as we have seen, Kripke introduces the skeptical argument by having the skeptic challenge the conformity of "125" to what I meant by "+" when I used it earlier, there is widespread agreement that this temporal dimension is essential neither to the argument nor to the thesis that meaning is normative.[10] All that is required in order for me now to mean addition by "+," and by implication to understand "+" as meaning addition, is, on this interpretation, for me to have in mind a standard which determines some uses of "+" as correct and the rest as incorrect. I need not be capable of recognizing any kind of relation, normative or otherwise, between my present uses and those which I made or observed in the past.

Now Wittgenstein's discussion suggests that, if a child is to succeed in learning the meaning of an expression from examples she has been given, she must be capable of coming to recognize new uses of the expression as correct in the light of those examples. Hearing "duck" used for ducks in Central Park might engender a disposition to apply "duck" to ducks on Hampstead Heath, but this would count as learning only in the very undemanding sense used by some psychologists and cognitive scientists, in which any acquisition of a disposition counts as learning. It would not be learning in the sense in which we normally think of learning in human children, which requires intelligent appreciation, on the part of the child, of what she should do in response to the teacher's examples, and, relatedly, the ability to recognize when she is being corrected and to modify her behavior as a conscious response to correction. Such learning, in the case of language, requires the ability to grasp, in particular cases, whether one's uses are appropriate to previous uses. The child who says "duck" to a duck on her first visit to London does not count as having learned from her previous duck-experiences in Central Park unless she is in a position to register a normative connection between her "duck"-utterances now and the ones she observed earlier. But someone might

---

[9] Note that this does not require that, at the time of use, I consciously recall any past uses; it requires only that, if I am reminded of past uses, I can recognize that my present use conforms to them. Thanks to Gary Ebbs for prompting this clarification.

[10] McGinn (1984) is an exception, but my view of the relevant normativity differs from his. See Ginsborg (2022) for discussion and for a defense of my temporal reading of the normativity thesis.

accept this as a point about what is required for learning the meaning of an expression, while denying that it has any implications for grasp of meaning as such. Even though, as a matter of empirical fact, we do come to understand our most basic expressions by learning from examples, this is not necessary for the possibility of understanding. So, the objection goes, understanding an expression does not require that we be able to recognize a normative fit between our uses of the expression at one time and our, or others', uses at earlier times; all we need to be able to recognize is the normative fit between any one use and the meaning that we have in mind at the time of that use.

We can make the objection vivid by imagining that, rather than our coming to understand expressions by learning them from others, God grants us linguistic understanding by implanting the meanings directly in our minds. That is to say, for each expression, God puts into our minds an item of intentional content which both inclines us to use the expression in a specific way and which we recognize as constituting a standard for its use. If the objection is well-founded, the presence of this item in any one person's mind at any time should be sufficient for saying that she understands the expression, or, equivalently, grasps its meaning. So, even though the possibility of linguistic communication would depend on God's giving each of us the same meaning for any one expression, and also on his keeping the association between expressions and their meanings constant over time, this would not be required in principle for each of us, at any one time, to understand our own idiolect. We might allow that, perhaps in order to amuse himself, God could change my idiolect from day to day or from moment to moment. Today he has made it so that I mean addition by "+" and duck by the word "duck," but tomorrow, or in a moment, I might mean quaddition and duckog. This hypothesis satisfies the constraint that meaning is normative, as it is typically understood, since, at any one time, the meaning I have in mind normatively constrains my uses of the expression, and is recognized by me as doing so. Regardless of what I meant a moment ago or what I will mean tomorrow, I know now that, given what I mean by "+," the correct response to "68 + 57" is "125" rather than "5." It might seem, then, that we have all we need to make sense of my grasping the meaning of "+" in my idiolect-of-the moment. Admittedly, I am not grasping a public meaning, nor am I grasping a personal meaning which endures over time. The meaning I grasp may be a short-lived thing which exists only while I am asking myself and answering the question "what is 68 + 57?" But there is nonetheless something in my mind which I recognize as determining the correctness of my use of "+" on this occasion, and this is sufficient for me to count as understanding "+."

However, the idiolect-of-the-moment hypothesis fails to accommodate a distinction between two kinds of correctness, which is, I believe, essential to the idea of linguistic understanding. We can make sense, on this hypothesis, of my going wrong in responding "5" to "68 + 57?," or saying "That's a duck" about a dog on Hampstead Heath or under the Eiffel Tower, but we cannot distinguish between my going wrong because I am mistaken about the arithmetical or empirical facts, and my going wrong because of what Tyler Burge calls "linguistic or conceptual" error.[11] Ordinarily, we recognize two different kinds of mistake and conversely, two different kinds of correctness, in our use of an expression. We can be wrong in responding to a "+" question or in saying "that's a duck" because we have failed to calculate correctly (e.g. forgotten to carry) or because we have been misled by the poor viewing conditions (this distant object looks like a duck, but it is actually a floating log). But we can equally well be wrong because we lack sufficient understanding of the expression, or do not fully grasp the corresponding concept. A child might say, of something that is obviously a goose, "That's a duck," because she understands "duck" as applying to all water-birds; or she might refuse to apply "duck" to a mallard because, having learned the word in connection with her bathtime rubber duck, she understands it as restricted to yellow ducks. This kind of error is not limited to children. I might report that a house with a gabled roof has a "pediment" because, having learned the term "pediment" in connection with triangular structures on top of colonnades, doors, and windows, I have come to misunderstand it as applying to any triangular section of a facade. To borrow some examples from Burge, I might deny that someone entered into a "contract" because the agreement she made was verbal, and my acquaintance with the expression up until now has led me to understand "contract" as restricted to written agreements, or I might refer to a harpsichord resting on a table as a "clavichord" because I have come to understand "clavichord" as applying to any early keyboard instrument without legs.[12] In both kinds of cases, the upshot is, or can be construed as, a false assertion, but the error responsible for the falsity is different in each.

---

[11] Burge (1979: 82, 100). In invoking this kind of error, and the examples Burge gives of it, I am not necessarily endorsing Burge's account of how such error is to be understood, nor the use he makes of it in arguing for anti-individualism. What I am drawing from Burge is primarily the idea of a distinctive kind of error, in one's use of a word, that cannot be assimilated either to straightforwardly factual (paradigmatically empirical error) or to mistakes in which a word with one meaning is unintentionally substituted for one with another meaning (as in slips of the tongue, spoonerisms and malapropisms).

[12] Burge (1979: 80ff).

The ordinary idea of understanding depends on our being able to distinguish these two kinds of error, and, correspondingly, correctness. We attribute understanding, as opposed to effectiveness at discerning the relevant facts, to the extent that someone successfully avoids the second, rather than the first, kind of error.[13] Someone may be bad at arithmetic, or lacking in the observational skills that make for a good birdwatcher or naturalist, but still have a perfectly good understanding of "+" and "duck." Conversely, someone could be highly skilled in these respects – capable, say, of doing complex arithmetical calculations or creating detailed drawings and descriptions of birds – and still make false assertions because of deficiencies in their understanding of arithmetical and ornithological terms or in their grasp of the corresponding concepts. Indeed, as I understand Kripke, it is this distinction that he aims to capture when, in setting up the skeptical argument, he describes me as confident that "125" is correct in both the arithmetical and the "metalinguistic" sense (8). The worry that "125" is an "unjustified leap in the dark" (10), and hence that, for all I know, "68 + 57 = 125" is false, is not that I lack arithmetical justification for asserting the sentence "68 + 57 = 125," but rather that my understanding of "+" is deficient, so that I lack grounds for believing that "68 + 57 = 125" means what I think it does. But, on the idiolect-of-the-moment hypothesis, we cannot make sense of the distinction. The meaning now in my mind serves as a standard for determining whether "68 + 57 = 125" or "that's a duck" (uttered while pointing to a duck) is a true or false sentence. However, it does not determine whether falsity would indicate a lack of understanding or an ability to determine the arithmetical or empirical facts. This means that the idiolect-of-the-moment hypothesis does not allow for the distinctive kind of error whose avoidance is characteristic of understanding an expression. Consequently, the hypothesis is incoherent. God cannot grant us understanding simply by giving us a standard for the truth or falsity of our uses; what he needs to give us is a standard by which we determine whether our uses are correct in Burge's "linguistic or conceptual" sense. But on the idiolect-of-the-moment hypothesis, there is no standard simply because there is no such thing as being correct in the distinctive sense relevant to understanding.[14]

---

[13] Davidson concludes from his discussion of malapropisms that this distinction cannot be maintained: we must "erase ... the boundary between knowing a language and knowing our way around in the world generally" (1986: 445–446). I am arguing in effect that, without this boundary, we cannot make sense of meaning or understanding. Davidson would disagree, but discussion of this lies beyond the scope of the present chapter.

[14] Davidson's triangulation argument, as defended by Claudine Verheggen in Myers and Verheggen (2016), and helpfully summarized and discussed in Verheggen (2023),

The idea that understanding – and not just learning to understand – depends on the recognition of conformity to previous uses is motivated by the thought that, if there is a standard of correctness in the "linguistic or conceptual" sense, it must be afforded by, or depend on, the history of past use. If, to cite Burge's most famous example,[15] Bert applies "arthritis" to the pain in his thigh, he is failing to go on appropriately from past uses of "arthritis" in the same sense in which Wittgenstein's aberrant pupil fails to go on appropriately from past uses of "+2." The main difference between the examples, aside from degree of psychological plausibility, is that Bert's error is localized and thus can be easily corrected, whereas the pupil's error is part of a systematic pattern of error, extending to the words (like "count" and "same") which we might use to try to explain where he is going wrong. (We could make Bert more like the pupil by supposing that he resists correction: when we explain that arthritis is a disorder of the joints, he might insist that his thigh is a "joint" and that this use of "joint" is consistent with its use for his knees and elbows; if we point out that joints are like hinges, and his thigh is not like a hinge, it might turn out that he applies "hinge" to doors and jewel-box lids, and so finds it natural to think of his thigh as "like a hinge" as well.)

It might be responded that, although we might need a standard for correctness in the relevant sense, it does not have to be provided by previous use; it could instead be that Bert is going wrong because what he means by "arthritis" diverges from what the broader community means, or what the experts mean.[16] On this picture, what is distinctive about linguistic or conceptual error as opposed to factual error is that it has its source in this kind of divergence. We understand an expression, then, to

---

might seem to rule out the idiolect-of-the-moment hypothesis for a different reason, but one which also has to do with understanding: a speaker can assign meanings to her own expressions only through linguistic interaction with another speaker occupying a distinct point of view on how the first speaker should be interpreted. While adequate discussion of this point lies beyond the scope of this chapter, I am inclined to suspect that Davidson's commitment to what Verheggen calls the "primacy of idiolects" means that he cannot rule out the in-principle possibility of the idiolect-of-the-moment hypothesis. Even if, absent divine intervention, the meanings of our own expressions can be fixed only through our triangulation with others, it would remain possible, on Davidson's conception of meaning, for God to endow each of us directly with determinate meanings corresponding to our expressions and thus, by Davidson's lights, to make it the case that we understood those expressions. The difficulty I am raising for the idiolect-of-the-moment hypothesis goes deeper: God could not make our expressions meaningful because, in the absence of a standard for what we have been calling "linguistic or conceptual" correctness, there would be no such thing as understanding those expressions.

[15] Burge (1979: 77).
[16] Thanks to Paul Boghossian for raising this possibility.

the extent that the meaning of the expression in our idiolect matches the meaning of the expression in other idiolects, that is, those of the broader community or those of the experts. Now for some kinds of linguistic errors, this does seem like the right account: a very clear case is that of malapropism, where we confuse the meanings of two similar-sounding words (say, "epithet" and "epitaph"). But for reasons articulated by Burge, not all errors relevant to understanding are naturally assimilated to this model.[17] More importantly, this picture assumes as a starting point that individuals in a community can attach determinate meanings to their expressions, or possess concepts corresponding to those expressions: without that assumption, we cannot make sense of the idea that what one individual means by an expression at a given time matches, or fails to match, what other individuals mean by it. This assumption, however, is just what is in question when we ask what is required for understanding an expression. To make sense of the idea that what Bert means by "arthritis" or "contract" diverges from what the medical or legal experts mean, we have to assume that both Bert and the experts mean something by those expressions, which in turn requires that they understand them, at least in their own idiolects. So while in isolated cases, such as malapropisms, we can appeal to community or expert meaning as the standard of linguistic or conceptual correctness, we cannot appeal to that standard to account for the possibility of understanding in general.

5 A Response to the Skeptical Argument

I have defended a reading of the skeptical argument which, in line with Kripke's stated intentions, understands it as an interpretation of Wittgenstein. Specifically, the skeptic's conclusion that there are no facts of meaning is reached through his challenge to our supposed knowledge of the "right way to go on" from a past sequence of uses – a challenge which is implicit in Wittgenstein's example of the aberrant pupil. If we do not know the right way to go on in our uses of linguistic expressions, then we do not understand them, but if there is no understanding of them, then there is no meaning anything by them either: the idea of meaning thus "vanishes into thin air" (22). The skeptic's arguments to the effect that I cannot cite a fact in which my having meant addition consists are not intended, on this reading, to lead directly to the conclusion that there is no such fact. Rather, they are intended to undermine my supposed knowledge that I meant addition, which Kripke takes to

---

[17] Burge (1979: 90).

be a condition of my being able to know the right way to go on from my previous uses of "+." My lack of knowledge of what I meant in the past is not in itself a reason to suppose that there are no facts about what I meant, or now mean, by my expressions; rather, for Kripke, it is a reason to deny that I know how to go on from my past uses of expressions, and hence that I understand or mean anything by those expressions.

In addition to bringing Kripke's skeptic closer to Wittgenstein, this reading has the advantage of making the skeptical argument both more distinctive and stronger than the consensus reading allows. It interprets the argument as turning, not on familiar metaphysical concerns about how to account for meaning and understanding in more fundamental terms, but on an epistemological question which is, arguably, original with Wittgenstein: how do I know the right way to go on from a previous sequence of behavior? Thus construed, the argument is stronger in that it resists the often-cited objection from unargued reductionism. As I argued in Section 2, the skeptical problem, as standardly understood, can be answered simply by denying that meaning facts must be reducible to more basic facts, that is, by allowing the possibility that meaning facts are primitive. But this answer does not work for the problem as I have construed it. In order to show that I know how to go on from my previous uses of "+" – for example, that the correct "next step" is to respond to "68 + 57?" with "125" rather than "5" – it is not enough, according to Kripke, for me to say that my having meant addition is a primitive fact. What I have to show, to satisfy Kripke's skeptic, is that I *know* that I meant addition – that is to say, I have to provide epistemic justification for my belief that it was addition, rather than quaddition, that I meant. Kripke is not, then, simply relying on the assumption that meaning facts have to be reducible to more basic facts; he could allow provisionally that meaning facts could be primitive, and still generate the skeptical puzzle by asking how we can justify our supposed knowledge that one rather than another such fact obtains. The nonreductionist might respond to this version of the argument by proposing, not just that meaning facts are primitive, but that we have a primitive capacity to know these facts. When the skeptic asks me to justify my confidence that I meant addition and not quaddition, I can reply that no justification is necessary: it is simply a fact about me that I know I meant addition, just as it is a fact about me that I meant addition. But in the context of the skeptical dialectic, this answer is unsatisfactory: it is not an answer to the skeptic, but a dogmatic refusal to engage with his argument.[18]

---

[18] For more on this point, see Ginsborg (2018: 158–159).

How, then, can the skeptic be answered? Recall that, on my reading of the argument, the skeptic's primary challenge is not to my knowledge that I meant addition in my past uses of "+," but to my knowledge that, given those past uses, I ought to say "125": it is my lack of this knowledge that leads to the conclusion that I do not understand "+" and, in turn, to the disappearance of meaning. My knowledge that I meant addition is important to the argument only because Kripke assumes that, if I do not know that I meant addition, I cannot know that I ought to say "125." If the assumption is correct, then the only way to answer the skeptic is to justify my claim to have meant addition: something which, as the skeptic argues at length, cannot be done. But we can also answer the skeptic by challenging the assumption, and this is the approach which I propose. I can grant the skeptic that I do not know that I meant addition, as opposed to quaddition, in my previous uses. But I can deny that this impugns my knowledge that I ought to say "125" rather than "5." In Wittgenstein's terms, I can "know how to go on" from my teachers' uses of an expression without first having to identify what my teachers meant when they used that expression, or what rule was governing their use of the expression. The question of whether responding "125" or "5" is the correct continuation of my previous uses of "+" is independent of the question of what I meant in those previous uses, so the skeptic's suggestion that I might have meant quaddition leaves untouched my prior conviction that I ought to say "125." This approach parallels what I take to be Wittgenstein's own response to the threat of skepticism implicit in his discussion of the aberrant pupil.[19] Wittgenstein rejects the idea that, in order to know what I should write after "1000" in the series 0,2,4,6,8..., I must be guided or justified by an antecedent grasp of the rule governing the series. I can recognize "1002" as appropriate to the sequence "0,2,4,6,8....1000" without first having to interpret that sequence, or the expression "+2," as meaning *add two* as opposed to, say, *add two up to 1000 and then add four*.[20] Similarly, we can answer Kripke's skeptic by rejecting the requirement that I need to interpret myself as having meant addition rather than quaddition in order to know that I should now say "125." This allows us to short-circuit the question whether I meant addition or quaddition. Even if I meant quaddition, in which case

---

[19] For more on this parallel, see §§5–6 of Ginsborg (2022).
[20] This is of a piece with Wittgenstein's remark – often taken, following McDowell (1984), to embody Wittgenstein's rejection of rule-following skepticism – that "there is a way of grasping a rule which is not an interpretation" (PI §201). I grasp the add-two rule, not by interpreting the expression "+2" or the sequence I was shown, but by knowing the correct way to continue the sequence, where this knowledge does not itself rely on interpretation.

"68 + 57 = 125" is false in the language I was speaking earlier, I can still know it to be the case that "125" is the correct next step in the sequence of my earlier responses to "+" questions.[21]

Where does this leave the skeptical challenge as it has typically been understood, that is, as a challenge to give an account of what meaning consists in? In earlier work, I argued that the approach I have just sketched allows the skeptic's interlocutor not only to defend the correctness of "125" as an answer to "86 + 57," but also to offer a "partially reductive" account of meaning addition in the form of a normatively enhanced version of the dispositional view.[22] Roughly, on this account, meaning addition by "+" is being disposed to respond to "+" questions with the sum, and, in so doing, to take one's response to be primitively appropriate to one's previous uses of "+."[23] Although I remain cautiously optimistic about the prospects of such an account,[24] I have come to believe that the task of giving an account of my meaning addition is inessential, and perhaps even irrelevant, to the task of answering the skeptical argument, properly understood. If, as the skeptic argues, there is no such thing as meaning and rule-following, it is not because I am not in a position to give an account, reductive or otherwise, of what meaning addition consists in. At most, my being able to give such an account might put me in a position to establish, against the skeptic, that I previously meant addition rather than quaddition, so that my saying

---

[21] This approach might seem to resemble that offered by James Shaw (this volume) in that both appeal to the idea of "going on" from previous uses. For Shaw, I meant addition rather than quaddition because "addition is the most regular and uniform continuation" of previous uses; responding "125" to "68+57" is more "similar" to my previous uses than responding "5." (As Shaw makes clear, his approach is like that of David Lewis (1983), but without the metaphysical underpinnings.) But there are two important differences. First, my approach turns on the idea not that responding with "125" is *similar to* what I did previously, but that it is *correct or appropriate* given what I did previously, where this appropriateness does not depend on its being similar. (I argue in §6 of Ginsborg (2020) for the conceptual priority of the idea of going on correctly over that of going on the same way; the same considerations apply with respect to Shaw's preferred notion of going on in a way that is similar.) Second, Shaw's idea that saying "125" is going on in a uniform or similar way figures, for Shaw, as part of an argument to the effect that I meant addition, whereas my approach bypasses altogether the question of what I meant. This means that Shaw's answer does not address the problem as I understand it, since it does not account for the immediacy of my ordinary knowledge that "125" is correct in the relevant sense: for Shaw I can know this only by a stretch of philosophical reasoning to the effect that I must have meant addition because addition is the more uniform continuation of my previous uses.

[22] See Ginsborg (2011b).

[23] Or, as I might now put the last clause, "to take oneself to be going on as one ought in one's use of '+'."

[24] In spite of criticisms raised, for example, in Miller (2019), Sorgiovanni (2018), Sultanescu (2021) and Myers and Verheggen (2016: 50–53).

"125" accords with the meaning I previously ascribed to "+." But the skeptical challenge to the possibility of meaning, I have argued, turns not on whether my present use of "+" accords with my earlier *meaning*, but on whether it accords with my earlier *uses*, in the sense highlighted by Wittgenstein's examples of going on. The project of providing a wholly or partially reductive account of meaning is an interesting one, but, as I see it, tangential to addressing the very real challenge to meaning posed by Kripke's Wittgenstein.[25]

---

[25] I presented earlier versions of this chapter at a seminar led by Saul Kripke and Romina Padro at CUNY in 2021, and at a workshop organized by Claudine Verheggen at York University, Toronto, in 2022. I am grateful, for comments and discussion, to the participants at both events, especially Paul Boghossian, Chris Campbell, Anandi Hattiangadi, Saul Kripke, Dan Isaacson, Henry Jackman, Alex Miller, Bob Myers, Romina Padro, Olivia Sultanescu, Claudine Verheggen, Ben Winokur, and José Zalabardo. Thanks also to John Campbell, Naomi Ginsborg-Warren, and Daniel Warren for helpful conversations, and to Gary Ebbs for detailed and illuminating criticisms.

3 Answering Kripke's Skeptic
Dispositions without 'Dispositionalism'

Henry Jackman

1 Introduction

In his *Wittgenstein on Rules and Private Language*, Saul Kripke famously presented us with a novel type of skeptic who suggested that, given what we meant by "plus" in the past, the correct answer to "68 + 57" was not 125, but 5. Kripke asks us to accept for the sake of argument that we've never added a number over 56 before (and notes that there must be *some* number for which this assumption is true), so his skeptic can point out that all of our past applications of "plus" are compatible with our meaning *quus* by "plus," where *quus* functions just like *plus* for numbers under 57, but for every number 57 and over, gives the result of 5. The skeptic doesn't deny that we *now* mean *plus* by "plus," but he challenges us to find some past fact about us in virtue of which we are entitled to claim that we meant *plus* in the *past*, since, after all, all of our past applications of "plus" are as much in accordance with *quus* as they are with *plus*.

A naive, natural, and indeed obvious response to this skeptic is to note that, even if I had never responded to the question "what is 68 + 57?" before, *if I had been asked*, I *would* have answered "125" and not "5," and that this gives me good reason to say that I meant *plus* rather than *quus* in the past.[1] Kripke, however, is unmoved by this obvious response. This seems to be largely because he cashes out the natural appeal to my past dispositions to use the term in order to justify my claim that I meant *plus* rather than *quus* by "plus" in this case as an attempt to *identify* what I meant with how I would have answered. As he puts it:

> The dispositional analysis I have heard proposed is simple. To mean addition by "+" is to be disposed, when asked for any sum 'x + y' to give the sum of x and y as the answer (in particular, to say '125' when queried about '68 + 57'); to mean quus is to be disposed when queried about any arguments, to respond with their

---

[1] I initially thought of this as *the* naive response, but see the contributions to this volume from Shaw and Sultanescu for two other candidates for that title.

quuum (in particular to answer '5' when queried about '68 + 57') .... To say that in fact I meant plus in the past is to say ... that had I been queried about '68 + 57', I *would* have answered '125'. (Kripke 1982: 22–23)

Kripke argues that the resulting view, which he labels "dispositionalism," is inadequate for at least three reasons.

The first of these is that it seems incompatible with the fact that we can be *disposed to make mistakes,* and so ignores the fact that the question of whether I meant *plus* or *quus* in the past is related not to whether I *would have* answered "125," but rather whether I *should have* answered "125" (Kripke 1982: 37). To satisfy the skeptic, what we need to show is not just that we would have answered "125" to the question, but that we would have been *correct* in doing so (Kripke 1982: 57), and Kripke argues that the dispositionalist is unable to do this. Kripke often bundles this with a closely related worry. An answer to the skeptic must show not just that we would have answered "125" to the question, but that we would have been *justified* in doing so. Kripke argues, once again, that the dispositionalist is unable to do this. As he puts it, "the fact that our answer to the question of which function I meant is *justificatory* of my present response is ignored in the dispositional account" (Kripke 1982: 37). The third problem that Kripke brings up is that our dispositions are *finite*. There are numbers (such as those that would take more than a lifetime just to read out) that are so large that we have no actual disposition to add them together. Even if the dispositionalist answer were enough to deal with *quus* itself, there would be *some* other function out there that swerved off in the same way when it reached some extremely large number which we had *no* dispositions relating to.

I don't think that the first two of these are particularly compelling rejoinders to the 'naïve' response to the skeptic (at least once we separate it from 'dispositionalism'), and while the objection relating to the finiteness of my dispositions touches on a real issue, it's not clear that it is one that leads to any conclusions about meaning that would properly be called *skeptical*. Consequently, in what follows, I'll discuss why the 'naïve' response is a justified reaction to Kripke's initial skeptical challenge (as, of course, it is), even if 'dispositionalism' is not.

2   Dispositions, Dispositionalism, and Interpretation

While Kripke's skeptic has been presented as someone who potentially undermines any theory that takes meaning to be determined by use, his objections tell more against some use-based theories than others. In particular, while Kripke's focus on the 'dispositionalist' targets more 'atomistic' use-based theories (which tie the meaning of particular words to particular dispositions), more holistic theories (such as those that try to understand meaning via some notion of radical interpretation),[2] don't get much attention.

In many ways, it's surprising that Kripke gives the dispositionalist the monopoly on the naive response since these more holistic metasemantic theories were hardly obscure at the time his book was published.[3] Indeed, one might think that interest in Davidson's account of radical interpretation was then near its peak,[4] and Kripke's own colleague David Lewis had famously defended a version of the radical interpretation account almost a decade earlier.[5] Kripke claims that some version of dispositionalism was just what was, in fact, proposed by his interlocutors when they suggested the naive response (Kripke 1982: 22–23),[6] but this doesn't seem like enough on its own to explain why a more holistic appeal to dispositions would not have occurred to Kripke at some point.[7]

A possible explanation for why Kripke ignored the more holistic appeals to dispositions associated with radical interpretation may be his understanding these questions about meaning by analogy with the 'intelligence tests' by which we must determine which number comes next in a series like: 1, 4, 7, 10, 13, ...[8] There are two features that seem characteristic of such intelligence tests: first, the members of the initial

---

[2] Most notably Quine (1960), Davidson (1973), and Lewis (1974), though the general holistic approach can be seen in other theories (such as Burge 1986) that don't explicitly mention radical interpretation.

[3] Kripke does say that the book grew out of thoughts from 1962 and 1963 (Kripke 1982: 1), but while the full-blown Davidsonian view might not have been developed then, the sort of holistic metasemantics coming from Quine (see Quine 1951, 1960) should have still been very familiar.

[4] See for instance, Davidson (1973, 1984). The massive Rutgers conference on Davidson (whose papers were collected in Lepore and McLaughlin 1985 and Lepore 1986) was just two years later.

[5] Lewis (1974).

[6] And, once again, this might have been a little more plausible if they were responding to him in 1962 or 1963.

[7] It's possible that these holistic accounts struck Kripke as similar to the 'descriptive' theories of reference (or at least the 'cluster' version of them) of the sort that he criticized a decade earlier in his *Naming and Necessity* (Kripke 1972), and so perhaps he thought that such non-'dispositionalist' appeals to dispositions didn't need to be discussed. Indeed, Wilson's original formulation of charity ("We select as designatum [of a name] that individual which will make the largest possible number of [the speaker's] statements true" (Wilson 1959: 532)) can seem like a cluster version of the descriptivist view, and see McGinn (1977: 527) for an early statement of the view that Davidson's theory of radical interpretation involved such a commitment to descriptivism. However, while I'm sympathetic with Kripke's criticisms of descriptivism, they don't really tell against many holistic metasemantic theories in the interpretational tradition. I don't have room to go over all the reasons here, though see Jackman (2003a).

[8] And to some extent he is undoubtedly following Wittgenstein here (see Wittgenstein 1953a: par 185).

set of numbers *can't be wrong*,⁹ and second, only things that *can't* be wrong can serve as justifiers for how to go on. If past use is understood by analogy with the initial sequence of numbers, then it would seem that past use can't be mistaken as well, and Kripke seems to encourage this understanding by insisting that 68 + 57 "is a computation that I have never performed before" (Kripke 1982: 8). Kripke accuses the dispositionalist of equating performance with correctness (Kripke 1982: 24), but he implicitly seems to do precisely this with past usage. If our past use is incorrigible in this way, then we might think that whatever the skeptic's interlocutor appeals to must be incorrigible in that way too (as dispositions are for the 'dispositionalist'). Dispositions manifestly do not fit this bill,[10] but it should be clear that past use doesn't either, as our past applications can clearly be mistaken. Consequently, the analogy with intelligence tests isn't a good one here, and an account that allows past use to contribute to what we mean without being incorrigible will likely allow dispositions to do so as well.[11]

If we break away from the analogy with "intelligence tests," and allow more holistic theories to be considered, how does the skeptical challenge look? Broadly speaking, radically interpretive metasemantic frameworks take meaning to supervene on use by starting with *all* of the sentences "held true" (which will reflect *both* our past applications and our dispositions) and taking the meanings to be the set of semantic values that would (in some sense to be determined) best satisfy all of the held-true sentences. What best satisfies the set is usually understood in terms of some notion of 'maximization',[12] and among the candidates for what might ultimately be maximized are the total amount of truth in the set, the overall rationality or coherence of the set, the psychological typicality

---

[9] And, if we agree with Wittgenstein that if "whatever is going to seem correct to me is correct ... [then] here we can't talk about 'correct'" (Wittgenstein 1953a: par 258), it may follow that can't talk about the initial sequence in the intelligence tests as being correct either.

[10] Hence Kripke's objections to dispositions on the grounds that they are "not infallible" (Kripke 1982: 57).

[11] Independently of 'intelligence tests', the general focus on going on "in the same way" (Kripke 1982: 18, 19, 82, 118, 135) might encourage treating past usage as 'infallible', and thus drawing a sharp distinction between past uses and dispositions, since 'going on in the same way' tracks *actual* past behavior, not dispositions. Indeed, one could argue that 'going on in the same way' should actually replicate 'mistakes', and so all past use is 'right' for at least one sense of "the same way." That is, if, in the past, I called poorly lit raccoons at a distance "cats," then 'going on in the same way' would involve continuing to do so.

[12] The notion of maximization will not, of course, be strictly numerical (if that even makes sense in this case), since some sentences will be more important to make-true than others. Some of our beliefs are central, and/or deeply held, and some are peripheral and inconsequential, and all else being equal, an interpretation is better if it preserves the central beliefs at the expense of the peripheral ones rather than vice versa.

("humanity") of the set, or some combination of these.[13] Further, there is considerable variation in terms of just how 'reductive' one takes the project to be with Quine (1960) being at one extreme with a behavioristically respectable notion of 'assent' sitting at the bottom of the theory,[14] and Davidson (1973, 1984) at the other extreme, with his 'taking *true*' arguably being a semantically loaded attitude.[15] With all this in mind, I'll just use the term "Charity" for whatever the function is that takes us from the total set of sentences held true to a set of semantic values for the words in those sentences. I won't go into any more of the details of the various holistic metasemantic accounts here,[16] since while there are clearly many different candidates for just what 'Charity' could be, on all of the versions of it, not *all* of the sentences *held* true will actually *be* true on the resulting assignment. Furthermore, even at this level of generality, it should be clear that if meaning is determined by use along some sort of holistic line, *both* our past applications and dispositions can help determine what we mean, and because of this, such past applications and dispositions, while not infallible, will have an at least *prima facie* claim to be correct. Consequently, on all candidate accounts, if you are, say, disposed to call something a "cat," that will make it more likely that, all else being equal, that object falls within the extension of "cat." Finally, on all these holistic accounts, meaning is, in some sense, the 'center of gravity'

---

[13] For a discussion of some of these competing approaches about what should be maximized, see Jackman (2003a).
[14] Lewis (1974) might fall within this more reductive camp, though without the commitment to behaviorism.
[15] And it is probably something like this that would better capture the naive response. Further, while having a 'semantic' attitude at base may make such accounts non-reductive in some sense, they would certainly be a far cry from the view that semantic facts are *primitive* and incapable of analysis (a position that Kripke, with some justification, calls "desperate" (Kripke 1982: 51)). The view would be non-reductive not in the sense of treating meaning states as being primitive states, but in the sense of not taking meaning and content as being elucidated in terms of things that don't presuppose meaning and content. (For a related discussion, see Sultanescu's chapter [Chapter 9] in this volume.)
[16] Though see Jackman (2003a) for an argument in favor of maximizing truth and measuring whether a belief is central or peripheral in terms of the agent's *own* dispositions to revise these beliefs if they were aware of all of the conflicts. This would leave us with something like the following principle, which I'll call "Peircian Charity" (or "PC"), to take us from sentences held true to semantic values.

PC: The semantic values of the words in a speaker's language are the values that would make true the set of sentences held true that would survive a process of (idealized) belief revision on the speaker's part.

Still, nothing in what follows rests on cashing out Charity in this particular way. Furthermore, the skeptic can't require that we have a completely worked out metasemantic theory in order to answer them; instead they need to show that the factors appealed to in the naive reply to them *can't* be filled out in a workable way (which, arguably, they succeed in doing with 'dispositionalism').

of our use, and if our past applications really are balanced between *plus* and *quus*, then our dispositions will be able to tip the scales one way or the other.

Now, from the perspective of a more holistic metasemantic theory, let's look again at Kripke's objections to the naive response.

3 The Arguments from Error and Justification

Of Kripke's objections to dispositionalism, his appeal to the fact that we can be disposed to make mistakes has garnered the most attention (largely relating to its purported connection to the 'normativity of meaning'). However, if one presupposes a more holistic metasemantics rather than dispositionalism, merely pointing out that we can be disposed to make mistakes doesn't have that much bite against the naive response. It certainly is true that we can be disposed to make mistakes, but that hardly shows that appeals to dispositions can't justify my claim that I meant *plus* by "plus" in the past. In particular, on the holistic view, an appeal to dispositions doesn't commit one to any particular set of dispositions being *identified* with what we mean.

As noted above, on the holistic model, *all* of our dispositions contribute, holistically to what we mean, and while it's always possible for some *particular* aspect of our usage to be out of line with what we mean, showing that that particular piece of usage is mistaken requires showing it to be out of line with *other* aspects of our (dispositions to) use. So, for instance, my disposition to call a poorly lit raccoon in the distance a "cat" may count as a mistake because it conflicts with my more firmly entrenched disposition to call it a "raccoon" when the light is better and I'm a little closer (and my disposition to affirm things like that "cats don't turn into raccoons when you come near them or shine a light on them"). In much the same way, it's certainly *possible* that my former disposition to answer "125" when asked "What is 68 plus 57?" was a *mistaken* disposition, but for that to be so, there must be some other (more deeply entrenched) aspect(s) of my past (dispositions to), use "plus" that it conflicts with. Since the debate with the skeptic is supposed to be taking place under conditions of cognitive idealization,[17] I can assume that both the skeptic and I know *all* the facts about my past dispositions and usage, so if I can bring up a *plus*-favoring disposition, the burden of proof is on the skeptic to show that there are other more entrenched facts about my use that are incompatible with my disposition to answer "125." As a matter of fact, I don't think that there are

---

[17] Kripke (1982: 14, 21, 39).

any such entrenched facts about my past dispositions or use, and even if the skeptic were to find enough such facts, that would only show that (surprisingly) I did mean *quus* by "plus" in the past, not that there was no fact about which of the two I meant.

Kripke seems to ignore this sort of possibility by saddling the naive response with dispositionalism and its commitment to simply *identifying* meaning with specific dispositions. The dispositionalist's response to the problem of error seems limited to trying to specify a privileged set of 'meaning determining' dispositions, and understanding mistakes as use that is out of line with the privileged set. There are, undoubtedly, dispositionalist theories that try something like this,[18] and I'm inclined to accept Kripke's arguments (or arguments he has inspired) against such views.[19] But, once again, this gives us reason to reject understandings of the naive response that commits one to dispositionalism, not to reject appeals to our dispositions *tout court*.

After all, and as mentioned above, it's not just the case that we can be *disposed* to make mistakes, it's also the case that we often *actually do* make mistakes. However, the fact that we have occasionally misapplied our words in the past doesn't lead us to think that our past usage isn't relevant to what we meant at the time. If the mere possibility of error were enough to rule out the relevance of past dispositions, then the possibility of past errors would rule out the relevance of past use as well, and Kripke's skeptic could argue that by "plus" in the past we meant *fuss*, a function for which the answer was *zero* for *whatever* two numbers were 'fadded' together. (In the same way, such a skeptic could argue that in the past, by "table," we meant not *tabair* (a table not found under the Eifel Tower and a chair found there) but rather just *chair*, insisting that we've just *always* misapplied the term.) If one thought that meaning was somehow *so* independent of use that neither one's past applications nor one's dispositions contributed to what one meant, then appeals to such things obviously wouldn't answer the skeptic, but if one does think that meaning is a function of use, then it seems natural to think that appeals to one's use (and dispositions to use) are fair game in determining what one means, and thinking that the justifiers need not be infallible seems to be the price we must pay, and unless one is really in the grip of the "intelligence test" model, it isn't that high a price.

This brings us to Kripke's related suggestion that the dispositionalist response to the skeptic fails to capture the intuition that we should be

---

[18] The candidates include dispositions we would have under certain ideal conditions, the dispositions that the other dispositions are "asymmetrically dependent upon" etc. See for instance, Dretske (1981) and Fodor (1990a).
[19] For a discussion of these, see Boghossian (1989).

able to *justify* our answer of "125" rather than "5."[20] However, Kripke often cashes out this demand for justification in terms of a need to show that a response follows from 'instructions' that determine it, along with all other correct answers, but such a restrictive account of justification seems unmotivated.[21] Showing that "125" is not "a mere jack-in-the-box unjustified and arbitrary response" or "no better than a stab in the dark" (Kripke 1982: 23) is not a matter of finding the "instructions" (Kripke 1982: 23) or "directions" (Kripke 1982: 11) which "*tell* me what I ought to do in each new instance" (Kripke 1982: 24). Rather, it is a matter of showing how it fits best with the rest of one's use. If one works with the more holistic metasemantic picture outlined above, *all* of one's past-applications and dispositions to use are at least *prima facie* justified, and since the way that they lose that justification is by being shown to be inconsistent with enough of one's other applications or use, one can show that one's use is *justified* (all things considered) by showing how it coheres with the rest of one's use. One's dispositions aren't justified in terms of their flowing from something else, but one isn't left with a position where "whatever is going to seem correct to me is correct"[22] because any particular disposition (or instance of past use) can still be shown to be wrong by such appeals to the rest of one's (dispositions to) use.[23] As Kripke puts it, "The fundamental problem ... is ... whether my actual dispositions are 'right' or not, is there anything that mandates what they *ought* to be?" (Kripke 1982: 57), and for the holist, we can evaluate whether each individual disposition is "right" or not, depending on how it coheres with the rest of one's dispositions (including dispositions coming from the gathering of new information). The collective whole mandates what dispositions you ought to have in particular cases, and showing that it coheres with the whole justifies any particular disposition within that whole.

4 The Argument from Finitude

Once one's dispositions are allowed in, one's use of "plus" will rule out most 'bent' responses mentioned in the literature, in particular, it will clearly rule out "5" in the case of "68 + 57." However, it isn't clear that

---

[20] See for instance, Kripke (1982: 11, 23, 24).
[21] Though Kripke may, to some extent, be following Wittgenstein here. (See Shaw [this volume] on Wittgenstein's particular notion of justification as involving a 'thing' that you interact with which results in your application of a word.) In any case, the analogy with 'intelligence tests' might be part of the problem here as well, since in most of those cases, the 'following instructions' model seems plausible.
[22] Wittgenstein (1953a: par 258).
[23] As I put it elsewhere (Jackman 2003b), justification has a coherentist rather than foundationalist structure.

it will rule out *every* response to *every* set of possible numbers that could be plugged into the addition function. Indeed, this brings us to the most serious problem that Kripke brings up for *any* dispositional responses to his skeptic (not just "the dispositionalist"), namely that our dispositions are *finite*.

As he puts it, the problem is not just that my actual dispositions are "not infallible" but also that they do not "cover all of the infinitely many cases of the addition table" (Kripke 1982: 57). Even if we were entitled to trust our dispositions, there will always be numbers so large that we seemingly wouldn't have any dispositions related to calculating with them. Specifically, there are numbers so large that not only could we not complete calculations with them, we also couldn't read them from end-to-end even if we spent our entire lifetime trying to do so. (Let's call these, following Boghossian,[24] "inaccessible numbers.") We have a sense that *plus* is a function that gives a determinate answer even with arbitrarily large inputs, including pairs of inaccessible numbers, and it may seem as if our dispositions aren't able to underwrite that. As Kripke puts it:

> The dispositional theory attempts to avoid the problem of the finiteness of my actual past performances by appealing to a disposition. But in doing so, it ignores an obvious fact; not only my actual performance, but also the totality of my dispositions, is finite. It is not true, for example, that if queried about the sum of any two numbers, no matter how large, I will reply with their actual sum, for some pairs of numbers are simply too large for my mind – or my brain, to grasp. When given such sums, I may shrug my shoulders for lack of comprehension; I may even, if the numbers involved are large enough, die of old age before the questioner completes his question. Let 'quaddition' be redefined so as to be a function which agrees with addition for all pairs of numbers small enough for me to have any dispositions to add them, and let it diverge from addition thereafter (say, it is 5). Then, just as the sceptic previously proposed the hypothesis that I meant quaddition in the old sense, now he proposes the hypothesis that I meant quaddition in the new sense. A dispositional account will be impotent to refute him. As before, there are infinitely many candidates the sceptic can propose for the role of quaddition. (Kripke 1982: 27)

A mathematical function like addition is supposed to be *determinate* in that it has a value for *any* two numerical inputs (the proverbial 'rails to infinity'),[25] and it might seem like our dispositions can't fund this level of determinacy, given that there are manifestly pairs of numbers we have no disposition to add.[26]

---

[24] Boghossian (2015: 335).
[25] Wittgenstein (1953a: par 218).
[26] Indeed, the numbers themselves need not actually be large, since if one had two small numbers (say, between 1 and 2) whose decimals went on long enough, their sum would still be uncomputable by us.

Attempts could be made to show that we have dispositions to add even such large numbers in some 'idealized' sense (say, if my brain were somehow altered to increase its computing capacity, and my life were somehow extended indefinitely), but as Kripke argues, there seems to be no noncircular way to do this, since there may be ways of expanding my brain capacity and lifespan that might also result in me computing in a nonstandard fashion, and just allowing increases to my capacity that kept me giving answers in accordance with the rule for *plus* would seem question begging.[27] (And further, even if such a drastically altered successor of mine did mean *plus*, what would that really have to do with what *I* meant by the term *now*?)[28]

While the issue of 'finiteness' is most salient with mathematical terms, our use seems unable to produce completely determinate meanings for our nonmathematical terms as well. For instance, our use of, say, "red" or "table" doesn't seem up to the task of, respectively, producing a *completely* sharp line between items which are red and which or not, or determining *precisely* which number of atoms can be removed from any particular table and still have it count as a table. When we think about language in general, we often assume that our terms have determinate extensions (each term partitions the world into two: that what falls under it and what does not). Our logic seems to suggest that this must be so,[29] but when we actually think about what such determinacy would require in particular cases, our use doesn't seem up to the task.[30]

However, there is an important way in which these nonmathematical cases are different from the mathematical ones. It's not *obviously* a bad thing that our use doesn't seem able to produce completely determinate meanings for terms like "red." There certainly are philosophical arguments in favor of thinking that all of our terms must have determinate meanings, but most people (even most philosophers) are comfortable with the idea that most of our terms fail to have completely precise extensions. Indeed, if anything, it's the view that terms like "red" have *completely* determinate meanings that is viewed as "paradoxical" by most people working in the area. Unlike, say, the mathematical case, where we do have a sense that if our mental capacity were somehow expanded 'properly', we would continue on the *plus* track for the calculation

---

[27] See Kripke (1982: 27–28) and the discussion in Boghossian (2015: 334–345).
[28] See, once again, Boghossian (2015: 345–346).
[29] See the arguments for 'epistemic' conceptions of vagueness (e.g., Williamson 1996; Sorensen 2001).
[30] See some of the literature against epistemic accounts of vagueness (e.g. Keefe 2007; Boghossian 2015), or those defenders of epistemic accounts who argue that we should conclude that this simply shows that meaning *isn't* determined by use (Sorensen 2001; Ebbs 2000).

problems that are currently beyond our reach, we don't have the same intuition with terms like "red" or "table." We don't assume that, if my capacities for discrimination were improved indefinitely, there would be just *one* 'determinate red' waiting for me to extend my current term "red" to, or one particular cutoff point where I would inevitably decide that the removal of a single atom stopped a particular table from being a table.

This still leaves us, of course, with the mathematical cases, but even these don't seem *quite* as worrying as the original skeptical puzzle.[31] It is no coincidence that the finiteness objection to dispositionalism hasn't generated as much excitement as the ones based on justification and error. The idea that there was no fact of the matter as to whether I meant *plus* or *quus* (in its original sense where it veers off from *plus* while we are still dealing with 'accessible' numbers) by "plus" is shocking precisely because it's 'obvious' to most of us that we don't mean *quus*. We have a clear idea what the quus-function is and a clear sense that we *never* meant that function by "plus." On the other hand, the 'skeptical scenario' that leans on the finiteness objection can't be formulated in such a stark way. We might be left with a vague sense that things are underdetermined far in the distance, but we can't give any concrete examples. As far as any two numbers *we can comprehend* go, there is no difference between *plus* and its supposed skeptical alternative, and so a lack of determinacy at this level is less obviously 'paradoxical'. Nevertheless, while it may be *less* paradoxical, the idea that our mathematical terms are indeterminate remains at least *somewhat* paradoxical. We are fine with our regular terms not being completely determinate, but our mathematical ones do seem to have that determinacy behind them, so where does that leave us?

Fortunately, even with inaccessible numbers, more work can be done with our dispositions in this area than Kripke allows. After all, the only dispositions that Kripke lets 'the dispositionalist' work with are the dispositions to perform complete computations when faced with pairs of numbers. As Kripke puts it, for the dispositionalist, "To mean addition by "+" is to be disposed, when asked for any sum 'x + y' to give the sum of x and y as the answer" (Kripke 1982: 22), and these dispositions do seem to simply run out when we are faced with inaccessible numbers. However, there are other dispositions that the more holistic theories might also allow. Certainly, we have dispositions that would tell against the revised version of "quaddition" that Kripke suggested in the paragraph quoted above. Even if I don't have the disposition to

---

[31] After all, there are people who seriously endorse finitism in mathematics, while no one seriously endorses the possibility that we might have meant *quus* by "plus" in the past.

perform a complete calculation that involves two inaccessible numbers, it remains the case if I see two such numbers stacked on top of each other and the number 5 as the sum, I'll be concluding that the calculation is in error, and just *that* disposition is enough to rule out the new version of the quaddition function that Kripke introduces.[32] Of course, there will always be other potential functions that aren't ruled out as easily as that,[33] but this case points to the fact that there are dispositions that can be treated as contributing to how our arithmetical terms are best interpreted that don't involve the sorts of complete calculations that the 'dispositionalist' is strictly limited to.

For "plus," we have, by definition, no disposition to come up with an answer when presented with a calculation involving one or more 'inaccessible' numbers, but we have a number of other dispositions that would give the interpreter reason to treat us as meaning *plus* rather than an alternative even for this range. So, for instance, if I am to add 1 to a number that ends with "7," I'll get that very number but with the final "7" replaced by an "8." I haven't performed many such 'calculations', but they point to a sense in which I *can* provide a solution to some calculation problems that include inaccessible numbers without performing a 'full' calculation. So if I'm asked to add 1 to an inaccessible number that ends with "7," I can erase the "7" at the end of the initial number, replace it with an "8," and call it a day. In some sense, I don't know what this new number is, but I'm still convinced that it's the right answer to the question. I am convinced of this because I'm also convinced that I *don't need* to actually see all the numbers that come before the "7," since if I'm just adding 1, then they aren't going to change. This lack of concern with what comes ahead of the "7," no matter how large the number is, tells in favor of "plus" over its traditional quus-like rivals. Note that this response to the skeptic above is not just *saying* things like "it doesn't matter what is to the left of the '7'," which could be reinterpreted to cover just the smaller range. Rather, it relies on the fact that I'm actually disposed to ignore the numerals coming before the "7," even when those numbers are larger than the skeptic's proposed turning-point. We have these open-ended dispositions, and in this sense, they seem to apply to arbitrarily large numbers.

The same could be said for how one might interpret our commitment to the successor function. Kripke (1982: 16) considers responses

---

[32] See also Boghossian (2015: 335) for the same suggestion that our use couldn't rule out a function that had two inaccessible numbers as inputs and "5" as an output.

[33] Such as ones where you have two inaccessible numbers which are added together and the 'bent' conclusion is just one digit off the correct result.

to the skeptic that appeal to our commitments to *plus* being understood in terms of the successor function ("S") through "recursion equations" for +, such as the following:

$$(x)(x + 0 = x)$$
and
$$(x)(y)(x + Sy = S(x + y))$$

However, his response to such appeals seems to focus only on explicit *statements* of such general equations, statements which can, in turn, be interpreted in a quus-like way. So, for instance, the quantifiers in the formulas above could be reinterpreted by the skeptic so that "(x)" just means "for all x below 57" etc. (Kripke 1982: 17). However, just as with the general disposition to add 1 discussed in the paragraph above, our commitment to the recursion equations isn't just a matter of our *saying* the formulas, it includes our willingness to endorse them for any values we are given for "x" and "y," even when those numbers are 'inaccessible'. For instance, if I'm shown that x = 78... and y = 25... (where the "..." stands for a set of numerals long enough to make the numbers involved inaccessible), I'll still agree that $x + Sy = S(x + y)$ even if I can't read to the end of the two numerals listed. The fact that I see no need to check how large x and y are before endorsing the formula is reason for the holist *not* to interpret me as taking (x) to be "for all below 57" (or any other number) in the recursion equations above.

So, for instance, when Boghossian[34] argues that, given that *plus* and the 'new' (inaccessible) sense of *quus* were in agreement for all of the *accessible* numbers, our dispositions couldn't determine that we meant *plus* without making it metaphysically impossible for us to ever mean *quus*, his argument seems to presuppose that if our meaning something different between the two were to supervene on our dispositions, then those dispositions would have to relate exclusively to the completion of an actual calculation (which, by definition, is supposed to be the same for all of the accessible numbers). However, the difference between the two could lie elsewhere; in particular, it could lie in the presence (or, in our case, absence) of a need to check into more detail just how big a number is before agreeing that it could be plugged in for x in a formula like $x + Sy = S(x + y)$. Boghossian remarks:

Surely, it needs explaining why it is metaphysically impossible for a human being to refer to this other function rather than to plus. What makes plus so special? Why, given that everything about my dispositions is compatible both with plus

---

[34] Boghossian (2015: 352–353).

and all of these other functions, do my thoughts nevertheless gravitate inexorably to the plus function, ignoring every one of these other functions? (Boghossian 2015: 353)

But the impossibility of our referring to the new version of *quus* that veers off at an inaccessible number while we can refer to plus is precisely because it is *not the case* that "everything about my dispositions is compatible both with plus and all of these other functions." Our dispositions to perform complete calculations may be in line, but once we break from 'dispositionalism', those are not the only dispositions we have access to.

This is, admittedly, only a start,[35] but while I think that a lack of determinacy would be more problematic in the mathematical case than, say, the perceptual one, I'm inclined to think that dispositions when embedded in the more holistic framework have, at least, more *potential* to produce a determinate content for a term like "plus" than they do for a term like "red." By contrast, it's fairly clear that they would have *no* chance of doing so on the dispositionalist's model. It is his casual slide from the appeal to our disposition to answer "125" when queried to "dispositionalism" that proves to be the proverbial "decisive move" in Kripke's skeptical conjuring trick,[36] and once we resist this move, the skeptical challenge seems considerably less threatening.

---

[35] And one should never underestimate the ways for philosophers to find some kind of underdetermination if they really want to (see for instance, Putnam 1981).
[36] Wittgenstein (1953a: par 308).

4 Wittgensteinean Notions of Uniformity and Kripkensteinean Skepticism*

James R. Shaw

The threat of semantic skepticism that Kripke (1982) extracts from Wittgenstein's remarks on rule-following is as trenchant as it is troubling. Still, Kripke's reading of Wittgenstein as grappling with such skepticism is on shaky exegetical grounds.[1]

My point of departure here is a reading of Wittgenstein that I defend elsewhere, on which he never engaged with semantic skepticism in his texts.[2] While this reading distances Wittgenstein from Kripke, an intriguing indirect connection between their work remains. Certain concepts like *regularity*, *constancy*, and *(qualitative) sameness* – what I will call "notions of uniformity" – play a significant role in addressing questions in the foundations of semantics for Wittgenstein. If Wittgenstein's appeal to these notions is legitimate, they may also be of use in defusing semantic skepticism.

1 Notions of Uniformity in the *Investigations* and a Naive Reply to the Skeptic

Let me *very* briefly sketch the reading of Wittgenstein I am working from. On it, Wittgenstein asks and addresses two logically distinct questions in his rule-following remarks.

The first of Wittgenstein's questions is (roughly) in semantic epistemology. Imagine an interlocutor who is liable to systematically misinterpret any overt definitions or examples you give that are supposed to

---

* Some of the material in this chapter appears, sometimes in a slightly altered form, in chapters 4 and 10 of Shaw (2023). I'm grateful especially to participants at 2019 *Rules, Norms, and Reasons* conference at the University of Milan, and to the participants at the 2022 conference on *Kripke's* Wittgenstein on Rules and Private Language *at 40* at York University, for extremely helpful comments and criticism on earlier versions of this work.

[1] See for example, the exegetical criticisms coming on the heels of Kripke's work in Baker and Hacker (1984), McDowell (1984), McGinn (1984), Anscombe (1985), Goldfarb (1985), and Tait (1986). I give my own reservations in chapters 3 and 8 of Shaw (2023).

[2] Shaw (2023). From here on out, "Wittgenstein" is perhaps best thought of as "Wittgenstein as I read him."

explain how some words (like "add 2") are to be applied to new cases. Wittgenstein's first question is:

THE JUSTIFICATORY QUESTION: What justification did you possess when meaning your words, such that if a bizarre but sincere misinterpreter were to possess that justification, even they would have reapplied the words as you would to new cases?

"Justification" here is used in a special sense, largely divorced from its role in contemporary epistemology. Wittgenstein takes model justifications to be things like ostensive definitions or like schematics, diagrams, or images that – engaged with in certain processes – can be used to rectify misconstruals of verbal instructions.[3] So the question is whether we can produce something *like those* that will avoid bizarre misinterpretations.[4] Wittgenstein is principally concerned with the actual effects of producing a justification on a given interpreter.[5] The reason for asking this unusual question with this focus is to probe a latent idea: that when I mean my words in a particular way, the way that I do that is by having something in mind which *shows* how the words are to be used, so that sincere engagement with "what I have" must lead to the same usage I make.

Wittgenstein's technique in engaging with this question is one of trial-and-error: Run through possible justifications (especially "internal" mentalistic ones), and see whether any can do this work. And Wittgenstein's conclusion is that none can. We possess nothing on the model of what Wittgenstein calls a "justification" such that, if the sincere bizarre misinterpreter were only to have had that justification, their applications would have coincided with ours. Note that however surprising that conclusion may be, no radical concerns about meaningfulness (e.g. threats of non-factualism or non-truth-conditionality) are immediately pressed by it.

The second of Wittgenstein's questions is (roughly) in the foundations of semantics. I call it the "Grammatical Question" for reasons we needn't get into here. It suffices for now to note that Wittgenstein almost always frames his foundational semantic questions metalinguistically (not: "what is meaning?", but: "how do we use the word 'meaning'?").

---

[3] This construal of justification is made clearest around (Wittgenstein 1958: 14) – though Wittgenstein there uses the (for him interchangeable) language of reasons.

[4] The role of a *bizarre* misinterpreter is to make salient the range of possible misunderstandings a justification of this kind would have to remove. Indeed, considering the variety of such misinterpreters, such a justification seems like it would have to be *immune* to misinterpretation – something which Wittgenstein thinks contributes to a sense of the activity of meaning as strange and almost supernatural.

[5] Notably, on this reading Wittgenstein is not concerned with an abstract normative justification relation. In anticipation: I am also tempted not to read Kripke's Wittgenstein as dealing with distinctively normative issues either – see n17.

THE GRAMMATICAL QUESTION: When "everything is open to view", what conditions influence your willingness to say "such-and-such was meant" ("such-and-such a rule was followed," etc.) on a particular occasion?

The methodology Wittgenstein uses to address this question is one he reserves for family resemblance terms – that is, the methodology of case studies. These often take the form of thought experiments involving contrast cases: a "good," clear case of meaning or rule-following, and a case where some single feature from the good case is removed. We are then asked to see if removing the relevant feature makes a difference to our willingness to apply semantic terms in the context imagined. His conclusion from a series of such case studies is that there is an assortment of different things that can matter, in different contexts, to how we use semantic terms (the presence of training, the presence of repeated usage, the presence of "ordinary human behavior," the presence of regularity in usage, etc.). But no set of features provides anything like the necessary and sufficient conditions. This last idea is, of course, bound up with a treatment of meaning, rule-following, etc. as family resemblance concepts.

The Justificatory and Grammatical Questions are related ones to Wittgenstein. He thinks the presupposition of the Justificatory Question (that there is some justification we have that our imagined perverse interlocutor lacks) stands in relationships of mutual support with a tempting misconception of meaning as a "local" event. On this view, criteria for meaning a word in a particular way center around the happenings at the time and place the word was meant. The grammatical investigation aims to dislodge that misconception by bringing to the foreground nonlocal criteria (training that precedes acts of meaning, regularity that extends beyond it, etc.). But, again, nowhere is it ever countenanced that there is a problem for meaning attributions of the kind Kripke raises (e.g. in the truth-conditionality of such attributions).

The above is the barest sketch of a reading of the rule-following remarks, and is compressed even as such. Still, it can serve to frame the significance of a thought experiment engaging with the Grammatical Question at §207 of the *Philosophical Investigations*.[6]

Let's imagine that the people in [an unknown country] carried on usual human activities and in the course of them employed, apparently, an articulate language. If we watch their activities, we find them intelligible, they seem 'logical'. But when we try to learn their language we find it impossible to do so. For there is no regular connection between what they say, the sounds they make, and their activities; but still these sounds are not superfluous, for if, for

---

[6] Henceforth *PI*. I employ the translations from Wittgenstein (1953b), sometimes with minor modifications of my own.

example, we gag one of the people, this has the same consequences as with us: without those sounds their actions fall into confusion – as I feel like putting it.

Should we say that these people have a language: orders, reports, and so on? (*PI* §207)

This passage exhibits the methodology of constructing contrast case studies that I alluded to earlier: Wittgenstein takes the good case (a community of ordinary speakers) and subtracts exactly one feature, namely regularity of usage, and finally asks if this makes a difference to whether we say meaningful language is present. One way to imagine the people Wittgenstein has in mind is to take an extended span of interactions from a group of actual human speakers and imagine a counterfactual circumstance differing only in that the usage of words is chaotically permuted (perhaps along with anything needed to effect the permutation – e.g. some causal bases for the chaotic usage). Outwardly, by hypothesis, this counterfactual group of people looks exactly like the original group of ordinary language users up to the sounds they emit or the symbols they inscribe. Do these people speak a language? This thought experiment is a rare case where we have an unequivocal verdict from Wittgenstein.

There is not enough regularity for us to call it "language". (*PI* §207)

I agree. It can help to see the point by focusing on just one "word." Supposing the original, un-permuted speech was English, a word like "knight" might be used by one of the permuted users in a setting where they are testing avocados for ripeness at the supermarket, by another when they are selecting paint colors for a bedroom, by another in the middle of what looks like a counting procedure, and so on. The word does not occur in any discernible pattern. If this word is part of a language, it should have meaning. But what could its meaning be?

If there is no regularity in the use of "knight" whatsoever, then there can be no words in our language to say directly what its meaning is. We could try to define the meaning indirectly as "whatever people seem to be using it for (or are disposed to use it for) on each occasion." But this presumes we can first figure out what "knight" is used for on *any* occasion, which on reflection is completely unclear. For example, imagine there's a case where some speakers seem to treat the word "knight" as having a possible application, but one that they are as yet ignorant of (e.g. an astronomer appears to conjecture tentatively with "knight", observing a point of light through a telescope). How do we settle on a correct application, which should be possible if "knight" has a meaning here? There's no help from actual usage, actual dispositions, or even "ideal" dispositions – how are we ever going to pick out ideal dispositions for these completely bizarre agents? And even if we could identify ideal dispositions, what if on such dispositions we find speakers are not disposed to use "knight" in ideal circumstances (e.g. where they have better eyesight, more astronomical experience, etc.)? Is that due to the word failing to apply to (say) the heavenly body, or is it due to the oddly permuted linguistic usage of this people, which appears to be sensitive to *any* change of circumstances?

Due to concerns like this, I'm inclined to agree with Wittgenstein that even though *all* other features of meaningful linguistic use are present, in the absence of regularity, we lose our grip on how this people could be construed as speaking a language.

More could be said to bolster this lesson from *PI* §207 and to bolster the exegetical significance of regularity and other notions of uniformity (like "sameness", etc.) for Wittgenstein.[7] But for now, let's just take this as a given: Wittgenstein thinks regularity of usage is one of the features that influences our willingness to say words have meanings, rules are followed, etc. And for him, that means that regularity of use is something that sometimes helps "constitute" the presence of meanings (at least in whatever sense of constitution his grammatical, family resemblance methodology allows).

Wittgenstein, as I alluded to before, draws out many more concepts than just regularity in investigating which features play a role in attributing meaningfulness. These include: the presence of training, repetition, general harmonious "agreement" in good cases, similar harmonious reactions to "justifications," and so on. The reason I focus here on regularity is because it appears to have a distinctive power against the kinds of skeptical considerations Kripke adduces on Wittgenstein's behalf.

Kripke's skeptic asks of Kripke's past use of the word "+": "what fact it is (about [Kripke's] mental state) that constitutes [his] meaning plus, not quus,"[8] where "quus" denotes a function that deviates from addition for arguments greater than the greatest number figuring in Kripke's past explicit computations. The definition of "quus" ensures Kripke's past usage doesn't distinguish between addition and quaddition. So the question is in effect: What *else* could do the work of settling that Kripke meant the first function rather than the second? Kripke adduces an impressive array of arguments, seeming to show that no fact is suited to the task.

However, if we help ourselves to the use of notions of uniformity like regularity in addressing questions in the foundations of semantics, as

---

[7] To give one other example, at *PI* §237 Wittgenstein says we could not count a procedure in which someone produces one line on the basis of another as following a rule if there is no discernible regularity in how the features of the first line relate to the second.
[8] Kripke (1982: 11).

I've claimed Wittgenstein does, then it seems like we have the following relatively straightforward reply.

NAIVE REPLY
What determines that I meant addition by "+" rather than quaddition? While there may be no general answer as to what facts determine someone's meaning addition by their words, we can point to many features of past use and its circumstances (ordinary human responses of approval and disapproval, expectation and frustration, and so on) that help us determine a range of "core, good" applications of "+" by myself and other calculators that accords with a substantial (albeit 'gappy') initial segment of the addition function. Of course, as Kripke notes, all this usage accords just as well with many quaddition-like functions. But *addition is the most regular and uniform continuation* of the core, good applications we make. Indeed, it is the most regular and uniform continuation of even the smallest segments of addition that we use in elementary instruction. And that is one of the factors that influences our willingness (that is, my willingness, and that of ordinary speakers like me) to say that addition is meant by users of "+", including my past self. It is not that it is impossible to mean a quaddition-like rule, but rather that its irregularities must be manifest either in original use or dispositions for use, in order for us to be willing to say that it was meant on an occasion. Otherwise addition, because the most regular continuation, wins by default. And that is just a feature of how we use the word "meaning".

What can we say about this somewhat simple-minded attempt to head off the skeptic's arguments?

2   Lewisian Natural Properties

To those familiar with the literature on meaning skepticism, the NAIVE REPLY should look familiar. With some fiddling, it could be viewed as a variant on the reply offered by Lewis (1983). (Indeed, I've borrowed the language of "naivité" from him.) For this reason, Lewis's views serve nicely as a contrast for the "Wittgensteinean" position we're exploring.

Here is the barest sketch of Lewis's position. Lewis accepts a broadly "interpretationist" picture of mental content, on which such contents are assigned to an agent's mental states via principles of functional fit designed to optimize the decision-theoretic rationality of that agent. But (even independently of Kripkensteinean worries) Lewis thinks there will be many unrelated contents that satisfy the principles of functional fit for any given thinker. So to avoid radical underdetermination, we need to introduce what he calls "principles of humanity": "*a priori* – albeit defeasible – presumptions about what sorts of things are apt to be believed and desired."[9]

---

[9] Lewis (1983: 375).

Lewis says that to wield these principles, we need a metaphysically privileged class of properties: the natural properties.

> It is here that we need natural properties. The principles of [humanity] will impute a bias toward believing that things are green rather than grue, toward having a basic desire for long life rather than for long-life-unless-one-was-born-on-Monday-and-in-that-case-life-for-an-even-number-of-weeks. In short, they will impute eligible content, where ineligibility consists in severe unnaturalness of the properties the subject supposedly believes or desires or intends himself to have. (Lewis 1983: 375)

So, the content of a mental state (which, for Lewis, will be a property) is determined by a combination of the content's functional fit and metaphysical naturalness. This, familiarly, is supposed to help with meaning skepticism.

> The naive solution [to Kripkensteinean skepticism] is that adding means going on in the same way as before when the numbers get big, whereas quadding means doing something different; there is nothing present in the subject that constitutes an intention to do different things in different cases; therefore he intends addition, not quaddition. We should not scoff at this naive response. It is the correct solution to the puzzle. But we must pay to regain our naiveté. Our theory of properties must have adequate resources to somehow ratify the judgement that instances of adding are all alike in a way that instances of quadding are not. The property of adding is not perfectly natural, of course, not on a par with unit charge or sphericality. And the property of quadding is not perfectly unnatural. But quadding is worse by a disjunction. So quaddition is to that extent less of a way to go on doing the same, and therefore it is to that extent less of an eligible thing to intend to do. (Lewis 1983: 376)

Some clarifications: I follow Schwarz (2014) in thinking that Lewis is not claiming that the addition function is more natural than the quaddition function. He is rather claiming that the property of being an adder is more natural than the property of being a quadder. Second, Lewis initially frames his resolution by saying that adding is "going on in the same way." But "same" here cannot mean *numerically identical*. That would be tantamount to saying that we were always adding, which would beg the question against the skeptic. "Same" is better construed as expressing qualitative sameness – that is, sufficient similarity in certain respects. This comes out more clearly when Lewis talks of instances of adding being "all alike" in ways that instances of quadding are not. Qualitative sameness and likeness are, of course, notions of uniformity.

Seen in this way, Lewis's naive response and the Wittgensteinean one sketched in §1 run parallel. Lewis's functionalism is the souped-up, modern, mentalistic counterpart to Wittgenstein's seemingly more behaviorist and linguistically focused methods of establishing "core applications." Then both appeal to notions of uniformity to help smooth out some remaining cases. The key difference at present, of course, is that Lewis posits a metaphysical distinction of naturalness to "ratify" (as he puts it) our judgments of uniformity. Wittgenstein would posit no such distinction. Of course, Wittgenstein thinks some things are more similar than others, some continuations of patterns are more regular than others, and so on. But the notions of uniformity are just ordinary, intuitive concepts. There's no concern to "ground" or "ratify" them in Wittgenstein, even when they surface in foundational semantic investigation, and certainly not with the help of a metaphysical distinction.[10] So the contrast between Wittgenstein and Lewis forces us to confront the question: What work are universals doing for Lewis? I believe that probing this question reveals that Lewis's appeal to universals is not only superfluous, but in fact counterproductive.

A first, simple concern is that it is far from obvious that Lewis's proposal gets us the right results. Lewis takes perfectly natural properties to be those figuring in fundamental physics like spin, charge, and spatiotemporal distance. It might also be worth noting what kinds of properties seem to be excluded from the category of perfect naturalness: being exactly alike or alike in some respect, set and class membership, and so presumably more generally properties of numbers.[11]

So Lewis's claim seems to be something roughly like this: When we write up a definition of the properties of "being an adder" and "being a quadder" in terms of things like spin and charge, we will find the former involves (say) a shorter definition than the latter.[12] But complexity in the definition of a property applying to all and only (actual and possible) adders in terms of spin, charge, etc. seems like it will exhibit an absurd degree of complexity. What does a young child grouping together apples and an accountant in the midst of furiously mashing on a keyboard share in terms of fundamental properties like charge and spin? And how can we extend this to cover all actual *and merely possible* adders, human or otherwise?

---

[10] As one might anticipate, Wittgenstein is in fact hostile to such a distinction – see for example, I.X of Wittgenstein (1974).
[11] Lewis (1983: 345). See discussion of this point at Schwarz (2014: 24).
[12] Lewis develops his solution by appealing to a relative notion of naturalness, which he never developed in great detail. He sometimes suggested (Lewis 1984: 66, 1986: 61) that we can ascertain the relative naturalness of two properties by comparing the lengths of the definitions of those properties in terms of perfectly natural properties, which is the provisional understanding I work with here given Lewis's talk of the property of intending to quadd being "worse by a disjunction." See the citations in Schwarz (2014: 25) for some alternative characterizations that may or may not be equivalent. I do not think these differences in a characterization of naturalness help with the general concern developed here.

Grant for the moment that there are such definitions. What do we know about them – in particular about their lengths? Do we even know that they are finite? Couldn't it be that the definitions in question exhibit some "surprising" results – for example, that the quadders form a more natural class than the adders? And what importance would this have for how we use the term "intends to add"? Would we say, in the face of this surprising result, that such talk referred to quadders all along? I find this incredible.

These worries for the role of naturalness may seem to be exacerbated by the fact that Lewis's candidate natural properties (spin, charge, etc.) are distantly removed, by chains of definition, from intuitive applications of notions of uniformity to rule-followers or the rules they follow. But the core of the objection I'm making actually has little to do with definitional distance. And this is important, since the interpretation of Lewis I've been working with is controversial.[13] Some philosophers have attributed to Lewis a much simpler account of the role of naturalness in semantics.[14] On this view, naturalness arbitrates directly between possible *linguistic* contents for an expression (rather than indirectly influencing linguistic contents by first arbitrating between the contents of mental states). Naturalness does this by privileging a subset of the contents compatible with certain actual privileged uses of particular words. Let's call a view of this form: *Reference Magnetism*. Sometimes philosophers see Lewis as holding not only a magnetic view of linguistic reference but also holding that naturalness is applicable directly to mathematical entities like functions, so that (say) the property of being the addition function would be more natural than that of being the quaddition function.

Whether or not this view is properly attributable to Lewis isn't of great concern here. One can still wonder: Wouldn't this view escape the worries I've given above? Couldn't it help reveal more clearly how fundamental metaphysical facts could be of great importance to the meaning of "meaning"?

But actually, the objection to this sketched form of Reference Magnetism is essentially the same as the objection against the view I originally attributed to Lewis. In fact, I think a decisive objection to both appeals to naturalness can be found (with minor variations) in a footnote of Kripke's.[15]

In the footnote in question, Kripke considers an attempt to revitalize a dispositionalist reply to semantic skepticism by appealing to a notion

---

[13] For example, for some criticisms of Schwarz's reading of Lewis, which I've been following here, see Janssen-Lauret and MacBride (2020).
[14] Cf. Weatherson (2003) and Sider (2009).
[15] Kripke (1982: 39, n25).

of simplicity from computer science. The idea is that perhaps addition would come out to be a simpler function than quaddition along some metric computer science would supply, and that this could arbitrate which of several dispositions we count as manifesting on a particular occasion. Kripke's main response to this idea invoked a hypothetical: Suppose (after developing the relevant technical simplicity metric) that on investigating the structure of the brain we found the simplest program instantiated in it, to our surprise, was computing quaddition. Kripke asked: "Would this show that I did not mean addition by '+'?" Would it show that I meant quaddition instead? The answer to both questions, obviously, is "no." Kripke thought this sufficed to show that any technical notions offered by computer science are not part of the *actual* foundations of our practices of attributing meanings in linguistic usage.

It is important to recognize that the force of Kripke's objection here is not hostage to the future development of science. The objection to the use of simplicity metrics would not have been met by doing computer science and developing a suitable notion of simplicity that showed that programs computing addition were generally simpler than those computing quaddition. It would not have been met even if we could wield this hypothetical characterization of simplicity to show that quaddition was a relatively less simple program instantiable in our brain structure. The point of Kripke's hypothetical was not to raise a likelihood, but to make a conceptual point: that we regard the outcome of the project of developing a notion of simplicity in computer science and applying it to our brains with relative indifference when it comes to actually ascertaining our intentions. The failure of that project to vindicate our intuitive judgments would not dislodge them. So, correlatively, the success of the project can in no way support them.

Similarly, the objection I raised above for appeals to naturalness – which involved raising the hypothetical outcome of metaphysical inquiry turning up the "surprising" result that quaddition is more natural than addition – is not an objection which banks for its efficacy on a bet about the development of metaphysics. It is not met by successfully defending a metaphysics on which (say) addition really is more natural than quaddition. The point of the hypothetical is to show that, on reflection, we view the result of technical, metaphysical investigation with indifference. We use the term "meaning" without any regard for it. The failure of the metaphysical project to vindicate our intuitive judgments about meaningfulness would in no way dislodge or alter them, and so the success of the metaphysical project in no way supports them either.

The same points apply to my imagined reference magnetist. Maybe it is less in doubt that their notion of naturalness, which applies directly to functions, will make an addition function (as opposed to the property of being an adder) more natural than its competitors. The objection is not that the result of metaphysical investigation won't pan out. The objection is that the investigation's possible failure (even if this possibility is merely conceptual) would do nothing to influence our application of "means". And that shows that it is not part of the actual foundation of that word's use. The Kripkean point that our ordinary notions of meaningfulness are not, in the first instance, responsive to any sophisticated technical analogs of notions of uniformity stands, whether those analogs come to us from computer science or metaphysics.

For reasons like this, I think that Lewis's foray into distinctly metaphysical foundations for semantics was a mistake. (It is worth noting that this foray was new to Lewis at the time – beforehand, he seemed happy to take the relevant principles of humanity as unjustified givens.) It is abundantly clear from the examples Lewis gives that he wants the *deliverances* of the application of naturalness to be ordinary, intuitive notions of similarity, regularity, and the like. Trying to ground those appeals in a metaphysical distinction provides no extra support, when it is clear that it is ordinary notions that are doing the real work. Better to let the ordinary notions play foundational roles themselves, as Wittgenstein frequently seems to do.

So much for the relationship between Wittgenstein and Lewis. What can we say about how Kripke's skeptic might view the NAIVE REPLY?

3   Skeptical Responses to the Naive Reply

Notions of uniformity appear sufficient to respond to Kripkensteinean semantic skepticism, provided three claims hold.[16]

(i) The present language of uniformity can be used to state (truth-conditional) facts.
(ii) Notions of uniformity privilege non-skeptical continuations of actual usage.

---

[16] I am here glossing over the extremely complex issue of whether there are distinctive normative or epistemic dimensions to the form of skepticism Kripke develops. I tend to think that Kripke's epistemic and normative language can be "deflated." (cf. Fodor 1990b: 135–136, n35) Whether or not this is what Kripke intended, I think any formulation of skepticism that incorporates substantive epistemic or normative constraints can and should be dealt with simply by rejecting the constraints. I recognize this requires much more defense than I can supply here. But even if I am wrong about this point, it would be interesting to show that the NAIVE REPLY is sufficient to cope with the "purely metaphysical" formulation of semantic skepticism. I focus on that issue here without further comment.

(e.g. the total function that is the most regular extension of the partial function picked out by past privileged use of "+" is in fact addition.)
(iii) It is dialectically permissible to appeal to the language of uniformity while engaging with the skeptic.

If (iii) holds, we are free to use the language of uniformity in the dialectic with the skeptic. Then, if (i) and (ii) hold, we can use these notions in stating facts that privilege the actual meanings of our words over bizarre skeptical interpretations, roughly as the NAIVE REPLY seeks to do. Given this, where should the skeptic put up resistance?

Significantly, as far as I know, there is *no* explicit discussion in Kripke's text that bears on *any* of (i)–(iii). Kripke discusses issues relevant to notions of uniformity at three places in his text, but none of these discussions cast doubt on the claims needed for the NAIVE REPLY to succeed.

The footnote discussed in §2 is an example. There, we saw Kripke criticize an appeal to a simplicity metric from computer science for being at a conceptual remove from actual practices of meaning attributions. But while this objection carries over to metaphysical correlates, it does not carry over to ordinary notions of uniformity. These are not technical notions belonging to a specialized domain like computer science or metaphysics, but mundane concepts that even a grade schooler is expected to understand and deploy in elementary instruction. Not only this, but these notions seem directly conceptually tied, in ways evinced by those kinds of instructional settings, to the continuations that yield up reapplications of words consistent with how they are meant.

For example, if we want a student to learn the even numbers, it is a normal first attempt to show them the first few evens and, after noting some features of the series, to tell the student to "continue on *like* I did." When a student makes a mistake, a common way of showing them why is to demonstrate an *irregularity* in their continuation, and describe it as such. We might also, for example, say that they didn't continue in the *same way* as they were before. In short, the ordinary notions of uniformity (unlike those of computer science or metaphysics) are directly conceptually tied to the continuations of usage that we regard as giving the meanings of our words. So the style of objection Kripke raises in the footnote discussed in §2 cannot be extended to rule out their foundational relevance.

A second place Kripke comes close to considering something like the NAIVE REPLY occurs in a second footnote given below.

Few readers, I suppose, will by this time be tempted to appeal to a determination to "go on the same way" as before [...]. Some followers of Wittgenstein [...] have thought that his point involves a rejection of 'absolute identity' [...]. I do not see that this is so, whether or not doctrines of 'relative' identity are correct on other grounds. Let identity be as 'absolute' as one pleases: it holds only between each thing and itself. Then the plus function is identical with itself, and the quus function is identical with itself. None of this will tell me whether I referred to the plus function or quus function in the past, nor therefore will it tell me whether to apply the same function now. (Kripke 1982: 18, n13)

Here Kripke notes that appealing to *absolute identity* is of no help in resisting the skeptic. Despite a superficial appearance of relevance to the position of §1 in attacking an appeal to "going on the same way," Kripke's remarks here are not germane to the NAIVE REPLY since numerical identity (absolute or relative) is not a notion of uniformity like qualitative identity or similarity (or, at any rate, numerical identity is not a notion of uniformity used in the NAIVE REPLY).

Of course, one might wonder whether Kripke's point here might be *extended* to notions of uniformity. Kripke claims that a past *intention* (which is roughly what I take him to mean by "determination") to go on in the "same way" would be ineffective. Isn't that right, whether the sameness in question involves numerical or qualitative identity? Indeed, Kripke does make the analogous point in a third footnote – the final passage that comes closest to engaging with the NAIVE REPLY.

[I]t is important to see that, even if 'absolutely similar' had a fixed meaning in English, and 'similar' did not need to be filled in by a specification of the 'respects' in which things are similar, the sceptical problem would not be solved. When I learn 'plus', I could not simply give myself some finite number of examples and continue: 'Act similarly when confronted with any addition problem in the future.' Suppose that, on the ordinary meaning of 'similar' this construction is completely determinate, and that one does not hold the doctrine that various alternative ways of acting can be called 'similar', depending on how 'similar' is filled out by speaking of a respect in which one or another way of acting can be called 'similar' to what I did before. Even so, the sceptic can argue that by 'similar' I meant *quimilar*, where two actions are quimilar if .... (Kripke 1982: 59, n46)

Kripke notes that notions of uniformity like regularity, similarity, etc., can be subjected to a key maneuver in the skeptic's toolkit: that of skeptical reinterpretation. Past overt use of "regular" is compatible with meaning *schregular*, where schregular continuations conform to explicit past applications of "regular" but diverge in irregular ways beyond them. This means that replies to the skeptic cannot appeal to *past* usage of the language of uniformity, including past intentions that take concepts of uniformity as objects, to circumvent the skeptical paradox.

While I agree with Kripke on this point, it has no bearing on the NAIVE REPLY, which makes no use of theses about past usage of the language of uniformity or past intentions to use terms uniformly but only applies *present* standards of uniformity to arbitrate between competing meanings. These present standards are fair game, and not subject to skeptical reinterpretation at the first stages of the skeptic's dialectic (when the NAIVE REPLY is intervening).[17]

Lewis recognized the importance of this point as well, when he said: "there is nothing present in the subject that constitutes an intention to do different things in different cases; therefore he intends addition, not quaddition." It is in contexts where we find the *absence* of further intentions – not the presence of intentions to "do the same" or "do what is natural" – in which naturalness gets to play its arbitrating role for Lewis. Notions of uniformity function analogously in the NAIVE REPLY. So the last footnote of Kripke's just discussed has no force against it.[18]

I mention these footnotes not to point to a deficiency in Kripke's arguments. On the contrary, I agree with Kripke on all the points he makes. I have merely emphasized that their force is directed against positions other than that offered by the NAIVE REPLY. So these passages motivate a rather different conclusion about Kripke's relation to the NAIVE REPLY: That he never seemed to consider anything like it in his text. This is already a noteworthy fact, especially given the strikingly broad range of positions Kripke does engage with. I think it is interesting to ask *why* this simple reply never gets considered (though I won't be able to explore that question here).

In any event, any reply on the skeptic's behalf seems like it will have to go substantially beyond Kripke's explicit argumentation. Given this, which of (i)–(iii) should the skeptic target?

---

[17] Kripke (1982: 12) – I elaborate this point further below.
[18] In this footnote Kripke also seems concerned about whether sameness (and so perhaps other notions of uniformity) exhibit a relativity to respects (e.g. sameness in color, rather than shape), though he does not explain why this would matter. As far as I can see it would not, as long as the respects are not themselves semantic. As long as the respects are not semantic in nature, the facts stated by suitably relativized notions of uniformity could still not be disqualified as tools in rebutting skepticism. I suppose one might also worry that respects will sometimes vary from case to case. That could impede the statement of a precise, general recipe specifying meaning-constituting facts in necessary and sufficient terms. But this only seems problematic if we are precluded from treating meaning and rule-following as family resemblance concepts, as Wittgenstein does. For in that case it would be perfectly natural to expect that we would not specify respects for all terms, but rather that we would elaborate elements of a network of usages bearing various relationships to each other. The skeptic might claim that treating semantic terms, or the notions of uniformity underlying them, as family resemblance concepts somehow lands us in skepticism anyway. I find it hard to see why this would be so. (There is no indication that Wittgenstein, e.g. thought that family resemblance terms were *as such* precluded from stating truth-conditions or facts.)

I find it hard to see how (iii) can be rejected. As alluded to above, at the first stages of the dialectic, the skeptic gives us access to all our present language with its standard interpretation. As Kripke puts it: "[the skeptic] is not questioning my *present* use of the word 'plus'; he agrees that, according to my *present* usage, '68 + 57' denotes 125. Not only does he agree with me on this, he conducts the entire debate with me in my language as I *presently* use it" (Kripke 1982: 12 emphases in the original).

Granted, the skeptic *eventually* wants to call into question present usage as well. But doing this requires first casting sufficient doubt on past meaning facts, and this is precisely what the NAIVE REPLY would block.

Could some variation on the technique of skeptical reinterpretation be applied here? Well, the skeptic calls into question whether we can find facts that underlie *all past* meanings, and then leverages our eventual failure to further call into question *all present* meanings. But perhaps the skeptic shouldn't first call into question past meanings for all symbols, including those like "+", and should instead first specifically attack our ability to ground the meanings of more fundamental terms like "regular" or our other past expressions of notions of uniformity. If the skeptic could undermine the facts governing the past use of the language of uniformity first, perhaps he could leverage that into a case that there is no fact about what we mean by such terminology in the present. Once we are deprived of these present resources, the skeptic could go *back* to undermine the existence of past (and then eventually present) facts underlying the meanings of other terms like "plus" without fear of the NAIVE REPLY.

But it is not obvious how the skeptic can execute the first stages of this plan successfully. Here is how I imagine the skeptic trying to formulate the challenge.

Consider your past use of the word "regular" or even "regular continuation of a series", and consider some series to which you didn't yet apply these terms. For example, since you only applied these terms to finitely many cases in the past, there is some number n such that you never considered a "regular continuation" of a series whose first few members count by n. We can say, for the sake of argument, that n is 5, so that you never considered the initial segment given by "5, 10, 15, 20, 25, 30, 35". I will grant you that your *present* use of "regular continuation" is one on which the most regular continuation of this series follows with the number 40. But what fact determines that your past use accords with that present one?

This is a new challenge. The problem is that meeting it doesn't call for new argumentative resources. For the series of past applications of the term "regular" *itself can admit of more and less regular continuations by present standards*. We are *given* (say) that some past use of "regular" applies to the continuation "14, 16, 18 ..." of "2, 4, 6, 8, 10, 12" and to the continuation "21, 24, 27 ..." of "3, 6, 9, 12, 15, 18" and to the continuation "28, 32, 36 ..." of "4, 8, 12, 16, 20, 24". We can ask, in the *present* use of the word "regular" (which the skeptic must grant us): "what would be the most regular way of continuing to use the past word 'regular' when confronted with the initial segment '5, 10, 15, 20, 25, 30, 35'?" It would obviously be a slightly irregular (in the present, accepted sense) continued use of the past word "regular" to go on to apply it to the continuation "45, 55, ..." or the continuation "36, 37, 38 ...". It is not that these represent impossible ways for us to mean the word "regular" in the past. It is rather that to mean it in those ways would require special circumstances, just as would be required to use a word to express quaddition. Absent such circumstances, "regular" as used in the past will take on the meaning corresponding to the most regular continuation of its past privileged use. And that is the continuation that corresponds to the present use of the term "regular" – that is, a continuation of the use of "regular" on which the continuation of "5, 10, 15, 20, 25, 30, 35" by "40, 45, 50, ..." counts as most regular. In short, *present* applications of notions of uniformity can be used to salvage *past* ones via the NAIVE REPLY. So the skeptic makes no progress by trying to target those notions specifically.

Given that the NAIVE REPLY appeals to present usage that the skeptic grants, the only other reason I can see for trying to forbid appeal to the language of uniformity would be to claim that it is used to state *semantic* facts. Semantic terminology, presently used or not, is dialectically ruled out because we are supposed to answer the skeptic with *non*-semantic facts to ground the semantic ones, lest we lapse into a form of semantic primitivism.

But notions of uniformity plainly state non-semantic facts. Water can drip from a leaf in a more or less regular pattern. That fact about the dripping is hardly a semantic one. The colors of two flowers can be more similar to each other than they are to the color of a third flower. This is a fact about colors, and their relationships, not about meanings. There would be innumerable regularities, irregularities, similarities, dissimilarities, etc. present in a world with *no* physically realized semantic properties – no beings that spoke or inscribed their thoughts, for example. So there is no hope of claiming that notions of uniformity are out-of-bounds for smuggling in semantic concepts.

For reasons like this, I feel the skeptic will have a hard time denying (iii). Denying (ii) is perhaps even harder. It is clear that ordinary speaker judgments involving concepts of uniformity track the extensions of past usage that match the interpretations we would assign to words. If you give even a young student the first eight evens and ask them to continue the series in the "most regular" way, it is perfectly clear what counts as satisfying that command. For the same reason, virtually any other series of past applications of terminology will have a "most regular" extension, or one which applies to "most similar" things, etc., that lines up with the terminology's standard interpretation. This is probably why Lewis hardly elaborates on how naturalness – insofar as he presumed it would track ordinary notions of uniformity – will give us the results we need to avoid skepticism. He took this to be obvious. What needed defense, he thought, was the legitimacy of appealing to the notions in the first place.

If we also grant (i) (on which more in a moment), then the skeptic requires some kind of error theory for these judgments. He must acknowledge that there are facts about which continuations of past usage are most regular or most similar, and then deny what appear to be obvious, ubiquitous claims about what those facts are. I do not know what the basis for this error theory could be. It seems desperate and ad hoc.

Given all this, I think the skeptic's best response to the NAIVE REPLY is to try to deny (i): to say that notions of uniformity aren't usable to state facts. In what sense of "fact" must the skeptic claim this? Well, in whatever sense they want to deny that there are "meaning facts" in the first place.

Here we run up against the tricky issue of how to interpret the nature of the skeptic's desired threat. While there are subtleties here,[19] I don't think we need to enter into them. This is because there is a strong *prima facie* case that the language of uniformity is fact-stating, and usable to state truth-conditions, in just the way that any other area of apparently factualist discourse does. What I take to be essential for a predication to express truth-conditions (even broadly inflationary ones) is that there be "conditions under which" what was said or expressed through the predication is true. That is to say, there is a partition among possibilities into those that accord with what was thereby said, and those in which are not in accord with it. And (again *prima facie*) notions of uniformity meet that standard. Notions like "similar" (perhaps relative to a respect) partition the world into pairs, notions like "regular" partition processes and events, and so on. True, there will be vagueness and ambiguity. But this is fine as long as there is parallel vagueness and ambiguity in the semantic case (which, to all appearances, there is).

---

[19] For example, Kripke eventually countenances a "skeptical solution" on Wittgenstein's behalf that may end up deflating the notions of fact or truth along the line of a redundancy theory (Kripke 1982: 86). See Byrne (1996) and Wilson (1998) for a discussion of the resulting complexities in trying to attribute a form of non-factualism to Kripke's Wittgenstein.

Here is another way to put the matter. There was no special reason *prior* to skeptical inquiry to doubt that the language of uniformity was usable to state facts or truth-conditions in a manner like any other clearly factualist form of discourse. And there do not appear to be any reasons, *post* skeptical inquiry to do so either. What I've been arguing so far is that the kinds of techniques Kripke deploys on behalf of the skeptic (like skeptical reinterpretation) cannot *establish* the non-factuality of the relevant sphere of discourse. Rather, if anything, the success of skeptical techniques *presupposes* this independent form of non-factualism.

This leaves open the possibility that the skeptic could construct an inventive case against the factuality of the language of uniformity. I won't try to prejudge the existence of such a case here. I merely want to emphasize that it would have to be novel. Nothing in Kripke's text gives us any reason to doubt the factuality of the language of uniformity, since the skeptical arguments for forms of non-factualism can only succeed *given* that the language of uniformity is not fact-stating. Surely, given that dialectical situation, the burden of proof here is on the skeptic to kick-start the non-factualist argumentative machinery. What could motivate an independent skepticism distinctly for notions of uniformity I am not entirely sure.

There is obviously more to be said on all the matters I've been discussing. I certainly haven't explored all the possible worries one could raise for the NAIVE REPLY. But I think it is interesting to see how resilient this loosely Wittgenstein-inspired reply can be in a confrontation with the semantic skeptic, especially if Wittgenstein in fact never countenanced any such form of skepticism. Wittgenstein was exceedingly cautious in formulating his response to foundational semantic worries, and in spite of this, he made open use of notions of uniformity in spelling out his views.[20] Those notions appear to have a power against the skeptic that Kripke never really considered. Whether or not something can ultimately be said to firmly shore up the skeptic's position in light of this attempted reply, there is good reason to think we will have something interesting to learn from the confrontation.

---

[20] To be fair, Wittgenstein *did* qualify the use of notions of uniformity in important ways – notably at *PI* §208. But, as I read him, he is there qualifying the relevance of notions of uniformity for the *Justificatory* Question, and so not qualifying their relevance to skeptical inquiry as I have construed it.

5   Wittgenstein's Naturalism and the Skeptical Paradox

Marie McGinn

1   Introduction: Naturalism and Kripke's Skeptical Solution

In the subtitle to *Wittgenstein on Rules and Private Language*, Kripke describes his book as *An Elementary Exposition*. One way to understand this is as an exposition which aims to identify the key elements – the principal philosophical ideas – which shape the discussion carried on in the remarks that make up the *Philosophical Investigations* (henceforth *PI*). The primary elements Kripke identifies are three: (1) the skeptical paradox – there is no such fact as meaning something by a word – "the most radical and original skeptical problem that philosophy has seen to date" (Kripke 1982: 60) and "the fundamental problem of *Philosophical Investigations*" (Kripke 1982: 78); (2) the skeptical solution to the paradox, which draws on the third element; (3) the idea that the meaning of a statement is given by a description of the conditions in which we are justified in asserting it (or, more generally, the meaning of an expression is given by the conditions in which we are justified in using it to make the relevant move in a language-game) and the role that the assertion (language-game) plays in our lives.

Within the overarching framework of these three organizing elements, additional key elements enter Kripke's account of Wittgenstein's understanding of rule-following and concept attribution, which when looked at together reveal a further, tacit element, whose philosophical significance I want to explore in this chapter. This tacit element is a form of naturalism which runs through Kripke's account of Wittgenstein's later philosophy. It has both a methodological and an ontological aspect. The methodological aspect consists primarily in an emphasis on *description* in his account of the assertability-conditions view of meaning and the skeptical solution to the paradox: On the description of the circumstances in which, in a particular case, we are, for example, justified in asserting that either I myself or another means addition by "plus," has continued a series correctly, has carried out an order as it was meant, and so on. It can also be seen in the claim, central to the skeptical solution, that the psychological accompaniments to the following of a rule are irrelevant to the language-game of concept attribution; everything that we need to understand the language-game of attributing meaning and understanding lies open to view in the circumstances in which the expressions of our language are used.[1]

The ontological aspect consists in the emphasis the skeptical solution places on our immediate reactions, on our ungrounded agreement in how we respond in new cases, on the way our concepts have developed as part of human natural history, on the way our use of linguistic expressions is woven in with other activities in human life, on the way in which agreement in reactions and responses binds us together in a community with a shared form of life, whose members implicitly rely on the responses of others to agree with their own, on the fact that our language-games depend in the end upon ungrounded ways of acting, that agreement in ungrounded ways of acting is sustained by nothing more than natural facts about us, and so on. These elements in Kripke's account could be taken to fall under the rubric of "remarks on the natural history of human beings," which Wittgenstein refers to in *PI* §415, and are connected with his aim of showing "that nothing extraordinary is involved" (*PI* §94). What they show, I believe, is that Kripke has identified an important theme in *PI*. The question is how the naturalism, which is undoubtedly present, is to be understood.

What is interesting is that, although this tacit naturalism in Kripke's account is woven into his development of the skeptical paradox and his account of the skeptical solution to it, it is logically quite distinct from them. Kripke himself never claims that it is the discovery of the skeptical paradox about meaning that motivates Wittgenstein to abandon the view of meaning he held in the *Tractatus* and adopt the assertability-conditions view that, in his narrative, is key to the skeptical solution. He acknowledges that in the opening sections of *PI*, the assertability approach is introduced to the reader through remarks that do not deal explicitly with the skeptical paradox. The same, I want to argue, holds for the naturalism which Kripke detects and which I want to claim is an important aspect of Wittgenstein's later work. Extracting the naturalism from the elements of Kripke's account gives a clear sense of its significance. However, the overarching structure of his account, which elevates the skeptical paradox to the position of the fundamental problem of *PI*, hijacks the naturalism into a narrative

---

[1] Although I shall argue for a different interpretation of Wittgenstein's naturalism, this anti-psychologistic element in Kripke's reading of it clearly taps into an important theme in *PI*. It is one of the aspects of Kripke's reading of Wittgenstein's remarks on rule-following that makes it difficult to identify, if it does go wrong, just where it goes wrong.

which serves the ends of the skeptical solution, in which normative notions are explicitly excluded. This inevitably has the effect of assimilating the naturalism that Kripke finds in Wittgenstein's later philosophy to a form of reductive naturalism, which sets out to provide an account of our normative practices using exclusively non-normative concepts.

The question I want to raise is whether Kripke's assessment of the significance of the paradox of *PI* §201 and its shaping of the narrative of *PI*, which puts the naturalism to work in a skeptical solution to it, is correct. The question is important not only for how we understand the philosophical aims of *PI*, but also for how we understand the nature of the naturalistic element in Wittgenstein's later philosophy. The reductionist interpretation of Wittgenstein's naturalism, which is made inevitable once it is pressed into service in a solution to the skeptical paradox, is made particularly clear by those, such as Crispin Wright, who made Kripke's naturalistic element explicit and used the non-normative notion of *primitive dispositions* in a constructive account of what going by a rule consists in that is intended to provide a direct reply to the skeptic.[2] The communitarian account of rule-following which Wright puts forward, which grounds the concept of following a rule in shared primitive dispositions to respond in a certain way in new cases, has been seen as simply equivalent to skepticism about norms[3] or, if it eschews constitutive definitions, unsatisfactorily quietist, in a way that appears merely to bury the skeptical problem.[4] I want to consider whether there is another way to understand Wittgenstein's naturalism and its relation to the paradox of *PI* §201, one which allows it to escape the charges of both reductionism and Wright's unsatisfactory form of quietism.

2   Wittgenstein's Naturalism and the Skeptical Paradox: An Alternative View

Wittgenstein's pivot toward some form of philosophical naturalism began in the early 1930s. In *Philosophical Grammar* (henceforth *PG*),

---

[2] For Wright's constructivist account developed as a straight solution to the skeptical paradox, see Wright (2001b), (2001c), and (2001d).
[3] John McDowell criticizes Wright's view along these lines in three papers. See McDowell (1984), (1992), and (1998a). In the wake of his compelling criticisms of the communitarian account, McDowell defends a reading of Wittgenstein's naturalism that is non-reductive but also platonistic and psychologistic, and to this extent goes against important themes in *PI* which Kripke and Wright tap into. The version of naturalism that I develop here differs from McDowell's in being neither platonist nor psychologistic.
[4] This is a view which Wright himself later develops. See Wright (2007).

based on a typescript written in 1933, he is already committed to the key methodological principle of his naturalistic approach:[5]

> We are only concerned with the description of what happens and it is not the truth but the forms of the description that interests us....
> I am *describing* language, not *explaining* anything. (*PG*: 66)

What he is describing is already conceived, not merely as the use of words in a calculus, but "the way the use meshes with our life" (*PG*: 65), "and the way it meshes with life is infinitely various" (*PG*: 66). This early reconfiguring of his philosophical method is described in a remark which survives into *PI* (*PI* §108): "We are talking about the spatial and temporal phenomenon of language, not about some non-spatial, non-temporal phantasm" (*PG*: 121). These methodological adjustments reflect what is widely accepted as the key idea of the later philosophy: "The use of a word in the language is its meaning" (*PG*: 60). It is an idea which directs our attention to how human beings operate with words in their everyday lives and away from any concern with the psychological accompaniments to the use of expressions. Wittgenstein recognizes the temptation to think it is the psychological accompaniments that are essential for meaning, but he believes this is mistaken: "The psychological processes which are found by experience to accompany sentences are of no interest to us" (*PG*: 45). Understanding a word means being able to apply it, being able to use it; the criterion of someone's understanding, or of how someone understands a word, is how they go on to use it: "To understand the grammar of the word "to mean" we must ask ourselves what is the criterion for the expression's being meant *thus*" (*PG*: 45).

This pivot away from the psychological realm of representations and towards a concern with how speakers operate with words in "infinitely various" ways within the kind of life that is natural for human beings is fundamental to the naturalistic approach that comes to characterize Wittgenstein's later philosophy. However, while Wittgenstein considers himself liberated from the idea of meaning as something that is coupled with a word, or as something that comes before the mind when we hear and understand it, he sees that his idea of meaning as use poses a number of questions. His naturalistic approach recognizes a temporal aspect to

---

[5] I recognize a danger in attributing a form of naturalism to Wittgenstein. I do not mean to claim that Wittgenstein had a project of determining what kinds of entity are included in the realm of nature. Still less that he aims to establish which forms of discourse are factual and which are not. His concern is to become clear about how certain of our concepts function. My claim is that the nature of his methods of clarification and what they reveal about how our concepts function make the description of naturalism, applied to his later philosophy, apt.

the phenomenon of meaning, expressed in the remark from *PI* §108/*PG*: 121 quoted above, and also in the following: "It might almost be said: 'Meaning *moves*, whereas a process stands still.'" (*PG*: 149). And this appears to raise a problem:

> If "to understand the meaning of a word" means to know the grammatically possible ways of applying it, then can I ask: "How can I know what I mean by a word at the moment I utter it? After all, I can't have the whole mode of application in my head all at once." (*PG*: 49)

The problem is one that arises insofar as there is something which seems to be present and yet which isn't present. The problem crops up again and again in *PG* in a number of different guises. If the meaning of a word is its use, if someone says he understands the word "blue," say, "how does *he* know he understands the word?" (*PG*: 81). Surely, the whole use would have to be before his mind, and yet it isn't present. Again, "the system of language seems to provide me with a medium in which the proposition [expressing a wish] is no longer dead," "still the whole of language isn't present during this expression, yet surely the wish is!" (*PG*: 149). "I said that it is the *system* of language that makes the sentence a thought and makes it a thought *for us*. That doesn't mean that it is while we are using a sentence that the system of language makes it into a thought for us, because the system isn't present then ..." (*PG*: 153).

Wittgenstein's approach to this cluster of problems reflects his naturalistic turn: His concern is to pay attention to "what happens" on particular occasions of use. What we come to see – to recognize – is that nothing has to be present to make the signs that we operate with alive. What matters, as we can see when we attend to the facts about how words are used, is the background against, or context in, which they are used. However, he recognizes that it is this cluster of problems that tempts us into inventing "a shadow" – an "intermediary" between an order and its execution, between a wish and its fulfilment, between a sentence and the state of affairs that makes it true, between a rule and its application – which will do the work of prefiguring the future. Not content with the mere sign and its use over time, we feel the need for something that is present before the mind and carries a determination of reality within it. He wants to say that "we mustn't think that when we understand or mean a word what happens is an act of instantaneous ... grasp of grammar" (*PG*: 49), but he acknowledges "[i]t can seem as if the rules of grammar are in a certain sense an unpacking of something we experience all at once when we use a word" (*PG*: 50). He recognizes that the naturalistic move that he describes when he says, "What I want to say is that to be a sign a thing must be dynamic, not static," exerts its own pressure towards a problematic idea of shadows, for he immediately goes on:

> Here it can easily seem as if the sign contained the whole of the grammar; as if the grammar were contained in the sign like a string of pearls in a box and we only had to pull it out. (But this kind of picture is just what is misleading us). As if understanding were an instantaneous grasping of something from which later we only draw consequences which already exist in an ideal sense before they are drawn. (*PG*: 50)

Despite the anti-psychologism that emerges as fundamental to his philosophical naturalism, Wittgenstein finds himself having to fight a rear-guard action against a new source of the pressure to picture meanings as something that comes before the mind, one which has its roots in the dynamism which is central to his naturalistic picture: "one will believe that here the future is in some strange way caught in the sense of a sentence, in the meaning of the words" (*PG*: 155). We are tempted to think, not merely of the sentence – the sign – but "'The sense of this proposition was present to me'" (*PG*: 155). The tendency of Wittgenstein's thought here is the reverse of the one Kripke imagines. The naturalism does not arise as a response to skepticism about a mentalistic conception of meaning, rather, a pressure toward a mentalistic conception of meaning – meanings as shadows – arises within the naturalistic approach of the later philosophy, which concerns itself with the way speakers operate with words in the course of their everyday lives. And his response to it is to use the tools of his naturalistic method to overcome the temptations the pressure represents. Ultimately, these temptations are shown to give rise to the paradox that Wittgenstein alludes to in *PI* §95, which I'll discuss further in Section 3.

There is a second temptation to misunderstanding that Wittgenstein recognizes arises in connection with his naturalistic approach to meaning, which begins to emerge in *PG*. Wittgenstein wants us to focus on the way we operate with signs, on the way their use "meshes with our life," and to forget the idea of shadows that mediate between a sign and its application. That is to say, he wants us to accept that all that comes to a speaker's mind when he hears and understands a word is the word itself.[6] However, if we imagine, for example, the order to square a series of numbers written in the form of a table:

---

[6] McDowell believes the skeptical paradox is inevitable once the step is taken of accepting that all that comes before a speaker's mind when he hears and understands a word is the word itself. That's why he believes it is essential to reinstate a mental state that contains within itself a determination of what counts as conformity with it: the key idea of his naturalized platonism. The naturalistic approach I'm attributing to Wittgenstein, with its emphasis on the way speakers operate with words, is intended to provide an alternative to McDowell's claim that naturalized platonism is the only way to preserve genuine normativity.

x 1 2 3

x^2

then, he suggests, it can seem to us that we have to add something to the order in order to be able to follow it, namely the interpretation of it:

> It seems to us as if by understanding the order we add something to it, something that fills the gap between command and execution. So that if someone said "You understand it, don't you, so it is not incomplete" we could reply "Yes, I understand it, but only because I add something to it, namely the interpretation." (*PG*: 47)

Wittgenstein's response to this is to point out that introducing an interpretation is just introducing another sign, and to suppose that it always takes place would be to suppose that no sentence could be understood without a rider. Whereas, "If someone asks me "What time is it?" there is no inner process of laborious interpretation; I simply react to what I see and hear" (*PG*: 47). Later on, he notes:

> What happens is not that this symbol cannot be further interpreted, but: I do not interpret because I feel natural in the present picture.
> ... it is a stopping-place that is natural to me, and its further interpretability does not occupy (or trouble) me. (*PG*: 147)

He comments:

> (While thinking philosophically we see problems in places where there are none. It is for philosophy to show that there are no problems.) (*PG*: 47)

These thoughts are clearly the origins of the remarks on rule-following in *PI*, which culminate in the paradox of *PI* §201. As they emerge in *PG*, they have not yet reached their paradoxical crescendo, and it is clear that, like the reflections on meanings as shadows, they arise in the context of Wittgenstein's naturalistic approach to questions of meaning and understanding, and that he intends to use the methodological techniques this approach comprises in order to overcome the mistaken temptation they represent. Interpretations, like shadows, are things that his naturalistic approach, which limits itself to signs and the way we operate with them in the context of the myriad activities that characterize our distinctive ways of living, can seem to be pressured into introducing as a supplement to the mere sign. There is a temptation to think there must be a process of interpretation between the sign and its application, and Wittgenstein's task is to show that the pressure is illusory: The problem doesn't exist.

Once again, his aim is to show the steps we want to take achieve nothing, and the explanations we are tempted to reach for are empty.

Ultimately, the aim of his naturalistic approach is to show that everything that we need to understand the phenomena of meaning, understanding, thinking, inferring, intending, wishing, expecting, and so on are there before eyes in the institutions of language, in the customary ways that human beings, as a result of their education and training, operate with the expressions of their language in the various activities of their everyday lives. Naturalism is not, as Kripke's account makes it appear, a response to a skeptical problem but a philosophical outlook that represents the methodological first principle of Wittgenstein's later philosophy. It is the foundation of the anti-platonist, anti-psychologistic, and non-reductive treatment of meaning and understanding that gradually unfolds there. It also forms both the ground on which the temptations that lead to the paradox of *PI* §95 and *PI* §201 arise, and the approach within which they are overcome. Clearly, this suggests a very different interpretation for the role of the paradox and Wittgenstein's response to it, one in which the latter is neither reductionist nor problematically quietist.

3   The Paradox of §201 as a Means of Illumination

I argued in Section 2 that the roots of Wittgenstein's remarks on rule-following in *PI* can be seen in his reflections of the early 1930s, when he acknowledges our tendency to feel dissatisfied with the resources of his philosophical naturalism: Signs and the way human beings operate with them in their everyday life with language. We feel that the mere sign requires supplementing, that there must be something present in the mind when we understand a sign in addition to the sign itself, something which mediates between a sign and its application. Wittgenstein focuses on two ideas as to what these potential intermediaries might be: first, the idea of shadows – the proposition, the thought, the sense of a sentence, the wish itself, and so on – and second, the idea of an interpretation, which must be added to a sign before it is applied. Both ideas are the subject of critical attention in *PI*, where both are now associated with the idea of a "paradox": shadows in *PI* §95 and interpretations in *PI* §201.

The central claim of Kripke's interpretation is that we should understand the paradox of *PI* §201 as a skeptical paradox, that is, as an argument from premises we accept as true to a conclusion that is contrary to common sense. The rule-following considerations, on Kripke's reading, have destroyed what we think of as meaning something by our words, by showing that any application that we go on to make of them can, on some interpretation, be shown to be correct. It is a paradox that leaves us confounded and in a place that cannot possibly be inhabited. The skeptical solution is intended to offer a way of living with the paradox, but the implicit accommodation with skepticism about meaning is a position Kripke himself believes is unsatisfactory, finding himself unwilling to give up on the idea that there is something in his present mental state that differentiates his meaning addition rather than quaddition by the plus sign (Kripke 1982: 66). I've already argued that this understanding of the relation between the paradox and Wittgenstein's naturalism gets things the wrong way round, but it is perhaps also instructive, as we approach the question of how to understand the paradox of *PI* §201, to look first at the paradox of *PI* §95.

Kripke himself sees there is a connection between these early sections of *PI* and the remarks on rule-following, when he points out that "the paradox of the second part of the *Investigations* constitutes a powerful critique of any idea that 'mental representations' uniquely correspond to 'facts', since it alleges that the components of such 'mental representations' do not have interpretations that can be 'read off' from them in a unique manner" (Kripke 1982: 85). I think this point is key when it comes to understanding *PI* §95:

"Thinking must be something unique." When we say, *mean*, that such-and-such is the case, then, with what we mean, we do not stop anywhere short of the fact, but mean: *such-and-such – is – thus-and-so*. But this paradox (which indeed has the form of a truism) can also be expressed in this way: one can *think* what is not the case.

The remark is obscure. What is particularly unclear is why Wittgenstein calls the thought expressed in the second sentence a "paradox," though it is clear that its paradoxical nature is linked to the fact that one can think what is not the case. This implies that the object of our thought cannot be the fact itself, which may not exist, but must be merely a representation of it: the shadow of the fact. That idea is supported by the remark preceding *PI* §95, in which Wittgenstein speaks of "the tendency to assume a pure intermediary between the propositional *sign* and the facts" (*PI* §94). As he says in the *Blue Book* (henceforth *BB*): "There are different names for this shadow, e.g., 'proposition', 'sense of the sentence'" (*BB*: 32). And he goes on to express precisely the worry Kripke alludes to:

But this doesn't remove our difficulty. The question now is: "How can something be the shadow of a fact which doesn't exist?"
I can express our trouble in a different form by saying, "How can we know what the shadow is a shadow of?" (*BB*: 32)

Wittgenstein compares the case with that of a portrait, and asks what makes a portrait a portrait of Mr N. After considering a number of possibilities, he arrives at the idea that what makes a portrait a portrait of so-and-so "is the *intention*" (*BB*: 32). He then gives expression to the fundamental problem:

> For describe whatever process (activity) of projection we may, there is a way of reinterpreting this projection. Therefore – one is tempted to say – such a process can never be the intention itself. For we could always have intended the opposite by reinterpreting the process of projection. Imagine this case: We give someone an order to walk in a certain direction by pointing or by drawing an arrow which points in the direction. Suppose drawing arrows is the language in which generally we give such an order. Couldn't such an order be interpreted to mean that the man who gets it is to walk in the direction opposite to that of the arrow? (*BB*: 33)

He points out that any interpretation is merely "a new symbol added to the old one" (*BB*: 33), but he does not at this stage connect this with the idea of paradox. He is still working against the idea of shadows, as he did in *PG*, by looking at the origins of this idea and then using a variety of techniques which characterize his naturalistic approach to philosophy to counter and overcome them. For example:

> We said that the connection between our thinking, or speaking, about a man and the man himself was made when, in order to explain the meaning of the word "Mr Smith" we pointed to him, saying "this is Mr Smith." And there is nothing mysterious about this connection. I mean there is no queer mental act which somehow conjures up Mr Smith in our minds when he really isn't there. What makes it difficult to see that this is the connection is a peculiar form of expression of ordinary language, which makes it appear that the connection between our thought (or the expression of our thought) and the thing we think about must have subsisted *during* the act of thinking. (*BB*: 38)

However, these reflections in the *BB* provide good reason for thinking that the paradox that Wittgenstein alludes to in *PI* §95 is the same paradox he explores in detail in *PI* §201. This suggests that we should see the paradox as something Wittgenstein evolves as another way of demonstrating what he has long been committed to showing: That shadows – intermediaries between the sign and its application which settle what counts as a correct application of it – are an illusion. The two strands of *PG* come together in the paradox, for what we find is that anything that is added to a sign – an interpretation or rule of projection – is just another sign, and therefore itself subject to a variety of interpretations. As he says in the *BB*, "What one wishes to say is: 'Every sign is capable of interpretation; but the *meaning* mustn't be capable of interpretation. It is the last interpretation'" (*BB*: 34). But this is just the idea of shadows again, and when he pursues it, all he finds is something that "could only consist in a repetition of our previous expression ..., or else in a translation into some other form of expression" (*BB*: 38).

The idea that this train of thought – the search for intermediaries to accompany the use of signs – leads to a philosophical paradox has not yet fully emerged in the *BB*, but he is clear that his whole purpose is "to remove the temptation to think there '*must* be' what is called a mental process of thinking, hoping, wishing believing, etc., independent of the process of expressing a thought, a hope, a wish, etc." (*BB*: 41). And he believes that once we can accept that meaning is dynamic, that the whole system from which a sentence gets its meaning, does not have to be present at the moment of use, then "there is no more point in *postulating* the existence of a peculiar kind of mental act alongside our expression" (*BB*: 42). The aim is "to rid us of the temptation to look for a peculiar act of thinking [meaning], independent of the act of expressing our thoughts, ... stowed away in some peculiar medium" (*BB*: 43). When the paradox does emerge in *PI*, it is just another way of expressing the problem of the regress of interpretations that the appeal to shadows leads to. Relief from the paradox lies in the naturalistic turn that eschews concern with the psychological accompaniments to the use of words and focuses on what speakers *do* – how they operate with expressions – and the *context* in which they do it.

All this suggests a completely different understanding of the dialogue which begins at *PI* §138 and culminates in the paradox of *PI* §201. The dialogue begins with the following thought:

But we *understand* the meaning of a word when we hear or say it; we grasp the meaning at a stroke, and what we grasp in this way is surely something different from the 'use' which is extended in time! (*PI* §138)

Kripke takes this as the expression of our common-sense view of meaning, which is about to come under skeptical attack. However, the evidence of Wittgenstein's earlier remarks suggests that we should see it as the expression of the familiar pressure to introduce an intermediary between a sign and its application and understand the whole of the subsequent dialogue as a unified attack on the idea of intermediaries, either meanings – which mysteriously "in some *unique* way predetermined, anticipated – in the way only meaning something could anticipate reality" (*PI* §188) – or interpretations. The voices of the dialogue are those of Wittgenstein's interlocutor, who gives expression to the pressure to introduce intermediaries, or to think of understanding as "something that occurs in a moment" (*PI* §151), and the naturalistic voice in which we have seen Wittgenstein responding to this pressure since the early 1930s.

Wittgenstein raises the key question for his interlocutor in *PI* §139:

And how can what is present to us in an instant, what comes before our mind in an instant, fit a *use*?

The essential problem, as we saw in the passages from the *BB*, is that the process of "projecting" what comes before the mind can be interpreted in different ways, and each interpretation can be reinterpreted, and so we are led, from the question raised in *PI* §139 to the paradox of *PI* §201. It is the paradox alluded to in *PI* §95, which arises when we are tempted to suppose that meaning involves a unique form of prefiguring of reality, which *PI* §201 is about to make explicit: Whatever we introduce is just another sign, "[i]nterpretations by themselves do not determine meaning" (*PI* §198). There is no skeptical intent, merely a refiguring of the regress of interpretations into a paradox, which Wittgenstein uses as a means to illuminate the pointlessness of introducing an intermediary between a sign and its application: "there would be neither accord nor conflict here" (*PI* §201). The instantaneous fixing of meaning in a mental act of intending is an illusion.

There is, therefore, no sense in which Wittgenstein accepts the paradox or believes that it calls, as the skeptical solution and communitarian account of rule-following claim, for a piece of constructive philosophy to repair the damage it has wrought. The second paragraph of *PI* §201 makes this clear, for what we hear is Wittgenstein's naturalistic voice telling his interlocutor he can see that the paradox arises out of "a misunderstanding." And he can see it rests on a misunderstanding by "the mere fact" that he has again and again been presented with interpretations which he has been ready to act upon, until it has been pointed out that there is another way to interpret the interpretation. As he was already observing in *PG*:

> If I see the thought symbol "from outside," I become conscious that it *could* be interpreted thus or thus; if it is a step in the course of my thoughts, then it is a stopping-place that is natural to me, and its further interpretability does not occupy (or trouble) me. (*PG*: 147)

Normally, the possibility that there are other applications of a rule that we are familiar with and employ in our everyday life with language does not even occur to us; we simply apply the rule in the way we have learned to use it – in the way that accords with our practice of using it – and nothing occurs to worry us.

If we want to understand what makes what someone does a case of following a rule, then we need to look, not at what comes before the mind of someone who grasps a rule, but at the *context* in which *doing this* is "what we *call* (my emphasis) "following the rule" or "going against it" in particular cases" (*PI* §201). We judge that someone has carried out an order, multiplied two numbers, fulfilled his intention, and so on, on the basis of how he *acts* on a particular occasion, in the context of an ongoing linguistic practice which provides the background to his action. The role of the paradox in *PI* §201 is not, as Kripke claims, to confound us, but to bring illumination, by bringing an end to our pursuit of intermediaries and sending us "[b]ack to the rough ground" (*PI* §107): the way we operate with expressions in the context of our everyday practices. Wittgenstein's naturalistic approach to meaning and understanding, which looks at the ways human beings have developed a way of operating with signs in "infinitely various" activities within their complex lives, essentially connects the concept of a rule with that of a practice of going by a rule. It is in the context of an ongoing practice of using expressions that what I do now, when I apply the expression in the way that I have learned to use it, counts as following a rule or going against it. The question is whether this form of naturalism, shorn of its connections with a skeptical solution to a paradox about meaning, and attentive to how speakers actually employ the expressions of their language, is either reductionist or problematically quietist about nature of normativity.

4 Does Human Agreement Decide What Is True and What Is False?

Wittgenstein's express purpose in *PI* is "to understand the nature of language" (*PI* §92). Central to Wittgenstein's naturalistic approach to understanding the nature of language is his commitment to a methodology which is concerned with the description of language-in-use. Language provides us with the means to describe, measure, calculate, infer, and so on. These are all practices in which only certain ways of operating with signs count as correct, and taking part in them is a matter of following rules. Understanding a language means knowing how to use words in appropriate contexts to perform intentional actions – describing, calculating, measuring, and inferring – in which an agent applies rules for the use of expressions (for the most part) correctly in the course of doing other things.[7] To understand the nature of language means achieving a clarified view of these practices of rule following, seeing more clearly what they amount to. One of the key remarks Wittgenstein makes about what it is to follow a rule is expressed at *PI* §199:

To follow a rule, to make a report, to give an order, to play a game of chess, are *customs* (usages, institutions).

---

[7] It is clearly very important to Wittgenstein that human beings are creatures who act with an end in view. It is important that our linguistic techniques of measurement, inference, calculation, description, expression of intention, and so on are used within human lives in which actions are done with a particular end that gives what is being done its point. Thus, "Our talk gets its meaning from the rest of our proceedings" (Wittgenstein 1977: §229).

To understand a sentence means to understand a language. To understand a language means to have mastered a technique.

Wittgenstein does little by way of unpacking the notions of "*customs* (usages, institutions)." However, they clearly carry the implication of *agreed, regular, stable, and established ways of acting with signs*. To describe following a rule as an institution is to draw attention to the fact that speakers of a language are bound together in a linguistic community by customary ways of operating with signs in the course of their everyday lives. The relation of a speaker to his linguistic community is one of active participation in stable and established linguistic practices, which Wittgenstein expresses in the idea that mastery of a language is mastery of a technique. A speaker becomes part of a linguistic community through a training in the employment of words – in how to describe what he sees, in how to count, calculate, infer and so on – which he then goes on to employ in ways that mesh with his life in infinitely various ways. It depends upon his responding to this training by going on independently to project these techniques into new contexts in ways that are correct, that is, that accord with the established, ongoing practice of employing them. There is nothing more than our natural propensities underlying our capacity to master these techniques, but it is essential to the existence of our practices of describing, measuring, calculating, inferring, and so on, that speakers acquire the ability to operate with signs, *autonomously*, in ways that agree with an ongoing practice of using them.

However, Wittgenstein recognizes that this naturalistic approach to rule-following may appear to pose its own puzzles. We have already seen how he uses his naturalistic voice against his interlocutor's temptation to create intermediaries between a sign and its application. We also see him using his interlocutor to pose challenges to his naturalistic approach to language and linguistic mastery.[8] The challenges I want to look at focus on two areas of perplexity: (1) The question we saw him posing in *PG*: How can I know what I mean by a word at the moment I utter it? How do I know I understand a word when I say, "Now I understand?"; (2) Whether his naturalistic approach to language entails that human agreement decides what is true and what is false. I'll take the second issue first.

Wittgenstein's interlocutor raises the question at *PI* §242: "'So you are saying that human agreement decides what is true and what is false?'" Wittgenstein's response is clearly intended to repudiate the charge:

---

[8] The interlocutor's challenges often take the form of a charge that Wittgenstein's anti-platonist, anti-psychologistic approach to meaning and understanding falls into a form of reductionism. A charge which he strenuously resists.

What is true or false is what human beings *say*; and it is in their *language* that human beings agree. This is agreement not in opinions, but rather in form of life. (*PI* §242)

The rebuttal directs the interlocutor once again to the institutions of language that are constituted by forms of human action which have established customary ways of operating with expressions which are used to say things that are true or false. When a speaker uses a sentence on a particular occasion in certain circumstances, its meaning – what makes it possible to use it to say things that are true or false – is settled, not by a mental act of projection that anticipates the future, but the *context* of an ongoing human practice. The sense of my statement, "This table is 3 feet long," is fixed, on a particular occasion in a particular context, by a practice of measuring which has existed for a very long time, which is deeply embedded in human life, and in which we all agree in getting the same results when we apply our methods of measurement. Agreement in getting results belongs to the essence of techniques of measurement, which make it possible to express senseful propositions about an object's length. In the same way, it belongs to the essence of what we call measuring that we can predict with certainty that we will agree in our judgment as to whether my statement "This table is 3 feet long" is true or false. But it is not our agreement that decides whether the statement is true. That is settled by our techniques of measurement, which we have all mastered, and the table to which we now apply them.

One of the key passages for understanding Wittgenstein's distance from the communitarian view occurs at *PI* §195:

"But I don't mean that what I do now (in grasping the whole use of a word) determines the future use *causally* and as a matter of experience, but that, in a strange way, the use itself is in some sense present." But of course it is, 'in some sense'! Really, the only thing wrong with what you say is the expression "in an odd way."

The first thing to notice is that Wittgenstein accepts the first half of the thought: That when I grasp the meaning of a word, it is not a matter of the future use being determined causally or as a matter of experience, as the communitarian picture suggests. The second thing to notice is that Wittgenstein does not reject the idea that the future use of a rule is "'in some sense'" present, but gives a naturalistic steer as to how this should be understood – that is, not "'in an odd way'" – but, as his acceptance of the first half of the thought implies, this is not a matter of reducing it, as the communitarian reading claims, to a mere disposition to respond. What makes the sentence seem odd, he suggests, is that we imagine "it to belong to a different language-game from the one in which we actually use it" (*PI* §195). We misunderstand the use of the word and take "it to signify an odd *process*" (*PI* §196), something which makes its appearance *in an instant*, or which takes place *when* we understand.

Wittgenstein goes on to spell the point out in *PI* §197:

"It is as if we could grasp the whole use of a word at a stroke." – Well, that is just what we say we do. That is, we sometimes describe what we do in those words. But there is nothing astonishing, nothing strange about what happens. It becomes strange when we are led to think that the future development must in some way already be present in the act of grasping the use and yet isn't present. – For we say that there isn't any doubt that we understand the word, and on the other hand that its meaning lies in its use.

Wittgenstein clearly does not want to deny that the words "I grasped the meaning at a stroke," "I suddenly understood," and so on are used, that is, that they are *correctly* used, on certain occasions. However, the question is *how* they are used. That, he believes, is something which calls for clarification, by reflecting on how we operate with these sentences. The move that he now makes asks us to compare the use of these sentences with the use of the words "Let's play a game of chess." He tries to get us to see that it isn't anything which happens "at the time," or which is intrinsic to my mental state, which makes it *chess* that I intend to play, but the human *context* – the particular circumstances, which include facts about my own history – in which I say the words, "Let's play chess." *PI* §197 continues:

There is no doubt that I now want to play chess, but chess is the game it is in virtue of all its rule (and so on). Don't I know, then, which game I want to play until I *have* played it? Or is it, rather, than all the rules are contained in my act of intending? Is it experience that tells me that this sort of game usually follows such an act of intending? So can't I actually be sure what I intend to do? And if that is nonsense – what kind of super-rigid connection obtains between the act of intending and the thing intended? – Where is the connection effected between the sense of the words "Let's play a game of chess" and all the rules of the game? – Well, in the list of rules of the game, in the teaching of it, in the everyday practice of playing it.

One of the primary facts about natural language that Wittgenstein points to over and over again is that it is something that has been spoken for a very long time and which meshes in infinitely various ways with many of the other activities that human beings engage in. The stability of these practices is something we take for granted in all our communications with others. We take it for granted, for example, that speakers who have undergone the usual training with the color words of English will, in the main, in standard viewing conditions, agree on how those color words are projected in new cases. The future use of the word "red" is not in some strange way foreshadowed by a meaning that accompanies the saying or the hearing of the word, but it is the case that human beings are brought by the normal training with color samples to master a linguistic technique in respect of the word "red" which results in an overall consensus when it comes to describing the color of objects seen in good light. The institutions of language which give expressions their meaning are dynamic and exist in time, and when Wittgenstein speaks of our "everyday practice," we should think of this as encompassing the ongoing use of expressions by autonomous agents who have mastered these techniques.

This ongoing practice is present in the same sense in which Wittgenstein holds the rules of chess and the everyday practice of playing it are present and make it chess that I intend to play when I say, "Let's play a game of chess." The future use is not present in anything that comes before the speaker's mind, or in his primitive dispositions to respond, but in the practice, which is ongoing and exists independently of him, which, in claiming to grasp the meaning of a word, he claims he has the *ability* to participate in. If he claims, for example, that he has grasped counting in 2s, well what is counting in 2s? It is *this*, and here we point to the ongoing, stable practice of mathematics, which we take for granted and which provides the background to our language-game with the words "I grasp the use of the word." However, this leads on to the question of the first perplexity: How does Wittgenstein's naturalistic approach understand the first-person case: How do I know I have understood when I say "Now I understand"?

5 How Do I Know What I Mean by a Word?

Pointing out that the public realm of a dynamic, on-going practice of employing expressions provides the context in which "what we call 'following the rule' and 'going against it'" (*PI* §201) acquire a meaning still leaves a whole series of questions about ascriptions of meaning and understanding *to oneself*. Over the course of the remarks on rule-following one sees Wittgenstein's interlocutor using the first-person case to raise a series of challenges to his naturalistic approach. On the one hand, there are questions that focus on the idea that there must be a psychological state which settles in advance what counts as correct at every new point of application, for surely, we want to say I know what I mean by a word without waiting to see how I go on to use it. When I say (in the example of *PI* §151), on the basis of the formula's coming to mind, that I can go on with the series, I don't mean that I've had an experience which has been known in the past to lead to my going on correctly. On the other hand, there are questions that focus on how I know how I am to use a word which I understand, if the rule itself does not guide me. What is my justification for following a rule in the way that I do? When I give the order "+2," how can I know at the time I give the order that he has to write 1002 after 1000, if the rule itself doesn't settle it?

To the extent that the interlocutor is hankering after a conception of understanding as a state which is the source of correct use, in a sense which involves the discredited picture of a formula or a picture which cannot be interpreted, he is clearly to be resisted. But the challenges he poses to Wittgenstein's naturalistic approach are nevertheless real, and the way Wittgenstein responds to them requires a better understanding of what is involved in recognizing that "'following a rule' is a practice" (*PI* §202), that "to understand a language means to have mastered a technique" (*PI* §199).

Wittgenstein makes the point that mastery of language is mastery of a technique in various forms and on numerous occasions. When the interlocutor says, at *PI* §147, "'... [i]n my own case at any rate, I surely know that I mean such-and-such a series, no matter how far I've actually developed it,'" Wittgenstein responds, "[b]ut what does this knowledge consist in?" (*PI* §148). If we take our cue from the idea that understanding language is mastery of a technique, then knowing that I mean such-and-such a series – the series "+2," say – is to be understood as giving expression to *practical knowledge*: I'm describing what I *am doing*, based on the ability I have acquired. Once I have mastered the relevant technique, when I'm developing the series "0, 2, 4, 6, 8, ...," I am in a position to say what it is I am doing: I am counting in 2s. What justifies me in laying claim to such practical knowledge is not anything that comes before my mind while I count, but the *particular circumstances* that warrant my laying claim to such practical knowledge, which have to do with the kind of background training I have received and the kind of mastery I have achieved with mathematical techniques. Given I have mastered the basic techniques of developing series of the form 0, n, 2n, 3n, and so on, – that is, have learned how to do it in the way that everyone else does – then I can, in an exercise of practical knowledge, say, *straight off, not on the basis of observation*, that I am developing the series 2n, and *in these particular circumstances*, my assertion will be warranted.

In this way, we can see that my ability to say that I mean addition by "+" is grounded in a more fundamental capacity – mastery of a technique – which I possess insofar as I'm able both to *do* something on particular occasions and able to say, in virtue of my being a participant in the community of mathematicians, that what I am doing is *adding*. When I say "I already knew at the time when I gave the order, that he should write 1002 after 1000," what that amounts to, as Wittgenstein observes in *PI* §187, "is something like: 'If I had then been asked what number he should write after 1000, I would have replied '1002'.'" There was nothing in my mind that prefigured this continuation of the series, but I have mastered a technique of adding in 2s which puts me in a position to say now, "If I had been asked then what number he should write, ..."

In the same way, my saying "Now I can go on," when the formula comes to mind, is warranted "under certain circumstances" (*PI* §179), which have to do with my having acquired a mastery of linguistic techniques: I "had learnt algebra, had used such formulae before" (*PI* §179). "But that does not mean," Wittgenstein makes clear, "that [my] statement is only short for a description of all the circumstances which set the stage for our language-game" (*PI* §179). Rather, I'm suggesting, we should understand "Now I can go on" as the confident expression of my capacity to exercise practical knowledge of the relevant mathematical techniques: I am ready to *do* something that we describe as "working out the series." We see these first-person statements in the right light when we see them not as reports of mental states which in some strange way prefigure the future, but as connected with the capacity of an agent, who has received a certain sort of training and mastered a given technique, to continue the pattern independently.

We learn to use the words "Now I can go on" in the context of becoming agents who can act confidently and independently – autonomously – without further guidance, as members of a linguistic community, taking part in a practice of using expressions according to the customary ways of employing them. When Wittgenstein remarks that when I apply a rule, I act "without reasons" (*PI* §211), "'This is simply what I do'" (*PI* §217), "I follow the rule *blindly*" (*PI* §219), he should not be understood as claiming that our reactions are brute and devoid of normative significance. He is simply describing what happens when autonomous agents who have been trained in the practices that characterize our human life together apply the techniques they have mastered.[9]

---

[9] There is clearly an echo in this reading of Wittgenstein's remarks on rule-following of Anscombe's account of intentional action. See G. E. M. Anscombe (1972). Anscombe's anti-psychologistic approach to clarifying the concept of intention and intentional action is not only in general harmony with the anti-psychologism of *PI*, but the seeds of Anscombe's account are to be found in the remarks on intention in *PI* §§618–660. For an interpretation of Anscombe's work that brings out its Wittgensteinian methodology, see Rachael Wiseman (2016). For an interpretation of Wittgenstein's remarks on intention, see M. McGinn (2013: 283–296). It is interesting to note that although Anscombe's account of intention is clearly anti-psychologistic no one should consider it either behaviorist or reductionist. I'm suggesting we should regard Wittgenstein's anti-psychologistic account of rule-following in the same light.

The key elements in Wittgenstein's naturalism are, on the one hand, a methodology that focuses on describing what is open to view in the way speakers – autonomous agents – learn to operate with words in the course of carrying out the sorts of intentional activities that human beings engage in. On the other hand, an anti-psychologistic approach to human agency that focuses not on the psychological accompaniments to actions but on the individual and social context in which they occur, which, on a particular occasion, warrants the description of a particular action as one of "Adding 68 and 57," which an agent makes *straight off* in virtue of his practical knowledge of the technique of addition and a third party makes on the basis of what he says and does and the context in which he says and does it. It represents a distinctive form of naturalism entirely at odds with both the reductive aims of scientific naturalism and the reductive naturalism of Wright's communitarian account of rule-following. It begins with the acceptance of human natural history as encompassing practices which in their nature involve the idea of human agents learning to go by rules: "Giving orders, asking questions, telling stories, having a chat, are as much a part of our natural history as walking, eating, drinking, playing." (*PI* §25) The purpose of Wittgenstein's naturalistic approach in his later philosophy is to achieve a clarified view of the essence of rule following, by coming to see more clearly what is there before our eyes in our practice of operating with signs. On the one hand, he wants us to recognize that what gives life to signs is the human practices in which their use is embedded, and on the other, that the psychological accompaniments to our use of words are of no significance when it comes to understanding the nature of language, meaning, understanding, and so on. The approach is not reductionist, but nor is it quietist, in the sense that there is no question about the nature of normativity that should be answered that remains unanswered.[10]

---

[10] I would like to thank Jen Hornsby for helpful comments on an earlier draft of this chapter. I would also like to thank contributors to the discussion of this chapter at the UEA Wittgenstein Workshop, whose comments led me to make several clarifications and revisions.

6 Kripke and Wittgenstein on Rules and Meaning

Gary Ebbs

I have been puzzled for years by Saul Kripke's endorsement of the loose sketches of our ordinary view of meaning that he presents in his brilliant and provocative book *Wittgenstein on Rules and Private Language* (Kripke 1982, henceforth *WRPL*). The sketches depend on examples from which it is unclear how to generalize. They also appear to commit him to one or more of several doubtful claims about the normativity of meaning.[1] Why then is Kripke so confident that the sketches are "natural and correct" (*WRPL*: 65)? Why does he not question or revise them even *after* he takes himself to have shown that they imply the "incredible and self-defeating" conclusion that our words are meaningless (*WRPL*: 71)?

I recently found what I think are plausible answers to these questions by developing a new interpretation of Kripke's understanding of our ordinary view of meaning. The interpretation is guided by his remark that

Nothing is more contrary to our ordinary view – or Wittgenstein's – than is the supposition that "whatever is going to seem right to me is right." (PI §258) (*WRPL*: 23–24)

The leading ideas behind my interpretation are that

- Kripke's sketches of our ordinary view of meaning are attempts to highlight the features of meaning that enable us to draw the distinction between what seems right and what is right.
- Kripke thinks that the best way to clarify these features of meaning is to describe metasemantic conditions that a speaker's words must satisfy if the speaker is to be warranted in asserting a sentence in which the words occur.

I'll start by presenting my interpretation and explain how it makes sense of Kripke's sketches of our ordinary view of meaning. I'll then argue that

---

[1] For criticisms of several different formulations of the idea that meaning is normative, see for instance, Boghossian (2008b), Gibbard (2012: Chapter 3), Hattiangadi (2007: Chapter 7), Horwich (1995), Verheggen (In Press), Wikforss (2001), and Zalabardo (1997).

the interpretation clarifies Kripke's skeptical arguments without attributing to him any doubtful claims about the normativity of meaning. The view of meaning I attribute to Kripke is compelling enough, I believe, to explain why he is unwilling to question or revise it despite its absurd consequences. As I'll try to show in the last part of the chapter, however, it rests on a subtle yet fundamental misunderstanding of the distinction between what seems right and what is right.

1 Kripke's Requirement for Being Warranted in Asserting a Sentence

Recall Kripke's central example, in which we calculate for the first time the sum 68 + 57 and arrive at the answer 125. He writes,

> Ordinarily, I suppose that, in computing '68 + 57' as I do, I do not simply make an unjustified leap in the dark. I follow directions I previously gave myself that uniquely determine that in this new instance I should say '125.' (*WRPL*: 10)

Kripke, in his role as meaning skeptic, then poses a skeptical challenge: could it not be that in the past, and perhaps even only a brief moment ago, just before I started calculating, I meant quus by '+', where quus is a function that yields the same values as the addition function for arguments less than 68 but yields the value 5 otherwise? If this is logically possible, as Kripke's meaning skeptic supposes, then if it is false there must be a fact that determines that it is false. Kripke challenges us to specify the fact, if any, that rules out that I meant quus by '+'. He then states the conditions that any adequate answer to the skeptical challenge must satisfy:

> An answer to the skeptic must satisfy two conditions. First, it must give an account of what fact it is (about my mental state) that constitutes my meaning plus, not quus. But further, ... any putative candidate for such a fact must ... in some sense, show how I am justified in giving the answer '125' to '68 + 57'. The 'directions' mentioned [in the above quotation] ... that determine what I should do in each instance, must somehow be 'contained' in any candidate for the fact as to what I meant. Otherwise, the skeptic has not been answered when he holds that my present response is arbitrary. (*WRPL*: 11)

It is the second of these conditions that has generated the most controversy. Many readers interpret the meaning skeptic's second condition so that it implies that meaning is categorically normative in some sense and that to answer the meaning skeptic one must cite facts that determine the relevant categorical norms. I shall present a very different interpretation that I discovered while trying to answer the questions I posed at the start of this chapter.

My interpretation is guided by three additional features of Kripke's formulation of the meaning skeptic's challenge. First, Kripke's meaning skeptic grants that "if I use language at all, I cannot doubt coherently that 'plus', as I now use it, denotes plus" (*WRPL*: 13). The skeptic's argument therefore begins with the assumption that our words as we presently use them are meaningful. Second, and closely related, we can come to doubt that our word 'plus', as we now use it, is meaningful, the skeptic thinks, but only *indirectly*, as a result of (a) concluding that there are no facts that determined that my word 'plus' meant plus in the *past* and (b) acknowledging that "if there can be no fact about which particular function I meant in the *past*, there can be none in the *present* either" (*WRPL*: 13). It is solely for this reason that Kripke's meaning skeptic formulates his challenge as one concerning what I meant in the past, as follows:

> I am confident, perhaps after checking my work, that '125' is the correct answer. It is correct both in the arithmetical sense that 125 is the sum of 68 and 57, and in the metalinguistic sense that 'plus', *as I intended to use that word in the past*, denoted a function which, when applied to the numbers I called '68' and '57', yields the value 125. (*WRPL*: 8, my emphasis)

The "metalinguistic sense" of correctness that Kripke speaks of here is therefore not essential to the skeptical challenge, but an artifact of the meaning skeptic's need to present the challenge without immediately lapsing into the sort of pragmatic incoherence that would result from trying to doubt the meaningfulness of the very words that one uses to state it.[2] If and when we draw the radical skeptical conclusion that our words are meaningless, of course, "we pull the rug out from under our own feet" (*WRPL*: 13), or, in other words, we can no longer take ourselves to be able to use our words to make statements at all.

A third and widely overlooked feature of Kripke's formulation of the meaning skeptic's challenge is that it does not question our ordinary

---

[2] Each in their own way, McGinn (1984: 174) and Ginsborg (2022: 880–882) argue that the transtemporal metalinguistic formulation of the meaning skeptic's challenge is not just an artifact of Kripke's efforts to avoid incoherence; it is a theoretical expression of the meaning skeptic's requirement that the meanings of our words be settled in a way that is *temporally* prior to and independent of our new steps and assertions. On the interpretation I shall develop below, by contrast, the meaning skeptic requires that the meanings of our words be settled in a way that is *conceptually*, not necessarily *temporally*, prior to and independent of our assertions. Neither McGinn's nor Ginsborg's alternative readings fit well with Kripke's remark that he formulates the skeptical problem in temporal terms in order "to avoid confusing questions about whether the discussion is taking place 'both inside and outside language' in some illegitimate sense" (*WRPL*: 12). On this interpretive issue I agree with Paul Boghossian, who argues that the norms that are relevant to Kripke's meaning skeptic concern "relations between meaning something by [a word] at some time and its use at that time" (Boghossian 1989: 513).

or scientific standards for being epistemically warranted, or justified, in asserting meaningful sentences. In particular, Kripke writes, when we attempt to answer the skeptic's challenge, as exemplified by the case of calculating the sum 68 + 57, "scepticism about arithmetic should not be taken to be in question: we may assume, if we wish, that 68 + 57 is 125" (*WRPL*: 13). Since the skeptic's challenge concerns all meaningful uses of language, the point is general: with the sole exception of skepticism about what we meant in the past, skepticism about our ordinary or scientific standards for being epistemically warranted, or justified, in asserting meaningful sentences should not be taken to be in question.

In accord with these three features of Kripke's exposition of the meaning skeptic's argument I interpret the meaning skeptic's argument so that it does not challenge our ordinary standards for being warranted in asserting sentences about topics other than meaning, but instead seeks to render those standards irrelevant to our actual assertions of sentences, by establishing the following conditional: If, as the meaning skeptic argues, our word and sentences are meaningless, then the question whether we are warranted in asserting a given sentence is undefined and cannot arise; any "answer" to the question would be a "leap in the dark."

To formulate and clarify this interpretation I shall use the word "justified" differently from the way in which Kripke uses it. Kripke supposes that it is part of our ordinary thought and talk about meaning to take for granted that even in the most basic cases of applying words, when one's justifications give out, as in such cases as adding 1 to 8 or asserting that 8 + 1 is 9, our answers or assertions are not "arbitrary," not "leaps in the dark" – we are in some in some broad sense "justified" in giving them. It is more common these days for epistemologists to use the word "warranted" for this very broad category of good epistemic standings, to reserve the word "justified" for the special cases in which one can provide explicit noncircular support for one's acceptance of a given claim, and to use the word "entitlement" for cases in which one is warranted in answering or asserting as one does, but one is not justified in doing so.[3] Thus one can be *warranted* in asserting that 68 + 57 = 125 on the basis of an explicit calculation that, if done correctly, shows that one is *justified* in asserting that 68 + 57 = 125. Similarly, one can be *entitled* to assert that 8 + 1 = 9 if one has learned to add, one takes oneself to have arrived at one's answer by applying one's acquired ability to add, and the step one takes to arrive at one's assertion is so basic to one's ability to add that one cannot provide an explicit noncircular argument in support of one's

---

[3] Tyler Burge, among others, helped to codify these uses of "warrant," "justification," and "entitlement." For his summary of the uses, see Burge (2013: 1–3).

assertion. I'll use the terms "warranted," "justified," and "entitled" in this way.

I'll assume in what follows that to judge that p is to accept, whether in thought or in writing or speech, a sentence that (on a given occasion of judgment or assertion) expresses the thought that p, and that to assert that p is to write or utter a declarative sentence s that expresses one's judgment that p. To simplify my exposition, I'll focus on what is required according to Kripke for one to be warranted in asserting that p, for some p,[4] and abbreviate the phrase "write or utter a declarative sentence s that expresses one's judgment that p" as "assert s."

I'll also assume that for Kripke and his meaning skeptic, to say that I am warranted in *answering* '125' to the addition problem '68 + 57' is to say that I am warranted in *asserting* '68 + 57 = 125', and similarly for other sentences.[5] The same basic equivalence also holds, I'll assume, for taking new steps in a series, such as the series "+1." Such new steps, which amount to new applications of one's linguistic expressions, are in effect answers to questions. By the above equivalence, they therefore amount to assertions of corresponding sentences. Taking these equivalences for granted, to save words I shall focus on the meaning skeptic's requirements on being warranted in asserting sentences, leaving the corresponding versions of these requirements for taking new steps and making new applications of one's linguistic expressions unstated but implied.

My central interpretive thesis is that Kripke's arguments in *WRPL* are consequences of the following requirement (which I'll often refer to below as "Kripke's requirement"):

Requirement on being warranted in asserting a sentence. One is warranted in asserting a sentence s only if

(1) truth conditions of s are determined by the meanings of the words that occur in s, and
(2) the meanings of the words in s are determined by facts, including facts about one's mental states,[6] that together

---

[4] The extension of Kripke's reasoning to the case of judging that p is easy to see but including it would complicate my (already complicated) exposition.
[5] Similarly, Allan Gibbard writes, "I'll assume … that to say that I should have *answered* '125' amounts to saying that I ought to have *accepted* my sentence '68 + 57 = 125'" (Gibbard 2012: 55).
[6] I do not include in my formulation of Kripke's requirement on being warranted in asserting a sentence the requirement that *all* of the facts that together determine the meanings of one's words are facts about one's mental states. Although Kripke often insists that any fact we cite in an effort to answer the meaning skeptic must be a fact about mental states considered in isolation from our social or physical environment, it is not until Chapter 3

(a) are conceptually prior to and independent of one's assertion of s,
(b) constitute one's grasp of the truth conditions of s, and
(c) enable one to take reasonable steps to assert s only if s is true.

Clause (1), which on my interpretation is presupposed by all of Kripke's remarks about meaning, places an important semantical constraint on the application of clause (2). Clause (2), thus constrained, is the heart of the requirement. To explain clause (2) I shall start with Kripke's central example, in which we are by ordinary standards justified in asserting '68 + 57 = 125'. "In computing '68 + 57' as I do," he writes, "I do not simply make an unjustified leap in the dark. I follow directions I previously gave myself that uniquely determine that in this new instance I should say '125'" (*WRPL*: 10). This description of our "justification" for answering '125' or asserting '68 + 57 =125' is metalinguistic. Although we calculate sums by manipulating Arabic numerals in the base ten system, we do not ordinarily distinguish carefully between doing so and affirming the corresponding arithmetical claims. How are the things we actually think and say about when it is appropriate to assert that 68 + 57 = 125 related to Kripke's metalinguistic claims about the example, including his claim that we grasp a rule for applying the symbol '+' to new cases?

Here is one possible answer. Disquotational paradigms for denotation, satisfaction, and truth can be used to relate first-order reasoning to metalinguistic reasoning. If I accept a disquotational account of reference for my singular terms, for instance, I may immediately infer that '68 + 57' refers to 68 + 57 and '125' refers to 125, and so on. When I judge that 68 + 57 = 125, I may then infer that '68 + 57' and '125' have the same reference and that the answer to the addition problem '68 + 57' is '125', and vice versa. For the basic predicates of my language, satisfaction clauses are also easy

---

that he offers any support for this implausible claim. The support he offers is rooted in Cartesian intuitions about what we can make sense of doubting:

> Is not the grasping of a mathematical rule the solitary achievement of each mathematician independent of any interaction with a wider community? ... in grasping a mathematical rule I have achieved something that depends only on my inner state, and that is immune to Cartesian doubt about the entire external material world (*WRPL*: 79–80).

One problem for this reasoning is that Cartesian doubt may undermine our confidence that our arithmetical assertions are warranted. I can dream that the sum of 68 + 57 is 5 without finding this strange. Descartes himself used his Evil Demon hypothesis to cast doubt on our belief that 2 + 3 = 5. To describe a radical Cartesian skeptical possibility in which there is no external world and yet our capacity to do arithmetic is unaffected one must *stipulate* that our grasp of the meanings of arithmetical words and symbols remains unaffected in the scenario. The apparent intelligibility of such scenarios is not a discovery, but a mere consequence of our stipulation. And, of course, one does not provide support for a controversial thesis by stipulating that it is true.

to formulate disquotationally. For my basic predicate 'blue', for instance, I may stipulate that

x satisfies 'blue' if and only if x is blue.

Exploiting this trivial disquotational relationship, I may move back and forth between a metalinguistic claim that a given object x satisfies 'blue' and the first-order claim that x is blue. I may say that for any given object x, my grasp of when x satisfies 'blue' is the same at root as my grasp of when x is blue.

This answer to the question of how Kripke's metalinguistic descriptions of how we justify our assertions are related to our first-order justifications for them only goes so far. The first shortcoming is that a proper formulation of satisfaction conditions for complex sentences, especially sentences that contain quantifiers and bound pronouns (variables), is not trivial. Clause (1) of Kripke's requirement nevertheless implies that a speaker could not in general be warranted in asserting any given sentence s, including a sentence containing quantifiers and bound pronouns, if the truth conditions of s were not in some way determined by the meanings (such as the references and satisfaction conditions) of words that occur in s. The "directions" in one's mind that constitute one's grasp of the meanings of one's words must therefore somehow include a tacit grasp of a method such as Tarski's for deriving the truth conditions of one's sentences.

The second and more important shortcoming of the above answer is that it presupposes that one has *already* grasped the meanings (references and satisfaction conditions) of the logical constants and the basic terms and predicates of the language. This presupposition is appropriate and unproblematic in most ordinary circumstances in which we are able to justify our new steps or assertions. One cannot justify all of one's new steps or assertions, however. As Kripke emphasizes, following Wittgenstein, "eventually, the process [of justifying new steps or assertions] must stop, with 'ultimate' functions and rules that I have stipulated for myself only by a finite number of examples..." (*WRPL*: 18). Thus, suppose (as seems likely) that I have no noncircular grasp of the conditions under which a given object is blue. Lacking any "instructions" for applying 'blue' I cannot justify my basic applications of 'blue'. As Wittgenstein observes, however, "To use a word without justification does not mean to use it wrongfully" (PI §289). On my reading, Kripke understands this to imply that we may be *entitled* to use the sentence 'That's blue', for instance, to say of a given object that it is blue.

Kripke's requirement implies that for any sentence s that is basic for one in the way just described, one is entitled to assert s only if 2(a) and

2(b) are true. His reasoning, as I reconstruct it, is as follows: If conditions 2(a) and 2(b) are not met, then the question of whether one's assertion of s is true or false cannot be properly raised, since there is nothing that determines how to answer it. *A fortiori*, the question of whether one is *entitled* to assert s cannot be properly raised. To be entitled to assert s one must be able to take reasonable steps to assert s only if s is true without being able to justify those steps. In other words, clause 2(c) of Kripke's requirement must be true if one is to be entitled to assert s. But clause 2(c) is true only if clauses 2(a) and 2(b) are also true. In short, the question of whether or not one is entitled to assert s cannot be properly raised, there being nothing that determines how to answer it, unless there are facts, including facts about one's mental states, that together determine the truth-conditions of s and constitute one's grasp of them.

2 Kripke's Skeptical Arguments

On this interpretation of Kripke's remarks about meaning, the central problem with all the responses to the skeptical challenge that he considers in *WRPL* is that they fail to show that the above requirement is satisfied. I don't have the space here to reformulate all of Kripke's skeptical arguments in this way. I'll instead focus on three of the most important ones.

2.1   Kripke's Criticisms of Dispositional Accounts of Meaning

Consider first the naïve hypothesis that "To mean addition by '+' is to be disposed, when asked for any sum '$x + y$' to give the sum of x and y as the answer" (*WRPL*: 22). The heart of Kripke's criticism of this response is contained in the following passage:

> Well and good, I know that '125' is the response I am disposed to give (I am actually giving it!), and maybe it is helpful to be told – as a matter of brute fact – that I would have given the same response in the past. How does any of this indicate that – now or in the past – '125' was an answer *justified* in terms of instructions I gave myself, rather than a mere jack-in-the-box unjustified and arbitrary response? (*WRPL*: 23)

One might at first be tempted to read this passage so that it implies that to answer the meaning skeptic, one must cite facts that *by themselves* determine when we are justified (hence warranted) in asserting a given sentence, such as '68 + 57 = 125'. This interpretation may seem to fit the passage if one tacitly assumes that '68 + 57 = 125' is "analytic" or "true solely in virtue of meaning," where this is understood to imply that anyone who grasps the meaning of '68 + 57 = 125' is thereby warranted in asserting it. But the assumption that some sentences are analytic in this sense is controversial, and Kripke says nothing in *WRPL* to suggest he thinks his criticisms depend on it. The decisive problem with the reading, however, is that the skeptical problem he attributes to Wittgenstein "is completely general and can be applied to any rule or word" (*WRPL*: 58), and hence not just to our uses of words in sentences that some philosophers take to be analytic. The initially tempting reading therefore does not make sense of the passage.

The above passage makes sense if, as I suggest, we read it as an attempt to show that dispositional facts do not determine that Kripke's requirement for being warranted in asserting a sentence is satisfied. The basic idea is as follows. In its naïve form, a dispositional account of meaning provides a causal explanation of the responses that we *take* to be true. The problem is not that on the naïve dispositional account of meaning, the dispositional facts are not normative facts, but that they are not conceptually prior to and independent of our assertions. Kripke suggests this when he asks, "is the hypothesis to refer to my present dispositions alone, which would hence give the right answer by definition?" (*WRPL*: 23). I understand him to be pointing out here that if the hypothesis refers to my present dispositions alone, then it defines the meaning (truth condition) of a sentence that I now assert in terms of my assertion of it or, in other words, in terms of my *taking* it to be true; the hypothesis does not explain how the meaning of the sentence is determined by facts that are conceptually prior to and independent of my assertion of it.

Proponents of dispositional accounts of meaning agree with Kripke that any adequate dispositional account of meaning must explain the meaning of a sentence independently of any given assertion of it. They try to respond to Kripke's criticism of the naïve dispositional account of meaning by incorporating versions of Noam Chomsky's distinction between competence and performance. As Warren Goldfarb explains, summarizing a dispositional account of meaning suggested in Horwich (1984),

[A sophisticated dispositionalist] could claim that future physiological psychology might reveal two mechanisms, separable on scientific grounds. States of the first amount to a person's linguistic competence, and would, if untrammeled, always cause correct responses; states of the second are identifiable with interfering features, which explain why on particular occasions the first mechanism does not issue in an appropriate response (and the person errs). Of course, in the empirical work that leads to these identifications we must use our ordinary meaning ascriptions and practices of ascribing error. In the end, though, we can identify the physical states of the first mechanism as constituting meaning words in certain ways. To be sure, this is speculative; but nothing Kripke adduces rules it out in principle. (Goldfarb 1985: 477)

If we accept Kripke's requirement on being warranted in asserting a sentence, the central problem with this proposal is its circularity. For as Goldfarb notes, "in the empirical work that leads to these identifications, we must use our ordinary meaning ascriptions and practices of ascribing error" (Goldfarb 1985: 477): we identify as the meanings of our words just those hypothesized dispositional states that, if untrammeled (as we assume they are in the present case), *causally* explain our present disposition to assent to '68 + 57 = 125'. The problem is that according to the proposal our identifications of our linguistic competence in the uses of the numerals '68', '57', and '125' and the symbols '+' and '=' are not conceptually prior to and independent of assertions that we take ourselves to be warranted in making, including our assertion of '68 + 57 = 125'. It is not an adequate defense of the proposal to point out that once a given mechanism is identified in this way, we can describe it without mentioning the assertions we take ourselves to be warranted in making. The key problem of circularity remains: if a group of dispositional states that we can describe in purely physiological terms cause us to assent to an elementary arithmetical sentence that we regard as false, we will not second-guess our judgment that it is false, we will instead conclude that we had not identified the dispositional states that supposedly both explain and constitute our competence in using the words that occur in the sentence. Properly viewed, on my reading, Kripke takes this observation to imply that no dispositional mechanism *constitutes* our competence in the use of a sentence or a word.[7]

My interpretation of Kripke's criticisms of dispositionalist answers to Kripke's skeptical challenge differs from Paul Boghossian's influential interpretation, according to which Kripke's skeptical arguments depend on the assumption that meaning is categorically normative. Boghossian explains this assumption as follows:

Suppose the expression 'green' means green. It follows immediately that the expression 'green' applies correctly only to these things (the green ones) and not to those (the non-greens). The fact that an expression means something implies … a whole set of normative truths about my behavior with that expression: namely, that my use of it is correct in application to certain objects and not in application to others. (Boghossian 1989: 513)

The normative truths in question here are not merely hypothetical, as in "if your goal is to apply your words correctly, then you ought to apply your words in such and such ways," but categorical, as in "The meanings of your words by themselves, independent of your goals, determine that

---

[7] I don't think this criticism has been properly formulated or adequately answered by advocates for dispositional theories of meaning. See Warren (2020), however, for a more optimistic assessment.

you ought to apply them in such and such ways." Boghossian explains the relevant type of categorical norms about meaning that he attributes to Kripke's meaning skeptic as follows:

> The normativity of meaning turns out to be ... simply a new name for the familiar fact that, regardless of whether one thinks of meaning in truth-theoretic or assertion-theoretic terms, meaningful expressions possess conditions of correct use. ... Kripke's insight was to realize that this observation may be converted into a condition of adequacy on theories of the determination of meaning: *any proposed candidate for the property in virtue of which an expression has meaning, must be such as to ground the 'normativity' of meaning – it ought to be possible to read off from any alleged meaning constituting property of a word, what is the correct use of that word.* (Boghossian 1989: 513, my emphasis)

The italicized thesis, which Boghossian ascribes to Kripke, implies that the facts, if any, that determine what our words mean *by themselves* determine the correct uses of our words.[8]

On the reading I have developed, by contrast, Kripke's skeptical challenge is to cite facts that show that clauses (1) and (2) of his requirement on being warranted in asserting a given sentence are true. Suppose we could cite such facts generally and that we are considering whether to assert a given sentence, say, "There are more than 1000 kangaroos in Australia." Then, since Kripke's meaning skeptic does not challenge our ordinary or scientific standards for being warranted in asserting meaningful sentences, we could draw on ordinary methods – we could count the kangaroos in Australia – to decide whether or not the assertion is warranted. Now suppose we cannot cite facts that show that clauses (1) and (2) of Kripke's requirement on being warranted in asserting "There are more than 1000 kangaroos in Australia" are true. Then, for the reasons I explained above, we should conclude that the question of whether we are warranted in asserting that sentence is undefined and cannot be answered; any assertion we make would therefore be "arbitrary," a mere "leap in the dark." This, I think, explains the normative element in Kripke's reasoning.

In short, on the reading I have sketched Kripke's meaning, the skeptic does not demand that we cite facts that by themselves determine when we would be warranted in asserting a sentence. The skeptic demands, instead, that we cite facts that make clauses (1) and (2) of Kripke's requirement true. If there are such facts, then our ordinary and scientific standards for being warranted in asserting sentences apply; otherwise, not. The skeptic's conclusion that there are no such facts, if true, would have a disastrous

---

[8] Boghossian (2008b) retracts his own earlier endorsement of this claim but not his earlier attribution of it to Kripke. The other authors cited in note 1 each also attribute similar theses to Kripke. Allan Gibbard, for instance, writes, "Kripke's thesis of the normative nature of meaning ... [is that] '*Meaning* implies *ought*'" (Gibbard 2012: 55).

normative consequence, namely, that our ordinary and scientific standards for being warranted in asserting sentences do not apply since our assertions do not have truth conditions, and hence every "assertion" is "arbitrary," a mere "leap in the dark." But this disastrous conclusion, even if correctly drawn, does not presuppose that the facts that the skeptic challenges us to cite are, or by themselves determine, normative facts.[9]

There are several passages in *WRPL* that appear incompatible with this reading. When summarizing his rejection of dispositional theories, for instance, Kripke writes:

> The fundamental problem, as I have stated it earlier, is ... [this]: whether my actual dispositions are 'right' or not, is there anything that mandates what they *ought* to be? (*WRPL*: 57)

This passage appears to support the standard view that Kripke thinks the facts about meaning must *by themselves* "mandate" what one's answers "ought to be." This claim is problematic at best, and on some natural readings of the claim, it is clearly false.[10] We should therefore prefer any plausible and relatively clear reading of the above passage that does not rely on it. I read the passage as claiming, in effect, that

- the facts, if any, that make clauses (1) and (2) of Kripke's requirement true, *when supplemented by our unchallenged knowledge of the relevant topics and our unchallenged methods of evaluating claims about them*, mandate some particular answers and imply that others are wrong; and
- if there are no facts that together make clauses (1) and (2) of Kripke's requirement true, then for the reasons I explained in the previous paragraph the question of what my answer *ought* to be is undefined.[11]

On this sort of reading, the above passage and others like it are compatible with my interpretation.

---

[9] On my reading Kripke's meaning skeptic also need not take a stand on whether our ordinary and scientific standards for being warranted in asserting sentences are categorical norms, not hypothetical ones.

[10] See the references cited in note 1.

[11] In the most basic cases of language use, such as calling something blue or adding 1, one does not count as minimally competent unless one goes on the appropriate ways. Does this support the thesis that meaning is normative? I think not. The observation that in basic cases certain ways of going on are "required" need not be understood as dependent on a categorical norm. We might explain it, instead, as follows: To be competent in the use of language one must aim at asserting in accord with the truth at least some of the time; one's assertions in basic cases can then be evaluated relative to this aim. This then implies such hypothetical norms as: "if you are trying to take a correct new step in such and such a series, then the step you ought to take here is such and so." In Ebbs (1997: 18–19) I suggested that this is *all* there is to Kripke's claim that meaning is normative. This is on the right track but misses (what I now think is) the key point that

2.2 Kripke's Criticism of the Thesis That Meanings Are Determined by a Special Kind of Primitive Mental State

Another tempting response to Kripke's skeptical challenge is to claim that meanings are determined by a special kind of primitive mental state.[12] Kripke summarizes his criticism of this thesis as follows:

> It [is] mysterious exactly how the existence of any *finite* past state of my mind could entail that, if I wish to accord with it, and remember the state, and do not miscalculate, I must give a determinate answer to an arbitrarily large addition problem. (*WRPL*: 53)

This formulation of his criticism is not particularly helpful, in my view, because it focuses on just one way of finding the thesis mysterious – the "finiteness" of my mental states. On my reconstruction, Kripke's central problem with it is that it does not explain how clauses (1) and (2) of Kripke's requirement are satisfied in the most basic cases of language use. To satisfy these clauses for such cases, we need to explain how the truth conditions for our new assertions are determined by facts that are conceptually prior to and independent of them. The problem is that in these basic cases, for which we have no justifications, our new assertions are supposedly guided by our grasp of the truth conditions of the assertions, but we have no grasp of the truth conditions of the assertions, no way to say what those conditions are, that is conceptually prior, or independent of them. In short, in these cases, we are unable to say how we distinguish between what seems right to us and what is right. If there is a distinction between seeming right and being right, it is a purely formal one that we do not know how to apply. We are therefore unable to give any content to the theory that what explains our grasp of the distinction is that we possess some primitive mental states of a special kind.

2.3 Kripke's Criticism of Wittgenstein's Descriptions of Our Meaning-Ascribing and Rule-Following Practices

On my reading, Kripke's reasons for rejecting Wittgenstein's descriptions of our meaning-ascribing and rule-following practices are similar

---

the norms that are most important for Kripke's argument are the ones associated with being warranted in asserting sentences. In Ebbs (2017: 403–404), I emphasized that Kripke seeks an account that explains our experience that even in basic cases we are in some sense "guided" by our understanding of the meanings of our words. This is also on the right track, if my new interpretation is right – it is captured by clause (2)(c) of Kripke's requirement – but it misses the same key point.

[12] Boghossian (1989) and McDowell (1984) each defend versions of this sort of response.

to his reasons for rejecting the thesis that meaning is a primitive mental state.[13]

In the most basic applications of meanings and rules, according to Wittgenstein, where our justifications give out, our "grasp" of the idea that our new steps or assertions are in accord with the relevant meanings or rules is exhibited by the steps that we take and the assertions we make "as a matter of course" (1953b, §201, §238) without considering alternatives. For an individual considered in isolation, according to Kripke, Wittgenstein's descriptions of our most basic applications of meanings and rules collapse the distinction between thinking one is following a rule and actually following it. To draw this distinction at all, on Wittgenstein's view, according to Kripke, one must consider an individual in the context of a linguistic community: it is only other speakers who can judge, relative to their own unjustified applications of a given basic rule, that one is or is not obeying it.

The central problem with this account of meaning and rules, according to Kripke, is that it implies that no one in the linguistic community grasps the truth conditions of her assertions in a way that is conceptually prior to or independent of the assertions that members of her community accept.[14]

Kripke highlights this aspect of Wittgenstein's descriptions of our rule-following and meaning-ascribing practices by reading Wittgenstein as "inverting" such conditionals as "If Jones means addition by '+', then if he is asked for '68 + 57', he will reply '125'" (*WRPL*: 94). Such conditionals suggest (but do not require), in accord with Kripke's requirement, that their antecedents may be true prior to and independently of whether their consequents are true. Wittgenstein inverts such conditionals, according to Kripke, by treating their contrapositives (for instance, "If Jones does not come out with '125' when asked about '68 + 57', we cannot assert that he means addition by '+'" (*WRPL*: 95)), as *criteria* for ascribing meanings. On this way of applying the conditionals, the consequents of the conditionals provide us with our only grip on when the antecedents of the conditionals are true, so we cannot make sense of the antecedents of the conditionals being true prior to and independently of whether the consequents of the conditionals are true.

---

[13] This similarity makes sense of Kripke's comment that "if [the thesis that meaning is a primitive mental state] is understood in an appropriate way Wittgenstein may even accept it" (Kripke 1982: 51).

[14] According to Ginsborg (2020), and contrary to what Kripke argues, Wittgenstein thinks that in the most basic cases of going on there is a primitive notion of *the correct next step in a context* that is conceptually and explanatorily prior to any rule with which the step accords. In Ebbs (2022), I argue that this intriguing new reading of Wittgenstein does not fit well with what he actually says.

Kripke regards this as a shift from thinking that there are facts about meaning to thinking that we can only provide assertability conditions for ascribing meanings to speakers. Several writers have challenged Kripke's claim that, according to Wittgenstein, there are no facts about meaning.[15] I think they are right to do so. But if my reading of Kripke's arguments is correct, this exegetical question, though interesting and important, is not the key to evaluating Kripke's criticisms of the view he ascribes to Wittgenstein. On my reading, Kripke's central criticism of that view is not that it implies that meaning ascriptions are not factual, but that it implies that in basic cases of language use, we have no understanding of what it is for a new step to be correct or for the corresponding assertion to be true apart from someone's taking the step or making the assertion. It is for this reason, I suggest, that Kripke remains committed to his requirement even after he explains why our uses of words and sentences do not and cannot satisfy it.

3 A Wittgensteinian Critique of Kripke's Requirement

Kripke's complaints about Wittgenstein's descriptions of our meaning-ascribing and rule-following practices look better than they really are because of the way he portrays the circularity of the account he attributes to Wittgenstein. He sees that Wittgenstein offers no account of what "going on" consists in (*WRPL*: 111) and that "What follows from [Wittgenstein's descriptions of our practices of ascribing meanings] is not that the answer everyone gives to an addition problem is, by definition, the correct one, but rather the platitude that, if everyone agrees upon a certain answer, then no one will feel justified in calling the answer wrong" (*WRPL*: 112). He nevertheless suggests that if Wittgenstein's descriptions of our rule-following practices are correct, then we can imagine creatures who use their words in ways that are radically different from the ways in which we use our words:

> Beings who agree in consistently giving bizarre quus-like responses would share in another form of life. By definition, such another form of life would be bizarre and incomprehensible to us ("If a lion could talk, we could not understand him."...). However, if we can imagine the abstract possibility of another form of life (and no *a priori* argument would seem to exclude it), then members of a community sharing such a quus-like form of life could play the game of attributing rules and concepts to each other as we do. Someone would be said, in such a community, to follow a rule, as long as he agrees in his response with the (quus-like) responses produced by the members of *that* community. (WRPL: 96)

I think these reflections are off-track. I agree with Bernard Williams that

---
[15] See for instance, Goldfarb (1985) and Wilson (1994).

> The alternatives [that Wittgenstein invites us to consider] are not ... socially actual alternatives, relatively inaccessible or not, ... nor are they offered as possible objects of any kind of explanation. Rather, the business of considering them is part of finding our way around inside our own view, feeling our way out to the points at which we begin to lose our hold on it (or it, its hold on us), and things begin to be hopelessly strange to us. The imagined alternatives are not alternatives *to* us: they are alternatives *for* us, markers of how far we might go and still remain, within our world – a world leaving which would not mean that we say something different, but that we ceased to see. (Williams 1981: 160)

Thus understood, Wittgenstein's invitations to consider alternatives to our ways of going on do not presuppose, as beyond criticism, what Kripke takes to be purely *a priori* descriptions of how things might be for other language users; the invitations are instead designed to help us investigate, clarify, and in some cases revise or reject our preconceptions about what is possible. Kripke partly glimpses the possibility of such a reading of Wittgenstein when he writes

> What it seems may be unintelligible to us is how an intelligent creature could get the very training we have for the addition function, and yet grasp the appropriate function in a quus-like way. If such a possibility were completely intelligible to us, would we find it so inevitable to apply the plus function as we do? (*WRPL*: 98, fn78)

Kripke notes that this point is in tension with what he takes to be Wittgenstein's commitment to the claim that "there is no *a priori* reason why a creature could not follow a quus-like rule, and in this sense we ought to regard such creatures as conceivable" (*WRPL*: 98, fn 78). I suggest, instead, that Wittgenstein would urge us to investigate Kripke's supposition that there are *a priori* possible linguistic communities whose members go on in systematically quus-like ways. If the idea is that for *every* term in their language, the members of some imagined linguistic community "go on" in quus-like ways – a supposed linguistic community of beings whose "utterances" we could not translate into our language, whose "language" we could not learn, and who could not learn to communicate with us – then it's unclear in what sense, and by what criteria, we are supposing that we have imagined a linguistic community at all. In any case, if in the end, after a careful investigation, we find we cannot make sense of the idea of a linguistic community whose members apply their words in systematically quus-like ways, then we also cannot make sense of Kripke's companion implied criticism that on Wittgenstein's view, our most basic ways of going on are all radically contingent upon psychological or sociological facts that shape our "form of life" and, for that reason, are at root merely subjective "leaps in the dark."

A vestigial version of Kripke's challenge remains, however. One of Wittgenstein's central observations is that in basic cases of language use, we cannot make sense of doubting that our new steps are correct – we have no conceptually prior or independent point of view on the steps from which to evaluate them – but we also presuppose that our failure to be able to make sense of doubting them is not a noncircular reason to think they are correct or true. How can we make sense of this presupposition if Kripke's requirement is not satisfied?

The answer, I suggest, following Wittgenstein, is that once we have rejected the view that our ways of going on are radically contingent upon psychological or sociological facts, we can elucidate – without aiming to explain or ground – the distinction between our taking of a basic step and its being correct, or our acceptance of a basic sentence and its being true, by describing our steps and assertions from different points of view, including different points of view we *each* can take on our *own* assertions.[16] When evaluating a pupil's performance, we of course take for granted that our own steps and assertions are correct.[17] We remain open, however, to reconsidering them in light of challenges and corrections by other competent speakers or by ourselves at a later time. We therefore do not equate our taking of a basic step with its being correct or our acceptance of a basic sentence with its being true.

The grain of truth in Kripke's criticisms of Wittgenstein's descriptions of our meaning-ascribing and rule-following practices is that no matter how we redescribe or challenge our most basic new steps or assertions, we cannot evaluate them from a point of view that is independent of our acceptance of at least some of them. To make sense of and accept our ordinary view that the truth conditions for our most basic assertions can be evaluated independently of our own current confident acceptance of them, however, it is enough to describe the ways in which we and other speakers in our linguistic community may evaluate our basic assertions at different times and from different points of view and to cultivate an openness, at least in principle, to challenging and revising our assertions if and when we can make sense of doing so.[18]

---

[16] Blackburn (1984) argues out that competent speakers can rely on their present uses of their words to evaluate assertions they've previously made. Canfield (1996) argues against the claim that Wittgenstein's descriptions rule out the very possibility of solitary rule-followers and for the claim that the meaning-ascribing and rule-following practices we actually engage in are "essentially" social, in the sense that they include "two-or-more party language games" (479). Verheggen (2007) argues against Canfield's reading of Wittgenstein, and, more generally, against the very idea of a solitary language. My elucidatory remarks in the text are officially neutral on these difficult questions, though my sympathies lie with Blackburn and Canfield.

[17] "[L]et us suppose that after some efforts on the teacher's part he continues the series correctly, that is, as we do it" (PI §145).

[18] Thanks to Claudine Verheggen for inviting me to contribute to this volume and to Claudine, Kate Abramson, and Hannah Ginsborg for their comments on previous drafts.

7 Semantic Normativity, Properly So Called

Daniel Whiting

1 Introduction

Kripke finds in Wittgenstein a skeptical line of thought which leads to the "insane and intolerable" conclusion that there is no fact of the matter as to what any given expression means (1982: 60). On this view, for example, it is not true that "perro" (in Spanish) means *dog* or, for that matter, anything else. According to Kripke's Wittgenstein's skeptic,[1] there is simply "no such thing" as meaning (1982: 21).[2]

The skeptic's challenge is to identify some fact in virtue of which an expression means what it does. Crucially, the skeptic places a constraint on what that meaning-determining fact must be like: It must make it the case that certain uses of the expression are *permissible* or *justified*,[3] while others are *impermissible* or *unjustified*.[4] This, according to Kripke, is the skeptic's "fundamental requirement" (1982: 40). It expresses the idea that there is a "normative," not simply "descriptive," relation between the meaning of a term and its employment (1982: 37).[5] The skeptic's claim is that it is not possible to identify a fact that satisfies this requirement. As a result, as Kripke puts it, "The entire idea of meaning vanishes into thin air" (1982: 22).

---

[1] As this cumbersome phrase reveals, neither Kripke nor Wittgenstein (as Kripke interprets him) endorse the skeptical line of thought.
[2] Kripke sometimes talks of what an expression means – that is, of linguistic meaning – but more often he talks of what a speaker means by an expression – that is, of speaker meaning. I focus here on linguistic meaning.
[3] Kripke frequently expresses the requirement in terms of certain uses of an expression being *obligatory*, that is, of there being things a person "should" or "ought" to do with it (e.g. Kripke 1982: 11, 12, 21, 24, 28, 37, 40, 42). I set this aside, as the question of the normative strength of the relationship between meaning and use is tangential to the concerns of the chapter.
[4] To use Glüer and Wikforss's helpful phrase, this is *meaning-engendered normativity* (2009, 2018).
[5] In places, Kripke presents the skeptic's requirement as an *internalist* one, that is, as requiring that the justificatory force of the meaning-determining fact be in some way accessible to a person so as to guide their use of the relevant expression (e.g. Kripke 1982: 17, 24). For discussion, see Bridges (2014), Green (2018), Jones (2015), and Zalabardo (2009).

As Kripke anticipates, the skeptical conclusion strikes many as implausible or, worse, unintelligible. One response is to concede to the skeptic that there are no facts in virtue of which expressions have meaning – at least, none specifiable in more basic or independently intelligible terms – but deny that it follows from this that there are no facts as to what expressions mean. To put this in positive terms, facts about meaning are fundamental or primitive.[6] This response is worth exploring, but I set it aside here.[7] An alternative is to reject the normativity of meaning and thereby deny that the fact in virtue of which an expression means what it does must make it the case that certain uses of it are permissible or otherwise. To assess this response, we need to know what is being denied, that is, we need to know what the normativity of meaning amounts to. That question is the focus of this chapter.

Boghossian gives clear expression to what is arguably the standard or orthodox interpretation of the normativity of meaning (see also Blackburn 1984: 281; McDowell 2009a: 59–61; Thornton 1998: 32–33; Whiting 2009a: 537–540; Zhong 2017: 627):

Suppose the expression "green" means *green*. It follows immediately that the expression "green" applies correctly only to *these* things (the green ones) and not to *those* (the non-greens). The fact that the expression means something implies, that is, a whole set of *normative* truths about my behaviour with that expression: namely, that my use of it is correct in application to certain objects and not in application to others. (1989: 513)

To restate this in relation to the earlier example, the idea that meaning is normative is standardly understood as the idea that principles like the following hold:

(1) Necessarily, if (and because) "perro" means *dog*, then a person may apply "perro" to something if and only if it is a dog.

More generally, the norms that hold in virtue of what an expression means – semantic norms – are norms of *truth*. To use an expression in accordance with those norms is (only) to truly apply it.

In moving to and from talk of what it is *correct* for a person to do and talk of what they *may* do, I am assuming that correctness is a permissive notion (only) in the sense that it can be correct for a person to

---

[6] For versions of this view, see Alston (2000), Boghossian (1989), McDowell (1984), Stroud (1996), and Verheggen (2015).
[7] I also set aside the "sceptical solution" that Kripke's Wittgenstein proposes (1982: Chapter 3), in part because it is contentious how that solution is to be understood. For discussion, see Ahmed (2007: chapter 5), Boghossian (1989: Part II), Byrne (1996), Boyd (2017), Davies (1998), Hattiangadi (2007: chapter 4), Kusch (2006: chapters 5–6), Miller (2010b, 2020), and Wilson (1998).

do something without it being incorrect for them not to do it (Whiting 2010: 214–216). I am not assuming that semantic norms – however they are expressed – are *authoritative*. To adapt Foot's (1972) example, there might be a norm of etiquette stating that a person may not wear a hat at the dinner table, or that it is incorrect for them to do so. It does not follow that that norm has (in a sense to be spelled out) binding force for a person. Likewise, if the norm expressed by (1) holds – or, for that matter, any of the candidates to follow – that leaves open whether the norm has binding force.[8]

As I use the phrase here, the proponent of the orthodox account maintains that the norms of meaning are norms of truth. They are thereby committed to principles such as (1). They are not thereby committed to those norms being authoritative.

Orthodoxy, so understood, faces a challenge. One might grant that there are norms according to which it is (not) permissible (not) to apply an expression truly, but deny that those norms hold in virtue of meaning. Since they are norms of truth, an alternative is that they are grounded in the nature of *truth* (cp. Lynch 2004). Since the norms only govern applications of words – paradigmatically, in acts of assertion – a further alternative is that they are grounded in the nature of *assertion* (cp. Speaks 2009).

There is, however, a competing interpretation of the claim that meaning is normative, one which sidesteps this challenge (see Buleandra 2008; Glock 2005, 2019; McGinn 1984; Millar 2002, 2004: chapter 6; Moore 1954: 308–309; Schroeder 2008).[9] According to it, a person can use an expression in accordance with semantic norms without truly applying it, and a person can truly apply an expression without using it in accordance with semantic norms. Alternatively, using an expression in accordance with its meaning is not the same thing as using it in accordance with the facts.

What, then, are semantic norms, if not norms of truth? Those who reject the standard account differ among themselves on this issue. Elsewhere, in defense of orthodoxy, I argued against a number of answers to that question (Whiting 2016; see also Wikforss 2001; Glüer and Wikforss 2018). In this chapter, I explore two further recent proposals due to

---

[8] For discussion of the distinction between authoritative and nonauthoritative (formal) normativity, see McPherson (2018), Parfit (2011: 144–145), Wodak (2019), and Woods (2018). For application of the distinction to the debate about semantic normativity, see Hattiangadi (2007: chapter 3).

[9] In fact, there are several others. For an influential way of construing the normativity of meaning that differs from those I consider here, see Ginsborg (2011b, 2012, 2022). Assessing Ginsborg's account is beyond the scope of the present discussion. For discussion, see Haddock (2012), Miller (2019), Sultanescu (2021), and Verheggen (2015).

Millar (2014) and Reiland (2023a). To anticipate, I will consider a number of ways of unpacking those proposals and conclude that either they are unmotivated, or they do not amount to genuine competitors to the standard account.

To be clear, my aim is not to argue for or against the claim that meaning is normative – however it is best construed.[10] Nor is the aim to evaluate the skeptical argument in which that claim figures. Rather, the aim is to clarify the very idea of semantic normativity. This, I take it, is the prior task. It is not possible adequately to assess that idea or the role it plays in generating the skeptical conclusion until we have an adequate grasp of what the idea amounts to.

2 Nondeclarative Sentences

Neither Millar nor Reiland deny that there are norms of truth according to which some applications of terms are permissible while others are not. What they deny is that the normativity of meaning is to be understood in terms of such norms. In Reiland's words, a norm according to which a person may (only) apply a term truly is not one "that derives from the nature of linguistic meaning itself" (2023a: 2194). So, Millar and Reiland reject (1) as stated.

One rationale Reiland gives for rejecting the standard interpretation is that it is too narrow. Recall that a person applies a word to something via the use (in an assertion) of a declarative sentence.[11] For example, I might apply "perro" to Jake by uttering:

(i) Jake es un perro.

Now consider:

(ii) ¿Es Jake un perro?
(iii) ¡Camina un perro!

Since utterances of the interrogative sentence (ii) or the imperative sentence (iii) do not involve the application of "perro," the employment of

---

[10] For critical discussion, see Boghossian (2008a: chapter 4), Glüer (1999, 2001), Glüer and Wikforss (2009, 2018), Hattiangadi (2006, 2007, 2009, 2017, 2018b), Miller (2006, 2010b, 2012), Papineau (1999), and Zhong (2017). I defend the normativity of meaning in Whiting (2007, 2009a); see also Green (2021), Hlobil (2015), and Tracy (2020). For the record, I am less confident about the matter than I once was (cp. Whiting 2015).

[11] Arguably, there are cases in which a person applies a term without uttering a complete sentence, for example, by pointing to a dog and saying, "Perro!" For present purposes, treat this as a limiting case of a declarative sentence (perhaps with hidden constituents).

that expression is not assessable by reference to the norm of truth when it occurs in those sentences. More generally, uses of meaningful expressions in nondeclarative sentences need not be subject to norms permitting only true application.

This observation, according to Reiland, counts against the standard account of semantic normativity (see also Buleandra 2008: 180; Millar 2004: 166). He writes:

If you thought that there is a distinctively linguistic notion of correctness then, since it is supposed to derive from the nature of linguistic meaning, it should apply to all relevant uses of *all* meaningful expressions (2023a: 2195)

Here is a reconstruction of this line of thought:

(A) If a norm holds in virtue of the fact that an expression bears a certain meaning, then the norm governs all uses of that expression with that meaning.

(B) Norms of true application do not govern all uses of an expression with a certain meaning.

(C) So, norms of true application do not hold in virtue of the fact that an expression bears a certain meaning.

The first premise of this argument, (A), is false. In general, if a norm holds in virtue of the nature of something, it does not follow that that norm is operative in all contexts involving that thing, such that a person's actions may be assessed by reference to it. Suppose, for example, that in virtue of being a member of academic staff at a certain institution, a person is required to record their lectures. The academic is not subject to this requirement in all contexts, not even in all contexts in which they act in their capacity as a member of academic staff – the norm does not govern the way in which they research, say, or their conduct in meetings of the departmental board. Nevertheless, the requirement is one that holds in virtue of the academic role they occupy. Likewise, then, from the fact that norms of true application only govern some uses of meaningful expressions, not others, it does not follow that those norms hold in virtue of something other than the meanings of those expressions.

Reiland offers a further argument against the orthodox way of interpreting the normativity of meaning that also appeals to nondeclaratives. Expressions can be used correctly or incorrectly – permissibly or impermissibly – in the context of imperative sentences, interrogative sentences, and other nondeclarative constructions. But, Reiland says, "the orthodox construal can't capture this" (2023a: 2195). Again, on that construal, the norms that hold in virtue of what expressions mean only govern their use in declaratives.

It is no doubt the case that expressions as they occur in nondeclarative sentences like (ii) and (iii) can be used permissibly and impermissibly. This is a challenge to the standard account of the normativity of meaning only if the norms that deliver such verdicts are candidates for norms that hold in virtue of what those expressions mean – as opposed, say, to norms that hold in virtue of the corresponding speech acts of asking questions or giving orders, respectively. So, one way to respond to Reiland's argument is to concede that there are such norms, but deny that they qualify as semantic in the operative sense. Rather than pursue this, I will offer a more concessive response.

It is true that principles such as (1) are silent as to the conditions for the permissible use of expressions in nondeclarative sentences. But, at most, that shows that the standard account of the normativity of meaning is incomplete – that principles such as (1) capture some of the norms to which "perro" is subject but not all of them. More generally, to say that some norms other than those of truth hold in virtue of what expressions mean is not to say that norms of truth are not among those that hold in virtue of what expressions mean.[12] Compare: To say that an academic must record their lectures is only to offer a partial account of the norms they are subject to as a result of their role.

3   What Words Are For

I have suggested that Reiland's preliminary case for thinking that the norms of meaning are not norms of truth is at best inconclusive. However, Reiland offers a positive characterization of what he takes to be the norms of meaning, as does Millar. If those characterizations are independently plausible as characterizations of the norms that are supposed to hold in virtue of what expressions mean, that is a strike against the orthodox view and for the alternative. Accordingly, I turn now to their proposals.

Reiland suggests that a way to get a handle on what it is for a person to use an expression in accordance with its meaning – rather than in accordance with the facts – is via the notion of what an expression is *semantically for*. He explains:

---

[12] I do not have a worked-out account of how a defender of the normativity of meaning – as standardly construed – should characterize the norms governing expressions as they occur in nondeclarative contexts. But it seems in line with that construal to suggest that such uses are permissible only when some (so to speak) worldly condition obtains. By way of illustration, and as a first pass, it is permissible to use "perro" in (iii) only if there is sufficient reason for the addressee to walk a dog.

What an expression is semantically for doing in the particular language is what its meaning enables us to use it to *do*, such that we couldn't use meaningless expressions or expressions which have a different meaning to do these things. (2023a: 2197)

Returning in light of this to the earlier example, what is the word "perro" for? A natural answer is that "perro" is for talking about (referring to) things that are dogs.[13] So, if a person uses the expression for things that are, say, frogs or logs, they are not using the expression in accordance with what the expression is for. This seems of a piece with the standard construal of the normativity of meaning. Given what "perro" is semantically for, it is permissible to apply it to all and only dogs.

It is interesting to note that Millar also invokes the notion of what an expression is for, but as a gloss on what grasp of the conditions of true application involves:

What I mean by "grasp of the conditions" might more ordinarily be expressed by speaking of what a word is for. For instance, a somewhat partial grasp of the conditions of application of the term "flu" might be expressed by saying that "flu" is a word for a viral infection marked by fever and muscular aches. (2014: 801)

For Millar, talk of what an expression is for is just talk of what it stands for, that is, what it applies to. Again, then, this notion of what an expression is for seems to dovetail with the standard interpretation of semantic normativity: For a person to use "perro" permissibly, is to apply it to the things it is the word for, namely, the things that are dogs.

4   Use-Conditions

The notion of what a word is semantically for, at least on a natural reading of that phrase, does not point toward norms governing the use of expressions distinct from those concerning true application. However, although his initial gloss is in line with that reading, the examples Reiland goes on to offer by way of illustration suggest a different reading:

"Bertrand" is perhaps for using while you're thinking [about] or referring to Bertrand ... Similarly, "I" is for using while you're thinking of yourself in a first-personal or *de se* way, and "is British" while you're expressing the property of being British. Finally, a declarative sentence like "Bertrand is British" is for using when one is doing the above acts and further predicating the property of the person, resulting in your entertaining the proposition that Bertrand is British ... or judging it to be the case. (2023a: 2197)

---

[13] Compare: "'Bertrand' is for talking about some specific person." (Reiland 2023a: 2197)

As Reiland uses the phrase, then, an expression is semantically for using it while having certain thoughts or, more broadly, being in certain mental states.

If using an expression in accordance with its meaning – or in accordance with the semantic norms governing it – is a matter of using it in accordance with what it is for, and if what an expression is for is understood in Reiland's sense, then principles along the following lines hold:

(2) Necessarily, if (and because) "perro" means *dog*, then a person may apply "perro" to something if and only if they judge that it is a dog.[14]

More generally, the proposal is that the norms that hold in virtue of an expression's meaning specify the mental states or acts a person must be in or perform if they are to use the expression permissibly (see also McGinn 1984: 60; Schroeder 2008: 109). Those states or acts are what Reiland calls the expression's "use-conditions," in contrast to its truth-conditions (2023a: 2193; see also Reiland 2023b: 576).

It is clear how, on this view, a person might apply an expression in a way that violates the norms of meaning without applying it falsely – for example, by applying "perro" to a dog while judging that it is a frog. It is equally clear how, on this view, a person might apply an expression in a way that conforms to the norms of meaning without applying it truly – for example, by applying "perro" to a frog while judging that it is a dog.

I will grant that it is in some sense inappropriate when a person applies an expression without satisfying what Reiland calls its use-condition – that they fall short of some standard. And I will grant that it is in some sense appropriate when a person applies an expression while satisfying its use-condition – that they meet some standard. Still, I think that there is a way for the proponent of the orthodox interpretation to not only accommodate these points, but also explain them (cp. Whiting 2016: §7).

As a warmup, recall the longstanding debate in moral philosophy as to whether moral obligation is objective or subjective (see Hurka 2014: §3.3).[15] Moral obligation is objective if it depends on the facts of the situation; it is subjective if it depends instead on a person's beliefs about the situation. To illustrate, if moral obligation is objective, then whether a person ought (morally) to walk the dog will depend on such things as whether doing so keeps a promise, whether it promotes the dog's welfare, and so on. In contrast, if moral obligation is subjective, then whether a

---

[14] (2) speaks of "applying" the expression, which seems of a piece with Reiland's talk of "referring" and "predicating." However, Reiland also talks of (merely) "using" an expression, which need not involve applying it. I return to this shortly.
[15] Not to be confused with the debate as to whether moral obligations are *authoritative*. The objective/subjective and authoritative/nonauthoritative distinctions are cross-cutting.

person ought (morally) to walk the dog will depend on such things as whether they think that doing so keeps a promise, whether they think that it promotes the dog's welfare, and so on.

This issue might seem (merely) terminological. There are simply different senses of "ought," one objective, the other subjective. However, when a person engages in moral deliberation, they might ask themselves, "What ought I to do?" They might then draw a conclusion, which they express by saying such things as, "I ought to walk the dog." It is a substantive issue whether the "ought" that frames deliberation in this way is objective or subjective (Graham 2010: 95; Zimmerman 2008: 15).

Whatever the outcome of the debate as to which sense of "ought" is deliberatively prior, it is plausible that the objective sense is *explanatorily* prior. As one might put it, a person's beliefs about such things as fidelity and welfare matter only because such things as fidelity and welfare matter. Very roughly, a person has a subjective moral duty to act just in case, were their beliefs true, there would be an objective duty for them to act. So, subjective obligations are explained in terms of the corresponding objective obligations.[16]

To return in light of this to the issue at hand, a proponent of the standard construal of the normativity of meaning can accept (1), which concerns truth-conditions, and (2), which concerns use-conditions, but view (1) as explanatorily prior to (2).[17] More generally, they can maintain that there are objective norms which hold in virtue of what an expression means according to which a person may (only) apply that expression truly and that, as a result, there are subjective norms according to which a person may (only) apply that expression when they believe that it applies truly.

While this way of developing the standard account of the normativity of meaning recognizes additional norms, it does not view those norms as more intimately associated with the meanings of expressions; on the contrary, it views them as belonging later in the order of explanation than the norms of truth.[18]

---

[16] This is an oversimplification, though a harmless one in the present context. A more sophisticated approach is to define what a person objectively ought to do in terms of the objective reasons for and against the various options, to define subjective reasons in terms of objective reasons, and then to define what a person subjectively ought to do in terms of the subjective reasons for and against the various options. For theories of subjective reasons, see Hornsby (2008), Parfit (2001), Schroeder (2009), Sylvan (2015), Vogelstein (2012), Way (2009), Whiting (2014, 2021: chapter 6).

[17] If the "because" as it appears in those principles is nontransitive, then the story is a bit more complex. The proponent of the orthodox account will say that the subjective norm that (2) expresses holds because the objective norm that (1) expresses holds, and in turn that (1) holds because of the meaning of the relevant expression.

[18] Among defenders of the view that meaning is normative, Gibbard (2012: 81–84) argues that subjective norms are explanatorily prior to objective norms.

To pursue this point further, consider:

(3) Necessarily, if (and because) "perro" means *dog*, then a person may apply "perro" to something if and only if they have evidence that it is a dog.

It seems in some sense incorrect (wrong, impermissible) for a person to apply "perro" to something in the absence of evidence that it is a dog, even if they judge that it is dog, indeed, even if it is a dog. And it seems in some sense correct (right, permissible) for a person to apply "perro" to something in the presence of evidence that it is a dog, even if they judge that it is frog, indeed, even if it is a frog.[19]

The pattern continues. For example, it is in some sense correct for a person to apply "perro" to a dog when they *know* that it is a dog, and incorrect for them to apply "perro" to a dog when they are ignorant that it is a dog (cp. Williamson 2000: chapter 8).

These observations suggest that there is a spectrum of more or less objective norms governing the use of expressions. And, again, it is plausible that the less subjective are explanatorily dependent on the most objective, that is, the norms of truth.

It is an advantage of the standard account of the normativity of meaning – as I have developed it – that it does not just allow for this proliferation of norms but, together with some independently plausible ideas, predicts and explains it, and does in a way that accords with what theorists have to say about other domains of normativity.

While the reference to judgment in (2) is taken from Reiland's gloss on what an expression is for, quoted above, he also speaks there of mere thought. At the sentential level, a sentence is for using while entertaining the proposition it expresses. At the subsentential level, an expression is for using while thinking of what it refers to or picks out. This points to principles like the following (see also Reiland 2023a: 2203):

(4) Necessarily, if (and because) "perro" means *dog*, then a person may use "perro" if and only if they are thinking about dogs (or about that kind of animal).

Note that talk of *applying* an expression in (1) to (3) is replaced in (4) with talk of *using* it (cp. Reiland 2023a: 2199). If a person applies an expression, they thereby perform an illocutionary act – in the cases at hand, they assert something. If a person (merely) uses it, they thereby perform a locutionary act – they (merely) say something. While assertions are expressive of judgments, sayings are expressive of (mere) thoughts.

---

[19] This is a more liberal position than the one I defend in Whiting (2009b).

The kinds of examples proponents of nonstandard readings of the normativity of meaning typically give to illustrate the distinction between norms of meaning and norms of truth do not support principles like (4); indeed, those examples seem to count against such principles. Suppose that a person says, "Jake es un perro" in circumstances such that they qualify as speaking Spanish but while absent-minded or distracted, and so while not thinking of dogs. Suppose further that the person utters the sentence while their thoughts are elsewhere – they are thinking of the Prime Minster, rather than Jake, and of incompetence, rather than dogs. According to (4), the person is making a mistake or using "perro" impermissibly. But that seems false of the example (and not because there are competing considerations that justify the person's use). In general, it seems okay to say something while entertaining thoughts about something else.[20]

5 Intentions

The principles considered so far may not capture Reiland's interpretation of the normativity of meaning. Consider Reiland's later suggestions that one uses the proper name "incorrectly" when one "*tries* to use 'Bertrand' to talk about Gottlob," and that one uses the first-person pronoun "incorrectly" when one "uses 'I' while trying to talk about" another person (2023a: 2198). These remarks concerning what a person is *trying* to do point to principles such as:

(5) Necessarily, if (and because) "perro" means *dog*, then a person may apply "perro" to something if and only if they do so intending to apply it to a dog.

More generally, the idea is that according with the meaning of an expression is not a matter of applying it to the thing to which it applies but of intending to do so.

One might agree that a person makes some sort of mistake when they use "perro" while intending to apply it to a frog, for example, but object to (5) on the grounds that the norm that delivers this verdict holds in virtue of the intention, not in virtue of the fact that "perro" means *dog* (cp. Whiting 2016: 228). More generally, one might think that the situations Reiland considers involve violations of instrumental, as opposed to semantic, norms.[21]

---

[20] A person might use "perro" while thinking about, say, cats because they take "perro" to be a word for cats. Alternatively, they might use "perro" while thinking of it as a word for cats. In such cases, I agree that the person is making a mistake, but that mistake lies in their understanding. I return to this issue below.

[21] Principles such as (5) entail that, when a person intentionally misapplies an expression, say, when lying, they make a semantic mistake. Reiland embraces this implication (2023a: fn14). I will not consider whether he is right to do so.

I will not press this point. As discussed in §1, a proponent of the orthodox account faces a similar challenge, namely, that the norms which they postulate hold in virtue of the act of asserting, as opposed to the meanings of the relevant expressions. So, the point does not choose between the two accounts.

In assessing (5), it is instructive to consider again the moral domain. Suppose that a person morally ought to walk the dog, perhaps because they promised to do so. The person tries to walk the dog but inadvertently walks a cat. While the person has acted impermissibly, since they did not satisfy their moral obligation, their intention mitigates the extent to which they are open to criticism – it might even be grounds for praise. Suppose instead that the person ought to walk the dog and does so, but they were trying to walk the cat. In that case, while the person acted permissibly, since they satisfied their moral obligation, they are open to criticism, since they intended to act in violation of their moral obligation. To put this in Kantian terms, acting in conformity with duty is one thing, acting in a way that is morally worthy is another (Kant 1785; see also Ross 1930: chapter 1). The key point for present purposes is that the worth of an action depends on the motive with which a person acts, specifically, on whether their motive corresponds to their duty.[22]

To return in light of this to the issue at hand, a proponent of the standard account of semantic normativity need not deny that a person's intention in using an expression makes a difference to the assessment of their actions. On the contrary, if there are norms of true application, it is to be expected that there are further norms that concern *attempts* at true application. Crucially, the analogy with the moral domain suggests that the norms of (so to speak) trying that (5) concern are less fundamental than those of (so to speak) succeeding that (1) concerns. The motives that matter in using an expression are those that correspond to the norm of truth.

The analogy with the moral domain further suggests that norms like those (5) concerns are not best formulated in terms of permissibility but in terms of criticizability. To use the jargon, those norms are hypological, not deontic.

So, Reiland's point that there are standards governing a person's use of an expression that bear on, not whether they as a matter of fact truly apply it, but whether they are trying to do so, is a point that the proponent of the standard account of semantic normativity can accept; indeed, it is one that their view predicts and explains.

---

[22] This is deliberately noncommittal. For an influential analysis of moral worth, see Arpaly (2002).

In other remarks, Reiland locates intention in a different place. He considers a person employing an expression "with the intention to participate in the practice" of using a certain language. If that person with that intention is "not in the use-conditions," Reiland says, they "count as misusing the expression" (2023a: 2200). This suggests that principles such as the following hold:

(6) Necessarily, if (and because) a person intends to use (the Spanish word) "perro," then, because "perro" means *dog*, they may apply "perro" to something if and only if they judge that it is a dog.

According to Reiland, in order to count as using a certain language or participating in the practice of doing so, a person must intend to use that language or participate in that practice. In his words, "Absent such intentions there is no speaking a public language like English or Estonian" (2023a: 2193). For what it is worth, I doubt that it is necessary to possess or exploit such cognitive sophistication in order to qualify as using a language. Be that as it may, as I read Reiland's remarks, (6) is not opposed to (2). For Reiland, as just discussed, a person's intention to participate in Spanish by using "perro" is necessary for their use to qualify as the use of the Spanish word meaning *dog*. Moreover, according to Reiland, that intention is also sufficient. As he puts it, "the role of the intention is … to make it the case that the use is a use of the expression-type which has a meaning" (2023a: 2202). So understood, (6) is equivalent to (2).

The principles concerning intention considered so far, (5) and (6), speak of applying an expression (in illocutionary acts like that of assertion). One might object that this overlooks Reiland's suggestion that, in the first instance, norms of meaning govern the (mere) use of an expression. Consider, then:

(7) Necessarily, if (and because) "perro" means *dog*, then a person may use "perro" to say something if and only if they do so intending to use it to say something about dogs (or about that kind of animal).

In assessing (7), it is helpful to break it up:

(7a) Necessarily, if (and because) "perro" means *dog*, then a person may use "perro" to say something if they do so intending to use it to say something about dogs (or about that kind of animal).

(7b) Necessarily, if (and because) "perro" means *dog*, then a person may use "perro" to say something only if they do so intending to use it to say something about dogs (or about that kind of animal).

According to (5), given its meaning, a person may not apply "perro" unless they intend to apply it to a dog. Applying "perro" entails using it to say something. And intending to apply "perro" entails intending to use it to say something. So, (5) entails (7b). I have already explained how a proponent of the standard account can accept and accommodate (5). So, the dispute concerns (7b).

One challenge facing its proponent is to show that the norm that, according to (7b), holds does so in virtue of the relevant meaning rather than in virtue of the relevant intention. Again, I set this aside.

The key question is why a proponent of the thesis that meaning is normative should think that a principle such as (7b) is a more faithful expression of that thesis than the more orthodox (1). As introduced above, the guiding idea of the nonstandard interpretation is that semantic mistakes are distinct from factual mistakes. But (7b) does not vindicate that idea. The norm it introduces states a sufficient condition for the use of an expression to be permissible; it says nothing about when the use of an expression is impermissible, hence mistaken.

Another idea motivating the nonstandard account is that a semantic misuse is one that betokens a lack of understanding (see e.g. Glock 2005: 229). The orthodox interpretation, one might think, does not capture this thought. If a person applies "perro" to a cleverly disguised cat, their application is impermissible according to (1), but it need not betray a lack of understanding. On the contrary, their adequate grasp of what "perro" means might explain why the person applies that expression to a dog lookalike. In Section 6, I will show that (7), hence, (7b), fails to capture the (alleged) link between misuse and misunderstanding, hence, fails to capture another motivation for the nonstandard interpretation.

6 Grasp of Meaning

Meaning and understanding are coordinate notions in the sense that what an expression means is what a person who understands the expression understands. Perhaps, then, one way to get a handle on the notion of a semantic norm is by appealing to the notion of understanding.

In light of this, consider Reiland's suggestion that "uses by speakers who are mistaken about an expression's meaning constitute misuses" (2023a: 2198). The claim here is that if a person applies an expression in a way that reveals a misunderstanding of its meaning, then they use it in a way that fails to accord with its meaning.

The principles emerging from Reiland's remarks on the normativity of meaning do not vindicate this idea. Suppose that a person understands "perro" to mean *dog or cat*. On the basis of this understanding, they apply "perro" to a dog while judging that it is a dog, while thinking of dogs, while trying to apply it to a dog, and while trying to say something about a dog. According to (2), (4), (5), and (7), the person uses the expression permissibly, notwithstanding their mistaken understanding of its meaning.

At this point, it is helpful to turn to Millar, who offers an account of what it is to use an expression in accordance with its meaning – where this is supposed to differ from applying it truly – by appeal to the notion of understanding or, in his preferred term, grasping. According to Millar:

Correct use in this sense is a use of the term that respects the relevant conditions of correct (= true) application. (2014: 801)

What is it to respect those conditions? Millar tells us:

A use of a term respects the relevant conditions of correct application only if its use on the occasion in question manifests an adequate grasp of those conditions. (2014: 801)

Putting the two ideas together, Millar's claim is that the use of an expression is correct or permissible only if it manifests an adequate grasp of the conditions of true application.

Millar adds to this that the norms for the use of an expression "prescribe" respect for the conditions of its true application, hence they prescribe manifesting a grasp of those conditions (2014: 804). Presumably, if the norm prescribes this, then it is (according to the norm) correct or permissible. So, for Millar, using an expression in a way that manifests a grasp of the conditions of its true application is both necessary and sufficient for correctly using it in the relevant sense.

In motivating this proposal, Millar appeals to cases like the following:

A child might be disposed to apply the term ["fox"] to foxes and to dogs that look a little like foxes. Applying the term to a young Alsatian dog on some occasion the child speaks falsely but the error lies not just in the false application but in the fact that the false application derives from an inadequate grasp of the relevant conditions of correct (= true) application. The child uses the term as if it correctly applied not just to foxes but to foxes and some dogs and so fails to adequately to respect the relevant conditions of correct application. The mistake is accordingly semantic. (2014: 801)

To relate this to the earlier example, Millar's proposal is that principles like the following hold:

(8) Necessarily, if (and because) "perro" means *dog*, then a person may apply "perro" to something if and only if their application manifests an adequate grasp of the conditions for its true application.

Consider a case – analogous to Millar's – in which a person applies "perro" to a frog because they understand it to mean *frog*. It should be uncontroversial that their use of that expression on this occasion involves two mistakes or errors. But, I suggest, a proponent of the standard account of the normativity of meaning need not deny this. First, the person misapplies "perro" in the sense that they falsely apply it to a frog. According to (1), they ought not to do so. Second, the person makes a false judgment about what the word means. In doing so, they judge incorrectly. This suggests that there is a norm of truth governing judgment – the interior counterpart to assertion.[23] So, it is possible to capture what is going on in cases of the sort Millar draws attention to – in particular, to characterize the two norm violations – without departing from the standard account.

A proponent of the orthodox construal of the normativity of meaning might add to this: One question is whether or not a person conforms to the relevant norms – in the case at hand, whether or not they apply an expression truly. Another question is why a person conforms or fails to do so – in the case at hand, why they do or do not apply the expression truly. If a person applies "perro" to a frog, that might be due to their misunderstanding its meaning. To return to earlier ideas, it might instead (or in addition) be due to false beliefs, misleading evidence, or indifference to the truth. No doubt the basis on which a person applies an expression – truly or otherwise – makes a difference to the assessment of their linguistic behavior, specifically, to whether and to what extent they are criticizable for their use. But, again, it is important to keep the deontic and the hypological apart.[24]

So far, the suggestion is that reflection on cases does not motivate (8) or count against (1). In addition, there are more principled reasons for rejecting (8) and, in doing so, the construal of semantic normativity it expresses. According to (8), given what an expression means, a person should only apply it *on the basis of* a certain understanding. I have argued elsewhere that (deontic) norms can require a person to act, but they cannot require a person to act-on-a-certain-basis (Whiting 2017). I will not rehearse those arguments here. The point is that, if they succeed, (8), as stated, is false.

7 Commitments

I formulated (8) in terms of what is permissible, which I take to be equivalent to Millar's talk of what is correct. But, one might object, this overlooks Millar's appeal to the notion of *commitment*. Consider:

---

[23] This might seem to overlook Millar's claim that the relevant understanding is *practical*. But it is consistent with what I say here that the relevant judgement is in the relevant sense practical too.

[24] According to Schroeder (2018), there are standards for right action and standards for acting well, and the former are always explanatorily prior to the latter.

The normative dimension of the meaning of predicative terms is captured by the claim that just in virtue of using a term in a particular sense one incurs a commitment to following a rule for its use prescribing respect for the conditions of correct application that display the relevant meaning. The commitment arises from being a participant in a practice of using the term in the relevant sense. To have such a commitment is a matter of its being the case that one ought to avoid continuing in the practice while flouting the rules. (2014: 808–809)

For Millar, if a person does something that generates a commitment to doing something else, this corresponds to an obligation to avoid the combination of doing the first thing while not doing the second. So, to stick with the working example, perhaps the following better captures Millar's view:

(9) A person ought, if they participate in the practice of using the Spanish expression "perro" meaning *dog*, to follow the rule governing its use.

Here "ought" has wide scope; that is to say, it governs the conditional, not its antecedent or its consequent.

For Millar, as discussed earlier, the rules governing the use of a predicative expression prescribe what he calls respect for its conditions of true application, and to do that is to apply the expression in a way that manifests an adequate grasp of those conditions. So, (9) is equivalent to:

(10) A person ought, if they participate in the practice of using the Spanish expression "perro" meaning *dog*, to manifest an adequate grasp of its conditions of true application.

More generally, the idea is that a person ought to avoid the combination of continuing to use an expression in a certain language that bears a certain meaning while manifesting an inadequate grasp of the conditions under which that expression applies.

Introducing (10) only postpones the earlier concerns. First, consider a case in which a person is unable to withdraw from the practice of using the relevant expression – they cannot but, for example, engage in the employment of the Spanish word "perro." In that case, the only way to satisfy the obligation that (10) concerns is to use "perro" while manifesting an adequate grasp of its conditions of true application. So, they ought to do so.[25] In that case, (10) requires a person, not just to act, but to act-on-a-certain-basis.

Setting this aside, (10), like (8), is motivated (solely) by the observation that there is something problematic about a situation in which a

---

[25] In general, if a person is subject to an obligation to do one of two things, and only one of those things is an option for them, then they are under an obligation to do that thing. For this point, see Greenspan (1970), Setiya (2007), and Way (2010).

person applies an expression – truly or falsely – as a result of misunderstanding its conditions of true application.[26] I argued above that a proponent of the standard account of the normativity of meaning can accommodate that observation. Revising the scope of the deontic operator does not speak to this.

8 Conclusion

The challenge Kripke's Wittgenstein's skeptic presents is to find a fact that makes it the case that an expression bears a certain meaning, one which also "determines in advance what I should do to accord with this meaning" (1982: 65). According to the skeptic, that challenge cannot be met. So, there is no fact that makes it the case that an expression bears a certain meaning. So, there is no such thing as meaning.

A central premise in this skeptical argument is that, in some way, meaning is normative. In what way? That question was the focus of this chapter. While working out how best to formulate a view is not neatly separable from evaluating the view as formulated, my primary focus in this chapter has been the former task. So, I have not tried to defend the claim that meaning is normative, only to determine its content. My conclusion is the orthodox one: If meaning is normative, it is normative in the sense that there are norms of truth governing the application of expressions (in assertion) that hold in virtue of the meanings of those expressions. A recurring theme in the discussion is that to say this is not to say that truth is the *only* standard of assessment for the use of meaningful expressions. A proponent of the orthodox construal can allow – indeed, should expect – that there are other norms governing the use of expressions, in particular, norms that concern what the agent is like – specifically, their doxastic, epistemic, and motivational states. But they can – should – view those norms as explanatorily posterior to the norm of truth.

Does the claim that meaning is normative – on the interpretation defended here – lead to the "incredible and self-defeating" conclusion that there is no such thing as meaning (Kripke 1982: 71)? Answering that question is a task for another occasion, a task which, I hope, this chapter facilitates.[27]

---

[26] Millar is explicit about the motivation for his proposal (2014: 801fn5).
[27] Thanks to Claudine Verheggen and Indrek Reiland for comments on earlier versions. Extra thanks to Indrek Reiland for conversations on the issues it concerns.

8 What Is the Skeptical Problem? Wittgenstein's Response to Kripke

Claudine Verheggen

> I have been primarily concerned to explain the sense in which we are 'responsible' for the ways in which the rails are extended without destroying anything that could be called their objectivity.
>
> Stroud (1965: 16)

1 Introduction

In so far as Saul Kripke's *Wittgenstein on Rules and Private Language* (henceforth WRPL) has attracted nearly as many competing interpretations as has Wittgenstein's *Philosophical Investigations* (henceforth PI), it might be said that Kripke, who claimed to be presenting Wittgenstein's argument "as it struck him," did justice to Wittgenstein. This is not to say that Kripke got Wittgenstein right.[1] Indeed, almost everyone agrees that, at least where Kripke's "skeptical solution" to the skeptical problem about meaning embodied in Wittgenstein's rule-following paradox is concerned, Kripke got Wittgenstein wrong.[2] The most widespread interpretation has been that Wittgenstein dissolved the problem, by revealing it to be based on mistaken assumptions. I agree with this interpretation. But I disagree with many commentators' claim that what follows from this dissolution is simply quietism about meaning – the claim that nothing philosophically constructive can be said about it.[3] Revisiting Kripke's writings has convinced me anew that Wittgenstein was not a quietist about meaning.[4] Paradoxical as this may seem, I actually take the quietist

---

[1] Kripke himself did not insist that his interpretation was accurate, nor did he endorse the views he developed. For these reasons, they are often attributed to "Kripke's Wittgenstein" or "Kripkenstein." I shall stick with "Kripke," simply referring to the author of WRPL.
[2] There are of course also many commentators on Kripke who take no stand on his interpretation of Wittgenstein.
[3] See, among others, Fogelin (1987), Diamond (1989), and McDowell (1992). A notable exception is Child (2019). See also Moyal-Sharrock (2017), though her focus is not on Wittgenstein's remarks on meaning but more generally on his philosophical methods.
[4] I first suggested this interpretation in Verheggen (2000), on grounds different, however, from those developed here.

and Kripke to have much in common. For I take the challenge leading to the paradox to be a meta-semantic challenge, calling for a foundational account of meaning. I think that both the quietist and Kripke share this conception of the challenge. However, whereas the quietist argues that the challenge is fundamentally misguided, Kripke argues that it is legitimate and cannot be met. Consequently, whereas the quietist rejects the skeptical problem and its ensuing skeptical conclusion, Kripke accepts them. Yet, what then follows from these verdicts is remarkably similar in both cases: we are left with purely semantic, descriptive remarks about meaning. It is in fact Kripke's sharing a conclusion with some of those who maintain that Wittgenstein dissolved the skeptical problem that has prompted me to reconsider the question whether Wittgenstein really was a quietist about meaning, and to conclude that he was not. Here are, in brief, what I regard as the main contrasts between Kripke's and Wittgenstein's views.

I believe that, though Kripke's reading of what leads to the paradox is right in many respects, in particular, right in suggesting that Wittgenstein rejects semantic reductionism, he is wrong to conclude, once he has shown that the skeptical challenge cannot be met, that there is no such thing as meaning. As I see it, the conclusion Wittgenstein draws once he has reached the paradox is only that meaning cannot be explained by any of the theories or pictures, both reductive and nonreductive, he has considered, since they all lead to the paradox. But once their deficiencies are acknowledged, and thus once the skeptical problem embodied in the paradox is dissolved, a new meta-semantic challenge, and hence a new problem, arises, connected to the essential link Wittgenstein emphasizes between meaning and use, a challenge, and hence a problem, which Kripke does not recognize. As a result, he does not see that the positive remarks Wittgenstein makes after dismissing the paradox are meant to do some constructive, not just descriptive, work, in response to the problem newly arisen. In particular, he does not see that the notion of agreement plays an important meta-semantic role in Wittgenstein's remarks, rather than being a brute notion about which nothing can be said.

The chapter will proceed as follows. I start, in Section 2, by reviewing the remarks of PI that lead to Wittgenstein's paradox and the skeptical problem embodied in it. I argue that what at bottom leads to the paradox is a certain conception of what it is for words to have meaning. The question then is whether rejecting this conception amounts to rejecting semantic reductionism. In Section 3, I elucidate the notion of reductionism that is at play, in particular, what kinds of claims about meaning are apt to be reductionist. I argue that Wittgenstein has repudiated reductionism, as all reductive views fall under the erroneous conception.

The question then becomes whether this repudiation also amounts to quietism. I start, in Section 4, by clarifying the notion of quietism, in particular, what kinds of philosophical questions the quietist deems to be misguided and thus not in need of an answer. I argue that, once Wittgenstein has rejected the problematic conception of meaning and advocated a strong link between meaning and use, a new problem arises, which is how to reconcile this link with the claim that meaning is objective, and thus presumably, in some sense, independent of use. I then turn to Wittgenstein's positive remarks, and I argue that they can be understood as suggesting constructive claims about meaning, intended to meet this new meta-semantic challenge. I continue, in Section 5, with a review of what Kripke takes to be the skeptical challenge and how the views he considers cannot meet it. Again, I see Kripke's arguments as a rejection of reductionism. However, as I argue in Section 6, Kripke fails to realize that the reason to reject reductionist views, and more generally to denounce a certain conception of meaning, is no reason to reject non-reductionism about meaning, and thus no reason to be skeptical about meaning. And thus he fails to realize that Wittgenstein's positive remarks are meant to address a new problem, which arises from an alternative conception, rather than provide a skeptical solution to a problem Wittgenstein has shown to be incoherent.

2   Wittgenstein's Path to the Paradox

Wittgenstein writes: "A philosophical problem has the form: 'I don't know my way about'" (PI: #123). It is important to make clear, to begin with, what philosophical problem it is that prompted the opening sections of PI. This should eventually help us to assess whether this is the problem that is allegedly denounced as misguided by Wittgenstein. (To anticipate, I do not think that this is the problem Wittgenstein dissolves. What he does dissolve are the problems that arise from certain answers to the original question.) I see the path to the paradox as coming in three main steps, each of which is an attack on a received theory of meaning.[5] I shall be brief with the exposition of these critiques, as they have all already been much discussed.[6] What has seldom been recognized, let alone emphasized, is what they have in common, and hence the real target of Wittgenstein's attacks.

---

[5] As we shall see, there is actually a fourth step, which might be understood as an attack on the view Wittgenstein himself is suggesting.
[6] Which is not to say that there is consensus as to whether they lead to a skeptical problem. I have given a more thorough exposition in Verheggen (2017).

2.1 The Case against Referentialism (PI: ##1–36)

Wittgenstein starts PI by rejecting what he calls a "picture of the essence of human language" that can be summarized thus: (1) Every word stands for something, and sentences are combinations of such words. (2) The object for which a word stands is its meaning. (3) There is no difference between kinds of words. This picture has been called referentialism,[7] since the words that seem prima facie to fit the picture are words that refer to things like tables and chairs and persons. But the picture is so unelaborated that it could be said to stand for all the pictures and theories Wittgenstein will eventually reject. For, as we shall see, it embodies the essence, so to speak, of the problem with all those pictures and theories. However, sticking for now with referentialism, it is clearly intended to be an answer to the question what it is for words to mean what they do or what it is for words to have meaning, a question which preoccupied Wittgenstein his entire life. The immediate puzzle with the basic picture he has presented is that, even if it is partly correct, it could not apply to all kinds of words. As he says, we are thinking of some "kinds of word as something that will have to take care of itself" (PI: #1).

Consequently, the basic picture is contrasted with the example of a use of language in which different words have different uses and hence, it might be surmised, got to mean what they do in different ways, not always by standing for something. Thus, in the example, when the shopkeeper is given a slip marked "five red apples," he "opens the drawer marked 'apple'; then he looks up the word 'red' in a chart and finds a colour sample next to it; then he says the series of elementary number-words ... up to the word 'five', and for each number-word he takes an apple of the same colour as the sample out of the drawer" (PI: #1). But this is only the first step in Wittgenstein's rejection of referentialism, which receives its final blow in sections ##28–30 of PI.

There Wittgenstein argues that an ostensive definition cannot by itself endow a word with meaning unless "the role the word is supposed to play in the language is already clear" (PI: #30). If it is not clear, "an ostensive definition can be variously interpreted in *any* case" (PI: #28). Thus, I succeed in defining 'sepia' by pointing at a sample of sepia only if my interlocutor knows that 'sepia' is a color-word. Presumably the link between the discussion of ostensive definition and the rejection of referentialism is this: If words could have meaning just by standing for something, then we could define them ostensively independently of the

---

[7] See Fogelin (1996: 37).

rest of language. Ostensive definitions would be the basis of language and not dependent on it, as they in fact are.

2.2 The Case against Essentialism (PI: ##65–88)

In section #67 of PI, Wittgenstein introduces the notion of family resemblances in answer to the interlocutor's objection, in section #65, that Wittgenstein has not said what the essence of language is, what it is that all languages have in common. Wittgenstein denies that there is such a thing as the essence of language to be discovered. Rather, the concept of language is like the concept of game, a paradigmatic family concept. There are "similarities overlapping and crisscrossing" all the things that fall under the term 'game', but no set of necessary and sufficient conditions we could use to define 'game'. Likewise for all family terms or concepts.

Wittgenstein's argument, however, does not target only family terms or concepts but all general terms or concepts.[8] For what he is attacking here is the idea of essence, or universal, or common property, or Platonic form, allegedly that which is shared by all things falling under a given general term or concept, which guides our applications of the term or concept, indeed, which serves as the standard against which applications are deemed to be correct or incorrect. Thus, to take the example of a word that may be thought easily to fit the bill, viz., that again of a color-word like 'green', the idea is that the abstract universal of greenness determines what 'green' means and thus provides it with a standard of correct application. Again, Wittgenstein's argument against what may be called essentialism is two-fold, both indicating how words get to mean what they do and revealing the fundamental problem with the essentialist view.

Thus, on the one hand, Wittgenstein presents a myriad of examples that show that appealing to universals to explain the meaning of words is neither needed nor useful. For instance, we explain to someone what a game is, and presumably the meaning of 'game', by describing games to her, and maybe adding to the description: "This *and similar things* are called 'games'" (PI: #69). Importantly, the lack of rigid boundaries of application, which allegedly universals would be setting, does not prevent us from understanding the word. On the other hand, Wittgenstein asks us to consider what the consequences would be of postulating a universal as what determines the meaning of a word. This would be equivalent to saying that a sample of, say, pure green, determines the meaning of 'pure green'. Wittgenstein then asks, in section #73, what would the sample

---

[8] See Goldfarb (1997) for a brilliant demonstration of this claim.

have to be like in order to be a sample of pure green rather than a sample of all that is greenish, or, for that matter, a sample of a shape, or of a leaf, or whatever? The fact is that unless the sample is being used as a sample of pure green, it cannot provide any standard for the application of 'pure green'. Indeed, unless it is used in a certain way, the sample can be variously interpreted and so is such that whatever application we may make of the word connected to it is correct, or not, as the case may be. Samples cannot by themselves provide words with meaning any more than objects that might be pointed at while defining the words that stand for them.

2.3 The Case against Mental Occurrences (PI: ##138–201)

Interestingly, at this stage, Wittgenstein starts having second thoughts about the use picture of meaning he has been proposing. Among other questions, he asks, in section #139: How can the use of a word determine its meaning? One of the problems he seems to have in mind here is pretty clearly the idea that "the whole use of a word" cannot "come before my mind" when I understand a word. Yet, if I understand a word, if I know its meaning, I have the ability to assess as correct or incorrect an indefinite number of its uses. Simply put, then, the problem is this: If the use of a word determines its meaning, how can its meaning determine which uses are correct or not? The problem is pressing enough that it prompts Wittgenstein further to consider traditional views of meaning, all of which postulate a mental occurrence[9] – a picture coming before the mind, such as the drawing of a cube (PI: #139), or a formula grasped by the mind, such as an algebraic formula (PI: #146) – in order to explain what determines the meaning of a word. Wittgenstein's strategy, in response, is the same as before. On the one hand, these mental items are shown to be useless as determinants of meaning, neither necessary nor sufficient; indeed, unless such an item is taken as an item of a specific kind, it cannot serve as the standard governing the application of the word of which it allegedly determines the meaning (just as the object pointed at or the essence allegedly represented by the sample cannot do so if they are not taken to be an object or a sample of a specific kind). On the other hand, Wittgenstein reiterates the idea that if we want to figure out the meaning of a word, if we want to figure out "how the formula is meant," we must look at "the kind of way we always use it, were taught to use it" (PI: #190).

[9] There is also a shift of emphasis here. Wittgenstein is for the first time considering understanding, that is, words as they are understood, and not just as their meaning may be reflected in a speaker's behavior, and thus paying attention to the point of view of the speaker herself.

2.4 The Case against Reductively Characterized Use

Presumably, when Wittgenstein asks initially how the use of a word can determine its meaning, the kind of use he has in mind is the production of signs that are not yet meaningful, the meaningless use of signs. But the remarks he has made against the idea that words get their meaning simply by being somehow connected to either objects or properties in the world around us, or essences of those objects or properties, or mental items of one kind or another, also apply to the idea of words getting their meaning simply by being used in certain ways. As we have seen, none of those candidates can by itself provide a word with meaning, because unless it is taken, interpreted, as Wittgenstein says, in a certain way, it could serve as the standard for numerous incompatible applications, all of which could be said to be correct, or not, as the case may be, so that none of them could by itself provide a word with a standard of application, and hence with meaning.

Similarly, use, if it is thought of as consisting simply of non-semantically described applications of a word, regular though they may be, is not sufficient to determine or constitute the meaning of a word. For non-semantically described applications of a word are compatible with the word having different meanings, indeed, with different applications of the word being correct, or incorrect, as the case may be. Conceiving of meaning in terms of uses, non-semantically described, leads to the skeptical paradox just as straightforwardly as conceiving of it in terms of any of the items postulated by more traditional views as determinants of meaning. To put it in the way Wittgenstein expresses the paradox, if we think of the meaning of a word as being determined exclusively by an object or property, external or internal, or by the essence thereof, or by use, non-semantically characterized, then no application of a word could be determined by the meaning because every application of a word can be brought into accord with the meaning. Wittgenstein concludes: "The answer was: if everything can be made out to accord with the rule [or meaning], then it can also be made out to conflict with it. And so there would be neither accord nor conflict here" (PI: #201). And so there would be no meaning.

At bottom, then, what leads to the paradox is a certain conception of what it is for words to have meaning – call it the associative conception: their being somehow associated with items that do not wear a meaning on their sleeves, but which rather can be understood as providing standards of correct application only in so far as they have been interpreted as doing so. This demand is hopeless, indeed incoherent, as we need a language in order to do the associating it requires, and so the associating could not by itself establish a language. Now, all the items Wittgenstein considers are semantically empty, with one possible exception, though: essences. These might be thought of as wearing meaning on their sleeves; they are meanings by definition. However, Wittgenstein's concern, as I see it, is how words come to be associated with those meanings. How is it established that a given word's meaning is determined by one or the other of a myriad of "meanings"?[10] Thus, the incoherence affects not just views that are reductionist.[11] Still, it is worth emphasizing that any reductionist view does lead to the paradox, including the view that meaning can be reduced to non-semantically characterized use. For Wittgenstein is sometimes thought to be a reductionist of this kind.

3   Wittgenstein's Non-Reductionism

3.1   What Is Semantic Non-Reductionism?

To begin with, it is important to make clear what kind of theory of meaning is apt to be reductionist or not. Thus, it is important to distinguish between descriptive theories of meaning (or semantic theories), theories that tell us what the meanings of all the expressions of a language are, and foundational theories of meaning (or meta-semantic theories), theories that give us an account of the nature of meaning.[12] This distinction has recently been more and more recognized,[13] in part, I think, due to the renewed interest in questions about the foundations of meaning. These questions are admittedly varied, and, accordingly, different philosophers may understand the terms 'foundational' or 'meta-semantic' in different ways. Different philosophers may also conceive of the relation between the two types of theory in different ways, and they may indeed disagree as to what questions are the proper business of one or the other type of theory.[14] Here I follow the lead of Michael Dummett

---

[10] Cf Wilson (1998), who gives this as an interpretation of Kripke's interpretation of Wittgenstein, but which I see as an accurate interpretation of Wittgenstein as well, though Wilson's interpretation does not cover all the theories or pictures Wittgenstein and Kripke consider.
[11] Obviously the kind of non-reductionist view that is being affected here is different from that which I take Wittgenstein to endorse, and which we are about to examine.
[12] A related distinction was first introduced by Lewis (1970), followed by Kaplan (1989), and Stalnaker (1997).
[13] See Burgess and Sherman (2014), Glüer (2018), and Speaks (2019).
[14] It may be asked whether 'descriptive' and 'semantic' should be used interchangeably, since there may be an explanatory element in semantic theories, in so far as they are supposed to tell how the meanings of complex expressions depend on the meanings of simple ones. I shall use them interchangeably here, following Robert Stalnaker, who in his distinction between "foundational-semantic questions" and "descriptive-semantic questions" includes explanatory questions of the above kind on the descriptive side (Stalnaker 1997: 904).

and Donald Davidson, who made clear that they were interested in figuring out how to construct a descriptive theory because the construction of such a theory would illuminate the nature of meaning; it would, in effect, yield a philosophical account of meaning. As Dummett writes:

> a [descriptive] 'theory of meaning' for any one entire language is a detailed specification of the meanings of all the words and sentence-forming operations of the language, yielding a specification of the meaning of every expression and sentence of the language ... once we can enunciate the general principles in accordance with which such a construction could be carried out, we shall have arrived at a solution of the problems concerning meaning by which philosophers are perplexed. (1974: 97)

And as Davidson makes clear in the introduction to his collected essays on truth and interpretation:

> [We could answer the question] what it is for words to mean what they do ... in a philosophically instructive way if we knew how to construct a theory satisfying two demands: it would provide an interpretation of all utterances, actual and potential, of a speaker or group of speakers; and it would be verifiable without knowledge of the detailed propositional attitudes of the speaker. (1984: xv)

I believe that the distinction between semantic and meta-semantic queries and statements can be applied to Wittgenstein's remarks, with an important caveat. Whereas, at the semantic level, Dummett and Davidson are seeking a systematic semantic theory, which would tell us for any utterance of a speaker what its meaning is, all Wittgenstein is doing, at the semantic level, is describing how we teach, or explain, the meaning of words to others, and how we ascribe meaning to their words. These semantic remarks are neutral with respect to non-reductionism and non-quietism, as they are purely descriptive and non-philosophical.[15] However, as Wittgenstein says, the descriptive remarks "get [their] light – that is to say [their] purpose – from the philosophical problems. These are of course not empirical problems; but they are solved through an insight into the workings of our language" (PI: #109). This, to my mind, strongly suggests that, according to Wittgenstein, we may shed light, in particular, on the nature of meaning by looking at how we get to specify the meanings of someone's expressions. And thus it suggests that some of the remarks Wittgenstein makes belong to a meta-semantic theory that is both non-reductionist and, per force, non-quietist.

To say that the meta-semantic theory is non-reductionist is to say that the construction of the semantic theory, or the specification of the

---

[15] Strictly speaking, it could be said that Wittgenstein is a quietist at the semantic level, whereas Dummett and Davidson are not, in so far as Wittgenstein makes no attempt to provide a systematic theory of meaning. Nothing here turns on this difference, however.

meanings of someone's words, through which the meta-semantic theory is arrived at, cannot fully be done outside of a semantic context. That is, it cannot be done without including, in the construction of the semantic theory, or in the specification of someone's words' meanings, what the expressions whose meanings are specified are used to mean. For instance, it cannot be done simply by considering the dispositions a speaker has to utter words in certain circumstances, or simply by considering the relations that obtain between a speaker's utterances and features of her environment. The question, of course, is going to be, how can we provide an account of the nature of meaning if the account is given in terms that presuppose meaning? That is, how can we avoid quietism, which is to ask, how can we still have a meta-semantic or foundational theory? I shall address this question in Section 3.2. For now, let us see why Wittgenstein is sometimes considered a reductionist.

3.2   Wittgenstein's Reductionism?

What prompts some philosophers' claim that Wittgenstein is a reductionist are the multifarious descriptions he gives of how we assign meaning to speakers' expressions. Recall the exchange with the shopkeeper, in section #1 of PI, where different words are used in different ways and thus presumably get to mean what they do in different ways. The basic idea is that we assign meaning on the basis of the uses people make of their expressions. For example, a novel use of 'game' will be understood as meaning game on the basis of the activity (which may be quite complex) it is applied to, noticing that this activity has similarities with other activities that are called games, activities which in turn have been deemed to be games because of certain features they exhibit, including our roles in playing them. We apply 'chair' to an object in virtue of how it looks and what we can do with it. If an object we otherwise might have called a chair has been disappearing and reappearing, we are at a loss as to what to call it.[16] If asked what one's expression means, no one will answer, "It means what I use it to mean." Nor would anyone be content with that answer.

Paul Horwich mentions the shopkeeper's exchange of section #1 of PI as an example of an "illustration" that vindicates his interpretation according to which "meaning-facts *reduce* to underlying non-intensional facts of word use ... The meaning-constituting uses of the words [Wittgenstein considers] are invariably described in non-semantic terms" (Horwich 2010: 19).[17] It seems to me, however, that there is no reason to think

---

[16]   Cf. PI: #80.
[17]   See also Dummett (1978), and arguably Ginsborg (2020).

that the behaviour that is being described there is sufficient to fix the meanings of the words being used. Given the description, we are able to understand what the interlocutors mean by "five red apples" (provided of course we ourselves understand the words). But this does not tell us what makes it the case that, say, 'red' means red. The same behavior – associating 'red' with a sample of red – is compatible with 'red' meaning, say, round (which is not to say, though, that the behavior had no role to play in determining the meaning of 'red').

In short, when we are doing the purely semantic work of figuring out what someone's words mean, we of course do not appeal to meanings; meanings are what we are looking for. But it does not follow from this that meaning can be reduced to non-semantically described use. To mean something by an expression is not just to apply it correctly to some items and not others. It is to take it to apply correctly to some items and not others, and so to take it to mean what it does. And so, when we specify the meaning of an expression and say what the standards are that govern its applications, this specification reflects what we take the expression to mean, even though this is in part arrived at on the basis of its non-semantically characterized use. Somehow, among the many meanings it could have, we have isolated one, which can be described only semantically.

However, the process of specifying the meanings of someone's words elicits foundational claims about what it is for words to mean what they do, and so about what it is for words to have meaning. For it is not just any uses of expressions that will enable us eventually to say what a speaker means by them. If uses are to be understood as meaningful, certain conditions must be met. This is where, as I see it, Wittgenstein's non-quietism comes in.

4 Wittgenstein's Non-Quietism

4.1 What Is Semantic Quietism?

I take semantic quietism to be the refusal to give any explanation *of any kind* of any phenomena connected to the nature of linguistic meaning. It is, in effect, the refusal to develop a meta-semantic theory of any kind. In particular, I take it to be the refusal to answer the question of what makes it possible for words to mean what they do or indeed to have any meaning. Refusing to answer this question is not tantamount to refusing to address it, however. John McDowell, a prominent defender of the claim that Wittgenstein is a quietist about meaning, believes that Wittgenstein does address questions of the form "How is such and such possible?,," but that he reveals them to have no tenable basis. Someone who asks a question of that form should not immediately seek to answer it but should investigate instead why "we are expected to find a difficulty in the possibility of such and such" (2009b: 371). Often, it turns out that this expectation is the result of neglecting what is open to view, what we in fact know, such as the fact that signposts are things that "point in one direction or another" (2009b: 369). This realization in turn prompts us to reject the question or problem, for instance, by dissolving the puzzle that seems to lead to it. Thus, quietism "urges us not to engage in certain supposed tasks, but precisely because it requires us to work at showing that they are not necessary" (2009b: 371). Therefore, according to McDowell, quietism is a well-earned philosophical stance, contra those who believe that Wittgenstein does uncover genuine philosophical problems, but that he refuses to solve them because he is independently committed to quietism.[18] I believe that, though sometimes Wittgenstein proceeds exactly as McDowell says he does, in the case of meaning, he has uncovered a problem that calls for a constructive answer, and not just for dissolution.

4.2   Wittgenstein's New Problem

With many commentators, I agree that the skeptical problem embodied in the paradox has been dissolved. The conception on which it is grounded has been dismissed as incoherent. In so far as there might have been a difficulty in the possibility of words having meaning, it was revealed that this was due to an erroneous conception of what it is for them to have meaning. Moreover, once we pay closer attention to how we do ascribe meanings to words in ordinary practice, we cannot but recognize how by and large unproblematic these ascriptions are. Still, it might be complained that the answer to the initial question of what it is for words to have meaning is rather lacking. All we are left with is the platitude that meaning is semantically characterized use; meaning is meaningful use. We may be tempted to agree with Warren Goldfarb, another proponent of quietism, who writes, "[g]iven that invoking use by itself carries little information, I take [Wittgenstein's] remark in #43 [that the meaning of a word is its use in the language] to be, by and large, a denial of the possibility of theorizing about meaning" (Goldfarb 1983: 279). It seems to me, however, that it would be a mistake to be content with this denial. For the simple answer that meaning is use carries its own difficulty.

---

[18] McDowell cites Crispin Wright as providing "a variant version of this tendency" (2009b: 370).

To say that meaning is use is to say that meaning is intrinsically connected to people's activities. It is to say, in effect, that people at the very least contribute to determining what they mean by their words. But as we saw, and this is crucial, they do so, not just because they use their words in certain ways in certain circumstances – this would be compatible with a reductionist account. Rather, more importantly, they do so because they take their uses to have certain meanings rather than others – this conclusion was forced on us once we had to relinquish reductionism and, more generally, the associative conception.[19] Their uses are the meaningful uses they are because they take them to be that. Now, for words to have meaning, their applications must be governed by standards of correctness; therefore, to take one's words to have certain meanings is to take their applications to be governed by certain standards of correctness. Such standards must of course be objective, that is, capable of being met or not independently of people's say. If they were so dependent, there would, after all, be no distinction between correct and incorrect applications. Whatever application someone would deem to be correct, or incorrect, would be correct, or incorrect, so that, as Wittgenstein says, there would be neither accord nor conflict; and so there would be no meaning. But then we seem to have a puzzle: How can words have meaning, their applications be governed by objective standards of correctness, if people have to contribute to establishing what these are? Wittgenstein's answer, I believe, is encapsulated in one word: agreement.

4.3   Wittgenstein's Treatment of the New Problem

Wittgenstein writes:

The word "agreement"[20] and the word "rule" [and hence "meaning"] are related to one another; they are cousins. (PI: #224)

It is not only agreement in definitions, but also (odd as it may sound) agreement in judgments that is required for communication by means of language. (PI: #242). (Cf. *Remarks on the Foundations of Mathematics* (RFM below): 336, 342)

If there did not exist an agreement in what we call 'red', etc. etc., language would stop. (RFM: 196)

---

[19] I take it that even the quietist accepts this conclusion, though this is, for her, the end of the enquiry.
[20] The same word, 'Übereinstimmung', is sometimes translated as 'accord', sometimes as 'agreement'. Here, following Anscombe, I prefer 'agreement', as it better conveys the requisite sense of activity.

The agreement of ratifications is the pre-condition of our language-game. (RFM: 365)

[Someone] has learnt to operate with written signs according to rules. – Once you have described the procedure of this teaching and learning, you have said everything that can be said about acting correctly according to a rule ... Admittedly going according to a rule is also founded on agreement.

To repeat, what the correct following of a rule consists in cannot be described *more closely* than by describing the *learning* of 'proceeding according to the rule'. (RFM: 392)

These remarks bespeak the connection I mentioned earlier between semantic inquiry and meta-semantic inquiry. Clearly, to my mind, Wittgenstein endorses this connection. According to him, describing how the meaningful uses of words are taught and learnt, how words are applied correctly (which presumably requires distinguishing between correct and incorrect applications), is all it takes to be in a position to say what it is to use words meaningfully – what makes this possible – and what it is for their applications to be governed by the standards of correctness they are governed by. Investigating the "workings of language," not only how languages are taught and learnt, but also how they are used by people to communicate with one another, illuminates the nature of meaning. The semantic work yields meta-semantic results. Now, if this investigation is to shed light on what makes meaning possible, it should do so by addressing the specific difficulty we found in the possibility of meaning, to repeat: How can words have meaning, how can their applications be governed by objective standards of correctness, if people have to contribute to establishing what these are? Wittgenstein says that agreement is required, but what for exactly, and why, and what kind of agreement is required?

According to Wittgenstein, to begin with, agreement is required for communication by language. To be sure, if we reflect on how we communicate with each other and how we inculcate first languages, we soon must acknowledge that a kind of agreement is necessary. In order to communicate, we must agree on what we mean by the words we use.[21] As Wittgenstein says, there must be agreement in definitions, and in what certain things are called. When we teach someone a first language, we teach her how to mean what we do by the words we teach her,[22]

---

[21] At the very least in the sense that speaker and hearer must agree on what the speaker means by her words. Whether Wittgenstein thought that speaker and hearer must also agree on meaning the same things by the same words is a tricky issue I shall not address here. I have discussed this in Verheggen (2006).
[22] Or at the very least we teach her how to mean things by her words that we recognize her as meaning.

which, again, will ensure future communication. This much should be obvious. But Wittgenstein thinks that communication requires not only agreement in definitions, or more generally agreement in what we mean by the words we use, but also agreement in judgments. Moreover, he thinks that agreement in meanings and agreement in judgments are required, not just for communication, but for there to be any language at all. Again: "going according to a rule [using a word meaningfully] is founded on agreement." First, then, in what kind of judgment must there be agreement for communication to be possible?

Wittgenstein does not say, but, as with agreement in meanings, there is a trivial way of understanding the requirement that there be agreement in judgments. What there must be agreement in are, obviously, not any kind of judgments, but basic, what have been called bedrock, judgments. For communication to be possible we must agree, not only in what we call, say, pink, but in whether this, the pink rose, is pink, and in whether the pink rose is the same color as the pink blouse, or whether, when writing down the series +2, writing 1,002 after 1,000 is doing the same thing as writing 1,000 after 998. This agreement in judgments is what makes agreement in meanings and definitions possible. But why must there be agreement in judgments (and hence meanings) for there to be any language at all? Why, in effect, must language be shared for there to be any language at all? The short answer is that thinking of language as being shared is the only way to make sense of the idea that the existence of objective standards is perfectly compatible with these standards being established, in part, by language users. It is, in short, the only way to address Wittgenstein's problem. Here is the longer answer.

Recall once more that, since nothing they may associate their words with could by itself determine their meaning, language users must somehow contribute to establishing what their words mean, that is, what standards of correctness govern their applications. A socially isolated individual cannot do this because, by herself, there is no way she could distinguish between what are correct applications and what seem to her to be correct applications. As Wittgenstein says, on her own, "whatever is going to seem right to [her] is right. And that only means that here we can't talk about 'right'" (PI: #258). Thus, the socially isolated individual cannot establish objective standards. It may then be asked how, together with another person, she can succeed in doing this. And the answer is that two or more people can agree and disagree on what they are talking about. As a result, they can isolate the features of the world to which their words are referring. They can agree that their verbal responses to these features are correct, or incorrect, as the case may be. Importantly, they can also resolve disagreements in ways that are not dependent uniquely on one or the other person's say. Through the resolution of their disagreements, they get the idea that features of the world constrain their judgments, and that the distinction between what seems right and what is right is objective, independent of what they think it is.[23]

Thus, there is an answer to the often-heard opponent's complaint that we still do not get objective standards once we introduce a community, for, as the complaint goes, the interlocutors cannot draw an objective distinction between what is correct and what seems to *them* to be correct.[24] However, they can do so because they have to negotiate how to draw the distinction, against the constraints of the features of the world around them to which they are responding. The isolated individual has only herself to "disagree" with, and thus she can draw the distinction in any way she likes. Moreover, though language users contribute to fixing the standards governing the applications of their words, once these standards are fixed, whether they are met or not is not up to them. In short, though language users' contribution is essential, the world plays an equally crucial role in determining both the meaning of their words and the truth-value of the judgments they make about it. But there is another objection looming.

This is that in order to agree or disagree in their judgments, language users must obviously have a language. Thus, are we not saying in effect that, in order to have a language, language users must have a language? In response, it must be granted that we are saying something circular, which was after all to be expected, since a reductionist account of meaning has proved to be impossible to give. But the circularity is not vicious. We are not saying simply, and tautologically, that language is necessary for language. We are trying to make intelligible the idea that the standards that govern the applications of words are objective, which they have to be if they are to be standards at all, even though language users contribute to establishing them. And we are saying that reflecting on how interlocutors can share judgments about the world around them, judgments which are constrained by features of the world in such a way that they can recognize that their truth or falsity is in part dependent on the way the world is, allows us to make sense of that idea. As I see it, this is the core of Wittgenstein's non-quietism about meaning:

---

[23] Those familiar with Donald Davidson's triangulation argument will recognize the parallels between Davidson's view and the view I am attributing to Wittgenstein. No doubt, I am here influenced by Davidson. Equally no doubt, however, Davidson was himself influenced by Wittgenstein, whom he repeatedly refers to while developing his argument and the related social view of language. See, in particular, Davidson (1994) and (2001d). I also think that Davidson can provide an answer to Kripke's skeptic – see Sultanescu and Verheggen (2019).

[24] See for example, Blackburn (1984).

Language is essentially social, because only in a social context can we solve Wittgenstein's problem.[25]

In sum, according to Wittgenstein, we are in a position to say of someone that she has a language if we can think of her as having used some of her words in communication with others about the world they share, if she has shared some basic judgments about it. This entails that meaning is to be understood in externalist terms, not only, as we just saw, in social externalist terms, but also in physical externalist terms, since the world, as we also just saw, makes an essential contribution to determining meaning as well.[26]

5   Kripke's Path to the Paradox

Let us now briefly review what, according to Kripke, leads to the paradox. As I said at the outset, I take the bulk of Kripke's arguments against received views to be close to those developed by Wittgenstein. What I dispute is the overall skeptical conclusion Kripke draws from those arguments, and hence his treatment of the skeptical problem embodied in the paradox. Kripke introduces this skeptical problem by imagining a skeptic who challenges me, who, by hypothesis, has never computed numbers larger than 57, to cite a fact about myself that would constitute my meaning plus by 'plus', a fact I could also invoke to justify my answering "125" when asked to add 57 and 68.[27] Is there a fact about me that constitutes my meaning plus rather than quus, where 'quus' is defined as a function yielding the sum for numbers lower than 57, and 5 for numbers larger than 57? To begin with, Kripke argues, I cannot point to the ways I have used 'plus' in the past; my past uses of 'plus' are compatible with my meaning quus by 'plus' (WRPL: 10–11). Moreover, he continues, I cannot appeal to instructions I previously gave myself to use 'plus' in certain ways. These would themselves have to be interpreted as instructions to mean plus in order to do the job (WRPL: 15–16). Nor can I invoke an irreducible experience or mental image I have when I use 'plus'. I could have the same experience,

---

[25] There are other constructive claims Wittgenstein makes in connection to this, which, for want of time, I cannot discuss here. Central among them is the idea that to be a language user is to be involved in a custom. (See PI: ## 198-9.) I have discussed this a bit in Verheggen (2017). I have also discussed a bit Wittgenstein's remarks on agreement in Verheggen (2003). In neither piece, however, though I thought that there is a problem left over after the skeptical problem embodied in the paradox has been dissolved, did I appreciate the real nature of the new problem.

[26] See Child (2010) as another proponent of the physical externalist interpretation of Wittgenstein.

[27] Thus the challenge is two-fold; the facts that would meet it must both be constitutive of what I mean by my expressions and justify my applications of them. My focus here is on the constitutive part of the challenge.

or the same image could occur to me, if I meant quus instead of plus; also, I could mean one or the other in the absence of any experience or image (WRPL: 41–42). Invoking a Fregean sense or abstract entity I grasp when I mean plus by 'plus' will not do either. What I grasp is a "finite object," which also needs to be interpreted in a certain way in order to determine which of a potential infinity of applications are correct, and so in order to constitute my meaning plus rather than quus by 'plus' (WRPL: 54).

The meta-semantic question that leads to the paradox, as Kripke presents it, is different, narrower, than Wittgenstein's. Whereas Wittgenstein starts with the general question of what it is for words to mean what they do, or to have meaning, Kripke seems to assume that, for words to have meaning, there must be individual facts that constitute their meaning.[28] Still, his repudiation of all such potential facts is pretty much in line with the way Wittgenstein rejects traditional accounts of what it is for words to mean what they do. None of the items considered will do, because none of them wears a meaning on its sleeves. Each is such that, until it is taken in a certain way, it cannot provide one standard rather than another, and so it cannot determine one meaning rather another. But then each can always be taken in such a way that the application it yields is correct, or incorrect, as the case may be. And so none of the items considered can be meaning-constituting. As I have argued elsewhere,[29] this is true even of dispositions to use words in certain ways, to which Kripke devotes considerable time, though Wittgenstein did not discuss them at all. Dispositions, too, non-semantically characterized, are compatible with meaning one thing rather than another by a given word. No non-semantic characterization could be such that it determines which of all possible applications of the word are correct. Only semantically characterized dispositions, that is, dispositions described as dispositions to use words with certain meanings, would do.[30] But then, Kripke has reached the same conclusion as Wittgenstein: He has repudiated reductionism and, more generally, what I have called the associative conception of meaning. However, whereas Wittgenstein takes this to call for a dissolution of the skeptical problem embodied in the paradox, Kripke takes it as one important step toward a skeptical conclusion. Why is this so?

This is because there is something else that Kripke wants to reject as a potential meaning-constituting individual fact: that of a "primitive state of 'meaning [say] addition by "plus"'." Postulating this state, though he

---

[28] Interestingly, Kripke does not consider external facts to which individuals are related.
[29] See Myers and Verheggen (2016: chapter 2).
[30] I take Kripke to suggest this as well (see WRPL: 28), though he also argues that there are other problems with reductive dispositionalism, having to do with the second part of the challenge as well. (See WRPL: 22–37 for the discussion of dispositionalism.)

admits that it might well be the best move against the skeptic, would still leave its nature "completely mysterious" and, more importantly, would be equally problematic, for a primitive state, too, is finite, and thus it cannot determine that I mean plus for an infinite number of applications of 'plus'. As Kripke asks, "Can we conceive of a finite state which could not be interpreted in a quus-like way?" (WRPL: 51–52). If we cannot, then we must conclude that there is no such thing as meaning anything by any word, as we have not found any individual facts of any kind that could constitute their meaning. However, as we have seen, this skeptical conclusion is not Wittgenstein's. Where then has Kripke gone wrong?

6 Kripke's Misunderstanding of Wittgenstein

First, as I see it, Kripke misdiagnoses the conclusion to be drawn from the paradox. To repeat, the overall conclusion Wittgenstein draws after acknowledging that the theories or pictures of meaning he has considered all lead to the paradox is not that words have no meaning, but that their meaning cannot be explained in the terms appealed to by those theories or pictures. Wittgenstein has dissolved the paradox, rather than accepting a skeptical problem that needs to be solved. Furthermore, Wittgenstein, while repudiating the associative conception of meaning, has introduced an alternative conception, according to which meaning is meaningful use, a conception which in turn generates a new challenge. Kripke, on the other hand, never envisages a conception of what it is for words to have meaning other than the associative conception he has rejected. However, what are we to make, on Wittgenstein's behalf, of Kripke's complaint concerning primitive states of meaning? Does Wittgenstein not accept the claim that states of meaning are primitive, as Kripke suggests that he might? I think he does, but we must be clear on what accepting this amounts to, which should make it plain that the claim is neither mysterious nor problematic, let alone therefore "desperate" (WRPL: 51).

To begin with, I see no reason for Wittgenstein to deny that it is true that I mean game by 'game', pink by 'pink', +2 by '+2'. What makes any of these ascriptions true? In each case, it is simply the fact that this is what I mean. And this fact may be regarded as my being in a certain state. But this is not a mysterious state, nor is it a problematic one.[31] It is not mysterious, for it is not supposed to be the mysterious source of my meaning what I do by any given word. Rather, Wittgenstein gave us

---

[31] McDowell gives a similar interpretation in McDowell (1992) and (2010), though he does not think that we can have an explanation of what makes it possible to be in those states of meaning. I discuss McDowell in Verheggen (2000), where I first suggested this interpretation of Wittgenstein.

some explanation of what makes it possible for me to be in that kind of state. Less misleadingly put, Wittgenstein gave us some explanation of what makes it possible for language users to mean what they do by their words. It is to have used them in communicative interactions with others and features of the world around them. But, again, this strikes me as perfectly compatible with my being in a state of meaning when I use a word meaningfully. However, it is also not the problematic state Kripke envisions, which would lead to skepticism about meaning. The key here is not to understand 'being in a state' as having a finite object in my mind, which would be open to interpretation, but as having a certain ability. To mean what I do by a word involves precisely being capable of deeming an indefinite number of applications to be correct or not. As Wittgenstein writes, how one means one thing or the other by a word is "how meaning it can determine the steps in advance" (PI: #190). And we have seen how he thinks it is that one means one thing rather than another by a word.

If the above interpretation is right, there is no remaining skeptical problem that should somehow be addressed. However, Kripke takes Wittgenstein's remarks on agreement to be doing just that: "Wittgenstein's skeptical solution to his problem depends on agreement" (WRPL: 99). But again, precisely because it is skeptical, the skeptical solution is not a meta-semantic solution; it is not intended to meet the foundational challenge the skeptic has set. Given this, it is no surprise that Kripke understands Wittgenstein's remarks on agreement to play a different role from what I have understood them to play for Wittgenstein. And it is no surprise that he does not recognize that the notion of agreement can be fleshed out, rather than being considered as a mere brute fact. For Kripke, the notion of agreement plays a major role in answering one of the questions he thinks should be asked once we have conceded that the skeptical challenge leading to the paradox, though legitimate, cannot be met and thus that ascriptions of meaning are neither true nor false, namely, the question "Under what conditions may this form of words be appropriately asserted (or denied)?" (WRPL: 73). And the answer is:

We say of someone else that he follows a certain rule [means what he does by an expression] when his responses [applications] agree with our own [in enough cases] and deny it when they do not. (WRPL: 92)

[I]f there was no general agreement in the community responses, the game of attributing concepts to individuals ... could not exist. (WRPL: 96)

There is no objective fact – that we all mean addition by '+', or that a given individual does – that explains our agreement in particular cases. Rather our license to say of each other that we mean addition by '+' is part of a 'language game' that sustains itself only because of the brute fact that we generally agree. (WRPL: 97)

Why, according to Kripke, is agreement needed? First, it is needed because without it, as Wittgenstein also points out, communication – attribution of concepts – would be impossible. Second, it is needed because it makes room for there to be a distinction between correct and incorrect applications of words, which, as also emphasized by Wittgenstein, an isolated individual could not draw. Kripke does not say, however, how a group of people succeeds in making the relevant objective distinction. This is to be expected; in the face of an insoluble problem about meaning, one can only be meta-semantically quiet and hence a kind of quietist about meaning, albeit, to be sure, for very different reasons from the traditional quietist's. And, once one is a quietist about meaning, it is to be expected that the notion of agreement, even though it plays a role in our understanding of how we ascribe meaning to speakers' utterances, cannot further be elucidated as an essential ingredient in language possession.

7 Conclusion

Reflecting anew on Kripke's WRPL has prompted me to think of the issues he raises in terms of distinctions he did not himself draw, at least not explicitly. This has led me to reconsider Wittgenstein's PI and to pin on him a label that many would maintain is mistaken. If Kripke was right about Wittgenstein's treatment of the skeptical problem embodied in the paradox, joining the quietist's ranks would be the only philosophical option. But if, as I think, he was wrong, that is not the only option. I very much doubt that this will be my last word about Wittgenstein, or about Kripke, as they both continue to provoke new thoughts. For now, it is just how Wittgenstein strikes me after rereading Kripke.[32]

---

[32] I am grateful to Robert Myers and Olivia Sultanescu for their comments on an earlier draft of this chapter and for much helpful discussion.

9 How Not to Brush Questions under the Rug

Olivia Sultanescu

Four decades ago, in his *Wittgenstein on Rules and Private Language* (hereafter WRPL), Saul Kripke offered an interpretation of Ludwig Wittgenstein's remarks about rule-following according to which they take the form of a skeptical paradox about meaning. The initial round of critical responses to the paradox focused on the difficulty of accounting for the standards of correctness that are essential for the meaningful use of expressions. Some commentators claimed that this difficulty calls for the adoption of non-reductionism, according to which meaning states, understood to be states individuated by standards of correctness, are *sui generis*, and cannot be accounted for in more basic terms. But some of the earliest proponents of non-reductionism, such as Paul Boghossian and Crispin Wright, have grown more pessimistic about its prospects.[1] For, they claim, even though its adoption might make it possible to vindicate the idea that an individual has a determinate rule or standard of correctness in mind, this does not shed any light on the possibility of a rule being *followed* by that individual. While the puzzle articulated by Boghossian is general, having to do with the fact that rule-following seems to require inference, which is in turn alleged to require the application of a rule, Wright, inspired by Wittgenstein, focuses specifically on the prospects of conceiving of our uses of basic expressions as instances of rule-following. In such cases, Wright argues, we are not guided by any rules. These recent expressions of pessimism about the non-reductionist approach are in fact aligned with the earlier diagnosis offered by Kripke himself in the articulation of the paradox. He represents the non-reductionist approach as dubious, insofar as "it brushes ... questions under the rug" (WRPL: 52). There is some ambivalence in his attitude, for he also says that "if [non-reductionism] is taken in an appropriate way, Wittgenstein may even accept it" (WRPL: 51).

---

[1] This is not to say that they have renounced their commitment to non-reductionism. I have primarily in mind Boghossian (2012) and Wright (2007, 2012).

My topic is not what Wittgenstein might accept, but rather what it might be to take non-reductionism in an appropriate way. What are the prospects of addressing Kripke's challenge in a constructive and illuminating way from within a view of meaning and content that resists any ambition to account for them in more basic terms? I shall begin by examining Kripke's treatment of non-reductionism, and I shall argue that Kripke is concerned with the nature of one's application of a rule to a new case, and not just with the nature of one's internalization of it. I shall then try to show that the proponent of non-reductionism about meaning need not be seen as brushing philosophical questions under the rug. She is in a position to grapple with Kripke's challenge in all its complexity, provided that she does not confine herself to an austere approach.[2]

1 Kripke's Treatment of the Non-Reductionist Response

It is not clear how to understand the question that Kripke raises through his famous exchange with the meaning skeptic. Many interpreters agree that Kripke is articulating a constitutive problem, but the agreement typically ends there.[3] Some interpreters wonder why the question cannot be dealt with by defending a non-reductionist view.[4] Kripke does not think that such a response is satisfactory, and the goal of this section is to explain why.

Envision the following scenario: I visit the Eiffel Tower for the first time, and I see a table at its base, which I am about to point out to

---

[2] Here I am using the notion of austerity in a different way than Hannah Ginsborg uses it in her characterization of Barry Stroud's conception of meaning. She takes non-reductionism to be austere if it maintains that the semantic domain cannot be reduced to the merely intentional or normative domain – "the use which gives "life" or meaning to an expression can be characterized only in terms which presuppose meaning." On a "less austere and partly reductionist approach ... we could account for meaning in terms of a more basic idea of goal-directed human activity" (Ginsborg 2011a: 153). By contrast, I take non-reductionism to be austere if it deprives itself of explanatory resources. One way in which it might do this is by presupposing a conception of philosophical elucidation according to which to elucidate is, necessarily, to confine oneself to notions that are more basic (and independently intelligible) – in other words, to offer a reduction. Such a conception is not compulsory, and the philosopher who subscribes to austerity in Ginsborg's sense of the term need not endorse it.

[3] See Boghossian (1989) for the received interpretation of the paradox as a constitutive problem.

[4] For example, Ginsborg motivates her resistance against the received interpretation by drawing on the apparent easiness with which the paradox can be dealt with via a non-reductionist response. As she sees it, "it can simply be pointed out that Kripke is operating with an unwarrantedly narrow conception of fact, or that he is refusing to accept that meaning facts could be primitive and irreducible" (2018: 153). See also Goldfarb (1985), Boghossian (1989), and McGinn (2002).

the friend accompanying me. Kripke proposes that we consider the following (undoubtedly bizarre, but intelligible nonetheless) supposition: "by 'table' in the past I meant tabair where 'tabair' is anything that is a table not found at the base of the Eiffel Tower, or a chair found there" (WRPL: 19).[5] If this is what I meant, then I should not apply the word to the table; I should presumably apply it to the chair. What sort of facts about my mind or behavior would disprove this rather unusual supposition? For, unless it is disproved, there seem to be no grounds for my application of 'table' to the table at the base of the Eiffel Tower, and ultimately no grounds for thinking that I mean anything by 'table'. The supposition that I meant tabair by 'table' is subsequently represented (in the second chapter of WRPL) as impossible to disprove, for it seems that all the facts about my mind and behavior – such as dispositions, mental images, previous instructions that I might have given myself, and so on – are consistent with my having meant tabair, given that they can be interpreted in a way that secures that meaning. Now, I might of course settle on a different expression in order to pick out the table (I might even switch to a different language), but a similar skeptical supposition can be advanced about that expression, such that, unless I am able to defeat it, I will once again find myself prevented from applying it to the table. I will indeed find myself unable to pick out the table at all! The reasoning concerning 'table' easily generalizes, which leads to the skeptical conclusion that "the entire idea of meaning vanishes into thin air" (WRPL: 22).

In what follows, I shall bracket the issue of the significance of the skeptical dimension of the argument, and I shall not discuss the skeptical solution that Kripke subsequently proposes. Moreover, I shall not hesitate to attribute claims to Kripke himself, as opposed to Kripke's Wittgenstein. Even though Kripke insists that he does not articulate his own views in WRPL, and even though he represents himself as not endorsing the skeptical line of reasoning that he expounds, he also says that the problem that he was struck by when reading Wittgenstein, regardless of whether or not it is Wittgenstein's own problem, is "important, deserving of serious consideration" (WRPL: 5). My aim is to shed light on the nature of this problem.

As I suggested earlier, a natural response to the challenge to disprove the bizarre supposition is to say that it is simply a fact about me that I meant table by 'table', and that my meaning table by 'table' is a *sui generis* state. Meaning states – and content-involving states more generally – constitute a distinctive kind, and the expectation that there

---

[5] In developing the argument, Kripke primarily relies on a mathematical example, involving the functions of addition and quaddition, which I shall not rehearse here.

is a set of facts to which meaning facts can be reduced is misguided. Kripke rejects this response, raising two complaints against it. The first is that the non-reductionist owes us an account of self-knowledge, and, given the austerity of her view – for, again, all that she is represented as saying is that the state of meaning something by an expression is "simply a primitive state ... of a unique kind of its own" (WRPL: 51) – she is bound to lack resources for developing it. But Kripke does not assign much significance to this complaint. The second complaint involves a difficulty that he takes to constitute a serious obstacle for the proposed non-reductionist response:

> Even more important [for the assessment of non-reductionism] is the logical difficulty implicit in Wittgenstein's sceptical argument. I think that Wittgenstein argues ... that it is logically impossible (or at least that there is a considerable logical difficulty) for there to be a state of 'meaning addition by "plus"' at all. (WRPL: 51–52)

What is the nature of the logical difficulty? In Kripke's words, "such a state would have to be a finite object, contained in our finite minds," and even though "it does not consist in my explicitly thinking of each case of the addition table," we would have to concede that "in a *queer* way" each such case is "in some sense present." Kripke goes on to ask: "What can that sense be? Can we conceive of a finite state which *could* not be interpreted in a quus-like way? How could that be?" He concludes that the proposal that there are *sui generis* states of meaning "brushes such questions under the rug, since the nature of the supposed 'state' is left mysterious" (WRPL: 52).

It might be thought that Kripke fails to appreciate that the power of meaning states to classify performances into correct and incorrect is intrinsic to their nature, so there is no additional explanatory task regarding that power that needs to be discharged once we take such states to be *sui generis*. Alternatively, it might be thought that Kripke's position depends on an assumption that it is open to us to reject – indeed, we ought, in light of its disastrous consequences, to reject it – namely, that guidance by an item always requires assigning an interpretation to that item. If something can issue guidance without being interpreted, the fact that it can be interpreted in more than one way does not pose a problem; we have no reason to think that it is not possible for a finite state to guide.[6] What is at issue, on each of these two readings, is the nature of the state of meaning something by an expression. Consequently, it

---

[6] The claim that Kripke assumes that understanding always requires interpretation, failing to see that this assumption in fact serves as a target for Wittgenstein's remarks, is made in McDowell (1984).

might seem that the question that Kripke raises is how it is possible for "finite minds like ours to instantiate [this] sort of state" (Boghossian 2012: 33). But if this is the question, then it is indeed hard to see why non-reductionism cannot be the answer.

A crucial aspect of this line of interpretation is that we are supposed to investigate the nature of meaning states – their power to sort indefinitely many uses of expressions into correct and incorrect, their ability to guide, even the very possibility of their being instantiated – without attending to whether and in what way expressions are *actually* used by the speaker.[7] This is what allows Wright, for instance, to take himself to be presenting a new set of puzzles, which target "the transition from a rule 'in mind'… to its (correct) application in a given particular context," and which are allegedly "different; and crucially so" (2012: 381) from the paradox raised by Kripke. But it seems to me that the significance of the ordinary perspective of the language-user for Kripke's argument is undeniable, and that this interpretation fails to capture it.[8] What is at issue is the way in which we might make philosophical sense of the possibility of using an expression in a new scenario from within that perspective. As Kripke describes it, the challenge he presents is supposed to be seen as a challenge "from the 'inside'" (WRPL: 15). In his discussion of the Eiffel Tower example, he characterizes the problem as being about the way in which I "determine my use of the word ['table']" in this scenario, or "the basis of my present particular response" involving that word (WRPL: 20–21). This in turn suggests that the problem is not (just) about the nature of meaning states; it is (also) about the nature of meaningful uses. In other words, it concerns not (just) the internalization of the rule, but (also) its application to a new case. Kripke recognizes that the two issues are connected. For him, the question of the nature of meaning cannot be divorced from the question of the nature of meaningful use of words.

What is it for a response to have a basis in the relevant sense? It is a platitude that the use of words is governed by standards of correctness (or rules) that sort them into correct or incorrect. Standards are, by their nature, general. To put it crudely, they are not about this or that particular bit of reality. They cover indefinitely many potential bits of reality. To be a language user is to have internalized rules or standards governing the use of words, an internalization that allows one to understand those uses and deem them correct or incorrect. However, when I use language, I do so within a particular context – in response to a particular bit of reality,

---

[7] I do not intend to attribute this frame of mind to McDowell, whose criticism of Kripke's argument are issued, in part, from a careful consideration of actual use.
[8] I say more about this in Sultanescu (2023).

as it were. I must apply the rule I had previously internalized to that bit of reality. Kripke, drawing on Wittgenstein's remarks, seems to me to think that this leads to a puzzle. On the one hand, there must be a sense in which the relevant application is somehow contained in my mind, because, to repeat, internalizing the rule *just is* internalizing something that covers indefinitely many cases – indefinitely many bits of reality. This is what Kripke has in mind when he says, drawing on Wittgenstein's remarks, that "'in a *queer* way' each such case already is 'in some sense present'" in my mind (WRPL: 52). On the other hand, there must be a sense in which the relevant application is *not* already present in my mind. I have to *apply* the rule to the particular case I am confronted with, and to which I am able, in virtue of having internalized the rule, to respond appropriately. This is why Kripke's examples involve numbers that I have not computed before, or encounters with bits of the world that are unfamiliar. The response, it seems, has to be in some sense worked out. I am not already there; I have to think my way there. The question that Kripke raises concerns what it is to arrive at one's response, for example, to come to apply 'table' to the table. Any interpretation according to which Kripke is merely wondering about "how could there so much as be a correctness condition" (Boghossian 1989: 516), or about "how it is that anything we do, or can do, amounts to the constitution of unique meanings, autonomously so conceived" (Wright 2012: 380) fails to bring it into view.

If that question is (at least in part) what Kripke is after, the complaint that the non-reductionist is brushing questions under the rug is reasonable, especially if all she has to say is that meaning states are *sui generis*. Merely insisting on the *sui generis* nature of those states might plausibly strike one as akin to a refusal to engage with the question, rather than a way of grappling with it. But is Kripke right in thinking that the non-reductionist has no choice but to brush the question under the rug? There is a naïve reply that seems to be immediately available to her, and which can be motivated by appealing to the fact that, when we follow a rule and we are asked for a reason, we can cite the rule and the fact that the circumstances called for its application; we can provide an inferential justification. This is a feature of our ordinary way of conceiving of rule-following. The proponent of the non-reductionist response might, then, say that to work out one's response is simply to infer what the rule requires in a particular case and act accordingly. To mean table by 'table' is to follow the rule according to which 'table' applies correctly to tables; when one encounters a table at the base of the Eiffel Tower, one is seemingly in a position to infer that the word applies correctly to it, and thus in a position to use the word meaningfully in that context. The move from the generality of the rule, which accounts for indefinitely many contexts, to the particularity of the context in which one finds oneself can be elucidated in inferential terms. We are, of course, owed an account of the nature of this inference, so there is still philosophical work to be done, but there is no reason to think that resisting reductionism prevents one from doing it.

2   The Plausibility of the Naïve Reply

The trouble is that if we attend to our most basic classifications of the world, we will see, Wright argues, that the naïve view is unworkable. The argument relies on a picture of rule-following according to which it is comprised of two elements: the commitment to the rule, on the one hand, and the judgment that the circumstances that trigger its application obtain, on the other.[9] He proposes that we use what he calls "the *modus ponens* model" (a label that I shall borrow) in order to represent the elements involved: "The rule is stated in the form of a general conditional. A minor premise states that, in the circumstances in question, the condition articulated in the antecedent of the rule is met. The conclusion derives the mandate, prohibition, or permission concerned" (2007: 491). This corresponds to the kind of inferential justification characteristic of the naïve view mentioned earlier. For example, if I am committed to listening to the BBC news report about the war in Ukraine each morning at 6 am, then, if it is 6 am, I am required to listen to the BBC news report about the war. Consequently, my listening to the BBC news report is something that I do for a reason, supplied by my commitment to that rule. Whether, in any particular case, the conditions that trigger the commitment obtain is something that I am in a position to appreciate independently of that commitment. My behavior can be viewed as guided by the rule.

The question is why this intuitive way of thinking about rule-following is taken to lapse in basic cases of language use. Of course, in order to determine whether 'table' applies to the object in front of one, one must determine whether that object is a table. Determining this obviously requires that one deploys the very concept of table; one must possess the concept in order to be in a position to judge whether the situation calls for one's use of the word 'table'. On Wright's view, this suggests that in order for the model to capture uses of 'table' and other basic expressions, speakers must be viewed as being capable of thinking about the world prior to being capable of saying things about it. This in turn requires that we subscribe to "a general picture of thought as an activity of the mind,

---

[9] Cf. Boghossian's characterization: "In rule-following, I will say, there is, on the one hand, a *commitment*, on the part of the thinker, to uphold a certain pattern in his thought or behavior; and, on the other, some behavior that expresses that commitment, that is explained and rationalized by it" (2012: 31).

which language merely clothes" (2007: 496). This general picture, which Wright calls "the Augustinian picture of language," has been repudiated by Wittgenstein, whose *Philosophical Investigations* is described as pursuing "a journey of recoil" from it (2007: 495). Our reflection about the nature of language must be consistent with that journey. Wright thinks that we have no choice, then, but to reject the idea that our basic uses of language may be viewed as responses to the requirements of rules, which is allegedly tantamount to embracing the Wittgensteinian conclusion that our uses of language are ultimately blind, where the blindness of a response is contrasted to its being based on a reason. We might still say that rule-following is rational "in the sense that it involves intentionality and a willingness to accept correction in light of error" (Wright 2007: 498). But our basic engagements with the world cannot intelligibly be conceived of as instances of reason-responsiveness.

Even though the incoherence of the Augustinian picture is not in question, Wright's reasoning should still strike us as puzzling. On the face of it, all that we are entitled to infer from the rejection of the Augustinian picture, according to which language merely clothes thought, is that our "conceptual repertoire" ought not to be viewed as anterior to the "understanding of any particular rule" (Wright 2007: 496). But this leaves room for the possibility that it be viewed as concomitant to it. This is to say that nothing in the rejection of that picture prevents us from viewing the capacity to apply concepts as being on the same level as the capacity to be guided by standards of correctness for linguistic expressions: neither can be had without the other, and neither can be accounted for except in terms that exploit the intelligibility of the other. Wright appears to exclude this view from the outset.

What might the grounds for this exclusion be? They seem to involve the assumption that the *modus ponens* model is apt only when the two premises or steps are extricable.[10] In the basic cases, they are bound to be inextricable, and so the model allegedly fails to apply. But Wright's notion of inextricability calls for scrutiny. On one reading, the premises are inextricable when thinking or judging the content corresponding to the minor premise requires an application of the very rule specified by the major premise.[11] However, this cannot be the sense at play in Wright's

---

[10] See for example, Wright (2007: 495).
[11] For example, in earlier work, Wright writes: "I cannot always have concepts *other* than those whose governing rules I am trying to observe in a particular situation in terms of which I can formulate a separate judgment of the input to which these rules are to be applied" (1989b: 256). This passage is admittedly not very clear, but it seems to me to suggest that the problem is that the rule being followed is already involved in the appreciation of the obtaining of its input conditions.

argument, for one can judge or believe that something is red without deploying any linguistic standard. When explaining why the *modus ponens* model cannot apply to basic cases, Wright says that "the clean separation effected by the *modus ponens* model between what belongs to the rule and what belongs to the situation to which it is to be applied is possible only in (relatively complex) cases where the conditions which trigger the application of the rule – those described in the antecedent of the relevant conditional – can be *recognised and characterised in innocence of a mastery of the rule.*"[12] For the premises to be inextricable, the thinking or judging of the content corresponding to the minor premise must be able to be done by someone who has not already accepted the rule specified in the major premise. This is because discerning the circumstances that trigger the rule must be able to be done by someone who is not already committed to that rule, or so Wright seems to think. By contrast, in our example, discerning the fact that the object is a table requires a competence that can be had only by a subject who is already able to deploy 'table' (or some other word with the same meaning), and thus only by a subject who is already committed to the standard for the correct application of 'table' (or of some other word with the same meaning). This shows, in Wright's view, that one cannot be said to be genuinely guided by that standard. Indeed, one cannot be said to be guided by rules – or, more generally, to be acting for reasons – in one's uses of basic expressions.

On this view, we can locate our linguistic activity within the space of reasons only if we are successful in accommodating its "input-rationality," which amounts to such activity being "the product of a rational response to *anterior*, reason-giving states" (2007: 499, italics added). Reason-giving states can count as anterior to the states for which they give reasons only if the former can be individuated or constituted independently of the latter. This suggests that any rational relations they might bear to the latter are incidental to their integrity. On this view, reason-giving-ness operates as a layer that is extrinsic to contentfulness; it cannot be constitutive of contentfulness.

This conception of contentful states might seem mandatory only in the light of the assumption – which, as we have seen, Kripke shares – that all that a non-reductionist position can amount to is the bare idea that a thought's possessing intentional content is a primitive fact, and thus something that we are entitled to take for granted in our theorizing. On this picture, contentful thoughts might illuminate other mental phenomena, but are not themselves to be illuminated in any way. As Boghossian puts it, to "help [oneself] to an anti-reductionist view of mental content"

---

[12] Wright (2007: 494), italics added. See also Wright (2007: 493).

is simply to assume that "contentful thoughts are available" and that such thoughts "can be used to frame intentions – and so, it would seem, to account for our acceptance of rules" (2012: 39). This aligns with Wright's insistence, mentioned earlier, to the effect that the contentfulness of our basic engagements with the world remains unaffected by the revocation of the rational status of those engagements. Contentfulness is regarded as a basic datum whose integrity is not affected by philosophical moves made elsewhere, no matter how radical.

If one equates adopting non-reductionism with allowing oneself to rely on the notions of meaning and content, one will indeed seemingly have no choice but to take the fact that a state has intentional content as an explanatory primitive, incapable of receiving philosophical elucidation. Meaningfulness or contentfulness are viewed as providing basic materials for inquiry, but their nature and possibility cannot themselves serve as objects for that inquiry.[13] As a result, the full space of theoretical options within the non-reductive approach does not even come into view. But there is an alternative to viewing non-reductionism as a license to posit primitive meaning states. It is to view it as a commitment to the claim that the elucidation of what it is for us to use expressions meaningfully is bound to exploit the notion of meaningful use; it is thus bound to result in a conception of meaning and understanding that is given "from inside" meaning and understanding.[14] What this picture does not require is thinking that the nature of meaning and understanding – the nature and possibility of contentfulness more broadly – cannot be investigated.

To go back to Wright's reasoning, the idea that one must be able to make a rule-independent judgment about the context and subsequently determine whether the commitment to the rule requires that one apply it in that context is mandatory only if we are trying to give an account of what it is to follow rules "from outside" an understanding of those rules. But embracing non-reductionism, which is something that Wright represents himself as doing, requires recognizing the hopelessness of this ambition. The justification for using expressions in certain ways cannot always be given "from outside" an understanding of those expressions; the justification for applying a rule in a particular context cannot always be given "from outside" an understanding of that rule. More specifically, when it comes to basic cases of language use, the justification is bound to take for granted that the individual understands the relevant expressions. This does not entail that we have to conceive of basic cases of language

---

[13] But couldn't one posit contentfulness and subsequently inquire whether the posit was introduced at the appropriate place? The problem that I am raising does not concern the moment when the posit is made, but rather its status as a theoretical posit.
[14] Cf. Stroud (2012: 32).

use as *blind*, as not based on reasons. But it does entail that we have to conceive of the reasons for using expressions as being only within the reach of individuals who are already committed to standards for their use. Thus, we ought to reject the extricability requirement, and the aptness of the *modus ponens* model ought to be reassessed in light of this rejection.[15]

Now, it might turn out that this reassessment will lead back to the conclusion that the model does not illuminate basic cases. For example, one might object that the applicability of the idea of inference requires that one be viewed as making a cognitive advancement from premises to conclusion. If the premises already employ the concept of table, what room is there for saying that the conclusion, which concerns the use of the word 'table', counts as such an advancement? In deploying the concept of table (in the step corresponding to the minor premise), did one not already settle the question of whether to use the word 'table' in the particular context in which one finds oneself?

This is a legitimate worry, with which we must eventually wrestle. But we ought not to assume that a view lacks the resources for doing so merely as a result of resisting reductionism. I shall return to this issue in Section 3. For now, let us recall that what puzzles Kripke is the seeming tension involved in the conception of the application of a rule according to which it both is and is not already present in the mind that internalized the rule. The question is how to make philosophical sense, from within the language-user's perspective, of the transition from her general understanding of an expression to the particular context in which that understanding is deployed, in a way that preserves the intuitive idea that the application is somehow already contained in the language-user's mind. The appeal to the notion of inference helps us to deal with the puzzle, for it allows us to view the general understanding as inferentially connected to the application made in the particular context. This in turn allows us to preserve the intelligibility of a rational basis for the language-user's response, which amounts to its being assigned a location within a broader rational structure. The perspective of the language-user is a practical perspective, fully permeated by reason-responsiveness.[16] More generally, the point of defending the applicability of the *modus ponens* model is to vindicate the view that the use of language is a manifestation of our rational nature, of our capacity to act on reasons. This is what Wright suggests cannot be done.

---

[15] See Miller (2015) for a different response to Wright's position.
[16] I understand the practical point of view to be "a distinctively first-personal perspective defined by our interest in the deliberative question of what we ought to do" (Wallace 2006: 153). The fact that we do not usually deliberate about how to apply our expressions does not show that the point of view of the user of expressions is not practical. What matters for its practicality is that the question is intelligible.

What, more specifically, ought we to say in response to the puzzle concerning the application of a rule in a new case? To mean table by 'table' is to be committed to a standard according to which the expression applies correctly to some things, namely, the things which are tables. The fact that the expression is applicable to the object at the base of the Eiffel Tower might be something that one has not considered. But to notice that there is a table at the base of the Eiffel Tower is, given the aforementioned commitment, to conclude that the expression is correctly applicable to it. Sometimes, the task is to try to show that our naïve and intuitive understanding can survive philosophical scrutiny.

3 The Case of Judgment

Even if it is granted that we have rendered intelligible the transition from one's general grasp of a standard of correctness for the use of 'table' to a particular application of that expression, this elucidation presupposes that one is able to judge that the thing in front of one is a table; it thus presupposes that one is able to deploy the *concept* of table. One might plausibly complain that the question of how to make sense of the transition from a general grasp of the concept to a particular application of it has not yet been dealt with. And this is, the thought goes, the core of Kripke's problem.[17]

Let us spell out this line of reasoning in more detail. The distinction between correct and incorrect applications of concepts is parallel to the distinction between correct and incorrect uses of expressions. There are standards of correctness governing the application of concepts, just as there are standards of correctness governing the use of words. It seems plausible that when I notice that there is a table in front of me, I am guided by my grasp of the concept or by my mastery of it, just as when I use the word 'table' to say that there is a table, I am guided by my understanding of that word. Moreover, even though Kripke focuses on the use of language and the metalinguistic correctness characteristic of it (WRPL: 9), his line of reasoning targets the notion of content broadly construed.

But the idea of guidance that is at play in this line of reasoning needs careful handling. Is the sense in which one is guided, in one's application

---

[17] For example, Matthias Haase takes the rule-following problem to concern the application of concepts. As he sees it, "the root of the difficulty is a puzzle about the peculiar shape that the relation between the general and the particular takes on when it comes to the relation in which a *finite thinker* stands to the concept she deploys in her judgments" (2009: 284).

of a concept, by one's grasp of the concept the same as (or even in the proximity of) the sense in which one is guided, in one's uses of a word, by one's understanding of that word? On the face of it, there is a difference between the two cases: to use an expression is to act intentionally, but to judge is not to act intentionally. One might intend to say that there is a table at the bottom of the Eiffel Tower, and then execute that intention (or fail to do so). But one cannot intend to judge that there is a table at the bottom of the Eiffel Tower.[18] Now, it might be thought that this difference puts no pressure on the idea that both kinds of activities are instances of rule-following in the relevant sense, and that the need to account for the transition from the grasp of a concept, which is general, to the particular application of it in a determinate context is just as pressing as the need to account for the transition from the grasp of a standard of correctness for an expression to the particular use of it. In both cases, a general rule is brought to bear on a particular case. Moreover, it is indisputable that I am capable of judging not only that there is a table at the base of the Eiffel Tower, but also that there is a table in my living room, or on my friend's balcony, or in countless other situations. One does not grasp a concept unless one is able to deploy it in indefinitely many judgments. Surely, the thought goes, all these judgments must have something in common – the deployment of the same concept – and, surely, the explanation for each of them must somehow draw on that concept.

The explanation for a subject's judgments must indeed draw on the subject's having the concepts deployed in those judgments. But this does not show that it must belong to the same order as the explanations characteristic of the subject's use of language. That there is a difference can be seen by attending to the nature of the why-question that can be intelligibly asked in each case. Suppose that, as I am describing the items at the base of the Eiffel Tower, I am asked why I used the word 'table'. This question is different from asking why I said that there is a table at the base of the Eiffel Tower. The former might strike one as an odd question – it certainly comes less naturally to us than the latter – but it is not unintelligible. I can answer it by invoking what I mean by the word, that is, by pointing not to the table in front of me, but to the standard

---

[18] One might intend to assess the situation or to look for a table, but this is different from intending that one make a judgment with a determinate content. For example, I might intend to determine whether there is a cat in the garden, but I cannot intend to *conclude* that there is one. I do not take a stand on the question of the extent to which the notion of a mental act is helpful in spelling out what it is to make up one's mind about what is the case. The claim that there is a relevant disanalogy between deploying a concept and employing an expression does not require taking such a stand.

of correctness that governs the uses of the word 'table'. "I take 'table' to be correctly applicable to tables, and there is a table there!", I might say. Admittedly, this will not be a complete explanation of my use, but it goes some way toward that explanation. To say that the standard of correctness guides and explains my use is to say that I might appeal to it if asked to justify my use, and that I would not use the expression in this way if I did not view the use as supported by the standard. The standard need not be consciously contemplated when the word is used in order for it to be said to guide the use.[19]

At this stage, one might reasonably ask how the use of an expression can be justified by repeating that expression.[20] We must, once again, acknowledge that the justification is bound to be internal to the understanding of the expression; external justifications, justifications that draw on considerations that are antecedently intelligible, cannot be had. Our conception of the reason-responsiveness of the perspective of the language-user should not hinge on the possibility of providing justifications that are external in this sense.

Now, suppose that I am asked why I deployed the *concept* of table (as opposed to the corresponding expression). How might I deal with such a question? The only way in which it can be taken to be intelligible, it seems to me, is if it is taken to ask for a reason for judging that the thing in front of me is a table.[21] If it is construed in this way, the question is familiar enough. I might answer it by saying that it looks to me as though it is. I might draw on my general understanding of what it is for something to be a table: it has four legs, there are items placed on it, and so on. Thus, in response to the aforementioned question, I might make additional judgments, revealing my thinking that there is a table at the base of the Eiffel Tower to be supported by reasons. Ultimately, it is because the world is the way it is that I judge in the ways in which I do. It is the world that guides me in my thinking, and I will point to the world if I am pressed to justify my thinking.

The interlocutor might complain that I am misunderstanding her. She is not asking for the ground of the judgment that there is a table; her concern is not epistemological. She is asking for what might be regarded

---

[19] Ginsborg may be right that "the idea that we "follow directions" in our use of expressions looks like a philosopher's conception of what is involved in the meaningful use of language, not like something which language-users "ordinarily" suppose" (2022: 883), but this does not seem to me to show that the ordinary perspective of the language-user is not permeated by reason-responsiveness.
[20] Cf. McDowell (1984: 241).
[21] Or if it is taken as a demand for a reason for the use of the word 'table', discussed previously.

as the *metaphysical* ground of a particular deployment of the concept of table. But now it looks as though a shift has occurred, for what the interlocutor seems to be demanding is an account of my having the concept of table in the first place. More generally, the demand seems to be for an account of one's thoughts involving the concepts (or having the contents) that they do. But if this is the demand, then we seem to have moved from descriptive matters, concerning first-order explanations for acts and attitudes – explanations prompted by questions about why a particular action was performed or a particular judgment was made – to foundational matters, concerning the metaphysical underpinnings of those acts and attitudes. This shift is tantamount to a call for inquiry into the way in which the contents of thoughts are determined and, more generally, into the conditions that make language and thought possible. But this inquiry is of a different order than the first-order inquiry into the reasons for one's thoughts and attitudes, and so is the resulting explanation.

If we acknowledge the distinction between two levels of inquiry, pertaining to descriptive matters and foundational matters, respectively, it is not clear why we should accept that there is a relationship in which the thinker stands, *qua* thinker, with the concepts she deploys, such that she can be said to be guided by those concepts, or to be following the standards of correctness distinctive of them. Certainly, thoughts are essentially structured, and foundational inquiry must shed light on their being so.[22] Possessing the concept of table is a necessary condition for having thoughts about tables, thoughts that involve that concept. But possessing the concept might be a matter of having an understanding of what it is for something to be a table, which is tantamount to having thoughts about tables. The suggestion that there must be something over and above the judgments, a representation or an item in the mind – the concept or the rule – that guides the thinker in the making of those judgments, and for which foundational inquiry has to account, appears unmotivated. The guidance distinctive of the meaningful use of expressions might not be replicated at the level of concept application. Once we articulate a foundational account of the contents of our thoughts, we might very well discover that there is no remaining puzzle concerning the transition from the general to the particular in need of treatment.

---

[22] Here we might point to what Gareth Evans refers to as "the generality constraint," which he articulates in terms of the notion of a conceptual ability: someone "who thinks that John is happy and that Harry is happy exercises on two occasions the conceptual ability which we call 'possessing the concept of happiness'" (1982: 101). He adds: "And similarly someone who thinks that John is happy and that John is sad exercises on two occasions a single ability, the ability to think of, or think about, John" (1982: 102).

4 The Need for Foundational Inquiry

Let us now return to the naïve view, according to which the idea of an inferential connection helps us make sense of how a rule can be applied in a new case. We have seen that the adoption of non-reductionism makes it unsurprising that, in basic cases, the justification for the application of a rule can only be given "from inside" a commitment to that rule. But we have also noted that the aptness of the notion of inference, which seems intuitively to involve the idea of a cognitive advancement from premises to conclusion, is questionable. More generally, one might think that in order for a belief or action to be based on a reason, the appreciation of the reason must be anterior to it. To put it differently, the subject's access to the reason must be prior to the thought or action that the reason is for. If we insist on the applicability of the *modus ponens* model to basic cases, we risk a distortion of the notion of inference to the point of rendering it unrecognizable, or so the objection goes.

The idea that the justification for the application of a rule can only be given "from inside" a commitment to that rule, which enabled us to reject the demand that the premises in the *modus ponens* model be extricable, suggests that the contents of our thoughts are internally related; thoughts have their contents partly in virtue of patterns of reason of the sort captured by the *modus ponens* model. But if the contents of thoughts are so related, in basic cases there may be no advancement from premises to conclusions, or from the appreciation of the reason for a belief or action to that belief or action. Judging that the object in front of one is a table and judging that the word 'table' applies correctly to it, given one's commitment to the standard of correctness for the word, might not always be separable. We ought to abandon, then, the intuition that motivated the objection. A subject's access to the reasons for her thoughts or actions is not always prior to those thoughts or actions. Not all the elements of our intuitive conception survive philosophical scrutiny.

That thoughts stand in internal relations is a claim that many philosophers who resist reductionism might accept. But in order to defend it, we need a foundational account of the determination of the contents of thoughts that reveals thoughts as standing in such relations. The distinction between descriptive matters and foundational matters is not always observed, especially in debates concerning the prospects of reductionism.[23]

---

[23] For example, Stroud spells out the idea that meaning and understanding can only receive an "engaged, internal" specification in two different ways. On the one hand, he takes it to mean that specifying the meaning of an expression or specifying what someone means by an expression cannot be done without using that expression (or another expression with the same meaning). This is a claim belonging to the descriptive level. On the other hand, he takes it to mean that we cannot specify the facts in virtue of which

One philosopher who does observe it is Donald Davidson.[24] Davidson recognizes the hopelessness of the reductive aspiration, but unlike some of those who share that recognition, he does not abandon foundational inquiry. On his view, the contents of thoughts are internally related in just the way mentioned earlier: thoughts have the contents they do partly in virtue of patterns of reason of the sort captured by the *modus ponens* model. But he provides a foundational argument in support of his claim.

The argument purports to establish that someone cannot have thoughts with determinate contents or use expressions meaningfully unless she has interacted with another individual against the constraints of the world they share.[25] It starts from the premise that thoughts and utterances are caused by the world. If we want to understand how the contents of thoughts and the meanings of words are determined, we must attend to the way in which the world causally constrains one. But causal constraints cannot by themselves imbue minds with determinate thoughts and meanings. In order for one to think determinate thoughts and for there to be determinate meanings, the aspects of the world must be properly discerned. Davidson claims that if an individual confronts the world on her own, she is bound to be incapable of properly discerning its aspects. Engagement with another and, simultaneously, features of the shared world is required. Such engagement enables each participant, through the pursuit of the disagreements that it makes possible, to be in a position to appreciate the distinction between appearance and reality, and to make up her own mind about the world. This is the source of Davidson's metaphor of triangulation.

It is a crucial aspect of the argument that these steps are not supposed to be viewed as temporal stages in the acquisition of language and thought. Nor do they correspond to distinct layers of mindedness. Instead, they are supposed to reveal the necessary and mutually illuminating connections between certain capacities of ours (such as the capacity to think and to use language) and concepts that are central to the constitution of those capacities (such as the concept of truth, which is a primitive concept, and which Davidson takes to be intimately connected to the awareness of our own fallibility). If the argument goes through, we

---

expressions have meaning or in virtue of which someone means what she does by her expressions without drawing on the notions of meaning and understanding. This is a claim belonging to the foundational level. See Stroud (2017: 129–130).

[24] See for example, the papers collected in Davidson (2001c). See also Verheggen (2021), where Davidson's commitment to non-reductionism is discussed in light of the distinction between semantic theory and metasemantic theory, and Jackman (2005), where Davidson's commitment to holism is discussed in light of this distinction.

[25] I am drawing on Claudine Verheggen's reconstruction of the argument. See chapter 1 of Myers and Verheggen (2016).

can see how the holistic nature of our thoughts and commitments might be vindicated: the contents of thoughts cannot be determined unless the contents of many other thoughts are determined. A subject's conception of the world cannot be the product of a step-by-step acquisition of discretely individuated thoughts. Ultimately, what underpins the holistic structure of thought is the mind's deep aim of getting the world right, an aim that can only be pursued by inquiring into it (and conversing about it) with others.

Obviously, my aim here is not to defend the Davidsonian account that I just sketched but only to offer it as an example of the kind of foundational inquiry for which descriptive claims call. Kripke, followed by Boghossian and Wright, seem to assume that to espouse non-reductionism is to release oneself from the obligation of pursuing such inquiry. This saddles them with a narrow conception of meaningfulness that mirrors, in some respects, the sort of reductive structure that they seek to resist. But their assumption is mistaken. Non-reductionism need not brush foundational questions under the rug. It owes us answers to such questions.[26]

---

[26] I presented earlier versions of this chapter in the workshop "Kripke's *Wittgenstein on Rules and Private Language* at 40" at York University in June 2022, in the *Rule-Following and Normativity* Seminar held in the Winter of 2021 at CUNY, and in workshops at the University of Chicago in 2021 and 2022. I am grateful to all the participants in these events, especially to Chris Campbell, Melina Garibovic, Hannah Ginsborg, Matthias Haase, Anandi Hattiangadi, Henry Jackman, Gus Law, Alex Leferman, Alex Miller, Robert Myers, Ermioni Prokopaki, James Shaw, Samuel Steadman, Anubav Vasudevan, Claudine Verheggen, Ben Winokur, and José Zalabardo. I am most grateful to Claudine Verheggen for her comments on the chapter and for many illuminating discussions on its topic.

10 Quadders and Zombies
A Kripkean Argument against Physicalism

Anandi Hattiangadi

1 Introduction

I was introduced to Saul Kripke's *Wittgenstein on Rules and Private Language* (1982)[1] toward the end of the first year of my doctoral studies in Cambridge, when I was still casting around for a suitable dissertation topic, much to the dismay of my supervisors. I recall reading the book feverishly in a single sitting, as one might read a whodunnit, and I knew immediately what I would write my dissertation on. I was struck by the intuitive force of the argument Kripke presents and was perplexed by its paradoxical conclusion: that there is no such thing as *intentionality*, no such thing as meaning or content, no semantic or intentional properties or facts at all.[2]

Needless to say, I am not alone in taking an interest in *WRPL*. At the time of writing, it has been cited 6,094 times.[3] And yet, it seems to me that the force and significance of the argument has been systematically underestimated, particularly by mainstream philosophers of mind and language, who may have relegated it to the Wittgensteinian fringe. I hope, in this chapter, to take some steps toward remedying that situation. As I will argue here, *WRPL* contains the resources for a powerful argument against the physicalist thesis that meanings and contents exist but are in some sense "nothing over and above" the physical.[4] It thus has profound significance for the mind-body problem and foundational meta-semantics, two core issues in the philosophy of mind and language.

---

[1] Henceforth, *WRPL*.
[2] Though Kripke explicitly focuses on linguistic meaning, and concludes that "[t]here can be no such thing as meaning anything by any word" (Kripke 1982: 55), his argument broadly targets *intentionality*, the property of being *about* something or other; since this property is shared by mental and linguistic representations, Kripke's argument generalizes to the claim that there are no semantic or intentional properties and facts (Boghossian 1989; Hattiangadi 2007).
[3] Google Scholar, August 13, 2023.
[4] Kearns and Magidor (2012) similarly suggest that an argument for dualism might be developed on the basis of those in *WRPL*, though they do not develop such an argument in detail.

The argument I put forward here is inspired both by *WRPL* and by Kripke's discussion of the mind-body problem in *Naming and Necessity*[5] (1972, which, incidentally, celebrates 50 years since its first publication in 2022 as well). One might say that my argument is doubly Kripkean. However, the conclusion I will draw from the argument against physicalism is the semantic dualist thesis that intentionality is real and fundamental, and this clearly goes against the conclusion of the skeptical argument in *WRPL*.[6] Does this undermine my argument's claim to be Kripkean? Not at all! As Kripke reveals, the argument advanced in *WRPL* is not so much his own as one that struck him in the course of his reading of Wittgenstein (Kripke 1982: viii). Moreover, I have reason to believe that semantic dualism comes close to the view Kripke himself endorsed, beyond his clearly anti-physicalist arguments in *N&N*. I will never forget the moment, during the Q and A of a presentation of an earlier version of the present chapter,[7] when Kripke said in his distinctive voice, "regardless of what I say in the book, I really am rather sympathetic to your view." It seems fitting to mark the 40th anniversary of the first publication of *WRPL* by defending a view on the issues raised therein to which Kripke himself was sympathetic.

2   Supervenience, Quadders, and Zombies

I have glossed the target of the argument to come as the physicalist thesis that meanings and contents are real yet "nothing over and above" the physical. This gloss needs further refinement.

First, what is *intentionality*? Though I will have more to say on the essential nature of intentionality in what follows, we can take as our starting point the thought that intentionality involves being *about* something or other, and that core intentional properties are the properties of having a meaning or content. The main focus of the present discussion will be *original*, rather than *derived* intentionality:

Original Intentionality: x has original intentionality if and only if x has some intentional properties, and the fact that x has the intentional properties that it does is independent of the intentionality of anything else.

---

[5] Henceforth *N&N*.
[6] Strictly speaking, to provide a thoroughgoing defense of semantic dualism, I would have to discuss various alternative accounts of what constitutes intentionality, which take intentionality to be partly determined by some non-physical class of properties, such as the normative properties (Brandom 1994; Williams 2019) or phenomenal properties (Chalmers 2006; Loar 2003; Mendelovici 2018). However, for want of space, I set these views aside here.
[7] This occurred at the conference on Rules, Norms and Reasons 1: Kripkenstein's Paradox, held at the University of Milan, May 20–21, 2019, organized by Andrea Guardo and Andrea Raimondi.

In contrast, *x* has *derived* intentionality if and only if it has intentional properties, and its intentional properties *do* depend on the intentionality of something else (Haugeland 1998; Searle 1992). For instance, a signpost possesses derived intentionality, since it only has the meaning that it does in virtue of being interpreted by some thinking being, while the thoughts and systems of thought of a thinking being plausibly have original intentionality, since their having the content that they do is independent of the intentionality of anything else.[8]

Second, what is it to say that intentionality is *real*? I will take this to mean that semantic and intentional properties exist and are instantiated, as well as that they are "inflationary" or "robust" in the sense that they can serve as proper objects of investigation into their natures. Some physicalists, of a broadly anti-realist bent, either reject the reality of intentionality outright (Churchland 1981), or hold that semantic or intentional properties are in some sense "deflated," "minimal" (Field 1994; Horwich 1990, 1998), or merely "quasi-real" (Gibbard 2012; Price et al. 2013) and thus cannot serve as proper objects of investigation into their natures. Of course, a full defense of dualism would require a discussion of these forms of physicalism. However, since this is beyond the scope of this chapter,[9] I will simply assume here that there are some 'robust' or 'inflationary' semantic properties or facts, such as that Jones means *addition* by "plus" in her thought and talk.[10]

Third, what are the physical facts? A great deal could be said on this matter, but that would take us too far afield.[11] At any rate, we can assume that the physical facts are not essentially intentional, for that would be to commit to a kind of panpsychism that is at odds with physicalism.[12]

---

[8] Some philosophers deny that thoughts have original intentionality, such as Dennett (1981). Anand Vaidya raised an interesting question: if we acquire many of our concepts through the acquisition of language, does that make all intentionality derived? I am inclined to think not, since language acquisition merely enables the acquisition of original intentional understanding of linguistic expressions, but the understanding that one achieves is not dependent on the intentionality of anything else.

[9] For a critical discussion of anti-realist views, see Hattiangadi (2007). For a criticism of Gibbard's quasi-realist approach to meaning and content, see Hattiangadi (2015, 2018c).

[10] For simplicity, I will use quotation marks when I mention a representation, regardless of whether it is mental or linguistic.

[11] Answering this question notoriously raises Hempel's dilemma: if we go by current physics, we might be led astray, because current physics is liable to be false; if we go by some ideal future physics, we remain in the dark about what the physical facts are. The positive characterization of the essential nature of physical properties due to Chalmers (1996) proposed in the main text is intended to avoid Hempel's dilemma because it does not characterize the physical in terms of the physical sciences.

[12] Note that Chalmers (2009) suggests that Russellian Monism, the view that the fundamental constituents of reality have intrinsic natures that suffice to give rise to the mental, *could* be viewed as a kind of materialism.

Furthermore, I will assume here that the physical facts are *structural and functional* (Chalmers 1996). On this view, the fundamental physical facts concern such things as the position, momentum, spin, charm, charge, and so forth, of subatomic particles (structure) as well as the fundamental laws governing their behavior (function). The derivative physical facts concern the structural properties of emergent, macrophysical objects and processes, such as DNA and digestion, as well as the functional properties of macrophysical objects and the laws governing their behavior. Though this characterization of the physical facts is undoubtedly incomplete, it will suffice for present purposes.

Finally, what is it to say that intentionality is "nothing over and above" the physical? I take it that the core view is that intentionality is just another derivative physical phenomenon, much like digestion or photosynthesis, which emerges from the complex interaction of fundamental physical entities. This is typically made more precise as the thesis that the intentional facts supervene on the physical with metaphysical necessity. Though there are many ways to characterize supervenience, I will focus on the weakest formulation, since it has the most widespread support among physicalists:

Supervenience: For any metaphysically possible world, w, if w is a minimal physical duplicate of the actual world, α, then w is an intentional duplicate of α.

A minimal physical duplicate of α is a world that is just like α in physical respects and which contains no nonphysical "extras," such as ghosts or ectoplasm (Jackson 1998).[13] Most physicalists accept Supervenience.[14] Reductive[15] physicalists hold that there is an analytic entailment from

---

[13] Some physicalists endorse Strong Global Supervenience (SGS): For any two metaphysically possible worlds, w and w^*, and any two objects x at w and y at w^*, any isomorphism between x and y that preserves physical properties preserves semantic and intentional properties. However, SGS is open to several objections stemming from the metaphysical possibility of nonphysical beings, such as ghosts. For instance, Kearns and Magidor (2012) advance several arguments against SGS along these lines. In response to such cases, physicalists sometimes prefer to endorse a minimal supervenience thesis. Kearns and Magidor (2012) also consider and reject a minimal supervenience thesis similar to the one presented in the main text on the basis of the assumption of *haecceitism*, the thesis that possible worlds may differ with respect to which individuals occupy the qualitative roles at those worlds. That is they argue against minimal supervenience by appeal to inverted worlds at which the individuals occupying qualitative roles differ from the individuals occupying qualitatively indiscernible roles at our world.

[14] Those physicalists who reject the robust reality of intentionality view Supervenience as trivial. If there are no intentional properties or facts, then no two worlds that are natural duplicates will differ in intentional respects simply because there are no intentional respects with which worlds may differ.

[15] The terms "reductive" and "non-reductive" are contested, and used differently in some cases. For instance, "reductive" is sometimes reserved for type-identity theory, according to which mental properties are identical to physical properties, while "non-reductive"

the physical truths to the intentional truths, which entails Supervenience, and though non-reductive physicalists deny that there is any such analytic entailment from the physical to the intentional, they hold that intentionality is constituted by or grounded in some class of physical properties or facts, which is also generally thought to entail Supervenience.[16]

The argument I will present here targets Supervenience, and thus both reductive and non-reductive forms of physicalism. It turns on the metaphysical possibility of *deviant worlds*: minimal physical duplicates of our world which differ from it in some semantic or intentional respects. It is possible to distinguish two ways in which a world may be deviant: *inverted worlds* are minimal physical duplicates of our world at which some semantic or intentional properties differ from those that are instantiated at our world;[17] *zombie worlds* are minimal physical duplicates of our world at which some semantic or intentional properties that are instantiated at our world are absent.[18] Obviously, if any deviant world is metaphysically possible, Supervenience is false.

We can describe an inverted world in more detail by appealing to the skeptical scenario Kripke envisages in *WRPL*. Let us suppose that, as a matter of fact, Jones means *addition* by "plus," and that when she computes sums in her head, she deploys a concept or mental representation, "plus," that denotes the addition function. Let us suppose further that Jones has only previously computed sums less than some number, n, which, for simplicity, we may assume is 57. Now she is asked to add 67

---

is used for physicalist theories that are committed to Supervenience, but not to type identity. This distinction is not, however, particularly useful for present purposes, since type identity theory is not a particularly prominent theory in the philosophical study of intentionality.

[16] Note that Leuenberger (2014) has argued that grounding does not entail supervenience. Recently, some have defended a form of non-reductive physicalism that rejects commitment to Supervenience (Bader In Press; Montero 2013; Moran 2021, forthcoming [manuscript]). I set aside these forms of physicalism here.

[17] The use of the term "inverted" here derives from an analogy with inverted spectrum cases in the philosophy of consciousness, that is, cases in which *a* and *b* are physical duplicates of one another, but where the phenomenal character *a* experiences when she sees grass is identical to the phenomenal character that *b* experiences when she sees blood and vice-versa.

[18] The notion of a zombie came to prominence in Chalmers' (1996) influential zombie argument against physicalism, in which zombies are defined as physical duplicates of conscious beings who lack consciousness. The zombies that figure in the present chapter are not zombies in Chalmers' sense, since they lack *intentionality* rather than *consciousness*. This raises a terminological issue to which I propose an irenic solution. Let's say that a zombie is a physical duplicate of a being with a mind who lacks some mental property. Then we can distinguish phenomenal zombies, who lack phenomenal properties, from intentional zombies, who lack intentional ones. The zombies that figure in the present chapter are thus intentional zombies. However, for simplicity, I will drop the qualifier "intentional" and use "zombie" to denote intentional zombies.

and 58, and she gives the answer "125." Kripke imagines that a skeptic comes along and puts forward the hypothesis that Jones means *quaddition* rather than addition by "plus," where:

Quaddition: x quus $y = x$ plus y, if $x, y \leq 57$

$\qquad\qquad\quad = 5$, otherwise

As Kripke formulates it, the skeptical scenario is a hypothesis about *our* world. What I suggest here is that we can appeal to the skeptical scenario to describe a merely possible inverted world at which Jones means *quaddition* by "plus," against the background assumption that Jones determinately means *addition* by "plus" in the actual world.[19]

Now, let us turn to zombie worlds. Kripke (1982: 24) alludes to a kind of zombie scenario when he imagines a situation in which Jones meant to denote *no* number-theoretic function by a particular symbol, "★," despite having dispositions to use it in such a way that it might be interpreted as denoting some such function. In this case, though the physical facts about Jones's use of "★" are compatible with an *interpretation* of it as denoting some number theoretic function, the symbol in fact means nothing whatsoever to *Jones*, because *she* did not intend it to mean anything by it at all. Now imagine that, in the actual world, Jones does mean some specific number theoretic function by "★." We can nevertheless imagine a minimal physical duplicate of our world at which "★" lacks any meaning or original intentionality for Jones.

The foregoing case involves what might be thought of as a zombie symbol, rather than a full-blown zombie world, at which no intentional properties are instantiated at all. However, we can characterize a full-blown zombie world by appealing to the skeptical conclusion in *WRPL*, that there are no semantic or intentional properties at all,[20] and by appealing to the various eliminativist, deflationary, or quasi-realist approaches to semantic properties cited above. Once again, though these philosophers purport to be describing *our* world, I suggest that we can hold fixed the assumption that semantic and intentional properties are instantiated at our world and take them to be characterizing a merely possible world that is a minimal physical duplicate of our world but at which no robust semantic or intentional properties are instantiated. When merely possible zombie worlds are viewed from our perspective, "from the outside",

---

[19] That the world described is a *minimal* physical duplicate of our world is implicit in the fact that the skeptic does not explicitly hypothesize any difference in Jones's physical state, nor the presence of any nonphysical extras.

[20] Note that some take the skeptical argument to target only truth conditional semantic theories (e.g. Wilson 1998; Zalabardo this volume).

as it were, the beings at those worlds behave exactly as we do, and thus would be naturally interpreted by us as meaning precisely what we mean by our words, and as having precisely the thoughts that we have. Yet, despite outward appearances, the minds of our zombie twins are blank; their words have no meaning, and their brain states are not accompanied by any contentful thoughts.

3   The Conceivability of Deviant Worlds

Reductive physicalists hold that the concepts of meaning and content are reductively analyzable and hence that there is an analytic entailment from the physical truths to the intentional truths. This is taken to justify the commitment to Supervenience (e.g. Lewis 1994). I will argue in this section that the considerations Kripke raises in *WRPL* concerning the essential natures of meanings and contents give us good reason to think that there is no analytic entailment from the physical truths to the intentional truths, and thus that deviant worlds are conceivable.

First, note that deviant worlds are logically possible: the set of propositions that constitutes a deviant world is logically consistent. At any rate, in the 40 years since the publication of *WRPL*, no one has, to my knowledge, complained that either the skeptical scenario or the skeptical conclusion is *logically* inconsistent.

Second, note that inverted worlds are prima facie conceivable: we can imagine a minimal physical duplicate of our world at which Jones means some quaddition-like function by "plus" without detecting any conceptual incoherence of the kind we might detect if we tried to imagine a vixen that is not a female fox. What about zombie worlds? These might initially seem prima facie inconceivable, since it has been argued that the skeptical conclusion is in some sense incoherent.[21] However, the apparent incoherence of the skeptical conclusion results from the self-referential nature of the thesis that there is no fact of the matter what any sentence means; it implies that a sentence stating this thesis itself lacks meaning. If only meaningful statements can be *true*, non-factualism about meaning seems to imply a liar-like incoherence. Perhaps this is why Kripke calls the skeptical conclusion "paradoxical." Nevertheless, this incoherence does not extend to zombie worlds thought of as merely possible, because there is no self-reference involved: we can imagine zombie worlds from the external perspective, holding fixed the semantic and intentional facts at the actual world;

---

[21] See also Boghossian (1990), Hattiangadi (2007), and Wright (1984a) for further arguments along these lines.

imagining or entertaining the possibility of a minimal physical duplicate of our world at which there are no meanings or contents does not entail that *our* words have no meaning.

The reductive physicalist might retort that though deviant worlds may be prima facie conceivable, they are not *ideally* conceivable, because we would detect an incoherence in them if we really did know all of the physical facts, or if we attempted to imagine deviant worlds under ideal conditions of rational reflection. However, as I will argue, Kripke presents two insights into the essential nature of meanings and contents which provide us with excellent reason to doubt that there is any analytic entailment from the physical truths to the semantic and intentional truths, and hence that deviant worlds are ideally conceivable.

The first insight is that meanings and contents are essentially *general*. As Kripke points out, since the addition function is defined for all pairs of positive integers no matter how large, if Jones means addition by "plus," then what she means determines the correct answer to sums involving arbitrarily large numbers (Kripke 1982: 18). This insight is inspired by Wittgenstein's suggestion that meanings lay down "rails to infinity" (1953b: §218). But the thought does not originate with Wittgenstein. As Willhelm von Humboldt famously put a similar point, language is a system that makes "infinite use of finite means" (Chomsky 1965; quoting Von Humboldt 1836).

Note that this generality or open-endedness is not exclusively a feature of meanings understood in truth-conditional terms. For instance, the introduction and elimination rules that inferentialists take to constitute the meanings of the logical constants are universally quantified, and apply to all well-formed formulae of a certain form (Brandom 1994). Indeed, even *singular* terms are inherently general. If a name is a *rigid designator*, it picks out the same object in *all* possible worlds in which that object exists (Kripke 1972). Moreover, though Kripke focuses in *WRPL* on semantic rules governing the use of atomic expressions such as "plus," compositional rules of most if not all human languages are recursive, so there is no upper bound to the length of meaningful sentences. This is the sort of generality that interests Chomsky (1965) and perhaps Von Humboldt too. If our *thoughts* are similarly compositional, as Fodor (1975) has argued, then there must be recursive rules for the construction of thoughts that are general in their application.

A consequence of the essential generality of meaning and content is that the semantic and intentional facts *transcend* the physical facts about actual and counterfactual use, even when the set of use facts is construed broadly, so as to include causal relations, dispositions, fine-grained and coarse-grained functional roles, evolutionary history, biological function – just about any physical phenomena that have been thought to determine meaning or content. As Kripke (1982: 26–27) points out, though the addition function may be defined for all pairs of positive integers no matter how large, there is an upper bound to the size of numbers Jones is capable of adding in her lifetime, and there is an upper bound to the length of meaningful sentences that any human being is capable of understanding or assenting to. Given the recursive nature of compositional rules, most sentences in a language such as English are too long for any human being to process (Hawthorne 1990: 118).

Though it has a much broader significance, Kripke raises this point specifically in relation to the dispositional account of meaning, which for present purposes can be understood as the view that "Jones means addition by 'plus'" is analytically equivalent to "Jones is disposed to respond with the sum of any two numbers when asked." Kripke's argument from generality can be presented as a dilemma. Consider the first horn. Let's say that a Very Large Number (VLN) is one which is represented by a numeral that is 1 mile long, when written out in full in a 12-point font (Lance and O'Leary-Hawthorne 1997). If asked to add two VLNs, Jones will get bored, fall asleep, or pass out instead of responding with the sum (Kripke 1982: 27). That is, Jones's dispositions are finite, in the sense that there are some VLNs too large for her to compute (Guardo 2022). She is quite simply *not* disposed to respond with the sum of any two numbers when asked. On the dispositionalist proposal under consideration, it follows that she does not mean addition by "plus."

The dispositionalist might regroup and say that "Jones means addition by 'plus'" is analytically equivalent to "Jones has dispositions D," where D denotes the (finite) dispositions that Jones in fact has in her use of "plus."[22] But then, the second horn of the dilemma comes into view. Let's say that quaddition* is a quaddition-like function that deviates

---

[22] Note that D can describe Jones's *extended* dispositions, such as her dispositions to correct errors when they come to light, and so forth. Some have suggested that formulating dispositionalism in terms of these dispositions avoids the difficulties Kripke raises (see Blackburn 1984; Coates 1997; Warren 2020; for versions of this response). However, appeal to extended dispositions does not resolve the problem for dispositionalism, since her making errors of correction too are compatible with her meaning addition by "plus" (as I have argued in Hattiangadi 2007). Moreover, D can be taken to describe Jones's *ideal* dispositions, that is, her dispositions under naturalistically specifiable ideal conditions, such as conditions in which the lighting is good, she is well-rested, sufficiently caffeinated, and so forth. Some have suggested that formulating dispositionalism in terms of these dispositions resolves the difficulties Kripke raises. See for example, Blackburn (1984), Chalmers (In Press), and Hattiangadi (2007) for versions of this response. However, even under such ideal conditions, there will be an upper bound to the numbers Jones is able to compute, so there remain VLNs she would not be able to grasp even in naturalistically specifiable ideal conditions.

from the addition function at some VLN (Kripke 1982: 27). If the dispositionalist has conceded that it is sufficient for Jones to mean addition by "plus" that she conforms to the addition function when asked to add small numbers, surely it is sufficient for Jones to mean quaddition★ by "plus" that she conforms to the quaddition★ function when asked to add small numbers. But since the addition and quaddition★ functions converge for small numbers, by parity of reasoning, the sentence "Jones means quaddition★ by 'plus'" must thereby be analytically equivalent to "Jones has dispositions D." It would be arbitrary and *ad hoc* to insist that the general form of the analysis that is given for meaning addition does not simply carry over, mutatis mutandis, to the analysis of meaning quaddition★.[23] Thus, the hypothesis that Jones means quaddition★ by "plus" is compatible with all of the dispositional truths. So, even if the dispositional analysis of "Jones means addition by 'plus'" is *true*, it remains conceivable that a minimal physical duplicate of Jones means quaddition★ by "plus."

The essential generality of meaning and content constitutes good reason to think that inverted worlds are ideally conceivable. If meanings and contents transcend use, the physical truths about use are compatible with multiple competing interpretations of agents, and there is no analytic entailment from the physical truths to the semantic and intentional truths. It follows that – even under conditions of ideal rational reflection, and with a full grasp of semantic and intentional concepts – we can conceive of any number of inverted worlds at which Jones is just as she actually is in physical respects but means some deviant quaddition-like function by "plus."

The second important Kripkean insight into the essences of meanings and contents is that they are *weakly normative*: they essentially give rise to standards of use whose normative authority is not absolute or objective but relative to and dependent on the intentional mental states of some agent or agents.[24] This insight may be inspired by Wittgenstein's suggestion that languages can be viewed as analogous to games, which are also weakly normative. For instance, consider the rules of chess: there is no robust, normative fact that you ought to conform to them. Rather, the fact that you ought to conform to the rules of chess on some occasion depends on your intending to play chess, or on your playing chess

---

[23] It is possible to respond to this objection by appeal to the claim that the addition function is objectively more "eligible" to serve as the referent of "plus" than the quaddition function, as Lewis (1984) does. I discuss this response in Section 5.

[24] This is a point on which there is widespread agreement (Boghossian 1989; Gibbard 2003, 2012; Glüer 1999; Glüer and Wikforss 2009; Hattiangadi 2007; Verheggen 2011; Whiting 2007; Wikforss 2001).

in the context of a conventional set up in which you are expected to play by the rules. In the absence of any such conventional set up, if you were not intending to play chess at all, but to clean the chess set, create a sculpture, or to play a different game altogether, the rules of chess would not have any normative authority over you. And if you happened to find yourself in a different conventional set up, in which you are expected to adhere to some other set of rules, then it would be those rules that would have normative authority over you, not the rules of chess.

Kripke makes the point that meaning and content are weakly normative in his discussion of the dispositionalist account sketched above. He argues that Jones's being disposed to respond with the sum of any two numbers when asked is not necessary for her to mean addition by "plus" because she may be disposed to make mistakes in calculating large sums, and yet still qualify as computing the addition function, rather than some bizarre function that just so happens to deliver the answers she is in fact disposed to give (Kripke 1982: 30). The fact that Jones means addition by "plus" does not imply that she *will* or *would* give answers that conform to the addition function, as Kripke puts it, it implies that she *ought* to do so. This "ought" is weakly normative in much the same way that the rules of chess are: its normative authority derives from the fact that Jones means addition by "plus," or from the fact that "plus" has this conventional meaning in Jones's linguistic community.[25]

Kripke's remarks on the normativity of meaning have frequently been interpreted to imply that meanings and contents are *robustly* normative, in the sense that they give rise to standards that have a normative authority that is absolute and independent of any agent's intentional mental states (Boghossian 1989; Glüer 1999; Wikforss 2001).[26] Indeed, I myself have subscribed to this interpretation, thinking that it was only if meaning and content were robustly normative that the argument against physicalism went through (Hattiangadi 2007). However, I have now changed my mind on this point. Indeed, I argue here that it is precisely because meanings and contents are weakly normative that the concepts of meaning and content cannot be reductively analyzed.

Crucially, *what it is* for meanings and contents to be weakly normative is for their normative authority to be relative to and dependent on the intentional states of some agent or agents. Thus, what it is for meanings and contents to be weakly normative essentially involves intentional states.

---

[25] I have argued elsewhere that correctness is not a robustly normative notion (Bykvist and Hattiangadi 2013).

[26] In (Hattiangadi 2007), I distinguish between norm-relativity and (genuine) normativity. I take this to map straightforwardly onto the distinction I draw here between weak normativity and robust normativity.

For instance, the fact that the addition function is weakly normative for Jones may consist in her *meaning* addition by "plus"; her *intending* to conform to the addition function; her being *expected* to conform to it by other members of her linguistic community, or its being *accepted* as a convention in her linguistic community. In all of these cases, what makes it the case that the addition function is weakly normative involves intentional mental states, either those of Jones or of her linguistic community. After all, when conceived of as abstract objects, as mappings from strings to meanings, there are infinitely many languages (Lewis 1975). In the absence of any intentional states at all, there is nothing that privileges English, as described by a particular formal language, or a small subset of them, as the language that Jones and her linguistic community actually speak.[27]

The weak normativity of meaning and content makes reductive analysis of meaning and content impossible. If meaning is weakly normative, then any adequate analysis of "Jones means addition by 'plus'" makes essential reference to semantic or intentional properties. If *all* intentional contents are weakly normative, then any adequate analysis of intentional content makes essential reference to some intentional properties, so no analysis can break out of the intentional circle. This constitutes a powerful reason to think that zombie worlds are ideally conceivable. If semantic and intentional concepts cannot be reductively analyzed, there is no analytic entailment from the physical truths to the semantic and intentional truths. It follows that – even under conditions of ideal rational reflection, with a full grasp of semantic and intentional concepts – we can conceive of zombie worlds that are physical duplicates of our world but at which no semantic or intentional properties are instantiated.

4 An Essentialist Argument for the Possibility of Deviant Worlds

The non-reductive physicalist may be impatient to point out that conceivability is a fallible guide to metaphysical possibility, and that it is the metaphysical possibility of deviant worlds that tells against Supervenience. For instance, familiar cases of Kripkean (1982) a posteriori necessities show how conceivability falls short: though it is conceivable that molecular motion occurs without being accompanied by heat, if heat really is identical to molecular motion, it is not metaphysically possible for molecular motion to occur without being accompanied by

---

[27] See Guardo (2022) for a version of this "privilege" argument developed in detail in relation to Warren's (2020) recent defense of dispositionalism. See also Hattiangadi (2023) for an argument against the dispositional account of the adoption of rules postulated as constitutive of the meanings of logical constants.

heat. Similarly, the non-reductive physicalist might argue, though deviant worlds are conceivable, they are not metaphysically possible (Cf. Soames 1998: 231–232).

One way to respond to this objection will be familiar to readers of *N&N*. Kripke (1972: 131) argues there that when we seem to conceive of a world in which there is molecular motion without heat, we are subject to a modal illusion, because what we are really conceiving of is a world in which molecular motion fails to give rise to the *sensation* of heat, which does not amount to the same thing. Moreover, he argues, we are susceptible to modal illusions in cases such as this because we identify heat by way of a contingent property of it, the property of producing certain kinds of sensations in us. Kripke (1982: 151) points out that the same does not hold for our phenomenal concepts, which we identify by their essential properties: their phenomenal character or qualitative feel. As a consequence, when we conceive of a situation in which the actual physical realizer of pain is not accompanied by a pain sensation, we are not subject to a modal illusion, but are conceiving of a genuine possibility. Similarly, our ability to conceive of minimal physical duplicates of our world that differ in intentional respects cannot be explained as a modal illusion, because we identify meanings and contents by their essential properties. It is essential to Jones's meaning addition by "plus" that she understands "plus" to denote the addition function, that "plus" has this original intentional content for her. So, when we imagine deviant inverted or zombie worlds, we really are imagining minimal physical duplicates of our world at which the original intentional content either differs or is absent, and that just is a world in which Jones does not mean addition by "plus."

Another way to respond to the non-reductive physicalist would be to rely on a modal rationalist framework, such as has been developed in detail by Chalmers (2002, 2009), and argue that in the special case of intentionality, conceivability entails possibility.[28] Though I am sympathetic to this approach,[29] the 2-dimensional framework Chalmers adopts to advance this argument is at odds with some of the views Kripke endorses in *N&N* (Mallozzi 2018b). Since I would like to put forward a *Kripkean* argument against physicalism here, I shall adopt a different tack, which proceeds from an essentialist account of metaphysical modality (Fine 1994; Rosen 2020) and an essence-first account of modal knowledge (Lowe 2012; Hale 2013; Mallozzi 2018a; Vaidya 2018;

---

[28] See also Yablo (1993), where Yablo argues that conceivability is a guide to possibility.
[29] I have for instance used this framework to argue against moral supervenience (Hattiangadi 2018a).

Vaidya and Wallner 2021).[30] Though this admittedly goes well beyond what Kripke explicitly says in *N&N*, it seems to me to fit well with the broadly essentialist approach Kripke takes in *N&N*.

An essentialist account of metaphysical modality begins with a primitive, non-modal concept of essence, where the essential truths are those that obtain in virtue of the nature or identity of some item or items (Fine 1994). In Fine's nomenclature, "it is in the nature of x that p" is written: $\square_x p$. Modal notions such as possibility and necessity are then analyzed in terms of essence: what it is for a proposition p to be metaphysically possible is for p to be compatible with all of the essential truths, and what it is for p to be metaphysically necessary is for p to be an essential truth or to be logically entailed by the essential truths (Rosen 2020). According to an analytic essentialist account of modal knowledge, we can acquire justified beliefs or knowledge of modal truths by deducing them from facts about essence (Lowe 2012; Hale 2013; Mallozzi 2018a; Vaidya 2018; Vaidya and Wallner 2021).

Within this framework, non-reductive physicalism can be characterized as the thesis that while semantic and intentional concepts cannot be reductively analyzed, semantic and intentional properties can be given *real definitions* in physical terms.[31] The notion of a real definition serves to cash out the non-reductivist's thought that what it is for something to have a semantic or intentional property *consists in* its being ϕ, where ϕ is a proposition with wholly physical constituents.[32] Of course, a non-reductive physicalist may hold that not all semantic and intentional properties can be given real definitions in physical terms. For instance, it is plausible that the real definition of some semantic properties, such as the property of having a certain meaning in a public language, might nontrivially refer to the intentional properties of the beliefs and desires of the speakers of the language. However, if semantic and intentional

---

[30] Vaidya and Wallner (2021) argue that essential truths are indispensable to the epistemology of modality, since they are needed to determine when some scenario that can be imagined or conceived of is genuinely metaphysically possible.

[31] As Alex Moran pointed out in a personal communication, an alternative would be for the non-reductive physicalist to claim that though semantic and intentional properties cannot be given real definitions in physical terms, they are nevertheless grounded in the physical. However (as he also acknowledged), because the considerations that I raise against the possibility of real definition of semantic and intentional properties has to do with the essential natures of semantic and intentional properties, these considerations tell against the alternative formulation of non-reductive physicalism in terms of grounding, particularly for those who hold that grounding relations must be mediated by facts about essence (Fine 2015).

[32] Of course, since non-reductive physicalists typically accept the multiple realizability of mental phenomena, ϕ will be a lengthy disjunction of all of the physical conditions that constitute physical realizers of the semantic and intentional properties.

properties are constituted by the physical, there must be a chain of real definitions that ultimately bottoms out in some basic semantic or intentional properties which have real definitions which make no nontrivial reference to any semantic or intentional properties. Let's say that F is one of those basic semantic or intentional properties. Then, non-reductive physicalism can be characterized as the thesis that F can be given a real definition of the following form:

(a) $\Box_F \forall x(Fx \leftrightarrow \phi)$
(b) The essences of the constituents of ϕ make no nontrivial reference to any semantic or intentional properties.[33]

With this in place, we can see that the two Kripkean insights into the essential natures of semantic and intentional properties canvassed above suggest that they have no adequate real definitions in physical terms, and hence that deviant worlds are metaphysically possible. First, Kripke's point about generality undercuts the possibility of satisfying condition (a) above. Since the property of meaning addition by "plus" transcends the physical facts about use, there is no proposition ϕ adequate to provide a real definition of the property of meaning addition by "plus," since any ϕ that mentions only physical properties of finite use will be compatible with the property of meaning any number of quaddition-like functions by "plus." This implies that any statement of the form of (1) is false, where F is the property of meaning addition by "plus."[34] This is because one cannot in general deduce from the fact that ϕ is true that someone means addition by "plus," rather than some quaddition-like function or other. This in turn renders the biconditional in (2) false:

(1) $\Box_F \forall x(\phi \supset x$ means addition by "plus")
(2) $\Box_F \forall x(x$ means addition by "plus" $\leftrightarrow \phi)$

Second, Kripke's point about the weak normativity of meaning and content undercuts the possibility of satisfying condition (b). If meaning and content are essentially weakly normative, and if the essences of weakly normative items make nontrivial reference to semantic or intentional properties, there is no proposition ϕ adequate to supply a real definition of weakly normative meanings and contents, which makes no nontrivial reference to any semantic or intentional property.

---

[33] This is adapted from Rosen's (2020) account of real definition.
[34] Though meaning addition by "plus" may not be a basic property, since generality is essential to content, we can stick with this example for simplicity.

If the foregoing is correct and semantic and intentional properties cannot be given a real definition in physical terms, then deviant worlds are compatible with all the facts about essence and thus are metaphysically possible. After all, the physical properties and facts are structural and functional, and thus do not mention any semantic or intentional properties. So, if semantic and intentional properties resist real definition in physical terms, their essences are similarly compatible with propositions representing deviant worlds. For instance, if we let P be a proposition stating the physical facts of our world and S_q be the proposition that Jones means some quaddition-like function by "plus," the proposition $P \wedge S_q$ is metaphysically possible because it is compatible with the essential truths about all of the items in both P, which makes no mention of any semantic and intentional properties, and S_q, which can't be given a real definition in physical terms. Similarly, if we let $\neg S$ be the negation of S, a proposition stating all of the semantic and intentional facts at our world, the proposition $P \wedge \neg S$ too is metaphysically possible because it is compatible with the essences of all of the items in P and S. In sum, if semantic and intentional properties resist real definition in physical terms, this shows that they are not constituted by the physical, by the essentialist's lights. This in turn implies that deviant inverted and zombie worlds are compatible with all of the facts about essence, and thus that they are metaphysically possible. And if deviant worlds are metaphysically possible, Supervenience is false.

5 Application: Radical Interpretation

I would like to close by considering, albeit briefly, the interpretationist program for naturalizing meaning and intentionality associated most famously with Davidson (1973) and Lewis (1974). This is a useful test case for the foregoing arguments for two reasons. First, it is expansive: Supervenience is defended on the grounds that it is possible for a radical interpreter, who knows all of the physical facts about Jones, to deduce the semantic and intentional facts about her, without recourse to any semantic or intentional information. So, no physical facts are ruled out from consideration. Second, though there is much commonality between them, Lewis carries out his program in an analytic reductive mode, whereas Davidson carries his out in a non-reductive mode. So, it is possible to consider a reductive and nonreductive account of intentionality in tandem. Though I have argued against interpretationist defenses of Supervenience elsewhere, (Hattiangadi 2020; Hattiangadi and Stefánsson 2021) I will focus here on how Kripke's two insights cast the adequacy of both programs into doubt.

According to interpretationists, radical interpretation is a two-step process (Williams 2007). In the first step, armed with knowledge of all the physical truths, the radical interpreter sets out to ascribe beliefs and desires to an arbitrary agent, such as Jones. Decision theory, which is taken to characterize *what it is* for an agent to have beliefs and desires, plays a vital role in this step. Both Lewis (1974: 337) and Davidson (1985: 93ff, 1990: 323–324) appeal to Bolker's (1966) representation theorem for Jeffrey's decision theory, which proves that if an agent's preferences satisfy the so-called Bolker-Jeffrey axioms, it is possible to deduce probability and utility functions that can be taken to represent the agent's degrees of belief and desire. Thus, at this step, the radical interpreter works out whether Jones's preferences indeed satisfy the axioms, and then goes on to ascribe suitable degrees of belief and desire.[35] In the second step, the radical interpreter sets out to ascribe meanings to sentences of Jones's language by deploying some kind of principle of charity. In Davidson's (1973) case, the radical interpreter is instructed to maximize truth in the set of sentences Jones holds true. In Lewis's case, the instructions are more complex but crucially involve maximizing "truthfulness and trust" in the language: making the users of the Jones's language out to be typically aiming to utter truths in the language and typically interpreting others as doing the same (Lewis 1974, 1975).

With this in place, we can see how Kripkean insights undercut the radical interpretationist enterprise. First, consider the point about generality, which implies that semantic and intentional properties are essentially use-transcendent. This provides the basis for an objection Hawthorne (1990) raises against Lewis.[36] As Hawthorne points out, given the recursive nature of the compositional rules of language, *most* meaningful sentences in any natural language such as English are far too long for any speaker to use (Hawthorne 1990: 118). This, Hawthorne argues, is at odds with Lewis' proposal that the radical interpreter assign meanings to the sentences of a language that maximize truthfulness and trust in the language. The trouble is that since ordinary language users use only a

---

[35] Of course, preferences are intentional mental states, so the radical interpreter does not know Jones's preferences at the outset, but must work them out on the basis of knowledge of the physical facts about her "raw behaviour" (Lewis 1974: 338). Davidson provides a decision-theoretic account of how this works, in which the radical interpreter begins by identifying an initially uninterpreted truth-functional connective in Jones's language as the Sheffer stroke, meaning "not both p and q," and then determines all other truth-functional connectives on that basis. From this, the radical interpreter is supposed to be able to determine Jones's preferences, or more precisely, which sentences of her language she prefers true. (See Davidson 1984, 1990) For critical discussion of this aspect of Davidson's proposal, see Rabinowicz (2002) and Hattiangadi and Stefánsson (2021).

[36] In his response to Hawthorne (1990), Lewis (1992: 106) refers to a similar objection raised by Stephen Schiffer, but provides no citation.

fragment of the language, maximizing truthfulness and trust in that fragment does not rule out the possibility that they are speaking English*, a variant of English with semantic and compositional rules that deviate from those of English only for sentences that are too long for any ordinary speaker to process. A similar objection can be raised against Davidson's suggestion that the radical interpreter should maximize truth in the sentences Jones holds true. Since there is an upper bound to the length of sentences Jones can hold true, an interpretation of Jones as speaking English* will be just as charitable as one that interprets her as speaking English. Thus, whether the interpretationist story is cast in reductive or non-reductive terms, it fails to rule out the possibility of a deviant world that duplicates our world in physical respects but in which Jones and her linguistic community speak English* rather than English.[37]

Lewis's response to Hawthorne (Lewis 1992) echoes his response to Kripke (Lewis 1984: 376–77): he claims that the addition function, and the rules of English, are objectively more "natural" than the bent rules of quaddition and English*, and thus more "eligible" to figure as the meanings of our utterances or the contents of our thoughts. There is a good deal to be said about the limitations of this response (Cf. Dorr and Hawthorne 2013; Hawthorne 2007; Hattiangadi, 2020; Williams 2007). I would like to highlight two objections to it here. The first objection is that this style of response does nothing to remove another indeterminacy that comes in at the ground-level, in the interpretationist's proposal for the assignment of beliefs and desires to agents. The interpretationist's appeal to Jeffrey's decision theory falls short, since this procedure delivers at best a non-singleton set **X** of *pairs* of probability and utility functions which rationalize Jones's preferences equally well, and where the probability functions do not even agree on how to rank some propositions. For instance, consider the following two propositions:

(a) *It will snow in London next December and I will have a successful career*, and
(b) *It will snow in Copenhagen next December and I will have a successful career* (adapted from Hattiangadi and Stefánsson 2021: 6485).

Though it is plausible that Jones believes (b) more strongly than (a), the radical interpreter who appeals to Jeffrey's decision theory cannot rule out the possibility that she believes (a) more strongly than (b). Moreover, this problem will arise in relation to any two logically independent propositions for which the probability/utility product is not close to 0. As a consequence, even if one of the probability functions x in **X** accurately

[37] Of course, this is a "permutation argument," involving an interpretation that permutes the meanings of the intended interpretation in such a way as to preserve the truth values of sentences of the language, of the sort made famous by Putnam (1980).

represents Jones's degrees of belief, there will be another probability function y in **X** that is inconsistent with x and yet rationalizes Jones's behavior equally well, and thus is an equally eligible contender for representing Jones's degrees of belief. Indeed, there will be many such functions (Hattiangadi and Stefánsson 2021). Moreover, there is no reason to think that the unique function (or subset of functions) in **X** that accurately represent Jones's beliefs is also uniquely most natural and therefore most eligible, since there is no reason to think that the probability functions that do not accurately represent Jones's beliefs are "bent". Thus, no appeal to objective naturalness will suffice to rule them out.

Furthermore, the appeal to naturalness does nothing to rule out the possibility of zombie worlds, which arises in light of the weak normativity of meaning and content. The trouble is that considerations of eligibility only serve to constrain *what* Jones is thinking against the background assumption that it has already been determined *that* Jones has intentional states in the first place. Once again, it is the appeal to decision theory that is intended to determine *that* the agent has intentional states at all, for both Lewis and Davidson. However, it is possible to use zombie cases to put pressure on the very appeal of decision theory as analytic or constitutive of the attitudes. This is because there are various systems and processes that can be modelled in decision-theoretic terms, yet plausibly lack original intentionality. Indeed, the cognitive sciences are replete with Bayesian models of a range of sub-personal processes in the brain, such as the resolution of low-level visual data into visual images (e.g. Yuille and Kersten 2006), sensorimotor learning (Körding and Wolpert 2004), and the acquisition of language (Tenenbaum et al. 2011). If the interpretationists are right that what it is to have beliefs and desires is to have states that can be modelled in decision-theoretic terms, it follows that any sub-personal processes which can be modelled in decision-theoretic terms must, as a consequence, realize beliefs, desires, and preferences in the minds of some intentional agents. However, since these processes are sub-personal, if they realize attitudes, the attitudes they realize must occur in the minds of homunculi. Of course, this is wildly implausible! But if it is possible for these processes to fail to realize attitudes, despite being modellable in decision-theoretic terms, then by the same token, it is possible that a minimal physical duplicate of Jones, who can be modelled decision-theoretically, nevertheless fails to realize any attitudes.

6 Conclusion

I have argued that Supervenience is false. Against the assumption of realism about intentionality, the argument supports dualism: intentional properties are both real and fundamental.³⁸ The dualist view that I favor is not the Cartesian substance dualism Kripke rejects (1982: 155, n77), but a property dualism, which postulates fundamental intentional properties and contingent psychophysical laws.

Though Kripke was sympathetic to dualism, as I suggested above, he argued against it in *WRPL*, objecting that "it remains mysterious exactly how the existence of *any* finite past state of my mind could entail that, if I wish to accord with it, and remember the state, and do not miscalculate, I must give a determinate answer to an arbitrarily large addition problem" (Kripke 1982: 53). Though I must confess that I have no snappy retort to this objection, what I can say on behalf of the dualist is that intentionality is at least no *more* mysterious from the perspective of dualism than it is from the perspective of physicalism. The physicalist faces the additional challenge of explaining how infinite content could be contained in a *physical* system and how intentional norms can be weakly normative for agents – which, as I have argued, seems to be insuperable. There is no doubt a residual mystery for the dualist to resolve, but I will have to attempt to resolve it on a later occasion.³⁹

7 Addendum

As this chapter was going to press, Saul Kripke sadly passed away, which was a huge loss to the profession, and to me personally. As is evident in this chapter, his philosophy has exerted a powerful influence on my work from the very start of my career, and will likely continue to inspire me well into the future. In the past few years, I have had the tremendous privilege of getting to know Saul as a person: he was brilliant, but also gentle, funny, and above all, intellectually generous. He will be sorely missed.

---

[38] Strictly speaking, the argument thus far only implies that dualism is true against the background of some qualifications made earlier. For instance, I set aside physicalist views which reject Supervenience (n15), as well as accounts according to which the supervenience base for the intentional includes normative or phenomenal properties in (n6). A full defense of dualism would have to address these views.

[39] Earlier versions of this chapter were presented at the following venues: the conference "Rules, Norms and Reasons 1: Kripkenstein's Paradox," organized by Andrea Guardo and Andrea Raimondi, on May 20–21, 2019, at the University of Milan; the "Rule Following and Normativity" seminar series, organized by Romina Padró and Saul Kripke, on Feb 24, 2021, at the Saul Kripke Centre, CUNY Graduate Centre; the workshop on "Kripke's *Wittgenstein on Rules and Private Language* at 40," organized by Claudine Verheggen, on June 17th–18th, 2022 at York University, Toronto; and at the seminar series, "*Naming and Necessity* at 50" seminar series, on 2022, Feb 24, 2021, at the Saul Kripke Centre, CUNY Graduate Centre, September 14, organized by Romina Padró and Saul Kripke, together with Corine Besson, Antonella Mallozzi, Yale Weiss, Michael Devitt, and me. I am grateful to the audiences on all of these occasions for insightful discussion.

11 Communitarianism, Interpersonalism, and Individualism in Kripke's "Skeptical Solution"

Christopher Campbell

1 Introduction

The "skeptical solution" Kripke attributes to Wittgenstein[1] to the problem of meaning skepticism has been described as "communitarian." I suppose it's fairly clear what this means: The skeptical solution is a response to the result of Kripke's (1982) Chapter 2 that "if one person is considered in isolation, the notion of a rule as guiding the person who adopts it can have *no* substantive content," and arises from "widen[ing] our gaze from consideration of the rule follower alone and allow[ing] ourselves to consider him as interacting with a wider community" (89). It is "communitarian" in the sense that, on its account, the ascription to an individual of rule-following (and hence *a fortiori* of meaning something by a word) only makes sense against a background of seeing that individual as a member of a community. In other words, "communitarian" here stands in contrast with something like "individualistic."[2]

But there is room for finer distinctions. On the view of meaning embodied in Kripke's skeptical solution, language is essentially social; but one might defend a claim articulated in those terms without arriving at it on Kripke's grounds. For example, Davidson argues that one can become a bearer of propositional attitudes – a thinker and a language-user – only through social interaction (e.g. Davidson 1999), but he does not agree with Kripke that ascriptions of content to one's words and attitudes

---

[1] In his (1982), to which otherwise unmarked page references will refer. Note that I will sometimes simply speak of "Kripke" or "Kripke's view" where I mean to refer to the skeptical solution he offers in his Chapter 3. As he makes clear, he does not straightforwardly endorse that view as his own.

[2] For just one example of many readers who make this sort of distinction, see Bloor's (1997), where he contrasts "collectivism" about rule-following with "individualism", and takes as paradigm instances Kripke's skeptical solution and McGinn's (1984), respectively.

depend on reference to one's linguistic community (e.g. Davidson 2001d). Verheggen (2006: 203) marks this difference by calling Kripke's view "communitarian" and Davidson's "interpersonalist."[3]

It is worth disentangling some further threads. Note that Davidson's positive account of the sense in which language is social concerns the *constitution* of an individual as a language-user (and more generally as a bearer of propositional attitudes, but let us stick to "language-user" for short): to become as much, she must interact with others. Meanwhile, his negative point – the sense in which, on his view, language is apparently "less social" than Kripke makes it out to be – concerns the question of *agreement* in meaning. At the same time, note that even with respect to the positive point, Davidson does not argue that interaction with a *community*, as such, is necessary for one's constitution as a language-user; indeed, the central kind of triangulating scenario by reference to which he illustrates his claims about what is necessary – simplified and idealized though it is no doubt intended to be – involves interaction with just one other individual.[4] I take it that this is what makes the term "interpersonal" apposite to describe his view. Meanwhile, Davidson denies not merely that one's words must mean what one's *community* means by them, but that they must mean what *anyone* else means by them: On this second dimension, Davidson's view might reasonably be described not even as interpersonalist but as individualist.

We may thus distinguish two questions concerning the sense in which language is social. First, the constitutive question: Can one (at least in principle) become a language-user (i) on one's own, (ii) only through interaction with other individuals, or (iii) only in virtue of one's membership in an entire community, where this transcends, in some way, mere individual interaction? Answer (iii) here may involve reference to such notions as customs, institutions, or practices, again if these are taken to involve more than a mere aggregation of individual interactions. Call these three views "constitutive individualism," "constitutive interpersonalism," and "constitutive communitarianism." Next, the question of agreement in meaning: (i) may the meanings with which one uses words (sometimes, often, or always) differ from those with which the people with whom one has interacted use them, or must they coincide either (ii) with those, or (iii) with those of one's community as a whole? I'll call

---

[3] Compare also the distinction between "I-thou" and "I-we" relations as a foundation for an account of the sociality of language, for example, in Brandom (1994: 39 and *passim*).

[4] While the other individual in these illustrative scenarios is sometimes a teacher (Davidson 2001d: 120), hence one who is already a concept-monger, more often it is simply another language-user-to-be, on equal footing with the first individual.

these views "meaning-individualism," "meaning-interpersonalism," and "meaning-communitarianism."[5,6]

In this chapter, I propose to try to clarify Kripke's "skeptical solution" with respect to these two questions. Now, Kripke doesn't really address the constitutive question head-on; indeed, in a sense, he explicitly rejects it. Thus: "there is no ... fact, no ... condition in either the 'internal' or the 'external' world [which constitutes my meaning addition by 'plus']" (69). In other words, *nothing* "constitutes" me as a language-user! But we can modulate the question so as to be raisable in Kripke's framework: In so far as I can be said to be a language-user at all, in what sense is sociality presupposed in so calling me? And I shall argue in Section 2 that there is nothing in his account that warrants taking it to yield a "communitarian" rather than an "interpersonalist" answer to this question. Meanwhile (Section 3), I shall also argue that the skeptical solution is not committed to meaning-communitarianism or even meaning-interpersonalism but is rather compatible with meaning-individualism.[7]

The result is that Kripke's skeptical solution, while no doubt differing in detail and in points of emphasis from Davidson's account, broadly coincides with it with respect to these two questions. This will come as good news to those who defend Davidson's approach (except in so far as it makes it awkward for them to use Kripke as a foil!). However, in the concluding section of this chapter, I shall suggest that a thinker who finds congenial the meaning-individualism of the Davidsonian and, now, Kripkean sort need not on that account immediately conclude also to

---

[5] Williams (2000: 317, n5) distinguishes between semantic, epistemic and constitutive "versions of the community view" of the sociality of language. Her explication of the first and, especially, the third of these don't *quite* line up with what I'm proposing to call meaning- and constitutive communitarianism respectively; and I'm not proposing to discuss anything corresponding to her second version. Still, her concerns are certainly in the same ballpark as the present chapter.

[6] I put "less social" in shudder-quotes in the previous paragraph because these distinctions are not really quantitative (certainly not a matter of counting heads) – not to mention that, once we separate the different questions, the temptation to think of sociality as a (single) matter of degree should wane in any case. Thus the real force of the colloquially phrased "How social is language?" is surely "*In what sense(s)* is language social?". – I owe to Olivia Sultanescu the observation that, in some respects, constitutive interpersonalism might be considered "*more* social" than constitutive communitarianism: for the former emphasizes the essential role played by actual social interaction in the constitution of meaning, whereas the latter, at least in some hands, can seem to posit an abstract "community" or "practice" oddly dissociated from actual behavior. Nevertheless, I should hope that a healthy philosophy of action can show to be unmysterious the notions constitutive communitarianism appeals to. My thanks to both Olivia Sultanescu and Louis-Philippe Hodgson for pointing out the need for more clarity on these issues – which, however, I haven't yet managed to achieve.

[7] Miller (2020: 12) has recently argued for a similar claim. I arrive at it a bit differently.

the falsity of constitutive communitarianism. While at first glance the two sorts of communitarianism I've distinguished here may appear to go hand in hand, the distinction opens up the notional possibility, at least, of accepting a communitarian answer to the constitutive question while giving a different answer to the question of agreement in meaning.

2 The Constitutive Interpersonalism of the Skeptical Solution

For what I take to be the canonical expression of Kripke's skeptical solution, I turn to the stretch of text beginning at p. 86. Kripke has already argued, citing Dummett, that a central thread in Wittgenstein's *Philosophical Investigations* is a general rejection of the truth-conditional approach to meaning. As Kripke has it:

> Wittgenstein replaces the question, "What must be the case for this sentence to be true?" by two others: first, "Under what conditions may this form of words be appropriately asserted (or denied)?"; second, given an answer to the first question, "What is the role, and the utility, in our lives of our practice of asserting (or denying) the form of words under these conditions?" (73)

Now, in the stretch of text beginning at p. 86, where the "skeptical solution" is canonically expounded, Kripke deploys this two-pronged analysis of meaning on statements of meaning themselves. The issue now is the meaning of an ascription such as "Jones means *addition* by '+'," given that Chapter 2 has already purported to establish, as we saw earlier, that "there is no ... fact, no ... condition in either the 'internal' or the 'external' world [which constitutes my meaning addition by 'plus']" (69). Kripke states the "assertability conditions" of meaning ascriptions at pp. 90–91: Briefly, it is appropriate for Jones to assert that he means *addition* (or whatever else) by 'plus' as long as he feels confident that he can use 'plus' correctly; while it is appropriate for someone else, say Smith, to assert that Jones means *addition* by 'plus' – that is, that he means what Smith does – only if Jones's responses involving 'plus', such as his answers to addition questions, tend to agree with Smith's. And Kripke gives an explanation of the "point of the practice" at pp. 91–93: Briefly, it is useful for each of us to be able to keep track, from among the people with whom we interact, of those whom we can expect to respond as we would.

It's interesting that the word "community" doesn't even appear in this stretch of text until p. 89, where, after a recapitulation of the negative result of Chapter 2, we find the sentence we've quoted before: "The situation is very different if we widen our gaze from consideration of the rule follower alone and allow ourselves to consider him as interacting with a wider community." But what is it to do this? This sentence introduces a discussion of three scenarios each involving *two people* – a child and a teacher, two adults ("I" and "him"), and Jones and Smith. And in this discussion, the word "community" never recurs. Its next appearance is in the paragraph straddling pp. 91–92:

> Of course if we were reduced to a babble of disagreement, with Smith and Jones asserting of each other that they are following the rule [for the use of the word 'plus'] wrongly, while others disagreed with both and with each other, there would be little point to the practice just described [*viz.*, the practice of asserting meaning-claims under the conditions Kripke has given]. In fact, our actual community is (roughly) uniform in its practices with respect to addition. Any individual who claims to have mastered the concept of addition will be judged by the community to have done so if his particular responses agree with those of the community in enough cases, especially the simple ones …. An individual who passes such tests is admitted into the community as an adder; an individual who passes such tests in enough other cases is admitted as a normal speaker of the language and member of the community …. One who is an incorrigible deviant in enough respects simply cannot participate in the life of the community, and in communication.

What work is the notion of "the community" doing in this passage? It seems clear that it is not introduced as some mysterious entity greater than the sum of its parts: For that, we should certainly expect some further explanation, which we are not given. Rather, it is deployed precisely as the sum of its parts. Consider: What are "its practices," as mentioned in the second sentence here? Well, clearly, this sentence is meant to mark a contrast with the scenario envisaged in the previous sentence, the "babble of disagreement"; and to call our community "uniform in its practices" is just to deny that scenario: to deny that each of us is in disagreement with all the others about particular applications of '+'. A community of adders just *is* a group of people each of whom agrees with each of the others in (most cases of) the application of '+', in the case-by-case sort of way Kripke has described in the previous pages; a linguistic community more generally just is a group of people each of whom agrees with each of the others in most cases of the application of most of their words. Indeed, this passage explicitly tells us that that's the condition of membership in the community!

This is followed immediately by Kripke's explanation of the "utility of the practice" – the second part of what Kripke claims is Wittgenstein's alternative style of story about the meaning of a form of words, in contrast with a story about its "classical realist truth conditions." To explain the practice of meaning ascriptions, we must not merely point out that one person ascribes to another the use of a word with a certain meaning on the basis of seeing that her uses tend to agree with one's own; we must also explain the point of such a practice. Noteworthily, Kripke's account here is articulated again in terms of a two-person interaction: As he says, "The utility is evident and can be brought out by considering again a man who buys something at the grocer's" (92). In other words, having just expounded the practice of meaning ascriptions in a one-on-one framework, Kripke now explains its utility also by reference to the usefulness for each individual of being able to rely on expectations for the behavior of others grounded in the meaning ascriptions that are themselves grounded in that one-on-one way. The practice is useful to a community because, or rather just in the sense that, it is useful to each member of the community.

At this point, however, the reader may wonder what to make of all this talk of "the practice" itself. You may grant that I was right to explicate that earlier reference to "the community's practices with respect to addition" in terms of individual speakers' uses of 'plus'; but it might seem as though the very structure of the skeptical solution presupposes the notion of a practice at, so to speak, a higher order. The very idea of replacing a story about truth conditions with one about assertability conditions and their utility might seem to depend on the idea of imputing a unitary practice, of assertion under certain conditions, to the community. (Compare also passages where Kripke refers to this as "[t]he entire 'game' we have described ... our game of ascribing rules and concepts to each other" (96). A description of "us" as "playing a game" might seem difficult to resolve into individual tendencies to behave in certain ways.) And since I began by defining "constitutive communitarianism" as an account of the sociality of language that makes reference to notions such as customs, institutions, or practices, if they transcend in some way mere interactions among individuals, it might seem that this appeal to the practice of assertion makes the skeptical solution communitarian in this sense after all.

Perhaps it is possible to read the skeptical solution in this way. Or more precisely, perhaps it can be read as, so to speak, "crypto-communitarian," in the sense that, while officially the story is meant to be erected on materials that are hygienic by the lights of Kripke's Chapter 2 – mere patterns of similarity among individual speakers' verbal responses and so on – it rests ineliminably on an unexamined notion of "community practice." But it seems to me more charitable, and in any case consistent with the text, to understand Kripke's approach as assigning the same status to the so-called "game," the "practice" of asserting meaning ascriptions under certain conditions, as to "the community's practices with respect to addition." The implication of Kripke's approach is that there is not so much as such a thing as "the practice" – some unitary entity behind or above the individuals and their several interactions – in which each finds it useful to engage. Rather, the aggregate of facts concerning each individual – to the effect that she keeps track of others in this way, imputing meanings to them on the basis of noted coincidences in their responses to cases – *just is* "the practice." Put another way, just as "the community's practices with respect to addition" are a mere aggregate of individual speakers' uses of 'plus', as we saw above, so "our game of ascribing rules and concepts to each other" is simply an aggregate of individual uses of locutions of the form 'Jones means *addition* by "plus"'. The notion of a practice is in effect implicitly defined in this way, analogously to the way in which, as I suggested earlier, the notion of "the community" is in effect implicitly defined in terms of the aggregate of coincidences in agreement in linguistic response taken severally. – And so it also makes sense that, as we saw, the notion of the *utility* of "the practice" should emerge merely aggregatively out of the usefulness for each individual of keeping track of others.

It is significant that the notions of "the community" and "its practices" are introduced without fanfare, in this aggregative way to which I have been drawing attention, rather than as additional concepts not reducible to individual interactions among "the community's" members. If Kripke had pursued the latter strategy, he would have run the risk of incurring a dilemma for the overall argument of the book. If, on the one hand, Kripke simply took for granted a notion of "community meaning" or "community practice," and presented his "skeptical solution" in terms of an individual's use of a word agreeing or not with the "community meaning," the reader would rightly wonder why the notion of "community meaning" is exempt from the destructive arguments of Chapter 2.[8] If the result of Chapter 2 was correct, that there can be no fact about what an individual means, shouldn't we worry that parallel considerations will show that there can be no fact about what "the community" means? At any rate, surely such notions should not simply be taken for granted, on the heels of the barrage of skeptical argumentation of Chapter 2. However, on the other horn of the dilemma, if instead of taking them for granted, Kripke were to succeed in giving a positive account of "community meaning," "community practice" and so on, an account which does not reduce them to interpersonal interactions among individual community members but on the basis of which ascriptions of

---

[8] Horwich (1984: 166) is one reader who *does* appear to suppose that Kripke operates with a notion of community meaning, without however pausing to wonder, as I am arguing that one ought, how he can justify it.

meaning to individual community members could be grounded, would this not constitute a "straight solution" rather than a "skeptical solution"? It would presumably emerge from such an account that it would be a matter of fact about me that I am a member of a certain linguistic community, one with this practice (or perhaps of more than one if I am multilingual, but anyway of at least one); and now, if it were also a matter of fact about that community that, say, '+' means *addition* for it, then it would seem to follow after all, on a story of this shape, that it is a fact about me that '+' means *addition* for me – a straight solution.[9]

A couple more examples will serve to drive the point further home that the skeptical solution is not robustly communitarian. Immediately after the passages I have been discussing comes the following:

This expectation [that others will behave as we do] is *not* infallibly fulfilled. It places a substantive restriction on the behavior of each individual, and is *not* compatible with just any behavior he may choose. (Contrast this with the case where we considered one person alone.) A deviant individual whose responses do not accord with those of the community in enough cases will not be judged, by the community, to be following its rules; he may even be judged to be a madman, following no coherent rule at all. When the community denies of someone that he is following certain rules, it excludes him from various transactions such as the one between the grocer and the customer. It indicates that it cannot rely on his behavior in such transactions. (93)

Now, here it may sound as though Kripke is treating "the community" as an agent with "its rules" after all. But again, this comes, without ado, following the passages I've been examining – which are discussions of two-person interactions, in which reference to "the community" is made without remark, in a way that suggests that Kripke is thinking of it basically additively. So this passage about "the community's rules" comes across as, in effect, *defining* that notion: To say that "[a] deviant individual whose responses do not accord with those of the community in enough cases will not be judged, by the community, to be following its rules" is to *explain* the notion of "a community's rules" (or indeed, more precisely, to explain the notion of "judging someone to be following the community's rules") in

---

[9] I suppose it is not entirely clear whether, on Kripke's view as it stands, it is a "matter of fact about me" (in the semi-technical sense in which he uses that phrase) that I am a member of a certain linguistic community. (For one thing, if it were a "matter of fact," it's hard to see why Kripke would make such heavy weather of the idea of *considering a person as* a member of a community, as he does for instance in his discussion of Crusoe at p. 110.) In any case, as I have been arguing, the most that that comes to is that my linguistic responses coincide with those of certain other individuals, together perhaps with our mutual recognition of that coincidence. But if we now envision supplementing the text with a straight, positive account of "community practice," it is hard to imagine such an account leaving it entirely indeterminate *whose* practice a given practice is.

terms of the idea of the *responses* of the community, where that in turn just means: the responses of the various individual people who have found that they usually give the same responses (to, say, addition problems).

Another passage which might at first seem to make a difficulty for my reading, but which I would diagnose in the same way as the previous one, is at p. 96: "[T]hat the community attributes a concept to an individual so long as he exhibits sufficient conformity, under test circumstances, to the behavior of the community ... would lose its point outside a community that generally agrees in its practices." Here Kripke is adverting to his earlier account of the point of the practice, the second element in a putatively *Investigations*-style account of the meaning of a form of words – in this case, of meaning ascriptions. And here, the repeated references to "the community" may again seem to depend on positing it as something over and above its members. However, "the behavior of the community" means the particular responses made by the individual people making up the community (what else could it mean, after all?) – where what it is for people to "make up the community" is, as we have already seen, just for them to agree in their responses to addition problems. Likewise, for a community to "attribute a concept to an individual" is just for those particular community *members* to attribute a concept to an individual: say, for Smith and Martínez and Kobayashi each to attribute *addition* to Jones, on the basis of the fact that his responses to '+'-queries generally agree with Smith's and Martínez's and Kobayashi's respectively – which in addition agree with one another, *ex hypothesi*: That's why they're called a community. Likewise for "a community that generally agrees in its practices": This is just, of course, a group whose *members* agree in their particular responses, as in the passage at the bottom of p. 91 that this quotation harks back to, which we examined earlier.

In short, despite the various – indeed relatively infrequent – references to "the community" in the course of Kripke's exposition of the "skeptical solution," the sociality it presupposes in characterizing someone as a language-user is only that which we have been calling "interpersonal," not communitarian. Those references to community are shorthand for references to individual interactions; indeed, the very idea of a community is implicitly defined as nothing more than an aggregate of severally interacting individuals, and the idea of a "community practice" nothing more than an aggregate of similar patterns in individual behavior.[10]

---

[10] In the terminology of note 3, one might phrase my claim as that the skeptical solution is an "I-thou" rather than an "I-we" view. In this sense, I disagree with Brandom (1994: 37ff) and Williams (2000: 317, n11), who both characterize Kripke's Wittgenstein as an "I-we" theorist – the first disapprovingly, the second approvingly. (There may however be subtle differences in the ways in which they understand the "I-thou"/"I-we" distinction.)

3 The Meaning-Individualism of the Skeptical Solution

Now, even if we're right to read the skeptical solution's answer to what I have been calling the "constitutive question" (or anyway, the version of this question that I have suggested can be raised in Kripke's framework) as interpersonal rather than communitarian, it may seem that our very argument for this has brought out that its answer to the "agreement question" might be communitarian. Our argument proceeded by showing that Kripke's talk of "agreement with the community," for instance, should be understood not by positing a separate "community meaning" but rather in terms of agreement in the responses of pairs of speakers taken severally – but agreement taken severally is still agreement; and if each member's responses agree with (most of) those of each of the others, then the result will end up complying with the definition we suggested of "meaning-communitarianism" in §1.[11] In any case, it may seem that, on this view, surely any successful meaning ascription will at least meet the requirement of meaning-*interpersonalism*, even if not meaning-communitarianism: for if it is right to argue that, on the skeptical solution, for me to call Jones a rule-follower at all requires that his responses agree with mine, it seems to follow immediately that there cannot be ascriptions of rule-following, nor hence *a fortiori* recognition of meaning, without agreement.

However, I maintain that the skeptical solution is actually compatible with meaning-individualism. I can begin with a passage where Kripke *says* as much: "Sometimes Smith, by substituting some alternative interpretation for Jones's word 'plus', will be able to bring Jones's responses in line with his own" (91). In other words, Smith can interpret Jones's word 'plus' as *minus*, say, if Jones's responses to 'plus' queries generally agree with what Smith would have responded to such queries in which the word 'plus' is replaced by 'minus'. It might be clearer, and less fanciful, to consider a case where Jones's word, rather than being homophonic with another word of Smith's, is altogether different: Perhaps, for instance, Jones responds to utterances containing the word 'lorry' in the way Smith would respond to corresponding utterances with 'truck':

[11] If I had defined 'meaning-communitarianism' so as to hold that, say, the meaning of a word in a speaker's mouth just is the "community meaning" of that word, then I would have had little work to do in this section. If §2 was on the right track, it should seem obvious already that, just as the skeptical solution gives no comfort to the idea of a "community practice" over and above individual behavior and interactions, nor does it posit "community meanings" over and above individual verbal behavior. But I chose to define 'meaning-communitarianism' in a weaker way, so as to hold simply that the meanings with which one uses words must coincide with those of others, without specifying precisely why that should be. There thus remains a substantive question to be confronted in this section.

Then Smith can say that Jones means *truck* by 'lorry'. Or, for that matter, perhaps Jones responds to utterances containing 'más' in the way Smith responds to utterances containing 'plus', and also differing systematically in other ways: Thus, Jones responds to "¿Cuántos son tres más cuatro?" with "Siete," while Smith responds to "What are three plus four?" with "Seven," and meanwhile, Jones's other responses involving 'siete' parallel those of Smith involving 'seven' (and likewise with the other words involved). Then Smith can say that Jones means *addition* by 'más'. Again, this is just a complicated version of the sort of case Kripke explicitly (if laconically) acknowledges at p. 91 – and I dare to suggest that this sounds almost like the Davidsonian view we adverted to in §1 as a paradigm of meaning-individualism.

Where could this be coming from? Well, there are two different questions we might ask of an agent: (1) Is she following a rule at all? (2) Is she following *this* rule (or *our* rule)? Surely Kripke's main concern is the former. Passages where he articulates the skeptical conclusion, such as those we have quoted earlier from pp. 69 and 89, suggest that the point is that seeing someone as *so much as a rule-follower at all* will depend on seeing her as part of a community in some sense; that is, on comparing her responses to others'. Now, an attempt to address even the *first* question will no doubt have to involve reference to some *particular* rule: I can hardly tell whether someone is *following a rule at all* without seeking to identify some pattern in behavior which, just in virtue of its being a pattern, I could presumably describe as instantiating a rule. And the typical, or anyway easiest, way to do this in turn will be to check whether she's following *my* rule for doing whatever it is I take her to be doing. For this reason, talk of "applying our criteria for rule following to [Crusoe]" (110), for instance, can easily seem to imply determining whether Crusoe is following *our* rules for doing something: say, for using some particular word. Nevertheless, the quotation about interpretation from p. 91 shows that the real question is (1), the general one, and that (2) is *not* really essential. I can perfectly easily account for someone's meaning something different from what I do by a word – cases of idiolectal variation, malapropisms, and such – by recognizing that, using that word, she is giving responses that I would give using a different expression.

And on reflection, it should be obvious that this has to be Kripke's view. Indeed, it should have struck us as mad when, three paragraphs back, we found ourselves attributing to him the idea that "for me to call Jones a rule-follower at all requires that his responses agree with mine." I can surely call Jones a rule-follower even if *none* of his linguistic responses agree with mine (say, because he and I are monolingual speakers of different languages, as we would ordinarily put it), as long as I can reliably map regularities in his verbal behavior on to my own. Any view that excludes this possibility and hence requires me to deny that he is following any rules is evidently absurd! If I use 'plus' to mean *addition*, then indeed I will only suppose Smith also means *addition* by 'plus' if Smith responds in more or less the way I do to utterances containing 'plus' (give or take a few understandable cases of error, etc.); but again, as Kripke tells us on p. 91, I can recognize Smith as using *a* rule, even if not *my* rule, by recognizing Smith's use of, say, 'más' as systematically related to my use of 'plus'.

In short, the "skeptical solution" is compatible with a "meaning-individualism" of much the same kind as Davidson's.

Perhaps, however, the reader will wonder at this point what is left of the "skeptical solution" on this reading. Wasn't the idea supposed to be that nothing about an individual speaker considered in herself settles what she means by her words, and instead, ascriptions of meaning rest essentially on agreement in usage with other speakers? And wasn't a communitarian account of *correctness conditions* supposed to emerge from this story, such that the correctness condition of a speaker's use of a word derived from other speakers' use of it? If I'm right in recommending this *rapprochement* with Davidson's view, haven't I thereby divested the skeptical solution of all that made it *skeptical*? Or contrapositively, given that the skeptical solution surely *is* skeptical, mustn't my reading be wrong?

Let me start with the point about the structure of the skeptical solution; below, I'll discuss correctness conditions. The reading I propose does not threaten that structure: It leaves intact the guiding idea, which Kripke expresses, for instance, with his analogy with what he presents as Hume's view on causation. On that view, there is no "secret connexion" between two events considered in themselves that constitutes the one's causing the other; rather, we say that the one caused the other only when they instantiate *types* of events that are constantly conjoined. Likewise, it remains the case on my reading that the result of Chapter 2 is left unquestioned, that there is no fact about a speaker considered in herself that constitutes her meaning *addition* by 'plus', and that meaning ascriptions are, rather, essentially grounded in the assertability conditions Kripke specifies, the speaker-to-speaker comparisons. All I am proposing is a kind of liberalization of those assertability conditions – or more accurately, I am proposing a corrective to the excessive conservativeness with which some readers of Kripke's book have understood them. Admittedly, Kripke himself could be said to be largely responsible for this conservative misreading: He concentrates on cases where speakers' responses *do* coincide, or alternatively, on the fully contrasting case where *no* resemblance can be found and communication breaks down entirely. That seemingly throwaway remark on p. 91 is about all he gives us as a hint that there are intermediate cases: cases where there is a systematic relation between speakers' responses – not the relation of identity, but where the assertability conditions for meaning ascriptions are still met. Still, he *does* give us that remark, and as I've argued, he had better: It would be absurd to propound a view according to which I cannot so much as recognize someone as a rule-follower at all unless I find her to be following just the rule I follow. In any case, the point is that the solution is still *skeptical* on my reading. It is not that what Jones means by 'plus' is a fact about her, which holds regardless of how things are with Smith, but which Smith can only *discover* by comparing Jones's responses to his own. Rather, the story about assertability conditions is still meant to *replace* that truth-conditional picture of meaning ascriptions, even once we liberalize our understanding of the assertability conditions in question.

One way to see this is to recognize that the sort of skeptical worry that motivated Chapter 2 is still very much alive on my proposed reading. I argued earlier that it is consonant with the skeptical solution for Smith to find that Jones means *truck* by 'lorry'. But wait – does Jones mean *truck* or *quuck*, where a quuck is a truck if observed before now or a bus afterwards? Likewise, if Jones says "Tres más cuatro son siete" and Smith is inclined to say that Jones means *addition* by 'más', we can wonder how Smith is sure that Jones doesn't mean *quaddition* rather than addition. The specter of these skeptical hypotheses is in no way exorcised by recognizing that the assertability-conditional approach Kripke recommends is capable of accommodating cases of malapropisms, language variation, and the like. So if you were convinced by Chapters 2 and 3 of the need for this move to assertability conditions, you can remain convinced even on my reading of what Kripke intends those assertability conditions to be.

Now to the question of correctness. Recall the bipartite structure of the assertability conditions: Jones can say of herself that she means addition by 'plus' just in case she feels confident that she knows how to go on using 'plus', while *Smith* will say that of Jones just in case she has used 'plus' in more or less the same way Smith has – at least in the simplest case, though the passage from p. 91 reminds us that things can get more complicated. The point of the second clause here, the comparison between Smith and Jones, is that, if all we could say in defense of a meaning ascription were to advert to the speaker's own confidence, then what would seem right to her would be right, and as Wittgenstein said, "that only means that here we can't talk about 'right'" (1953b: §258). In other words, the second clause is doing the work of bringing back into the picture the *normativity* of meaning that Chapter 2 seemed to render incomprehensible. Thus, many readers have taken the skeptical solution to propound correctness conditions in terms of agreement with others: A speaker uses a word *correctly* just in case they use it in the way their *community* considers correct; that is, the speaker's correctness conditions are simply inherited from the community.[12] If I'm right that the skeptical solution is compatible with what I've called meaning-individualism, what becomes of its account of the correctness conditions of a speaker's use of a word? If they aren't given by the use *other* speakers make of the word, haven't we again lost the *skepticism* in the skeptical solution?

Well, here too, I think the answer is No. Consider the 'lorry' case again. I've argued that Smith can, by comparing Jones's responses with his own, conclude that Jones means *truck* by 'lorry'. Now, if Smith doesn't have the word 'lorry' in his vocabulary (or if he does, but not as a synonym of his word 'truck'), he won't take the correctness conditions of Jones's uses of 'lorry' to be given by his own – but he will take them to consist in agreement with his uses of 'truck'. So if Jones is staring down at her cellphone, and then looks up just as a bus turns a corner and disappears, and says, "That was an odd-looking lorry," Smith will judge Jones to have made an error. Similarly, if Smith takes Jones to mean *epithet* by 'epitaph', Smith will suppose Jones to have erred if she says, "One of Achilles's epitaphs was 'the man of twists and turns'": for that was an epithet of Odysseus, not of Achilles! But this seeming divorce of the correctness conditions of Jones's uses of words from Smith's need not drive us back to a non-skeptical understanding of Kripke's account in Chapter 3. Again, Chapter 2 purported to establish that "[there is no fact] which constitutes my meaning addition by 'plus'" (69), in particular by arguing that there is no fact

---

[12] Thus Horwich (1984: 166) writes that, on the skeptical solution, "[a speaker's] meaning is determined by the meaning of 'plus' within a community language which he speaks. Such a community is the external source of the normative standards that will permit some of a speaker's dispositions to qualify as mistaken." Likewise Verheggen: "in effect, the meanings of a speaker's words are determined by what the members of her community mean by those words. Correct applications are applications that conform to the conditions of correctness at play in her community. Kripke's answer [to the question how meanings are determined] is thus communitarian" (Myers and Verheggen 2016: 90). (Unlike Horwich, Verheggen recognizes that this reading raises a problem for Kripke, of the sort that I discussed earlier (in the text from which my note 8 hangs): namely, the question how in turn the *community*'s correctness conditions are determined.) – For a view which does have something like this structure, consider Burge's version of social externalism (Burge 1979). According to Burge, whether the word 'arthritis' in the mouth of the patient in his thought experiment applies only to inflammation of the joints or also to muscles is determined not by how things stand with the patient, but by how the word is taken to be correctly used by the rest of his speech community. – I am grateful to Claudine Verheggen for a substantial correction to an earlier version of this note, and for prompting me to clarify the text from which it hangs.

which distinguishes my meaning *addition* by 'plus' from my meaning *quaddition*. But if I mean *addition* by 'plus', then it is correct for me to assert that 68 + 57 = 125, and incorrect to assert that 68 + 57 = 5; while if I mean *quaddition* by 'plus', then the reverse is true. So if the result of Chapter 2 is correct that there is no fact about me that settles what I mean by '+', then there is no fact that constitutes the *correctness conditions* of my use of '+' either. And this persists through the skeptical solution of Chapter 3. Just as we have replaced a truth-conditional with an assertability-conditional account of meaning ascriptions, so must we replace a truth-conditional with an assertability-conditional account of correctness claims if we are to retain the skepticism purportedly forced upon us by the skeptical paradox. If Smith is entitled to assert of Jones that she means *addition* by 'plus', then Smith will likewise be entitled to assert of Jones that she is incorrect if she denies that 68 + 57 = 125. Just so, if Smith is entitled to assert of Jones that she means *truck* by 'lorry', then he will be entitled to assert that Jones has used 'lorry' incorrectly in applying it to a bus. But a quus-speaker[13] will also find Jones's responses to 'plus' queries to have agreed with his own so far, and so will be entitled to assert that Jones means *quaddition* by 'plus' (though of course the word the quus-speaker will use to express the concept of quaddition is 'addition'!). And such a speaker will also be entitled to assert that Jones would be *correct* in denying that 68 + 57 = 125. Likewise, if tomorrow Jones calls a bus "a lorry," Smith will be entitled to say that she is using 'lorry' incorrectly, while the quus-speaker, who we may suppose is also a quuck-speaker, will not. And again, if we accept the skeptical result of Chapter 2, there is no fact of the matter that can settle whether Smith or the quus-speaker is correct in these claims about the correctness of Jones's uses of words.

In short, it was never quite right to say that the skeptical solution *gives the correctness conditions* of a speaker's words in terms of other speakers' uses of those words; rather, what we should have said from the beginning was that the skeptical solution gives *assertability conditions for correctness claims* by reference to other speakers' responses. And now we can see that this is so whether we read the assertability conditions in question "conservatively" or "liberally," so to speak. Taking the hint from p. 91 and broadening our understanding of the assertability conditions to allow for speakers to recognize and correct for malapropisms, idiolectal variation, and so on does not render the skeptical solution any less skeptical. I thus conclude after all that the "skeptical solution" is compatible with a "meaning-individualism" of much the same shape as Davidson's.

---

[13] That is, a speaker who uses 'plus' to mean *quaddition* (not, of course, a speaker who uses the word 'quus').

4 Taking Stock So Far

The result is that Kripke's skeptical solution broadly coincides with a view such as Davidson's with respect to these two questions, the constitutive question and the question of agreement. This is, of course, not to deny that they differ in detail and in points of emphasis. I've already alluded to one still very significant difference: For Davidson, there is no need to "consider me as a member of a community" in any sense in order to recognize me as a language-user or to determine what I mean by a word, in the way Kripke insists on. On Davidson's account, once I achieve, with the help of others of course, the concept of objectivity, and hence the status of a proposition-monger, that achievement is a straightforward *fact* about me, as are the facts about what my words as I use them mean. So even if, in the broad sense in which I've been using the term, Kripke and Davidson are both "constitutive interpersonalists," this has a very different flavor for the two of them (and indeed, the label is less apt in Kripke's framework). Something similar can also be said of their "meaning-individualism": It could be said of Davidson too that I must in some sense compare Jones's responses to 'más'-utterances with my responses to 'plus'-utterances – or anyway to my beliefs involving addition – in order to determine whether Jones means *addition* by 'más', simply in light of the "charitable" nature of interpretation on Davidson's view. However, Davidson would not agree with what Kripke appears to insist is an implication of the "skeptical solution," that for this reason, it is only if I "consider Jones as a member of my community" that I can rightly make these meaning ascriptions; that "considered in isolation," there is no sense in asking what he means. In a word, we could say that, despite their commonalities, Davidson's account differs from Kripke's "skeptical solution" in not being skeptical. Still, my argument so far has suggested that Kripke is anyway less distant from Davidson than he may appear; to those who find views such as Davidson's congenial, this may be a welcome development.

In the final section of this chapter, though, I want to try to prepare the ground for the suggestion that there is more hope for some version of constitutive communitarianism than either of their accounts allows for. It seems clear enough that Wittgenstein, anyway, held that language use depends on something over and above individual interactions: as he variously put it, on customs, institutions, practices. It seems to me that part of the motivation some authors have had for the recoil against communitarianism as against interpersonalism has rested in a conflation of the constitutive question with the question of agreement. I want to suggest that when we distinguish the two, a version of constitutive communitarianism of the sort some of Wittgenstein's remarks seem to be hinting at can seem more plausible.

5 On the Possibility of Combining Meaning-Individualism with Constitutive Communitarianism (Some Brief and Polemical Remarks)

It seems to me that what I have been calling meaning-individualism has some intuitive points in its favor. I've already adduced some of them: the possibility (indeed actuality) and, often, smooth intelligibility of idiolectal variation; the familiar and straightforward phenomenon of malapropisms, both one-off and systematic; and indeed the possibility Davidson observes for speakers of completely different languages to achieve a degree of mutual intelligibility[14]. We might add the point Davidson (2001a: 287) says he learned from Quine but finds also in Wittgenstein: that "[a teacher] may think of herself as simply passing on a meaning that already attaches to the word. But from the learner's point of view, the word – the sound – is being *endowed* with a meaning" (Davidson 2001b: 14 [emphasis in original]). If we think of first-language acquisition from the point of view of the learner in this way, it will seem natural and unsurprising that the learner may sometimes "endow" a word with a meaning (and that is just to say, may come to use it in a way) somewhat different from the use to which her teacher puts it.

At the same time, constitutive interpersonalism seems to me to leave open a rather wider explanatory gap than we ought to be comfortable with. I only have the space to make the briefest of motivating polemical remarks, but consider the fact that Davidson rarely considers cases of teacher-learner interactions in his many discussions of the kind of triangular situation on which he suggests that the acquisition of language and propositional thought are grounded.[15] Davidson himself concedes that it's hard to explain how preconceptual creatures can bootstrap their way from preconceptuality into a grasp of the ideas of error, correctness, objectivity, and so on. This does not appear to worry him; he insists that we should not expect a full explanation of an organism's transition to conceptuality to be available in any case. He puts the point in terms of the impossibility in principle of reducing the intentional to the extensional.[16] But surely it helps – even if only by putting off the difficult question[17] – to recognize that in situations in which an organism

---

[14] "If you and I were the only speakers in the world, and you spoke Sherpa while I spoke English, we could understand one another, though each of us followed different 'rules'" (Davidson 2001d: 114).
[15] See footnote 4. Williams (2000: 313ff) has emphasized this surprising feature of Davidson's discussion.
[16] Davidson (2001b: 13); cf. Davidson (2001d: 120).
[17] I suspect that it can help with more than this, but I can't argue for that here.

acquires language, it acquires it from others who *already have* it. This at least encourages the suggestion that we need more than the idea of mere individual interactions to explain what's at work in language acquisition: We need something like the concept of initiation into a shared practice that is, so to speak, handed down from teacher to learner, rather than something easily reinvented by pairs of interacting prelinguistic human beings. (I don't claim to have given an argument here; only to have found encouragement for the suggestion.) The idea of two preconceptual organisms bootstrapping their way into conceptuality, even together through triangular interaction, strikes me as an order of magnitude more mysterious than the idea of one such organism inducted into conceptuality by other organisms for whom conceptuality is already a going concern, through initiation into a shared linguistic practice. The idea is that acting in accordance with a norm-governed practice is a *different kind of thing* from merely responding to one's environment; it is a kind of thing which comes naturally to human beings, of course, but only through a process of inculcation (initiation, induction). And it is a form of constitutive communitarianism to insist that the acquisition of language cannot be explained only on the basis of mere individual interactions, but also requires appeal to the concept of induction into a shared practice.

Some thinkers seem to find these two views – constitutive communitarianism and meaning-individualism – to stand in tension. Some, finding constitutive communitarianism appealing, suppose that induction into conceptuality as a going concern must involve the acquisition of the very patterns of use that constitute that going concern – and hence conclude to meaning-communitarianism. Others see this same inferential connection but, finding meaning-individualism (and hence the denial of meaning-communitarianism) intuitive, infer in the *modus tollens* to the denial of constitutive communitarianism: That is, they take it that, since we may perfectly well use words in ways different from those around us, we must not suppose to be available to us in our project of explaining the acquisition of language anything beyond the specific patterns of use individuals engage in, which may well vary from individual to individual.

But it seems to me that this conditional claim – "If constitutive communitarianism, then meaning-communitarianism" – is not obviously obligatory. Again, briefly and polemically: It seems to me that the requirement for conceptuality already to be on the scene in order for an individual to acquire it operates at a different level of generality from that at issue in meaning-communitarianism. When conceptuality is already on the scene, what learners are being brought into, or what is being inculcated in them, is *conceptuality itself* – or, to put a practical spin on it, the *practice of using words meaningfully*. But (contrary to the conditional claim) this doesn't obviously require that learners acquire the specific *contents* of the concepts of their teachers, much less that they use all the words they learn with just the same meanings as do their teachers. In any given case, a learner can come to use a word in a different way from the teacher. Davidson's Quinean observation that, so far as the learner is concerned, a word is *endowed* with a use in the learning situation is consistent with the idea that an organism could not so much as acquire the capacity *to use words meaningfully* except from others who already do so. But what we might have in mind by constitutive communitarianism is that the reason for which we need to appeal to "such notions as customs, institutions, or practices" to explain the acquisition of conceptuality is precisely that we need to explain the acquisition of *conceptuality in general*, or *language itself* – not the acquisition of specific words. And it could be true that we can acquire the very ideas of truth and error only by having inculcated in us a practice of using words – even if we end up using the specific words in question differently from our teachers.

Again, I don't claim here to have actually established constitutive communitarianism, or even to have demonstrated it to be independent of meaning-communitarianism. Of course, much ink has been spilled on both topics – the social nature of the constitution of language and the degree to which specific meanings must be shared – and no doubt some work on these topics can be read as arguing for, rather than tacitly and uncritically presupposing, a link between them.[18] But it seems to me that the topics often enough go undistinguished that it is worth insisting on this at least notional distinction. I leave for future work the question whether the hitherto underappreciated possibility that this makes visible, of combining meaning-individualism with constitutive communitarianism, yields a genuinely stable and satisfying view of the sociality of language.[19]

---

[18] For a couple of examples, the work of McDowell (1980, 1981, 1984, 1998b, *inter alia*) and of Williams (e.g. her 2000, and some of the papers in her 1999) are evidently relevant here.

[19] I am grateful to Claudine Verheggen for instigating the writing of this chapter; indeed it originated in a conversation with her. I wish I had had the time and space to do justice to her work, much of which bears directly on the present topic. – I am also grateful to her for organizing the workshop "Kripke's *Wittgenstein on Rules and Private Language* at 40" in June 2022 at York University, at which several of the chapters in the present volume, including this one, were presented and discussed. I am very grateful to all the participants, from whom I learned much, though I'm afraid the present chapter does not reflect it.

12 "Considered in Isolation"

Arif Ahmed

Chapter 2 of *Wittgenstein on Rules and Private Language* argues that there are no facts about what anyone means by their words. So meaning is a fiction. But some fictions are useful. And Chapter 3 explains why this one is. One side-effect of that explanation is supposed to be the "Private and solitary language argument," which says that we cannot, or cannot usefully, ascribe meaning to an individual "considered in isolation." It thereby reveals something essentially communitarian about meaning.

This chapter briefly defends that fictionalist reading of Kripke's great work. It then argues at more length that no communitarian conclusion follows. Even if semantic ascriptions are all false, they may still be useful. They may still be even when made by, or applied to, or addressed by, an individual "considered in isolation" – whatever exactly this turns out to mean.

1   Semantic Ascriptions are False

If:

(1) It is not a fact that Jones means addition (or anything else) by "+" (or anything else)

does it follow that:

(2) Jones *doesn't* mean addition (or anything else) by "+" (or anything else)?

Not on the commonest reading of Kripke's "sceptical solution." On that reading, Kripke takes (1) to be true, but falls short of (2) because he thinks that

(3) Jones means addition by "+"

was never in the market for *being made true by facts*. Rather, what gives (3) meaning is not that it ever does or could reflect the facts, but that there are circumstances in which meaning-ascriptions of that sort are appropriately assertible, whereas their denials (like (2)) are not.

Kripke says so – or rather, says that his Wittgenstein says so – in this famous passage:

> As Dummett says, 'the *Investigations* contains implicitly a rejection of the classical (realist) Frege-*Tractatus* view that the general form of explanation of meaning is a statement of the truth-conditions'. In place of this view, Wittgenstein proposes an alternative rough general picture ... Wittgenstein replaces the question, 'What must be the case for this sentence to be true?' by two others: first, 'Under what conditions may this form of words be appropriately asserted (or denied)?'; second, given an answer to the first question, 'What is the role and utility, in our lives of our practice of asserting (or denying) the form of words under these conditions?'[1]

There is a ready analogy in ethics. Queasiness about "ethical facts," whether acquired from Hume or Mackie or Stevenson or Ayer, might not force you to say, for example, that stealing apples *isn't* wrong. It is just that "Stealing apples is wrong!" was never in the market for stating facts in the first place. Ethical statements play a different role in our lives; and this role is what determines when they are appropriately asserted. When they are, "Stealing those apples is wrong!" might be an admirable thing to say; "Stealing them is OK!" not so much.

But this looks incompatible with a straightforwardly deflationary view of "facts" in general. Suppose we accept every instance of the following schema in which "p" gets replaced by a declarative English sentence:

(4) It is a fact that p = p

(5) It is not a fact that p = not-p

(4) and (5) are to be read as explanations of their left-hand-sides. "It is a fact that London is a city" is just a fancy way to say that London is a city. "It is not a fact that York is bigger than London" is just a fancy way to say that York *isn't* bigger than London.

Such "fact-deflationism" is in the spirit of Wittgenstein himself. He writes in *Philosophical Investigations* that:

(6) "p" is true = p

(7) "p" is false = not-p[2]

in the context of a passage attacking the idea that we can use "true" and "false" to explain what a proposition is. As if we had a pre-existing concept of true or false, and we explained what a proposition is by saying that it is whatever could be one or the other. Similarly, we might deny that we

---

[1] Kripke (1982: 73).
[2] Wittgenstein (1953b: sect. 136).

have a preexisting grip on "fact": as if we could explain a proposition as the kind of thing that could match "the facts". In reality I couldn't tell you what "facts" *are*, not beyond what is already implicit in (4) and (5).

But if we *do* take that attitude (as from now on I will), then we have to accept (5); but since (2) follows from (1) and (5), it seems that if we grant Kripke's argument for (1) then we must agree after all that Jones *doesn't* mean addition (or anything else) by the "plus" sign. Given (7), we must also grant that it is straightforwardly *false* to say that he meant anything by that word (or by any word). Kripke's argument leads directly to an error theory about meaning. This is just as he has the skeptic say at a climactic point in the book.[3]

Kripke's own discussion confirms this. He writes:

> Wittgenstein's sceptical solution concedes to the sceptic that no 'truth conditions' or 'corresponding facts' in the world exist that make a statement like "Jones, like many of us, means addition by '+'" true. Rather we should look at how such assertions are *used*. Can this be adequate? Do we not call assertions like the one just quoted 'true' or 'false'? Can we not with propriety precede such assertions with 'It is a fact that' or 'It is not a fact that'? Wittgenstein's way with such objections is short. Like many others, Wittgenstein accepts the 'redundancy' theory of truth: to affirm that a statement is true (or, presumably, to precede it with 'It is a fact that...') is simply to affirm the statement itself, and to say it is not true is to deny it: ('*p*' is true = p).[4]

The first sentence of this passage tells us briefly and clearly that Kripke's Wittgenstein assents to, and presumably would also assert, (1). The rest of the passage says, less briefly but just as clearly, that Kripke's Wittgenstein assents to (4)–(7). It seems, then, that he *must* be committed to (2). Kripke's Wittgenstein is an error theorist about meaning.

But then how can Kripke or his Wittgenstein also grant, as he plainly does, that we *can* appropriately assert that "Jones means addition by '+'" (and so too that it is a fact that he does)? Isn't that a contradiction?

I don't know what *he* had in mind, but whatever inconsistency there is might be tolerable if you are clear enough about it. The inconsistency is tolerable because there are times when it is appropriate to assert (and to assert the truth of) things that you know are false.

What I mean is this: It might be a good idea to say false things that have true consequences about what matters to you or your audience at the time, especially if no briefly stateable *truth* has all those consequences.

For instance, it is plausible that scientific progress can involve creating models that are inevitably idealized (so never strictly true) and which

---

[3] Kripke (1982: 55) ("There can be no such thing as meaning anything by any word").
[4] Kripke (1982: 86).

explain by implying observed, and predict by implying not-yet-observed, phenomena. Thus, the simple economic model of the firm describes it as a machine that maximizes expected profits. This idealization is false, but it might have sufficiently accurate consequences for what we care about, namely a firm's responses, for example, to shocks in factor prices, in demand, etc. What makes the model good is not whether it is *true* (we may know that it isn't), but whether *these* of its consequences are. And they might be; and if they are, then the textbooks that set out this model are appropriately asserting falsehoods.[5]

Similarly then: we might say in the seminar – and believe at all times – that "Jones means addition by '+'" is straightforwardly false; but still, we assert that sentence, and approve others' assertion of it, in the field. Not because there it somehow *stops* being false, but because there it has true consequences that are worth knowing.

And it may well do, if what matters is Jones's behavior. For presumably in the right circumstances, or given the right auxiliary assumptions,

(8) Jones means addition by "+"

can be seen to imply:

(9) If you ask Jones "What is 68 + 57?" he will answer "125"

and a range of similar things; and this range of (conditional) predictions about Jones's behavior might be useful for us to know and important for us later to rely on.

So I don't see any real tension after all between straightforwardly denying that anyone ever means anything by any word, and agreeing that there is a point to saying both that they do and what it is. I think Kripke's Wittgenstein does both of those things.

2   Semantic Ascriptions Can Be Useful

Fine, but then what *is* the point? According to Kripke, there are two types of conditions in which it is appropriate to assert (8) and similar things. These are: first, the first-personal assertibility conditions and second, the third-personal conditions.

On the first-personal case he writes:

Jones is entitled, subject to correction by others, provisionally to say, "I mean addition by '+'," whenever he has the feeling of confidence – "now I can go on!" – that he can give 'correct' responses in new cases; and he is entitled, again

---

[5] See for example, Friedman (1966). I make the same point as in this paragraph in Ahmed (2018: 1265–1266).

provisionally and subject to correction by others, to judge a new response to be 'correct' simply because it is the response he is inclined to give. These inclinations (both Jones's general inclination that he has 'got it' and his particular inclination to give particular answers in particular addition problems) are to be regarded as primitive. They are not to be justified in terms of Jones's ability to interpret his own intentions or anything else.[6]

Things are different from the third-personal perspective.

Smith will judge Jones to mean addition by '+' only if he judges that Jones's answers to particular addition problems agree with those he is inclined to give, or, if they occasionally disagree, he can interpret Jones as at least following the proper procedure.... If Jones consistently fails to give answers in agreement (in this broad sense) with Smith's, Smith will judge that he does not mean addition by '+'. Even if Jones did mean it in the past, the present deviation will justify Smith in judging that he has lapsed.[7]

These are the conditions under which it is legitimate to assert (8), in the first case for Jones himself and in the second case for Smith. But what is the *point* of the practice? Kripke writes:

> The utility is evident and can be brought out by considering ... a man who buys something at the grocer's. The customer, when he deals with the grocer and asks for five apples, expects the grocer to count as he does, not according to some bizarre non-standard rule; and so, if his dealings with the grocer involve a computation, such as '68 + 57', he expects the grocer's response to agree with his own. Indeed, he may entrust the computation to the grocer. Of course the grocer may make mistakes in addition; he may even make dishonest computations. But as long as the customer attributes to him a grasp of the concept of addition, he expects that at least the grocer will not behave bizarrely, as he would if he were to follow a quus-like rule; and one can expect that, in many cases, he will come up with the same answer the customer would have given himself.[8]

In the following discussion, I'll call the grocer G and the customer C.

It is worth being clear that Kripke is not, in this passage, explaining the point of C's asserting, to G, to himself, or to anyone else, a sentence like:

(10) G means addition by "+".

What would be the use of that? If C already possesses the grounds for saying so – having observed G's past behavior – then saying it to himself or to anyone else would be useless to *him*. But if C does *not* already

---

[6] Kripke (1982: 90–91). I have changed Kripke's "plus" to "+" for uniformity with my own notation.
[7] Kripke (1982: 91).
[8] Kripke (1982: 92).

possess the grounds for saying so, then saying it would be at best pointless, and it would be rash if he started to form expectations on the basis of it, expectations about the grocer's behavior that he didn't previously entertain. It might cause him to lose money, or apples.

Instead, the story illustrates the utility of the general practice of meaning-talk by alluding to the possibility that a *third* person, D, could tell the customer (10). Suppose the customer is new in town and has not had a chance to observe the grocer. The customer wants to buy a red apple costing 68p and a green apple costing 57p; he knows that the grocer will calculate the charge by computing "68 + 57." An aged local, who *does* know the grocer, might then say to the customer, "The grocer means addition by '+'." And this *would* be useful to the customer – it would assure him (or at least raise his confidence), on grounds that were not previously available to him, that he could trust the grocer's calculations.

Given its assertibility conditions, this story about the utility of a meaning-ascription like (10) relies crucially on two facts: (A) that the speaker and the hearer of (10) are both inclined to add in the same way; (B) that if the ascrib*ee* has added in the same way as the speaker in the past, then she will continue to add in the same way as the speaker in the future.

(A) and (B) are sufficient for the usefulness of (10) in these circumstances because if D observes that G uses the "+" sign in the same way as he, D, does then D will assert (10) to C. C will then form a new expectation, namely that G will continue to use "+" as C is inclined to; by (A) it follows that this expectation will be met if G will continue to use "+" as D is inclined to use it. But since G has in the past used "+" in the same way as D, it follows from (B) that G *will* in the future use "+" in the same way as D is inclined to use it. So, C's expectation *will* be met. By asserting the false sentence (8) to C, D has caused C to make a true and useful prediction about G's future behavior.

3 Two Comparisons

Before moving on to discuss the communitarian significance of this theory, it might help to locate it within or alongside two other accounts of the utility of linguistic expressions.

A great deal of fact-stating language can be useful because it permits a division of epistemic labor. Suppose that A, a successful businessman, is in a position to know whether the Porphyrion Insurance Co. is about to go bust, but B – who works there – is the one who really *needs* to know. Conversely, suppose that B is in a position to know whether M, the sister of his best friend, has any romantic attachments, but it is A – who is in love with M – who wants to know *that*. It is by means of fact-stating sentences in a common language ("The Porphyrion is in trouble," etc.) that A's evidence can be made to serve B's ends, and vice versa. Without a common language, both parties would be worse off. The fact that it is a mechanism by which one person can exploit the epistemic position of another, is of course, the reason why signaling games play such a central role in naturalistic theories of language.[9]

On my reading, Kripke's account of the utility of semantic ascriptions fits this general pattern. Semantic ascriptions are useful because they let one person (e.g. C) exploit the epistemic position of another (e.g. D): In the example, D's epistemic position – that is, having observed G's behavior – warrants the assertion of a statement (10) from which its hearer, C, can then infer true consequences about G that it is useful for C to know.

The only distinctive feature of Kripke's account – on this reading – is that the statement that serves this function is in fact false. But this is no problem: a statement can be assertable even though it is false if, in those circumstances, its important consequences are *true*. In fact, the grocer *doesn't* mean addition by "+," because nobody ever means anything; but she will say "125" when asked to compute "68 + 57"; and this *true* consequence of (10) is what matters to C.

The second point of comparison is Quine's account of *belief* ascriptions. In uttering,

(11) Jones believes that it will be apple pie for pudding

Smith needn't be *quoting* anything that Jones has said or is disposed to say (Jones might not speak English). Still, the sentence following "that" is a *kind* of impersonation.

[I]n indirect quotation we project ourselves into what, from his remarks and other indications, we imagine the speaker's state of mind to have been, and then we say what, in our language, is natural and relevant for us in the state thus feigned. An indirect quotation we can usually expect to rate only as better or worse, more or less faithful, and we cannot even hope for a strict standard of more and less; what is involved is evaluation, relative to special purposes, of an essentially dramatic act.[10]

Similarly, semantic ascriptions like (8) and (10) are based on matching the ascribee's past usage of "+" to *your* present disposition to add. Given a match, you then bring in the term that *you* are disposed to use, as the ascribee has used "+." You say that Jones, or G, means *addition* by "+." In this sense, you are *simulating* Jones or G: Not literally, because

---

[9] See for example, Skyrms (2010).
[10] Quine (1960: 218).

"addition" might not figure in *their* language, but because the word connects to dispositions on your part that correspond more or less closely to behavior that you expect on theirs.

Finally, on "more or less faithful" in the passage from Quine: The lack of clear and precise standards of correctness for indirect quotation is obviously what motivates *Quine* to deny, of (11) and its kind, any role in what he calls "limning the true and ultimate structure of reality" – that and his reservations about intensional objects, of course.[11] But these reasons for thinking (11) false are *not* Kripke's (or Wittgenstein's, or "Kripkenstein's") reasons for thinking (8) and (10) false. Kripke's reasons, which I have not discussed here, arise from the powerful argument in Chapter 2 of *Wittgenstein on Rules and Private Language*. I have argued elsewhere that the central argument of that chapter is that if (8) is true, then some object of Jones's awareness must *guide* his use of "+"; but no object of awareness *could* do that.[12] This is not the place to describe or assess that argument; I mention it only to mark the difference between it and Quine's route to a similar conclusion.

4   "Private" Semantic Ascriptions

Now: does anything follow from Kripke's account of (a) the grounds for, and (b) the utility of, semantic ascriptions, about the possibility of a language that is in some sense "private"?

Well, consider a congenital Robinson Crusoe, stuck on a deserted island all his life. Does anything follow, from (a) and (b), about whether there would be any grounds for, or any point in, ascribing a semantic meaning to Crusoe's activity, either by us or by Crusoe himself? I want to make four points about this.

(1) *I* can ascribe meanings to his words on the third-personal grounds that Kripke has set out; and doing so might be useful to *you*.

For instance, suppose Crusoe draws tally marks on the sand every day; suppose that I have observed (a) his use of the sign "+" in connection with those marks; and (b) a connection between those marks and his behavior. For instance, on Monday morning he writes "I + IIII," and on Monday evening he collects five coconuts from the trees on his island; on Tuesday he writes "III + III" and that evening he collects six coconuts, etc.

---

[11] See Quine (1960: chapter 6 generally). The quotation is from p. 220.
[12] Ahmed (2007: chapter 4).

Obviously, there might be some point in my telling you that he means addition by "+." Doing so will create expectations on your part about Crusoe's behavior on *Wednesday* evening, given observation of the marks that he made in the sand on Wednesday morning. It might matter to you that these expectations are fulfilled. (We might be putting bets on how many coconuts he gathers.) If so, my semantic ascription to Crusoe is obviously useful, even if it is false. – But still, if it is false for Kripkean reasons, it is no *more* false than an ascription of meaning to anyone else.

(2) Crusoe can make ascriptions of meaning to *his own past* self, and these too might be useful to *his own future* self.[13]

Suppose Crusoe comes across a diary that he'd written ten years before: On p. 258 he finds a map of a remote part of the island that he hasn't visited since. On the map, he sees an "S." "What did I mean by 'S'?" he wonders. Looking through earlier diaries, diaries for eleven or twelve years ago, he sees earlier maps, or sketches for maps, in which – he now notices – the "S" mark always appears on those areas of the map corresponding to regions that he knows to be swampy. He concludes: "I meant *swamps* by 'S'" and writes this semantic ascription on p. 258.

On what basis is Crusoe making this ascription? The same as the basis on which D makes a meaning-ascription to G: by observing his behavior. The fact that the person whose behavior is being observed is past-Crusoe, and not present-anyone-else, makes no difference to the essentially third-personal basis on which the ascription is made. Nor does the fact that present-Crusoe is observing past-Crusoe's behavior through the medium of reading his long-forgotten diary rather than by, for example, hearing his voice or seeing his bodily movements.

And as with G and D, Crusoe's license to make this ascription will expire in the face of suitable counter-evidence. If (in this hypothetical story counterfactually) Crusoe were to turn over, to p. 259, and see there repeated and confident uses of "S" on bits of the map corresponding not to *swampy* regions but to sandy ones, he himself would reject the ascription made by his 5-minutes-ago self, preferring to write, for example, "By 'S' I meant *swamp or beach*," or similar. The fact that this further thing *could* happen shows that a solitary Crusoe can subject his own semantic ascriptions to the same discipline that Kripke imagines in the communitarian case.

He can also find in them a parallel utility. Suppose that the counterfactual elaboration of the story does not in fact take place. Instead, suppose that one or two years after making the ascription on p. 258 of the diary,

---

[13] Here I am developing an important idea from Blackburn (1984).

Crusoe finds this page, now torn out blowing across the beach. He has quite forgotten about it. That is, he's forgotten about the maps that he originally drew and about the semantic ascription ("I meant *swamps* by 'S'") that he later wrote on the same page. Reading it now, he first sees the sign "S" and again wonders what it means. Reading the explanation, he can make predictions about where else "S" might appear, and what to do if it does appear, on maps that are drawn on other pages. It is in these ways that self-ascriptions of meaning to his past self will have utility for his future self.

(3) These same ascriptions of meaning to his past self might also be useful to *others*. Let us continue the story about the diary.

Three years after the events I just recounted, Crusoe has escaped the island. Explorers land, and they find the diary in Crusoe's abandoned cabin. Turning to p. 258, they see a map of what they recognize as a region of the island. Seeing a mark 'S' on the map, they wonder – what did the mapmaker mean by that? Looking further down, they see Crusoe's answer: "I meant swamps by 'S'." Again, you can imagine why it would be useful to *them* to read Crusoe's semantic ascription to his past self: It would be helpful for exploring the island.

(4) A fourth case is more complex and more controversial. Crusoe can ascribe meaning to his own *present* self.

Before saying anything about the basis on which he might do that, let me briefly state how such ascriptions might be useful, both to his own later self and to others. To see this, just imagine that when he is drawing a map, he writes "S," and then at the bottom of the map, as part of the key, he writes, "By 'S' I mean swamp"; or simply "S = swamp," but the effect is the same. That effect is that map-users, including his own future self, will get some idea of (a) where on the island they will find swamps and (b) where else on the map they will find "S." So the utility of semantic ascriptions extends not only to past tense or third-personal ascriptions, but also to present-tense first-personal avowals.

But what are Crusoe's *grounds* for such an ascription? One novelty that arises in this fourth case is that they are not the same as in (1)–(3). In those other examples, the ground for the semantic attribution is a comparison between the behavior of the object of the attribution and the dispositions of the person making the attribution.

For instance, in (1) our grounds for saying "Crusoe means addition by '+'" is that his use of the "+" sign resembles, or is systematically related to, our present disposition to use "add." Thus, the number of coconuts that he collects the evening after he writes "I + IIII," is the same as the number of coconuts that *we'd* collect if we were told to collect the number you get if you "add 1 to 4." Our grounds for making this attribution to Crusoe consist in a comparison between *Crusoe's actual* use of "+" and *our disposition* to use "add," where "use" includes dispositions to respond to utterances of others in which that word appears.

Similarly in (3), present-Crusoe's grounds for saying that past-Crusoe "*meant* swamps by 'S'" are that past-Crusoe put "S" on the map in the same places that present-Crusoe would put them if he (present-Crusoe) were asked to indicate "where the swamps are." Present-Crusoe's grounds for making this attribution to past-Crusoe consist in a comparison between past-Crusoe's actual use of "S" and present-Crusoe's disposition to use the word "swamp," where "use" again includes dispositions to respond to utterances of others in which that word appears.

But in this fourth case, *present*-Crusoe's grounds for saying that *present*-Crusoe "means swamps by 'S'" *don't* involve any comparison. That is because there *are* no such grounds, other than perhaps an unanalyzable feeling that he has "got it." As Kripke writes, not about Crusoe now but about Jones:

> *Jones* is entitled, subject to correction by others[14] provisionally to say, 'I mean addition by "+",' whenever he has the feeling of confidence – "now I can go on!" – that he can give 'correct' responses in new cases; and he is entitled, again provisionally and subject to correction by others, to judge a new response to be 'correct' simply because it is the response he is inclined to give. These inclinations (both Jones's general inclination that he has 'got it' and his particular inclination to give particular answers in particular addition problems) are to be regarded as primitive. They are not to be justified in terms of Jones's ability to interpret his own intentions or anything else.[15]

But even if we grant that first-person present tense semantic ascriptions are not made on any grounds, it doesn't follow that those ascriptions lack utility. As we have seen, they can be very useful, to Crusoe's or Jones's future selves or to the present selves of anyone else around. For those others – though not for present-Crusoe himself – such self-ascriptions can form the basis of reliable expectations about the speaker's future behavior; and why it might be useful to form such expectations is too obvious to need spelling out.

Semantic self-ascriptions are not the only kind of judgment that is made on no grounds at all. Wittgenstein gives the example of guessing what time it is – not on the basis of clues, like the position of the sun, etc., but just one's initial, offhand estimate. What really happens when you make such an estimate? Wittgenstein writes:

---

[14] I might seem to be overlooking the significance of this qualification: for discussion of self-correction in Crusoe's case, see "Seeming right and being right."
[15] Kripke (1982: 90–91).

One asks oneself, say, "What time can it be?", pauses a moment, perhaps imagines a clock face, and then says a time.... That's the sort of thing one does. – But isn't the hunch accompanied by a feeling of conviction; and doesn't that mean that it now accords with an inner clock? – No, I don't read the time off from an inner clock; there is a feeling of conviction inasmuch as I say a time to myself *without* a feeling of doubt, with calm assurance.[16]

The point of the example is to loosen the grip of the idea that every judgment not based on an outer perception is based on some kind of inner perception; sometimes, as in this case and as in the semantic case, the judgment might be based on nothing.

The doxastic comparison is perhaps even more apt, because present-tense self-ascriptions of belief resemble present-tense self-ascriptions of meaning in *two* respects. Both are made on the same (null) grounds; and both are useful for guiding expectations of behavior.

Of course, it's true that the act of uttering, or writing, "I mean addition by '+'," won't cause Jones *at that time* to form any new expectations about his own behavior. So it's true that present-tense semantic self-ascriptions are of no use to the ascriber *when he is making them*. But then present-tense *anything* self-ascriptions are of no use to the ascriber when he is making them. Jones's saying, for example, "I am thirty-six years old," even if it's true, won't tell *Jones* anything that he didn't know already: After all, if he hadn't known it, then he wouldn't have said it. This utterly banal fact does nothing to reveal the *especially* public or social character of linguistic meaning or ascriptions thereof; and given their availability and usefulness in the variously restrictive Crusoe-esque scenarios that we have discussed, it looks as if that social character is something of an illusion.

5   Distinct and Independent Wills

The argument is at odds with the idea that Kripke's skeptical solution establishes a communitarian conception of language and meaning, according to which it could not be true, or at least could not be assertable, or at least could not be usefully assertable, that "Jones means addition by '+'" – at least not if, as I will continue to assume, Jones is a solitary.

It is worth considering some important and representative communitarian writings, to get a sense of where they have gone wrong (according to me), or of where I have gone wrong (according to them).

---

[16] Wittgenstein (1953b: sect. 607). Moran (2001: chapter 1) is an insightful and informative discussion of this and similar examples.

Martin Kusch writes, of intra-subjective or 'time-slice' approaches like mine, that:

> The main problem is that intrasubjectivity can capture normativity only by either falling back on meaning-determinist concepts, or by distorting one's relation to oneself. It just is not true that meaning-attributions to myself and for myself have the utility of informing me under what circumstances I can rely on myself.[17]

In support of this claim he quotes the one passage in which Kripke himself addresses the point. Kripke writes:

> As members of the community correct each other, might a given individual correct himself?.... Ultimately, an individual may simply have conflicting brute inclinations, while the upshot of the matter depends on his will alone. The situation is not analogous to the case of the community, where distinct individuals have distinct and independent wills, and where when an individual is accepted into the community, others judge that they can rely on his response.... No corresponding relation between an individual and himself has the same utility.[18]

The argument seems to be that no individual can find the utility in ascribing meaning to himself that we find in ascribing it to others. Ascription of meaning to others can be useful because it can supply grounds for relying on the ascribee's responses in the future. Ascription of meaning to oneself presumably cannot be useful in *this* way, because you cannot do anything to reassure yourself that you can rely on your own responses in the future. Such reassurance would be quite unnecessary, since it is a tautology that your responses at any future time will match what you would be disposed to say at those times, and so, in that sense, can be "relied upon" by any future time slice of yourself.

But even if present-tense self-ascriptions of meaning could never have utility to the ascriber at the time of utterance, they certainly *could* have utility to the ascriber at a *later* time, as we already saw in connection with the fourth type of case discussed in the preceding section.

Maybe Kripke's point is not that I cannot usefully say of myself, now, "I mean addition by '+'" but that I cannot usefully say of myself, now, "My current use of '+' is in accordance with what I meant by it in the past." Maybe so, but then the reply is the same: it can be useful for Jones at t2 to say, of Jones at an earlier t1, that the latter was using "+" in a way that was faithful to, or that deviated from, what Jones meant by it at a still earlier t0. Saying so might be useful, for instance, to Jones at a later t3: No "community" needs to come into it.

---

[17] Kusch (2006: 193).
[18] Kripke (1982: 112, n88).

6   Seeming Right and Being Right

Alexander Miller writes:

> Consider the case of Jones, a lifelong solitary. If we initially think of the assertibility conditions of a sentence as conditions in which the participants in the practice of using S regard the utterance of S as justified, we can say that the assertibility conditions of
>
> (8) Jones means *addition* by '+'
>
> are conditions in which Jones is confident that he knows 'how to go on' in responding, e.g. to arithmetical queries featuring '+'. Now, the assertibility conditions of
>
> (12) It seems to Jones that he means addition by "+"
>
> will be identical to those of (8): the utterance of (12) will be regarded as justified by Jones when he is confident that he knows 'how to go on'.... The key point for Kripke's Wittgenstein is that the seems right/is right distinction necessary for the propriety of meaning-talk collapses.[19]

For Miller, semantic ascriptions require a seems right / is right distinction. That distinction is not available to a lifelong solitary. Hence semantic ascriptions are not available to a lifelong solitary.

But the seems right / is right distinction *is* available to a lifelong solitary. Or rather: there is a sense in which it is *not* available. And there is a sense in which it *is* available. And the sense in which it *is* available, I claim, is sufficient to ground the propriety of meaning-talk.

The sense in which the seems right / is right distinction is *not* "available" to Crusoe, is just the sense that Miller identifies. That is: no present-tense self-ascription of meaning can be distinguished, in point of justification, from the corresponding present-tense self-ascription of apparent meaning. Jones can never be justified in saying "I *seem* to mean such-and-such by so-and-so" without also being justified in saying "I *mean* such-and-such by so-and-so."

The reason for the collapse of the distinction from the first-personal present-tense perspective is that from *that* perspective, semantic ascriptions are not based on any criterion at all. They are, as Kripke says, primitive: "not to be justified in terms of Jones's ability to interpret his own intentions or anything else."

To illustrate the point by contrast: Visual experience might justify a desert traveler in saying, "There *seems* to be an oasis in the distance," without justifying the assertion, "There *is* an oasis in the distance," because he knows on other grounds that there couldn't be one, not over there. The seems/is distinction makes sense here, just *because* there are grounds that might prima facie justify the assertion, and grounds that

---
[19] Miller (2020: 3).

would undercut them, so that one could be justified in saying that it *seems* to be so but not justified in saying that it that it *is* so.

But for first-person present-tense semantic ascriptions, no such grounds exist (according to Kripke), neither *prima facie* grounds (like visual experiences) for saying "I seem to mean addition by plus," nor undercutting grounds for saying "I don't really mean addition by plus." The self-ascription is "primitive." That's why there isn't any room in our use of it for a situation where the "seems" and "is" come apart, at least not from the first-person present-tense perspective.

Present-tense *semantic* self-ascriptions are not the only kinds of statements that behave like this. For instance: what is the difference between: "I believe that it is raining" and "It seems to me that I believe that it is raining"? Is there any "criterion of correctness" here? No: I don't base this judgment *either* on an inner glance (at my brain) *or* on an outer glance (at the weather).[20] Nor are there any circumstances in which I am prepared to assert one but not the other. Here too, the seems/is distinction collapses, at least from the first-person present tense perspective. The same goes, arguably, for self-ascriptions of desires, motives, and many other mental states (though, of course, not all of them).

But now notice: In the case of first-personal belief reports, there clearly *is* a distinction between *being right* and *seeming right*. You needn't be a

---

[20] In asserting that self-ascriptions of belief are not made on any grounds at all, I am opposing an influential thesis of Evans's. Evans writes: "Wittgenstein is reported to have said ...: "If a man says to me, *looking at the sky*, 'I think it is going to rain, therefore I exist,' I do not understand him." ... Wittgenstein was trying to undermine the temptation to adopt a Cartesian position, by forcing us to look more closely at the nature of our knowledge of our own mental properties, and, in particular, by forcing us to abandon the idea that it always involves an inward glance at the states and doings of something to which only the person himself has access. The crucial point is the one I have italicized: In making a self-ascription of belief, one's eyes are, so to speak, or occasionally literally, directed outward – upon the world. If someone asks me "Do you think there is going to be a third world war?," I must attend, in answering him, to precisely the same outward phenomena as I would attend to if I were answering the question "Will there be a third world war?" I get myself in a position to answer the question whether I believe that p by putting into operation whatever procedure I have for answering the question whether p." (Evans 1982: 225). I agree with the first half of this but not with the second. That is, I agree that we do not base present-tense self-ascriptions on an inward glance. But contra Evans, I don't think we base it on an *outward* one either. "Do you think p?" can be taken as *merely* querying your state of belief now, at the time of asking, over whether p; but it can *also* be requesting you to *form* an opinion on p if you haven't yet done so. This latter request is what calls for "putting into operation whatever procedure you have for answering the question whether p"; but it only does that because it is not a request to tell the questioner about your present opinion but rather to form one. If the question really is about your *present* state of mind and nothing else, then in answering that question your (literal or metaphorical) eyes need not be directed (literally or metaphorically) outwards or inwards, because you don't answer *that* question by consulting *anything* – inner *or* outer.

full-blown Freudian to think that we sometimes are deluded, and sometimes we delude ourselves, about our motivations, beliefs, etc. Maybe Hamlet genuinely thinks, for most of the play, that what paralyzed him was indecision not cowardice – but seeing his actions before the final scene, we are at liberty to think differently; seeing them in retrospect, so is he. Charles Ryder *did* think himself free of religious belief; but he sees on his final return to Brideshead that it was always there inside him, an "unseen hook" on "an invisible line which is long enough to let him wander to the ends of the world and still to bring him back with a twitch upon the thread."

What these examples show is that a distinction between *seeming right* and *being right*, even if it is invisible from the first-person *present*-tense perspective, can still be visible from the first-person *past*-tense perspective. In the case of belief, for instance, one might easily have grounds for saying, at t1 about an earlier t0, *both* of the following:

(13) At t0 it *seemed* to me that I believed that p

(14) At t0 I did *not* believe that p

Thus a person might believe at t0 that they do not have any religious faith; at the later time t1, facts about their behavior in the intervening time – for instance, their response to a death in the family – might justify them in concluding that something worth calling religious belief *was* there all along. The person could not, at t0, have asserted the present-tense counterparts of (13) and (14), but they certainly can assert both at t1. This illustrates the sense in which, when it comes to ascriptions of belief, a distinction between seeming right and being right *is*, after all, available.

But if *that* kind of thing – that is, a discrepancy between a sincere report and other behavior – is enough to underwrite a difference between seeming right and being right in the case of belief, then we can also apply a similar distinction to semantic self-ascriptions made by a solitary individual. It *is* possible for a solitary to seem right without being right: for it to seem *as if* they mean addition by "+" – as if they "know how to go on," in Miller's formulation – when the right thing to say, as they later find out, is that they never did.

Wittgenstein himself describes just such a case. It is a variation on this example:

A writes down series of numbers; B watches him and tries to find a rule for the number series. If he succeeds, he exclaims: "Now I can go on!"[21]

---

[21] Wittgenstein (1953b: sect. 151).

In the variation, B says those words but is unable to continue the series. For instance, A writes "1, 5, 11, 19, 29…," B says "Now I can go on!," but when we ask B what the next number is, he gets it wrong, or says nothing. Wittgenstein writes:

> Are we then to say that it was wrong of him to say he could go on; or rather, that he was able to go on then, only now is not? – Clearly, we shall say different things in different cases. (Consider both kinds of case.)[22]

Consider both kinds of case.

(i) B is a learner; he has not practiced continuing sequences. He often says that he has understood how to do something – how to follow a recipe, ride a bicycle, play a game – when it is clear from his subsequent confident but failed attempts that he hasn't internalized the rules. On this occasion, despite saying "Now I can go on!" he is unable to continue the sequence.

(ii) B is mathematically proficient. He has proven successful at continuing sequences many times before. On this occasion, just after B confidently exclaims, "Now I can go on!" he is distracted by a sudden clap of thunder. A bit shaken, B returns to the problem but finds that now he cannot continue the sequence.

I think we'd be inclined to say that in case (i) B was *wrong* to say that he could go on, whereas in (ii) he was right.

The point of this example is, first: that (i) at least is a case where it makes just as much sense to say that there is a seems right/is right distinction with regards to B's semantic self-ascription as there is, in those other cases I mentioned, to say that there is a seems right/is right distinction with regards to Hamlet's *motivational* self-ascription, or Ryder's *doxastic* self-ascription.

Second: that the seems right/is right distinction seems to arise here independently of whether there is anyone else around: In case (i) B might very well be on his own – he might have been a lifelong solitary – when he says, "Now I can go on!"; but this in no way deprives him of the right to say, five minutes later, that he *couldn't* go on after all, that he *didn't* understand the sequence, or something similar.

This is also why, *even for a solitary speaker*, it can be called an *objective* matter whether a speaker can go on in one way, or another way, or at all – or in other words, whether they understand the "+" sign to mean addition, quaddition, or perhaps do not understand it to mean anything. It is objective in the sense that what justifies the solitary in saying, later

---

[22] Wittgenstein (1953b: sect. 181).

on, that he understood "+" to mean this or that at t0, are facts about the solitary's circumstances and about his actual performances both at t0 and at earlier times, that are independent of, and could easily undermine, appearances at t0.

I therefore disagree with Miller's assertion that for the lifelong solitary "the seems right/is right distinction necessary for the propriety of meaning-talk collapses." If he can later see his own present self from the perspective of his future self, the seems right / is right distinction is perfectly recoverable from Crusoe's situation.

7   Conclusion

Nothing in the foregoing argument is meant to show that language is not, *in fact*, what Quine called it: a social art. It is, as St Augustine and Wittgenstein both saw: we do in fact learn language from others, and we do in fact use it mostly to communicate with others. The point is rather that nothing about its social character follows from anything in Kripke's argument. More specifically, my purpose has been to sketch a tenable interpretation of Kripke's "sceptical solution" that is (a) genuinely skeptical in the sense that it denies that anything ever means anything; (b) genuinely a solution in the sense that it locates the utility in making (false) attributions of meaning; whist (c) remaining quite free of any communitarian baggage.[23]

---

[23] I am especially grateful to Claudine Verheggen for very insightful comments that greatly improved this chapter. I presented some of this material to a conference on Wittgenstein and the Social Sciences, held in Durham in November 2022, and I am grateful to attendants for their comments on that occasion, especially Ruby Main, Michael Wee, and Rachel Wiseman.

13 The Meaning of Meaning Ascriptions
Assertibility Conditions and Meaning Facts*

José L. Zalabardo

1   The Skeptical Problem

In Chapter 2 of *Wittgenstein on Rules and Private Language*, Saul Kripke presents an argument, inspired by Wittgenstein's rule-following considerations, for the conclusion that there can be no facts as to what a speaker means by a linguistic expression. Call these facts, whose inexistence the argument purports to establish, *meaning facts*. Kripke refers to the result that there are no meaning facts as the *skeptical paradox*. He doesn't endorse the argument or its attribution to Wittgenstein, but for simplicity, I'm going to refer to the argument and to the views expressed in the book as if they were Kripke's.

The skeptical paradox poses a problem for the task of explaining the meaning of meaning-ascribing sentences, such as "Jones means addition by 'plus'." The problem concerns the task of specifying what makes it the case that meaning-ascribing sentences have the meaning they have – the facts in virtue of which they have this meaning. I'm going to refer to the fact that plays this role with respect to a linguistic expression as its *meaning ground*. The problem posed by the skeptical paradox is that, if there are no facts as to what Jones means by "plus", we can't apply to the sentence "Jones means addition by 'plus'" a strategy for specifying the meaning ground of a declarative sentence which, according to Kripke, "may seem not only natural but even tautological" (Kripke 1982: 73). On this strategy, the meaning of a declarative sentence is given by its truth conditions – by the possible state of affairs on whose obtaining or otherwise the truth value of the sentence depends. A declarative sentence, on this approach, has the meaning it has by virtue of its relation to the state of affairs playing this role. Kripke sees the thought that the meaning ground of every declarative sentence is given by its truth conditions as the simplest and most basic idea of Wittgenstein's *Tractatus*:

---

* I've presented versions of this material at the Saul Kripke Center (online), the University of Sydney and York University, Ontario. I am grateful to these audiences.

a declarative sentence gets its meaning by virtue of its *truth conditions*, by virtue of its correspondence to facts that must obtain if it is true. For example, "the cat is on the mat" is understood by those speakers who realize that it is true if and only if a certain cat is on a certain mat; it is false otherwise. The presence of the cat on the mat is a fact or condition-in-the-world that would make the sentence true (express a truth) if it obtained. (Kripke 1982: 72)

Meaning ascriptions are expressed by declarative sentences, but if there are no meaning facts, there is no "fact or condition-in-the-world" that would make the sentence "Jones means addition by 'plus'" true. It follows that this sentence, and other sentences ascribing meanings to linguistic expressions, can't have a truth-conditional meaning ground. If we want to preserve the idea that meaning-ascribing sentences are meaningful, and that their meaning is not primitive, but grounded in some other fact, we must find alternative, non-truth-conditional meaning grounds for them.

2   The Skeptical Solution

Kripke's proposal is to employ for this purpose a strategy that he finds, following Michael Dummett, in Wittgenstein's *Philosophical Investigations*:

Wittgenstein replaces the question, "What must be the case for the sentence to be true?" by two others: first, "Under what conditions may this form of words be appropriately asserted (or denied)?"; second, given an answer to the first question, "What is the role, and the utility, in our lives of our practice of asserting (or denying) the form of words under these conditions?" (Kripke 1982: 73)

Kripke proposes to apply this strategy to the task of specifying the meaning grounds of meaning ascriptions. Thus, for the sentence "Jones means addition by 'plus'," he offers first a specification of its assertibility conditions, which are different for Jones himself and for other speakers:

Jones is entitled, subject to correction by others, provisionally to say, 'I mean addition by "plus",' whenever he has the feeling of confidence – 'now I can go on' – that he can give 'correct' responses in new cases. (Kripke 1982: 90)

Smith will judge Jones to mean addition by 'plus' only if he judges that Jones's answers to particular addition problems agree with those *he* is inclined to give, or, if they occasionally disagree, he can interpret Jones as at least following the proper procedure. (Kripke 1982: 91)

Then he provides an account of the role played in our lives by an assertoric practice with these rules – one in which "Jones means addition by 'plus'" is correctly asserted by other speakers when Jones's answers to addition problems agree with ours. He illustrates this role in terms of an interaction between a customer and a grocer:

The customer, when he deals with the grocer and asks for five apples, expects the grocer to count as he does, not according to some bizarre non-standard rule; and so, if his dealings with the grocer involve a computation, such as '68+57', he expects the grocer's responses to agree with his own. Indeed, he may entrust the computation to the grocer. (Kripke 1982: 92)

Asserting "the grocer means addition by 'plus'" in the conditions in which, on Kripke's account, it is correctly asserted enables interactions of this kind to take place.

3 Assertibility Conditions and Representation

The first component of Kripke's account is familiar from proposals put forward by other philosophers for specifying the meaning grounds of declarative sentences. Michael Dummett, on one reading of his ideas, proposed to specify the meaning grounds of the declarative sentences of certain discourses in terms of their assertibility conditions. The idea was also developed by philosophers in the 1960s and 1970s who sought to build a semantic theory on Wittgenstein's notion of a criterion.[1] However, in these proposals, the second component of Kripke's treatment of meaning-ascribing discourse is conspicuously absent. These philosophers seemed to think that a specification of the assertibility conditions of a sentence can serve as a full specification of its meaning ground, without needing to identify, in addition, the function that asserting the sentence in those conditions might play in our lives.

Kripke, by contrast, sees the second component of his account as indispensable. The reason he gives is that, in its absence, meaning-ascribing discourse would be without function:

granted that our language game permits a certain 'move' (assertion) under certain specifiable conditions, what is the role in our lives of such permission? Such a role must exist if this aspect of the language game is not to be idle. (Kripke 1982: 75)

The threat of idleness is generated by the skeptical paradox. If a sentence succeeds in representing things as being a certain way, then there is a state of affairs that the sentence represents as obtaining – on whose obtaining or otherwise the truth value of the sentence depends. If

---

[1] For Dummett's assertibility-based semantics, see for example, Dummett (1976). In some of his writings, Dummett appears to have no quarrel with a truth-conditional account of meaning, so long as the notion of truth is epistemically constrained. Crispin Wright highlighted the connections between anti-realist ideas and Wittgenstein's notion of a criterion in Wright (1982), but later distanced himself from this approach (Wright 1984b). For views based on Wittgenstein's notion of a criterion, see Pollock (1967); Lycan (1971).

there are no meaning facts, then there are no facts playing this role for meaning-ascribing sentences. It follows that these sentences cannot be construed as successfully performing the function of representing the world. If we want to avoid construing them as failed representations, we must ascribe to them an alternative non-representational function. I think this is the line of reasoning that leads Kripke to the inclusion of the second component of his account.

Advocates of Dummett-style accounts of meaning didn't see themselves as facing this challenge. They thought that their account of the meaning ground of a sentence in terms of assertibility conditions was compatible with the idea that the sentence successfully performs the function of representing the world. Crispin Wright puts the point very clearly, referring to Dummett's views:

it is consistent with anti-realism in this sense to retain the idea that a discourse is representational, and answers to states of affairs which, on at least some proper understandings of the term, are independent of us. (Wright 1992: 5)

Thus, according to Wright, specifying the meaning ground of a sentence in terms of its assertibility conditions is compatible with the idea that there is a state of affairs that the sentence represents as obtaining. Call this view *compatibilism*. Compatibilism faces two important challenges.

The first is what I've called elsewhere the *problem of harmony* (Zalabardo 2023). If the assertibility conditions of a sentence are what makes the sentence have the meaning it has, it follows that having those assertibility conditions is sufficient for the sentence to have that meaning. But if the sentence represents the world, there has to be a state of affairs that the sentence represents as obtaining. And its relation to this state of affairs has to be a necessary condition for the sentence to have the meaning it has – if the sentence didn't represent this state of affairs, it would not have the meaning it has. The problem is that these two claims are incompatible, unless its assertibility conditions are sufficient for the sentence to represent the state of affairs it represents. It follows that the compatibilist needs to offer an explanation of how the assertibility conditions that figure in the meaning ground of a target sentence necessitate the relation between the sentence and the state of affairs it represents.

The second challenge for compatibilism is to explain how the existence of a state of affairs that a sentence represents doesn't render an account of its meaning ground in terms of assertibility conditions redundant. If there is a state of affairs that a sentence represents, we should be able to ascribe to it a truth-conditional meaning ground, maintaining that the sentence has the meaning it has by virtue of its relation to this state of affairs. This suggests that whenever we ascribe an assertibility-conditional meaning ground to a representational sentence, a truth-conditional alternative will also be available.

In any case, a compatibilist treatment of meaning-ascribing discourse in particular seems to be blocked by the skeptical paradox. Even if we accept that it is in principle possible to treat a sentence with an assertibility-conditional meaning ground as performing the function of representing the world, we won't be able to extend this treatment to meaning ascriptions. This would require that there are facts for these sentences to represent, and according to the skeptical paradox, there can't be any facts playing this role.

My goal in this chapter is to outline a proposal for how the compatibilist can overcome these challenges. I'm going to argue that we can specify the meaning ground of a sentence in terms of its assertibility conditions and treat it as representing a state of affairs with the following features: on the one hand, the assertibility conditions of the sentence are a sufficient condition for the sentence to represent this state of affairs; on the other hand, this state of affairs would not sustain an alternative, truth-conditional account of the meaning ground of the sentence. I will then consider the application of this approach to meaning-ascribing discourse. I'm going to argue that if meaning facts are construed along the lines of my compatibilist proposal, Kripke's skeptical argument doesn't succeed in establishing that they don't exist. This paves the way for a compatibilist account of meaning-ascribing sentences, with their meaning explained in terms of the first component of Kripke's proposal, while the second component is rendered unnecessary by the existence of meaning facts. Meaning ascriptions will have assertibility-conditional meaning grounds but they will still succeed in performing the function of representing the world.

4 Assertibility Conditions

I'm going to focus on compatibilist views based on a specific type of assertibility-conditional meaning grounds. The assertibility conditions of a sentence are conditions under which the sentence is correctly asserted, and the notion can receive different construals depending on the kind of correctness on which it's based. One salient possibility is to construe the notion epistemically, as conditions in which assertion of the sentence will accrue some positive epistemic status, for example, justification or warrant. On this construal, if the meaning ground of a sentence is given by its assertibility conditions, it has the meaning it has by virtue of the fact that its assertion is justified/warranted under certain conditions.

Another possibility is to construe the notion semantically, as the conditions under which the sentence is actually asserted or the procedure by which assertion of the sentence is actually regulated. Correct assertion, on this reading, is assertion that's regulated by a procedure that makes the sentence have the meaning it has. On this construal, if the meaning ground of a sentence is given by its assertibility conditions, what makes the sentence have the meaning it has is the fact that it is asserted in these conditions, or that its assertion is regulated according to a certain procedure.

I think that advocates of assertibility-conditional meaning grounds typically have the epistemic construal in mind. This is of crucial importance for the anti-skeptical uses to which the proposal has been put by some of its advocates.[2] But here I'm going to concentrate on the semantic construal – on accounts of the meaning grounds of declarative sentences according to which they have the meaning they have by virtue of the fact that their assertion is regulated in a specific way. Notice that endorsing a meaning ground of this kind doesn't carry a commitment to the view that the target sentence is true whenever it is correctly asserted. The goal of the approach is to specify what makes it the case that a sentence has the meaning it has, without specifying, in addition, what would have to be the case in order for the sentence to be true. Typically, conditions of correct assertion will be unsuitable for the second task, as they are relative to specific contexts. If you and I are regulating the assertion of the sentence in the same way, it might be correct for you to assert the sentence and for me not to assert it. And yet, for the compatibilist, the sentence will have the same meaning and truth conditions as understood by each of us.

5   An Idea of Quine's

I'm going to present a strategy for identifying the state of affairs represented by a sentence that has the resources for overcoming these challenges to compatibilism. The strategy I have in mind can be introduced in terms of the account of the meaning of an expression that W.V. Quine outlines in the following passage:

Just what the meaning of an expression is – what kind of object – is not yet clear; but it is clear that, given a notion of meaning, we can explain the notion of synonymity easily as the relation between expressions that have the same meaning. Conversely also, given the relation of synonymity, it would be easy to derive the

---

[2] See Pollock (1967); Wright (1982).

notion of meaning in the following way: the meaning of an expression is the class of all the expressions synonymous with it. No doubt this second direction of construction is the more promising one. (Quine 1943: 120)[3]

I want to focus on Quine's favored option – to define the meaning of an expression as the class of all the expressions that are synonymous with it.

My goal will be to explore a method for specifying the state of affairs represented by a sentence that follows the same general approach as the account of the meaning of an expression that Quine proposes in this passage. My proposal will differ in substantial respects from Quine's version, but before I go into these differences, I want to display the appeal that the approach might hold for the compatibilist, by pretending provisionally that equivalence classes of synonymous sentences can be regarded as states of affairs.

Notice that the meaning ground of a sentence generates synonymy conditions for it – conditions under which an arbitrary sentence would have the same meaning as the target sentence. In particular, if we identify the meaning ground of a sentence with the procedure that regulates its assertion, we are claiming that every sentence whose assertion is regulated in this way will have the same meaning as the target sentence. It will be useful for us to think of this sufficient condition for synonymy as also necessary – a sentence will have the same meaning as the target sentence only if its assertion is regulated in this way. If we want to make room for the possibility of several regulation procedures bestowing the same meaning on a sentence, we just need to treat as the meaning ground the disjunction of these.

If the state of affairs represented by sentence A were the class of sentences synonymous with it, all we would need to do in order to identify the state of affairs playing this role would be to specify synonymy conditions for A. But, as we've just seen, if A has an assertibility-conditional meaning ground, its meaning-grounding assertion procedure will generate synonymy conditions for A. Hence, by specifying the meaning ground of A we will have identified the state of affairs it represents.

Crucially, this identification will not be vulnerable to the problem of harmony, since now the assertibility-conditional meaning ground of A is a sufficient condition for A to represent the state of affairs it represents. So long as the assertion of A is regulated in this way, A will refer to the same state of affairs.

The threat of redundancy for the compatibilist also disappears with this proposal. If the state of affairs represented by A is the equivalence

---

[3] Similar views are defended in Ayer (1936: 88) and Carnap (1956: 152).

class of sentences synonymous with A, with synonymy conditions fixed by the assertibility-conditional meaning ground of the sentence, then saying that A has the meaning it has as a result of its relation to the state of affairs it represents doesn't provide a genuine alternative to the assertibility-conditional meaning ground but a misleading reformulation of the same meaning ground. If A has the meaning it has by virtue of its connection to the state of affairs it represents, and this state of affairs is the class of sentences whose assertion is regulated by the same procedure as A, then A ultimately has the meaning it has by virtue of the fact that assertion of A is regulated by that procedure.

Clearly, this vindication of compatibilism is based on the assumption that we can treat a class of synonymous sentences as a state of affairs, and this assumption is utterly implausible. My next goal is to articulate a version of Quine's thought that doesn't depend on this assumption but still holds the same promise for the compatibilist.

6   Abstraction

What Quine is proposing for meaning is a definition by abstraction. The method of definition by abstraction has been widely used in mathematics since the end of the nineteenth century. It's a method for defining a function from a domain of objects taken as given. The sentences in which definitions by abstraction are formulated are known as *abstraction principles*. If D is a given domain of objects, and f is a function with D as its domain (the *abstraction operator*), an abstraction principle has the form:

A   For all x, y in D, $f(x) = f(y)$ iff xRy.

Notice that an instance of A is logically false unless R is an equivalence relation.[4] In effect, an abstraction principle specifies necessary and sufficient conditions for two elements of D to have the same image under f.

Definitions by abstraction were discussed by Frege in the *Grundlagen* (Frege 1980). In one of his famous examples, D is the set of lines, and f is the function pairing each line with its direction. The proposed abstraction principle can be formulated as follows (Frege 1980: 74–75):

For all lines x, y, the direction of x = the direction of y iff x is parallel to y.

In the application that Frege focuses on, D is the set of concepts, and f is the function pairing a concept F with the number of Fs. The proposed abstraction principle here is based on Hume's principle (Frege 1980: 73–74):

---

[4] An instance of A is logically false also if R is inflationary. See Fine (2002: 4). This is an important fact in other contexts, but it won't play a role in our discussion.

For all concepts F, G the number of Fs = the number of Gs iff there is a bijection between the extensions of F and G.

If we take a function to be defined by an abstraction principle, one question that arises immediately is what the values of the function are. An abstraction principle tells us when two elements of the domain of the abstraction operator receive the same image, but it doesn't seem to tell us anything else about the identity of the objects playing the role of images under the function.

Paolo Mancosu has introduced a useful distinction between two options one might take regarding the range of an abstraction operator. The contrast concerns whether its elements can receive an explicit definition independently of the abstraction principle. Mancosu refers to definitions by abstraction for which this question receives an affirmative answer as *thin*, and to those for which the question is answered in the negative as *thick* (Mancosu 2016: 24). As Mancosu points out, it is often unclear whether a definition by abstraction is meant to be understood as thin or thick, but there are some clear cases on both sides.

Among those who proposed thin definitions by abstraction, there are two main traditions concerning the identity of the elements of the range of the abstraction operator. As Mancosu explains, in number theory, the dominant approach was to treat as the image under f of an element a of D a specific representative of the equivalence class generated by R to which a belongs. However, in synthetic geometry and the theory of cardinals and ordinals, where it's often not possible to pick a representative non-arbitrarily, the standard approach is to take the equivalence class itself as the image.[5] The latter is what Quine is proposing for the function pairing each expression with its meaning – a thin definition by abstraction in which the image of an expression is the equivalence class generated by the synonymy relation to which the expression belongs.

Other mathematicians clearly embraced thick definitions by abstraction. Thus, for example, Giuseppe Peano writes:

Let u be an object; by abstraction one obtains a new object ϕu; one cannot form an equality

ϕu = known expression

since ϕu is an object whose nature is completely different from all those that have hitherto been considered. (Peano 1894: 45)[6]

---

[5] For the theory of cardinals and ordinals the approach was later abandoned, due to the discovery of its paradoxical consequences.
[6] Cited in Mancosu (2016).

And again, on the definition by abstraction of direction:

The relation between two unbounded straight lines "a is parallel to b" has the properties of equality. It has been transformed into "direction of a = direction of b", or "point at infinity of a = point at infinity of b". One cannot define an equality of the form: "point at infinity of a" = "expression formed with the words of Euclid's Elements." (Peano 1894: 47)[7]

Notice that treating an abstraction principle as a thick definition by abstraction involves accepting that what the abstraction principle tells us about the identity of the values of the abstraction operator – that is, which arguments they are paired with – can be regarded as a satisfactory specification of the identity of these items.

The legitimacy of thick definitions by abstraction is hugely controversial. It is strongly rejected by Frege in the *Grundlagen*, and Russell's verdict in *The Principles of Mathematics* is equally negative (Russell 1903: 113–116). The debate on their legitimacy regained momentum in philosophy in connection with the proposals advanced by neo-Fregean philosophers of mathematics.[8] Here I don't intend to take part in this debate. I propose instead to treat it as an assumption that the debate has been settled in favor of the legitimacy of thick definitions by abstraction. I'm going to assume, specifically, that if an instance of A satisfies the conditions under which it can be used as a definition by abstraction of f in terms of R, then it can be legitimately used as a *thick* definition of f in terms of R, that is, f will have been successfully defined even if the items in its range cannot be defined independently of A. I'm going to refer to this as the *Peano assumption*.

Accepting thick definitions by abstraction enables us to formulate a variant of Quine's proposal. On this position, the meaning of an expression will be defined by abstraction in terms of synonymy, as Quine proposes, but, *contra* Quine, it won't be identified with an equivalence class of synonymous expressions. Meanings will be treated instead as sui generis entities whose identity is fully specified by the abstractionist link with synonymy. It follows from the Peano assumption that if Quine's original proposal is legitimate, then the same goes for this thick version.

7 Abstraction and Representation

My goal is to explore how this general approach can be used to overcome the challenges faced by compatibilism. On this proposal, if a sentence A

---

[7] Cited in Mancosu (2016).
[8] See Wright (1983), Hale (1987), Hale and Wright (2001), and MacBride (2003) for an excellent survey.

has an assertibility-conditional meaning ground, the item it represents will be identified by a thick definition by abstraction, as the item represented precisely by those sentences whose assertion is regulated by the same procedure as A. This definition will single out the item represented by A by specifying which other sentences represent it, but the item playing this role will not be identified with the equivalence class of these sentences, or with any other item in our ontology. Our only method for singling it out will be as the item represented by those sentences whose assertion is regulated in this way. But since it is the kind of item represented by a declarative sentence, it seems perfectly appropriate to describe it as a possible state of affairs.

The abstraction principle that we would need to use to implement this strategy would be:

R   For all representational sentences x, y, the state of affairs represented by x = the state of affairs represented by y iff x and y are synonymous.

On an intuitive construal of the notion of synonymy, the left-to-right direction of R has counterexamples, as, for example, with "Superman flies" and "Clark Kent flies," or with "there's water in this cup" and "there's H_2O in this cup." But if we make adjustments to deal with these cases, we are still left with a recognizable notion of synonymy, and on this construal of the notion, R is a true principle.

However, from the truth of R it doesn't follow that we can provide a definition by abstraction of the state of affairs represented by each representational sentence. This would require, in addition, that the synonymy relation can receive an independent definition – one that's not built on when two sentences represent the same state of affairs. This is the point Quine makes in the continuation of the passage we quoted earlier:

The relation of synonymity, in turn, calls for a definition or a criterion in psychological and linguistic terms. Such a definition, which up to the present has perhaps never even been sketched, would be a fundamental contribution at once to philology and philosophy. (Quine 1943: 120)

Now, Quine's subsequent work contains a multipronged attack on the availability of the independent definition of synonymy the passage calls for. His arguments against the analytic-synthetic distinction (Quine 1951) and in support of the indeterminacy of translation (Quine 1960: chapter 2) would show, if successful, that it's not possible to provide an independent definition of synonymy on which it comes out as an equivalence relation and hence as fit for sustaining a definition by abstraction of the meaning of an expression, or of the state of affairs represented by a sentence, in terms of synonymy.

This is not the place to assess Quine's arguments, but I'm going to work on the assumption that they don't succeed – that for at least some of our terms and sentences, it is possible in principle to specify synonymy conditions. Notice that a specification of the meaning ground of a sentence in terms of the procedure that regulates its assertion entails that it's possible to define independently of R the equivalence class of sentences that are synonymous with it. In what follows, I'm going to assume that there are no general reasons for thinking that individual sentences can't receive this treatment.

However, even if this is possible for some sentences, it's still the case that there are sentences that can't be treated in this way. There are sentences for which synonymy conditions cannot be provided in terms of assertibility conditions or, more generally, without invoking the states of affairs they represent. I take this to be a direct corollary of work on natural-kind terms by Hilary Putnam and Saul Kripke (Putnam 1975; Kripke 1972). The problem is that any characterization of the procedure that regulated our assertion of "there's water in this cup" in pre-Lavoisier times would also be satisfied by our twins' sentence, "there's twater in this cup." However, our sentence is not synonymous with our twins'. For sentences that exhibit this kind of behavior, an account of their meaning grounds in terms of assertibility conditions is not an option.

But although we can't use R to provide a general definition by abstraction of the state of affairs represented by each sentence, we can still aim for the more modest goal of treating specific sentences in this way. Thus, for a sentence A with an assertibility-conditional meaning ground, we could provide a definition by abstraction of the state of affairs it represents by means of the following principle:

R*   For every sentence x, the state of affairs represented by x = the state of affairs represented by A iff assertion of x is regulated by the same procedure as assertion of A.

Let's see how this would work in a specific example. Consider the feelings of moral approval on which emotivists build their account of moral language (Ayer 1936), but instead of using them to define the function of moral sentences, take them simply as the basis for the procedure that we employ for regulating our assertion of moral statements: we assert "killing one to save five is morally right" just in case we feel moral approval toward the killing of one to save five. The proposal I want to consider would treat this procedure for regulating the assertion of the sentence as its meaning ground – the sentence has the meaning it has by virtue of the fact that its assertion is regulated by the speaker's feelings of moral approval toward the killing of one to save five. We can now use this procedure to formulate an instance of R*

MR For every sentence x, the state of affairs represented by x = the state of affairs represented by "killing one to save five is morally right" iff assertion of x is regulated by the speaker's sense of moral approval toward the killing of one to save five.

The compatibilist, unlike the emotivist, will go on to claim that the function of the sentence is to represent the world, and she will treat MR as a thick definition by abstraction of the state of affairs that the sentence represents as obtaining. It's the state of affairs represented by those sentences whose assertion is regulated in this way.

We can easily see how the challenges faced by compatibilism would be handled by this proposal. First, harmony won't be a problem since now the assertibility-conditional meaning ground of the sentence is a sufficient condition for the relation between the sentence and the state of affairs it represents. So long as the assertion of the sentence is regulated by the speaker's feeling of moral approval toward the killing of one to save five, the sentence will represent the same state of affairs. The threat of redundancy also disappears. We might want to say that "killing one to save five is morally right" has the meaning it has as a result of its connection with the state of affairs represented by those sentences whose assertion is regulated by the speaker's feeling of moral approval toward the killing of one to save five, but this is not a truth-conditional alternative to the assertibility-conditional proposal but a misleading reformulation of the assertibility-conditional account.

8   Abstraction and Meaning Ascriptions

Let's now consider how the approach could work for meaning ascriptions. Take the sentence in Kripke's example: "Jones means addition by 'plus'." The compatibilist would specify the meaning ground of this sentence in terms of its assertibility conditions. She could use for this purpose the first component of Kripke's skeptical solution. We'll focus, for the sake of simplicity, on the third-personal assertibility conditions proposed by Kripke.[9] The proposal would be that what makes "Jones means addition by 'plus'," as meant by Smith, have the meaning it has, is the fact that Smith's assertion of the sentence is regulated by whether "he judges that Jones's answers to particular addition problems agree with those *he* is inclined to give, or, if they occasionally disagree, he can interpret Jones as at least following the proper procedure."

[9] This simplification may give the impression that third-person and first-person meaning ascriptions don't have the same meaning. The impression would disappear if we removed the simplification, treating as the meaning ground of the sentence a disjunctive procedure for regulating its assertion, with one disjunct for Jones and another for everyone else.

As we've seen, meaning grounds generate synonymy conditions, and with assertibility-conditional meaning grounds, the resulting synonymy conditions can be used in a definition by abstraction of the state of affairs represented by the sentence. In this case, the definition would be based on the following abstraction principle:

MA   For every sentence x, the state of affairs represented by x = the state of affairs represented by "Jones means addition by 'plus'" iff assertion of x is regulated by whether the speaker "judges that Jones's answers to particular addition problems agree with those *he* is inclined to give, or, if they occasionally disagree, he can interpret Jones as at least following the proper procedure."

The compatibilist would treat MA as a thick definition by abstraction of the state of affairs represented by the sentence "Jones means addition by 'plus'" (as understood by Smith). It would not be possible to provide an explicit definition of the state of affairs playing this role. It could be singled out only as the state of affairs represented by the sentences whose assertion is regulated in this way, but this would be regarded as an adequate specification of its identity.

It is important to understand the conditions under which MA dictates that a sentence, as understood by a speaker, represents the same state of affairs as "Jones means addition by 'plus'," as understood by Smith. Suppose that Miller regulates her assertion of "Jones means addition by 'plus'" by whether she judges that Jones's answers to particular "plus" problems agree with those she is inclined to give or whether she can interpret Jones as following the procedure she follows for answering "plus" questions. It will follow from this that Miller regulates her assertion of "Jones means addition by 'plus'," with the procedure required by MA *only if* the answers Miller is inclined to give to "plus" questions are the answers she is inclined to give to addition questions and the procedure she follows for answering "plus" questions is her procedure for answering addition questions. In other words, Miller will count as using the same procedure as Smith for regulating her assertion of "Jones means addition by 'plus'" only if she means by "plus" what Smith means by addition – that is, only if the state of affairs represented by "Miller means addition by 'plus'," as understood by Smith, obtains. Smith will form his view on this on the basis of the procedure he uses to regulate his assertion of sentences of the form "S means addition by 'ϕ'" – that is, by whether he judges that Miller's answers to particular addition problems agree with those *he* is inclined to give, or, if they occasionally disagree, he can interpret Miller as at least following the proper procedure. If he decides on this basis that Miller means addition by "plus," he will conclude that she regulates her assertion of "Jones means addition by 'plus'" with the same procedure that he himself uses, and that the sentence, as understood by Miller, represents the same state of affairs it represents as understood by him.

Notice that the compatibilist's proposal is fundamentally different from a view that tries to provide an explicit definition of the state of affairs represented by "Jones means addition by 'plus'" in terms of the assertibility conditions that figure in Kripke's proposal. On this approach, we would specify the truth conditions of "Jones means addition by 'plus'" along the following lines:

"Jones means addition by 'plus'" is true if and only if Jones's answers to particular addition problems agree with those we are inclined to give, or, if they occasionally disagree, we can interpret Jones as at least following the proper procedure.

This is a crude version of the so-called communitarian account. I think this proposal faces very serious problems,[10] but my goal here is not to assess it, but to highlight the fact that the compatibilist doesn't endorse a specification of this kind of the truth conditions of "Jones means addition by 'plus'." The compatibilist is not proposing to use the procedure that regulates our ascription of the sentence to specify its truth conditions. Her proposal is to use this procedure to specify synonymy conditions for the sentence, and to use these synonymy conditions in a definition by abstraction of the state of affairs represented by the sentence. Her position doesn't entail that we can use the procedure that regulates the assertion of the sentence to specify necessary or sufficient conditions for the truth of the sentence. More generally, her position doesn't entail any informative specification of necessary or sufficient conditions for the truth of the sentence.

As before, the proposal has the resources for dealing with the threats of harmony and redundancy. The fact that the assertion of the sentence is regulated in this way is treated as a sufficient condition for the sentence to have the meaning it has, and the fact that it represents the state of affairs it represents is a necessary condition for the sentence having this meaning. However, there is no tension between these two requirements, since having its assertion regulated in this way is a sufficient condition for the sentence to represent the state of affairs it represents. So long as the assertion of the sentence is regulated in this way, the sentence can't fail to represent this state of affairs. Redundancy is also not a problem, as our specification of the state of affairs represented by the sentence wouldn't sustain a truth-conditional alternative to the assertibility-conditional account of its meaning ground. We might want to say that what makes

---

[10] Problems with this approach are highlighted in Blackburn (1984).

the sentence have the meaning it has is the fact that it represents this state of affairs, but what makes the sentence represent this state of affairs is the fact that its assertion is regulated by the procedure specified in its assertibility-conditional meaning ground.

9   Compatibilism and the Skeptical Paradox

We've seen, however, that this application of the compatibilist approach faces an additional hurdle. Kripke claims to have shown that there is no fact of the matter as to whether Jones means one function rather than another by "plus." The compatibilist proposal is directly opposed to this. For the compatibilist, there is a fact of the matter as to whether the state of affairs singled out by MA obtains. If it does, then "Jones means addition by 'plus'" is true, and Jones means the addition function by "plus." If it doesn't, then "Jones means addition by 'plus'" is false, and Jones doesn't mean the addition function by "plus." It follows that the compatibilist has to reject the skeptical conclusion, which requires, in turn, finding a gap in the argument that Kripke deploys in its support.

I think this can be done. Kripke's argument is based on the implicit assumption that if "Jones means addition by 'plus'" represents a state of affairs, it has to be possible to provide an explicit definition of this state of affairs – an informative specification of what has to be the case in order for this state of affairs to obtain.[11] Kripke's argument takes the form of considering a list of plausible attempts to provide this explicit definition, and concluding in each case that they face insurmountable obstacles. In this way, he concludes that it's not possible to provide an adequate explicit definition of the state of affairs represented by "Jones means addition by 'plus'," and he then derives from this his ultimate conclusion – that there isn't a state of affairs that "Jones means addition by 'plus'" represents as obtaining.

However, as we have seen, the compatibilist rejects the assumption that underwrites the last step in Kripke's reasoning. She openly accepts that it won't be possible to provide an explicit definition of the state of affairs represented by "Jones means addition by 'plus'." On this point, she is in agreement with Kripke. However, unlike Kripke, the compatibilist doesn't think that it follows from this that "Jones means addition by 'plus'" doesn't represent a state of affairs. On her view, the sentence represents the state of affairs singled out by MA, treated as a thick definition by abstraction. For her, the assumption that a sentence can't represent a

---

[11] The reliance of the argument on this assumption has been highlighted by Paul Boghossian (Boghossian 1989: 540–541).

state of affairs unless we can provide an explicit definition of the state of affairs playing this role begs the question against her claim that the state of affairs represented by a sentence can be fully identified by an instance of R*, as MA does for "Jones means addition by 'plus'."[12]

It might seem, however, that the state of affairs singled out by MA violates a major requirement that Kripke wields against other accounts of meaning facts:

> A candidate for what constitutes the state of my meaning one function, rather than another, by a given function sign, ought to be such that, whatever in fact I (am disposed to) do, there is a unique thing that I *should* do. (Kripke 1982: 24)

Specifically, for every question of the form "m plus n?," the state of Jones' meaning one function rather than another by "plus" ought to be such that it singles out a unique answer to the question as correct. Jones will be disposed to give answers to some of these questions, and it has to be possible to say of these answers that they are either correct or incorrect. The state of Jones' meaning one function rather than another has to generate the standard of correctness with respect to which talk of correct and incorrect answers can be made sense of.

Suppose we accept, for the sake of the argument, that an instance of R* can in principle succeed in identifying the state of affairs represented by a sentence. The question now is whether MA specifically achieves this. Suppose it does, and suppose the state of affairs specified by MA obtains. Then this fact will have to single out a unique answer to each question of the form "m plus n?" as correct. Is this condition satisfied? I think the compatibilist can successfully argue that it is. If the state of affairs singled out by MA obtains, then each question of the form "m plus n?" is correctly answered by "p" if and only if "p" refers to the image of the referents of "m" and "n" under the addition function. Jones's answers will be correct or incorrect depending on whether they meet this standard.

The compatibilist's opponent might protest that this response is unsatisfactory. It amounts to specifying the correct answers to "m plus n?" questions, as meant by Jones, in terms of the conditions of correct use for our own terms. The compatibilist is saying, in effect, that "p" is the correct answer to "m plus n?" just in case "p" refers to the image of the referents of "m" and "n" under the function that "addition," as we understand it, refers to. And this, it can be argued, doesn't solve the problem, for what goes for Jones goes for us too. We have inclinations as

---

[12] If we reject, as I'm proposing, the reductionist assumption of Kripke's argument, we open the door to a range of non-reductionist accounts of meaning facts (Stroud 2000; Ginsborg 2011b; Hattiangadi this volume). A full defense of the compatibilist approach would require arguing that it is preferable to these alternatives.

to how to answer "addition" questions, but they are in principle no more likely to be correct than Jones's own inclinations. The compatibilist's line, the complaint goes, doesn't provide an effective identification of the conditions of correct use for Jones's responses.

I think this complaint is right in claiming that there's something that the compatibilist position doesn't provide, but I'm going to call into question the legitimacy of the demand for what the compatibilist fails to provide. What the compatibilist doesn't provide is an explanation of how we can access the conditions of correct use of "plus," as meant by Jones, without relying on his or our inclinations concerning how to use the expression or its synonyms. If Jones is inclined to answer the question "m plus n?" with "p," and we want to check whether his answer is correct, we need to draw on the procedures that regulate our assertion of the sentence "p is the sum of m and n." These are based on the same kind of inclinations that generated Jones's answer, and the answer we are inclined to give may or may not coincide with the correct answer. In the end, all we can do is check his inclinations against our own, without ever gaining direct access to the standard that determines whether Jones's answers, and our own answers, are correct or incorrect.

I think the compatibilist needs to concede this point, but she can protest that what she is being accused of not providing is something that cannot be reasonably demanded. What the complaint calls for is a way of determining which answers to "plus" questions are correct that bypasses the procedures that we employ to regulate our assertion of sentences in which "plus" figures.[13] The compatibilist should maintain that this is an illegitimate demand. The state of Jones' meaning one function rather than another by "plus" cannot be reasonably expected to determine conditions of correct use for the symbol that are directly accessible in this way.

The demand that meaning facts determine conditions of correct use is legitimate only if divested of this direct-access component. Now the claim is that the state of Jones' meaning one function rather than another by "plus" has to determine the correct answer to each question of the form "m plus n?," without having to make these answers available to us in the unmediated sense we've discussed. But when the constraint is understood in this way, the state of affairs singled out by MA does determine the conditions of correct use: "p" is a correct answer to "m plus n?" just in case "p" refers to the image of the referents of "m" and

---

[13] I think this unmediated access to conditions of correct use is what Kripke refers to when he speaks of these conditions being "read off" from the meaning-constituting fact (Kripke 1982: 26, 29).

"n" under the function that "addition," as we understand it, refers to. So long as this function exists – so long as "addition" as we understand it, has a referent – the state of affairs singled out by MA will determine conditions of correct use for "plus," as understood by Jones.[14]

10 Meaning Ascriptions in General

So far, we've discussed how to provide assertibility-conditional meaning grounds for individual sentences – in our examples, "killing one to save five is morally right" and "Jones means addition by 'plus'." The same approach can be applied to other discourses besides ethics and meaning ascriptions.[15] It can also be used to provide general specifications of assertibility conditions for every sentence of a given discourse. We could take this approach for meaning ascriptions, seeking to specify meaning-grounding assertibility conditions for every sentence of the form "S means A by 'B'." This would require identifying a single procedure-type for regulating the assertion of a sentence such that every meaning ascription has the meaning it has by virtue of the fact that its assertion is regulated with an instance of this procedure-type. The assertibility-conditional meaning ground of "Jones means addition by 'plus'" would then follow from this as a special case.

A general procedure for regulating assertion that could play this role would be a procedure for ascribing meanings to expressions such that a sentence would count as ascribing a meaning A to an expression "B" by virtue of the fact that the pairing of A with "B" resulted from the application of this procedure. I want to illustrate how this approach would work in terms of the procedure to which Donald Davidson refers as Radical Interpretation.[16] For the purposes of this illustration we only need a rough and ready characterization of what the procedure involves – something along the lines of:

Pair expressions with meanings in such a way as to maximize the truth of the sentences accepted by the speaker in which the expressions figure.[17]

---

[14] See in this connection the contrast that Paul Horwich draws between two senses in which the use of a predicate can be said to determine its extension (Horwich 1995: 361–363).
[15] I apply the approach to propositional-attitude ascriptions in Zalabardo (2019, 2023: chapter 5).
[16] See the essays in Davidson (1984). The notion is of course derived from W. V. Quine's notion of Radical Translation (Quine 1960: chapter 2).
[17] Notice that the reliance of this procedure on the principle of charity can also be discerned in the assertibility conditions that Kripke proposes for "Jones means addition by 'plus'." His proposal is that Jones should be interpreted as meaning addition by "plus" only if this makes most of the "plus"-involving sentences Jones accepts come out true.

The Meaning of Meaning Ascriptions 257

We can use Radical Interpretation to provide an assertibility-conditional account of the meaning grounds of meaning ascriptions:

RIA "S means A by 'B'" has the meaning it has by virtue of the fact that its assertion is regulated by Radical Interpretation.

The proposal shouldn't be confused with a truth-conditional account of the meaning grounds of meaning ascriptions that uses Radical Interpretation in a different way. On this account, Radical interpretation is used to define the state of affairs represented by a meaning ascription:

RIT "S means A by 'B'" is true if and only if Radical Interpretation recommends interpreting S as meaning A by "B."

The assertibility conditional account expressed by RIA doesn't carry a commitment to RIT or to any other specification of the state of affairs on whose obtaining the truth value of "S means A by 'B'" depends. And some major obstacles faced by RIT do not apply to RIA. One is the context-dependence of Radical Interpretation – the fact that it can issue different recommendations to different interpreters in different contexts. It follows from this that RIT doesn't provide a coherent specification of truth conditions for "S means A by 'B'," but the point poses no obstacle to RIA. RIA dictates that "S means A by 'B'," obtains its meaning from the fact that its assertion is regulated by Radical Interpretation. The fact that the verdict on this sentence recommended by Radical Interpretation depends on the interpreter's context doesn't in any way undermine the proposal.

As with the assertibility-conditional meaning grounds considered earlier, RIA doesn't force us to abandon the idea that meaning ascriptions are representations. This requires, as we have seen, that there is a state of affairs that each meaning ascription represents, but here the compatibilist can deploy the same strategy that we considered in previous cases. The meaning grounds postulated by RIA generate synonymy conditions for "S means A by 'B'," and these can be used in a definition by abstraction of the state of affairs represented by this sentence:

MF For every sentence x, the state of affairs represented by x = the state of affairs represented by "S means A by 'B'" iff assertion of x is regulated by whether Radical Interpretation recommends interpreting "B," as understood by S, as meaning A.

The compatibilist would take this as a thick definition by abstraction of the state of affairs represented by "S means A by 'B'." She would take the identity of this state of affairs to be completely specified by MF, as the state of affairs represented by every sentence whose assertion is regulated in this way. She would see no need for the definition by abstraction to be supplemented by an explicit definition – for the state of affairs defined by MF to be identified with some item in our preexisting ontological catalog. As we have seen, the proposal would have the resources to overcome the challenges posed by harmony, redundancy, and Kripke's argument against the existence of meaning facts.

I want to emphasize that my endorsement of this account of the meaning grounds of meaning ascriptions is only partial. We can see the proposal as involving two components. On the one hand, it provides an assertibility-conditional account of the meaning grounds of meaning ascriptions, using for this purpose the procedures for regulating their assertion generated by our general method of interpretation. On the other hand, it endorses a characterization of our method of interpretation along the lines of Davidson's Radical Interpretation. I am endorsing the first component but not the second. I'm proposing that our general method of interpretation can form the basis for a plausible assertibility-conditional account of the meaning grounds of meaning ascriptions, but I don't think that Davidson's characterization of our method of interpretation can be accepted without revisions. I think, however, that Davidson's characterization can be easily modified to produce a satisfactory account of our method of interpretation, which would sustain a promising assertibility-conditional account of the meaning grounds of meaning ascriptions.[18]

---

[18] I develop this point in Zalabardo (2023: Chapter 6, In Press).

Bibliography

Ahmed, Arif. 2007. *Saul Kripke*. Bloomsbury/Continuum.
Ahmed, Arif. 2018. "Review of T. Crane, The Meaning of Belief," *Mind* 127 (508): 1261–1270.
Alston, William. 2000. *Illocutionary Acts and Sentence Meaning*. Cornell University Press.
Anscombe, G. E. M. 1972. *Intention*. 2nd ed. Blackwell.
Anscombe, G. E. M. 1985. "Critical Notice: Wittgenstein on Rules and Private Language," *Canadian Journal of Philosophy* 15 (4): 103–109.
Arpaly, Nomy. 2002. "Moral Worth," *Journal of Philosophy* 99 (5): 223–245.
Ayer, A. J. 1936. *Language, Truth, and Logic*. Victor Gollancz.
Bader, Ralf. In press. "Grounding, Reduction, and Analysis."
Baker, Gordon P. and P. M. S. Hacker. 1984. "On Misunderstanding Wittgenstein: Kripke's Private Language Argument," *Synthese* 58 (3): 407–450.
Blackburn, Simon. 1984. "The Individual Strikes Back," *Synthese* 58 (3): 281–301.
Block, Irving (ed.). 1981. *Perspectives on the Philosophy of Wittgenstein*. Basil Blackwell.
Bloor, David. 1997. *Wittgenstein, Rules and Institutions*. Routledge.
Boghossian, Paul. 1989. "The Rule-Following Considerations," *Mind* 98 (392): 507–549. Reprinted in Alexander Miller and Crispin Wright, eds., *Rule-Following and Meaning* (2002). Acumen Publishing: 141–187.
Boghossian, Paul. 1990. "The Status of Content," *Philosophical Review* 99 (2): 157–184.
Boghossian, Paul. 2001. "How Are Objective Epistemic Reasons Possible?," in Paul Boghossian, ed., *Content and Justification: Philosophical Papers* (2008). Oxford University Press: 235–266.
Boghossian, Paul. 2008a. *Content and Justification: Philosophical Papers*. Oxford University Press.
Boghossian, Paul. 2008b. "Is Meaning Normative?," in Paul Boghossian, ed., *Content and Justification: Philosophical Papers*. Oxford University Press: 95–108.
Boghossian, Paul. 2012. "Blind Rule-Following," in Annalisa Coliva, ed., *Mind, Meaning, and Knowledge: Themes from the Philosophy of Crispin Wright*. Oxford University Press: 27–48.
Boghossian, Paul. 2015. "Is (Determinate) Meaning a Naturalistic Phenomenon?," in Steven Gross, Nicholas Tebben, and Michael Williams,

eds., *Meaning without Representation: Essays on Truth, Expression, Normativity and Naturalism*. Oxford University Press: 331–358.
Bolker, Ethan. 1966. "Functions Resembling Quotients of Measures," *Transactions of the American Mathematical Society* 124 (2): 292–312.
Boyd, Daniel. 2017. "Semantic Non-factualism in Kripke's Wittgenstein," *Journal for the History of Analytical Philosophy* 5 (9): 1–13.
Brandom, Robert. 1994. *Making It Explicit: Reasoning, Representing, and Discursive Commitment*. Harvard University Press.
Bridges, Jason. 2014. "Rule-Following Skepticism, Properly So Called," in James Conant and Andrea Kern, eds., *Varieties of Skepticism: Essays after Kant, Wittgenstein, and Cavell*. De Gruyter: 249–288.
Buleandra, Andrei. 2008. "Normativity and Correctness: A Reply to Hattiangadi," *Acta Analytica* 23 (2): 177–186.
Burge, Tyler. 1979. "Individualism and the Mental," *Midwest Studies in Philosophy* 4 (1): 73–121.
Burge, Tyler. 1986. "Intellectual Norms and the Foundations of Mind," *The Journal of Philosophy* 83 (12): 697–720.
Burge, Tyler. 1996. "Our Entitlement to Self-Knowledge," *Proceedings of the Aristotelian Society* 96 (1): 91–116.
Burge, Tyler. 2013. *Cognition through Understanding: Philosophical Essays*, Volume 3. Oxford University Press.
Burgess, Alexis and Brett Sherman. 2014. "Introduction: A Plea for the Metaphysics of Meaning," in Alexis Burgess and Brett Sherman, eds., *Metasemantics: New Essays on the Foundations of Meaning*. Oxford University Press: 1–16.
Bykvist, Krister and Anandi Hattiangadi. 2013. "Belief, Truth and Blindspots," in Timothy Chan, ed., *The Aim of Belief*. Oxford University Press: 100–122.
Byrne, Alexander. 1996. "On Misinterpreting Kripke's Wittgenstein," *Philosophy and Phenomenological Research* 56 (2): 339–343.
Canfield, John. 1996. "The Community View," *The Philosophical Review* 105 (4): 469–488.
Carnap, Rudolf. 1956. *Meaning and Necessity*. 2nd ed. University of Chicago Press.
Chalmers, David. 1996. *The Conscious Mind: In Search of a Fundamental Theory*. Oxford University Press.
Chalmers, David. 2002. "Does Conceivability Entail Possibility," in Tamar Szabo Gendler and John Hawthorne, eds., *Conceivability and Possibility*. Oxford University Press: 145–200.
Chalmers, David. 2006. "Perception and the Fall from Eden," in Tamar S. Gendler and John Hawthorne, eds., *Perceptual Experience*. Oxford University Press: 49–125.
Chalmers, David. 2009. "The Two-Dimensional Argument against Materialism," in Brian P. McLaughlin, Ansgar Beckermann, and Sven Walter, eds., *Oxford Handbook of the Philosophy of Mind*. Oxford University Press: 313–336.
Chalmers, David. In Press. "Inferentialism, Australian Style," *Proceedings and Addresses of the American Philosophical Association*.
Child, William. 2010. "Wittgenstein's Externalism," in Daniel Whiting, ed., *The Later Wittgenstein on Language*. Palgrave Macmillan: 63–80.

Child, William. 2019. "Meaning, Use, and Supervenience," in James Conant and Sebastian Sunday, eds., *Wittgenstein on Philosophy, Objectivity, and Meaning*. Cambridge University Press: 211–230.

Chomsky, Noam. 1965. *Aspects of the Theory of Syntax*. MIT Press.

Churchland, Paul. 1981. "Eliminative Materialism and Propositional Attitudes," *Journal of Philosophy* 78 (2): 67–90.

Coates, Paul. 1997. "Meaning, Mistake and Miscalculation," *Minds and Machines* 7: 171–197.

Davidson, Donald. 1973. "Radical Interpretation," *Dialectica* 27 (3–4): 313–328.

Davidson, Donald. 1984. *Inquiries into Truth and Interpretation*. Oxford University Press.

Davidson, Donald. 1985. "A New Basis for Decision Theory," *Theory and Decision* 18 (1): 87–98.

Davidson, Donald. 1986. "A Nice Derangement of Epitaphs," in Ernest LePore, ed., *Truth and Interpretation: Perspectives on the Philosophy of Donald Davidson*. Blackwell: 433–446.

Davidson, Donald. 1987. "Knowing One's Own Mind," in Donald Davidson, ed., *Subjective, Intersubjective, Objective* (2001). Oxford University Press: 15–38.

Davidson, Donald. 1990. "The Structure and Content of Truth," *The Journal of Philosophy* 87 (6): 238–279.

Davidson, Donald. 1994. "The Social Aspect of Language," in Donald Davidson, ed., *Truth, Language, and History* (2005). Clarendon Press: 109–125.

Davidson, Donald. 1999. "The Emergence of Thought," *Erkenntnis* 51 (1): 7–17.

Davidson, Donald. 2001a. "Comments on Karlovy Vary Papers," in Petr Kotatko, Peter Pagin, and Gabriel Segal, eds., *Interpreting Davidson*. Center for the Study of Language and Information: 285–307.

Davidson, Donald. 2001b. "Externalisms," in Petr Kotatko, Peter Pagin, and Gabriel Segal, eds., *Interpreting Davidson*. Center for the Study of Language and Information: 1–16.

Davidson, Donald. 2001c. *Subjective, Intersubjective, Objective*. Oxford University Press.

Davidson, Donald. 2001d. "The Second Person," in Donald Davidson, ed., *Subjective, Intersubjective, Objective*. Oxford University Press: 107–121.

Davies, David. 1998. "How Sceptical Is Kripke's 'Sceptical Solution'?," *Philosophia* 26 (1): 119–140.

Dennett, Daniel. 1981. *The Intentional Stance*. MIT Press.

Diamond, Cora. 1989. "Rules: Looking in the Right Place," in Dewi Zephaniah Phillips and Peter Winch, eds., *Wittgenstein: Attention to Particulars*. St. Martin's Press: 12–34.

Dorr, Cian and John Hawthorne. 2013. "Naturalness," in Karen Bennett and Dean Zimmerman, eds., *Oxford Studies in Metaphysics*, Volume 8. Oxford University Press: 3–77.

Dretske, Fred. 1981. *Knowledge and the Flow of Information*. MIT Press.

Dummett, Michael. 1974. "What Is a Theory of Meaning?," in Samuel Guttenplan, ed., *Mind and Language*. Clarendon Press: 97–122.

Dummett, Michael. 1976. "What Is a Theory of Meaning? (II)," in Gareth Evans and John McDowell, eds., *Truth and Meaning: Essays in Semantics*. Oxford University Press: 67–137.

Dummett, Michael. 1978. *Truth and Other Enigmas*. Harvard University Press.
Ebbs, Gary. 1997. *Rule-Following and Realism*. Harvard University Press.
Ebbs, Gary. 2000. "The Very Idea of Sameness of Extension across Time," *American Philosophical Quarterly* 37 (3): 245–268.
Ebbs, Gary. 2017. "Rules and Rule-Following," in Hans-Johann Glock and John Hyman, eds., *A Companion to Wittgenstein*. Wiley-Blackwell: 390–406.
Ebbs, Gary. 2022. "Ginsborg's Reading of Wittgenstein on Rules and Normativity," *Philosophical Investigations* 45 (3): 374–380.
Evans, Gareth. 1982. *The Varieties of Reference*. Clarendon Press.
Field, Hartry. 1994. "Deflationist Views of Meaning and Content," *Mind* 103 (411): 249–285.
Fine, Kit. 1994. "Essence and Modality," *Philosophical Perspectives* 8 (Logic and Language): 1–16.
Fine, Kit. 2002. *The Limits of Abstraction*. Oxford University Press.
Fine, Kit. 2015. "Unified Foundations for Essence and Ground," *Journal of the American Philosophical Association* 1 (2): 296–311.
Fodor, Jerry. 1975. *The Language of Thought*. Harvard University Press.
Fodor, Jerry. 1990a. *A Theory of Content*. MIT Press.
Fodor, Jerry. 1990b. "A Theory of Content II," in Jerry Fodor, ed., *A Theory of Content*. MIT Press: 89–136.
Fogelin, Robert. 1987. *Wittgenstein*. Routledge.
Fogelin, Robert. 1996. "Wittgenstein's Critique of Philosophy," in Hans D. Sluga and David Stern, eds., *The Cambridge Companion to Wittgenstein*. Cambridge University Press: 34–58.
Foot, Philippa. 1972. "Morality as a System of Hypothetical Imperatives," *Philosophical Review* 81 (3): 305–316.
Frege, Gottlob. 1980. *The Foundations of Arithmetic*. Translated by J. L. Austin. Northwestern University Press.
Friedman, Milton. 1966. "The Methodology of Positive Economics," in Milton Friedman, ed., *Essays in Positive Economics*. University of Chicago Press: 3–47.
Gibbard, Allan. 2003. "Thoughts and Norms," *Philosophical Issues* 13 (1): 83–98.
Gibbard, Allan. 2012. *Meaning and Normativity*. Oxford University Press.
Ginsborg, Hannah. 2010. "Review of A. Hattiangadi *Oughts and Thoughts: Skepticism and the Normativity of Meaning*," *Mind* 119 (476): 1175–1186.
Ginsborg, Hannah. 2011a. "Inside and Outside Language: Stroud's Nonreductionism about Meaning," in Jason Bridges, Niko Kolodny, and Wai-Hung Wong, eds., *The Possibility of Philosophical Understanding: Reflections on the Thought of Barry Stroud*. Oxford University Press: 147–181.
Ginsborg, Hannah. 2011b. "Primitive Normativity and Skepticism about Rules," *Journal of Philosophy* 108 (5): 227–254.
Ginsborg, Hannah. 2012. "Meaning, Understanding and Normativity," *Proceedings of the Aristotelian Society Supplementary Volume* 86 (1): 127–146.
Ginsborg, Hannah. 2018. "Leaps in the Dark: Epistemological Skepticism in Kripke's Wittgenstein," in G. Anthony Bruno and A. C. Rutherford, eds., *Skepticism: Historical and Contemporary Inquiries*. Routledge: 149–166.
Ginsborg, Hannah. 2020. "Wittgenstein on Going On," *Canadian Journal of Philosophy* 50 (1): 1–17.

Ginsborg, Hannah. 2022. "Going on as One Ought: Kripke and Wittgenstein on the Normativity of Meaning," *Mind and Language* 37 (5): 872–892.

Ginsborg, Hannah. In Press. "Skepticism and Quietism about Meaning and Normativity," in Matthew Boyle and Evgenia Mylonaki, eds., *Reason in Nature*. Harvard University Press.

Glock, Hans-Johann. 2005. "The Normativity of Meaning Made Simple," in Christian Nimtz and Ansgar Beckermann, eds., *Philosophy – Science – Scientific Philosophy*. Mentis: 199–241.

Glock, Hans-Johann. 2019. "The Normativity of Meaning Revisited," in Neil Roughley and Kurt Bayertz, eds., *The Normative Animal?*. Oxford University Press: 295–318.

Glüer, Kathrin. 1999. "Sense and Prescriptivity," *Acta Analytica* 14 (23): 111–128.

Glüer, Kathrin. 2001. "Dreams and Nightmares: Conventions, Norms, and Meaning in Davidson's Philosophy of Language," in Petr Kotatko, Peter Pagin, and George Segal, eds., *Interpreting Davidson*. Center for the Study of Language and Information: 53–74.

Glüer, Kathrin. 2018. "Interpretation and the Interpreter," in Derek Ball and Brian Rabern, eds., *The Science of Meaning: Essays on the Metatheory of Natural Language Semantics*. Oxford University Press: 226–252.

Glüer, Kathrin and Åsa Wikforss. 2009. "Against Content Normativity," *Mind* 118 (469): 31–70.

Glüer, Kathrin and Åsa Wikforss. 2018. "The Normativity of Meaning and Content," in Edward N. Zalta, ed., *Stanford Encyclopedia of Philosophy*. https://plato.stanford.edu/entries/meaning-normativity.

Goldfarb, Warren. 1983. "I Want You to Bring Me a Slab: Remarks on the Opening Sections of *Philosophical Investigations*," *Synthese* 56 (3): 265–282.

Goldfarb, Warren. 1985. "Kripke on Wittgenstein on Rules," *The Journal of Philosophy* 82 (9): 471–488. Reprinted in Alexander Miller and Cripsin Wright, eds., *Rule-Following and Meaning* (2002). Acumen Publishing: 92–107.

Goldfarb, Warren. 1997. "Wittgenstein on Fixity of Meaning," in William Tait, ed., *Early Analytic Philosophy: Frege, Russell, Wittgenstein*. Open Court: 75–90.

Graham, Peter. 2010. "In Defense of Objectivism about Moral Obligation," *Ethics* 121 (1): 88–115.

Green, Derek. 2018. "Semantic Knowledge, Semantic Guidance, and Kripke's Wittgenstein," *Pacific Philosophical Quarterly* 99 (2): 186–206.

Green, Derek. 2021. "Rules of Belief and the Normativity of Intentional Content," *Acta Analytica* 36 (2): 159–169.

Greenspan, Patricia. 1970. "Conditional Oughts and Hypothetical Imperatives," *Journal of Philosophy* 72 (10): 259–276.

Guardo, Andrea. 2022. "Yet Another Victim of Kripkenstein's Monster: Dispositions, Meaning, and Privilege," *Ergo* 8 (55): 857–882.

Haase, Matthias. 2009. "The Laws of Thought and the Power of Thinking," *Canadian Journal of Philosophy* 39 (Suppl 1): 249–297.

Haddock, Adrian. 2012. "Meaning, Justification, and 'Primitive Normativity'," *Aristotelian Society Supplementary Volume* 86 (1): 147–174.

Hale, Bob. 1987. *Abstract Objects*. Basil Blackwell.
Hale, Bob. 2013. *Necessary Beings: An Essay on Ontology, Modality, and the Relations between Them*. Oxford University Press.
Hale, Bob and Crispin Wright. 2001. *The Reason's Proper Study: Essays Towards a Neo-Fregean Philosophy of Mathematics*. Oxford University Press.
Hattiangadi, Anandi. 2006. "Is Meaning Normative?," *Mind and Language* 21 (2): 220–240.
Hattiangadi, Anandi. 2007. *Oughts and Thoughts: Rule-Following and the Normativity of Content*. Oxford University Press.
Hattiangadi, Anandi. 2009. "Some More Thoughts on Semantic Oughts: A Reply to Daniel Whiting," *Analysis* 69 (1): 54–63.
Hattiangadi, Anandi. 2015. "The Limits of Expressivism," in Stephen Gross, Nicholas Tebben and Michael Williams, eds., *Meaning without Representation*. Oxford University Press: 224–244.
Hattiangadi, Anandi. 2017. "The Normativity of Meaning," in Bob Hale, Alexander Miller, and Crispin Wright, eds., *Companion to Philosophy of the Language*, 2nd ed. Wiley: 649–669.
Hattiangadi, Anandi. 2018a. "Moral Supervenience," *Canadian Journal of Philosophy* 48 (3–4): 592–615.
Hattiangadi, Anandi. 2018b. "Normativity and Intentionality," in Daniel Star, ed., *Oxford Handbook of Reasons and Normativity*. Oxford University Press: 1040–1064.
Hattiangadi, Anandi. 2018c. "The Normativity of MEANING and the Hard Problem of Intentionality," Symposium on Allan Gibbard's *Meaning and Normativity*. *Inquiry*: 61 (7): 742–754.
Hattiangadi, Anandi. 2020. "Radical Interpretation and the Aggregation Problem," *Philosophy and Phenomenological Research* 101 (2): 283–303.
Hattiangadi, Anandi. 2023. "Logical Conventionalism and the Adoption Problem," *Aristotelian Society Supplementary Volume* 97 (1): 47–81.
Hattiangadi, Anandi and H. Orri Stefánsson. 2021. "Radical Interpretation and Decision Theory," *Synthese* 199: 6473–6494. https://doi.org/10.1007/s11229-021-03078-8.
Haugeland, John. 1998. "The Intentionality All-Stars," in John Haugeland, ed., *Having Thought*. Harvard University Press: 127–170.
Hawthorne, John. 1990. "A Note on 'Languages and Language'," *Australasian Journal of Philosophy* 68 (1): 116–118.
Hawthorne, John. 2007. "Craziness and Metasemantics," *The Philosophical Review* 116 (3): 427–440.
Hlobil, Ulf. 2015. "Anti-normativism Evaluated," *International Journal of Philosophical Studies* 23 (3): 376–395.
Horgan, Terry and Mark Timmons. 2006. "Cognitivist Expressivism," in Terry Horgan and Mark Timmons, eds., *Metaethics after Moore*. Oxford University Press: 255–298.
Hornsby, Jennifer. 2008. "A Disjunctivist Conception of Acting for Reasons," in Adrian Haddock and Fiona Macpherson, eds., *Disjunctivism*. Oxford University Press: 244–261.
Horwich, Paul. 1984. "Critical Notice: Saul Kripke: *Wittgenstein on Rules and Private Language*," *Philosophy of Science* 51 (1): 163–171.

Horwich, Paul. 1990. *Truth*. Oxford University Press.
Horwich, Paul. 1995. "Meaning, Use and Truth," *Mind* 104 (414): 355–368. Reprinted in Alexander Miller and Crispin Wright, eds., *Rule-Following and Meaning* (2002). Acumen Publishing: 260–273.
Horwich, Paul. 1998. *Meaning*. Oxford University Press.
Horwich, Paul. 2010. "Wittgenstein's Definition of 'Meaning' as 'Use'," in Daniel Whiting, ed., *The Later Wittgenstein on Language*. Palgrave Macmillan: 17–25.
Hurka, Thomas. 2014. *British Ethical Theorists from Sidgwick to Ewing*. Oxford University Press.
Jackman, Henry. 2003a, "Charity, Self-Interpretation, and Belief," *Journal of Philosophical Research* 28: 145–170.
Jackman, Henry. 2003b, "Foundationalism, Coherentism and Rule-Following Skepticism," *International Journal of Philosophical Studies* 11 (1): 25–41.
Jackman, Henry. 2005. "Descriptive Atomism and Foundational Holism: Semantics between the Old Testament and the New," *ProtoSociology* 21: 5–19.
Jackson, Frank. 1982. "Epiphenomenal Qualia," *Philosophical Quarterly* 32 (127): 127–136.
Jackson, Frank. 1986. "What Mary Didn't Know," *Journal of Philosophy* 83 (5): 291–295.
Jackson, Frank. 1998. *From Metaphysics to Ethics: A Defence of Conceptual Analysis*. Oxford University Press.
Janeway, Charles A. Jr. 2001. "How the Immune System Works to Protect the Host from Infection. A Personal View." *PNAS* 98 (13): 7461–7468. https://doi.org/10.1073/pnas.131202998.
Janssen-Lauret, Frederique and Fraser MacBride. 2020. "Lewis's Global Descriptivism and Reference Magnetism," *Australasian Journal of Philosophy* 98 (1): 192–198.
Jones, Matthew. 2015. "The Normativity of Meaning: Guidance and Justification," *International Journal of Philosophical Studies* 23 (3): 425–443.
Kant, Immanuel. 1785. *Groundwork of the Metaphysics of Morals*. Translated by Mary Gregor. Cambridge University Press.
Kaplan, David. 1989. "Afterthoughts," in Josph Almog, John Perry, and Howard Wettstein, eds., *Themes from Kaplan*. Oxford University Press: 565–614.
Kearns, Stephen and Magidor, Ofra. 2012. "Semantic Sovereignty," *Philosophy and Phenomenological Research* 85 (2): 322–350.
Keefe, Rosanna. 2007. *Theories of Vagueness*. Cambridge University Press.
Körding, Konrad P. and Daniel M. Wolpert. 2004. "Bayesian Integration in Sensorimotor Learning," *Nature* 427: 244–247.
Kotatko, Petr, Peter Pagin, and Gabriel Segal (eds.). 2001. *Interpreting Davidson*. Center for the Study of Language and Information.
Kripke, Saul. 1972. *Naming and Necessity*. Harvard University Press.
Kripke, Saul. 1982. *Wittgenstein on Rules and Private Language: An Elementary Exposition*. Harvard University Press.
Kusch, Martin. 2006. *A Sceptical Guide to Meaning and Rules: Defending Kripke's Wittgenstein*. Routledge.
Lance, Mark and John O'Leary-Hawthorne. 1997. *The Grammar of Meaning: Normativity and Semantic Discourse*. Cambridge University Press.

Leuenberger, Stephan. 2014. "Grounding and Necessity," *Inquiry: An Interdisciplinary Journal of Philosophy* 57 (2): 151–174.
Lepore, Ernie (ed.). 1986. *Truth and Interpretation: Perspectives on the Philosophy of Donald Davidson*. Blackwell.
Lepore, Ernie and Brian McLaughlin (eds.). 1985. *Actions and Events: Perspectives on the Philosophy of Donald Davidson*. Blackwell.
Lewis, David. 1970. "General Semantics," *Synthese* 22 (1/2): 18–67.
Lewis, David. 1974. "Radical Interpretation," *Synthese* 27 (3/4): 331–344.
Lewis, David. 1975. "Languages and Language," in Keith Gunderson, ed., *Minnesota Studies in the Philosophy of Science*. University of Minnesota Press: 3–35.
Lewis, David. 1983. "New Work for a Theory of Universals," *Australasian Journal of Philosophy* 61 (4): 343–377.
Lewis, David. 1984. "Putnam's Paradox," *Australasian Journal of Philosophy* 62 (3): 221–236.
Lewis, David. 1986. *On the Plurality of Worlds*. Wiley-Blackwell.
Lewis, David. 1992. "Meaning without Use: Reply to Hawthorne," *Australasian Journal of Philosophy* 70 (1): 106–110.
Lewis, David. 1994. "Reduction of Mind," in Samuel Guttenplan, ed., *Companion to the Philosophy of Mind*. Blackwell: 412–431.
Loar, Brian. 2003. "Phenomenal Intentionality as the Basis of Mental Content," in Martin Hahn and Bjorn Ramberg, eds., *Reflections and Replies: Essays on the Philosophy of Tyler Burge*. MIT Press: 229–258.
Lowe, Edward Johnathan. 2012. "What Is the Source of Our Knowledge of Modal Truths?," *Mind* 121 (484): 919–950.
Lycan, William G. 1971. "Noninductive Evidence: Recent Work on Wittgenstein's 'Criteria'," *American Philosophical Quarterly* 8 (2): 109–125.
Lynch, Michael. 2004. *True to Life*. Harvard University Press.
MacBride, Fraser. 2003. "Speaking with Shadows: A Study of Neo-Logicism," *British Journal for the Philosophy of Science* 54 (1): 103–163.
Mallozzi, Antonella. 2018a. "Putting Modal Metaphysics First," *Synthese* 198 (Suppl 8): 1937–1956.
Mallozzi, Antonella. 2018b. "Two Notions of Metaphysical Modality," *Synthese* 198 (Suppl 6): 1387–1408.
Mancosu, Paolo. 2016. *Abstraction and Infinity*. Oxford University Press.
McDowell, John. 1980. "Meaning, Communication, and Knowledge," in John McDowell, ed., *Meaning, Knowledge, and Reality* (1998). Harvard University Press: 29–50.
McDowell, John. 1981. "Anti-realism and the Epistemology of Understanding," in John McDowell, ed., *Meaning, Knowledge, and Reality* (1998). Harvard University Press: 314–343.
McDowell, John. 1984. "Wittgenstein on Following a Rule," *Synthese* 58 (3): 325–363. Reprinted in John McDowell, ed., *Mind, Value, and Reality* (1998). Harvard University Press: 221–262.
McDowell, John. 1992. "Meaning and Intentionality in Wittgenstein's Later Philosophy," *Midwest Studies in Philosophy* 17: 40–52. Reprinted in John McDowell, ed., *Mind, Value, and Reality* (1998). Harvard University Press: 263–278.

McDowell, John. 1998a. "Intentionality and Interiority in Wittgenstein," in John McDowell, ed., *Mind, Value, and Reality*. Harvard University Press: 297–321.
McDowell, John. 1998b. *Meaning, Knowledge, and Reality*. Harvard University Press.
McDowell, John. 2009a. *Having the World in View: Essays on Kant, Hegel, and Sellars*. Harvard University Press.
McDowell, John. 2009b. "Wittgensteinian Quietism," *Common Knowledge* 15 (3): 365–372.
McDowell, John. 2010. "Are Meaning, Understanding, etc. Definite States?," in Arif Ahmed, ed., *Wittgenstein's Philosophical Investigations: A Critical Guide*. Cambridge University Press: 162–177.
McGinn, Colin. 1977. "Charity, Interpretation, and Belief," *The Journal of Philosophy* 74 (9): 521–535.
McGinn, Colin. 1984. *Wittgenstein on Meaning: An Interpretation and Evaluation*. Basil Blackwell.
McGinn, Colin. 2002. "Wittgenstein, Kripke and Non-reductionism about Meaning," in Alexander Miller and Crispin Wright, eds., *Rule-Following and Meaning*. Acumen Publishing: 81–91.
McGinn, Marie. 2013. *The Routledge Guidebook to Wittgenstein's Philosophical Investigations*. 2nd ed. Routledge.
McPherson, Tristram. 2018. "Authoritatively Normative Concepts," *Oxford Studies in Metaethics* 13: 253–277.
Mendelovici, Angela A. 2018. *The Phenomenal Basis of Intentionality*. Oxford University Press.
Millar, Alan. 2002. "The Normativity of Meaning," *Royal Institute of Philosophy Supplement* 77 (Suppl 51): 57–73.
Millar, Alan. 2004. *Understanding People*. Oxford University Press.
Millar, Alan. 2014. "How Meaning Might Be Normative," in Julien Dutant, Davide Fassio, and Anne Meylan, eds., *Liber Amicorum Pascal Engel*. University of Geneva: 798–817.
Miller, Alexander. 2006. "Meaning Scepticism," in Michael Devitt and Richard Hanley, eds., *Blackwell Guide to the Philosophy of Language*. Blackwell: 91–113.
Miller, Alexander. 2010a. "Kripke's Wittgenstein, Factualism, and Meaning," in Daniel Whiting, ed., *The Later Wittgenstein on Language*. Palgrave Macmillan: 167–190.
Miller, Alexander. 2010b. "The Argument from Queerness and the Normativity of Meaning," in Martin Grajner and Dolf Rami, eds., *Wahrheit, Bedeutung, Existenz*. Ontos: 107–124.
Miller, Alexander. 2012. "Semantic Realism and the Argument from Motivational Internalism," in Richard Schantz, ed., *Prospects for Meaning*. De Gruyter: 345–362.
Miller, Alexander. 2015. "Blind Rule-Following and the 'Antinomy of Pure Reason'," *The Philosophical Quarterly* 65 (260): 396–416.
Miller, Alexander. 2018. *Philosophy of Language*. 3rd ed. Routledge.
Miller, Alexander. 2019. "Rule-Following, Meaning, and Primitive Normativity," *Mind* 128 (511): 735–760.
Miller, Alexander. 2020. "What Is the Sceptical Solution?," *Journal for the History of Analytical Philosophy* 8 (2): 1–22.

Miller, Alexander and Crispin Wright (eds.). 2002. *Rule-Following and Meaning*. Acumen Publishing.

Millikan, Ruth. 1990. "Truth-Rules, Hoverflies, and the Kripke-Wittgenstein Paradox," in Alexander Miller and Crispin Wright, eds., *Rule-Following and Meaning* (2002). Acumen Publishing: 209–233.

Montero, Barbara. 2013. "Must Physicalism Imply the Supervenience of the Mental on the Physical?," *Journal of Philosophy* 110 (2): 93–110.

Moore, George Edward. 1954. "Wittgenstein's Lectures in 1930–1933," *Mind* 63 (249): 289–316.

Moran, Alex. 2021. "Living without Microphysical Supervenience," *Philosophical Studies* 179 (2): 405–428.

Moran, Richard. 2001. *Authority and Estrangement*. Princeton University Press.

Moyal-Sharrock, Danièle. 2017. "The Myth of the Quietist Wittgenstein," in Johnathan Beale and Ian James Kidd, eds., *Wittgenstein and Scientism*. Routledge: 152–174.

Myers, Robert and Claudine Verheggen. 2016. *Donald Davidson's Triangulation Argument: A Philosophical Inquiry*. Routledge.

Nagel, Thomas. 1974. "What Is It Like to Be a Bat?," *Philosophical Review* 83: 435–450.

Papineau, David. 1999. "Normativity and Judgement," *Aristotelian Society Supplementary Volume* 73 (1): 17–43.

Parfit, Derek. 2001. "Rationality and Reasons," in Dan Egonsson, Jonas Josefsson, and Toni Rønnow-Rasmussen, eds., *Exploring Practical Philosophy*. Ashgate: 17–39.

Parfit, Derek. 2011. *On What Matters*, Volume I. Oxford University Press.

Peano, Giuseppe. 1894. *Notations De Logique Mathématique. Introduction Au Formulaire De Mathématique*. Bocca.

Pettit, Philip. 1990. "The Reality of Rule-Following," in Alexander Miller and Crispin Wright, eds., *Rule-Following and Meaning* (2002). Acumen Publishing: 188–208.

Pollock, John. 1967. "Criteria and Our Knowledge of the Material World," *Philosophical Review* 76 (1): 28–60.

Price, Huw, Simon Blackburn, Robert Brandom, Paul Horwich, and Michael Williams. 2013. *Expressivism, Pragmatism and Representationalism*. Cambridge University Press.

Putnam, Hilary. 1975. "The Meaning of 'Meaning'," in Hilary Putnam, ed., *Mind, Language and Reality. Philosophical Papers*, Volume 2. Cambridge University Press: 215–271.

Putnam, Hilary. 1980. "Models and Reality," *Journal of Symbolic Logic* 45 (3): 464–482. Reprinted in Paul Benacerraf and Hilary Putnam, eds., *Philosophy of Mathematics: Selected Readings*, 2nd ed. (1983). Cambridge University Press: 421–444.

Putnam, Hilary. 1981. *Reason, Truth and History*. Cambridge University Press.

Quine, W. V. 1943. "Notes on Existence and Necessity," *Journal of Philosophy* 40 (5): 113–127.

Quine, W. V. 1951. "Two Dogmas of Empiricism," in W. V. Quine, ed., *From a Logical Point of View* (1953). Harvard University Press: 20–46.

Quine, W. V. 1960. *Word and Object*. MIT Press.

Rabinowicz, Wlodek. 2002. "Preference Logic and Radical Interpretation: Kanger Meets Davidson," in Peter Gärdenfors ed., *11th International Congress of Logic, Methodology and Philosophy of Science* 2. Springer: 213–233.

Reiland, Indrek. 2023a. "Linguistic Mistakes," *Erkenntnis* 88 (5): 2191–2206.

Reiland, Indrek. 2023b. "Rules of Use," *Mind and Language* 38 (2): 566–583.

Rosen, Gideon. 2020. "What Is Normative Necessity?," in Mircea Dumitru, ed., *Metaphysics, Meaning, and Modality: Themes from Kit Fine*. Oxford University Press: 205–233.

Ross, David. 1930. *The Right and the Good*. Edited by Philip Stratton-Lake. Oxford University Press.

Russell, Bertrand. 1903. *The Principles of Mathematics*. Cambridge University Press.

Schiffer, Stephen. 1986. "Kripkenstein Meets the Remnants of Meaning," *Philosophical Studies* 49 (2): 147–162.

Schroeder, Mark. 2008. "Expression for Expressivists," *Philosophy and Phenomenological Research* 76 (1): 86–116.

Schroeder, Mark. 2009. "Means-End Coherence, Stringency, and Subjective Reasons," *Philosophical Studies* 143 (2): 223–248.

Schroeder, Mark. 2018. "Believing Well," in Conor McHugh, Jonathan Way, and Daniel Whiting, eds., *Metaepistemology*. Oxford University Press: 196–212.

Schwarz, Wolfgang. 2014. "Against Magnetism," *Australasian Journal of Philosophy* 92 (1): 17–36.

Searle, John. 1980. "Minds, Brains, and Programs," *The Behavioral and Brain Sciences* 3 (3): 417–424.

Searle, John. 1992. *The Rediscovery of the Mind*. MIT Press.

Setiya, Kieran. 2007. "Cognitivism about Instrumental Reasoning," *Ethics* 117 (4): 649–673.

Shaw, James R. 2023. *Wittgenstein on Rules: Justification, Grammar, and Agreement*. Oxford University Press.

Sider, Theodore. 2009. "Ontological Realism," in David Chalmers, David Manley, and Ryan Wasserman, eds., *Metametaphysics: New Essays on the Foundations of Ontology*. Oxford University Press: 384–423.

Skyrms, Brian. 2010. *Signals*. Oxford University Press.

Soames, Scott. 1998. "Skepticism about Meaning, Indeterminacy, Normativity, and the Rule-Following Paradox," *Canadian Journal of Philosophy, Supp* 23 (Suppl 1): 211–250.

Sorensen, Roy. 2001. *Vagueness and Contradiction*. Oxford University Press.

Sorgiovanni, Ben. 2018. "Rule-Following and Primitive Normativity," *Dialectica* 72 (1): 141–510.

Speaks, Jeff. 2009. "The Normativity of Content and 'the Frege Point'," *European Journal of Philosophy* 17 (3): 405–415.

Speaks, Jeff. 2019. "Theories of Meaning," in Edward N. Zalta, ed., *The Stanford Encyclopedia of Philosophy*, Spring 2021 ed. https://plato.stanford.edu/entries/meaning/

Stalnaker, Robert. 1997. "Reference and Necessity," in Bob Hale and Crispin Wright, eds., *A Companion to the Philosophy of Language*. Basil Blackwell: 534–554.

Stroud, Barry. 1965. "Wittgenstein and Logical Necessity," *The Philosophical Review* 74 (4): 504–518.

Stroud, Barry. 1996. "Mind, Meaning and Practice," in Hans Sluga and David Stern, eds., *Cambridge Companion to Wittgenstein*. Cambridge University Press: 296–319.
Stroud, Barry. 2000. *Meaning, Understanding, and Practice: Philosophical Essays*. Oxford University Press.
Stroud, Barry. 2012. "Meaning and Understanding," in Jonathan Ellis and Daniel Guevara, eds., *Wittgenstein and the Philosophy of Mind*. Oxford University Press: 19–36.
Stroud, Barry. 2017. "Davidson and Wittgenstein on Meaning and Understanding," in Claudine Verheggen, ed., *Wittgenstein and Davidson on Language, Thought, and Action*. Cambridge University Press: 97–122.
Sultanescu, Olivia. 2021. "Meaning Scepticism and Primitive Normativity," *Pacific Philosophical Quarterly* 102 (2): 357–376.
Sultanescu, Olivia. 2023. "Meaning, Rationality, and Guidance." *The Philosophical Quarterly* 73 (1): 227–247.
Sultanescu, Olivia and Claudine Verheggen. 2019. "Davidson's Answer to Kripke's Sceptic," *Journal for the History of Analytic Philosophy* 7 (2): 8–28.
Sylvan, Kurt. 2015. "What Apparent Reasons Appear to Be," *Philosophical Studies* 172 (3): 587–606.
Tait, William W. 1986. "Wittgenstein and the 'Skeptical Paradoxes'," *Journal of Philosophy* 83 (9): 475–488.
Tenenbaum, Joshua B., Charles Kemp, Thomas L. Griffiths, and Noah D. Goodman. 2011. "How to Grow a Mind: Statistics, Structure, and Abstraction," *Science* 331 (6022): 1279–1285.
Thornton, Tim. 1998. *Wittgenstein on Thought and Language: The Philosophy of Content*. University of Edinburgh Press.
Tracy, Eric V. 2020. "Unfollowed Rules and the Normativity of Content," *Analytic Philosophy* 61 (4): 323–344.
Vaidya, Anand J. 2018. "Analytic Essentialist Approaches to the Epistemology of Modality," in Ivette Fred-Rivera and Jessica Leech, eds., *Being Necessary: Themes of Ontology and Modality from the Work of Bob Hale*. Oxford University Press: 224–244.
Vaidya, Anand J. and Michael Wallner. 2021. "The Epistemology of Modality and the Problem of Modal Epistemic Friction," *Synthese* 198 (Suppl 8): 1909–1935.
Verheggen, Claudine. 2000. "The Meaningfulness of Meaning Questions," *Synthese* 123 (2): 195–216.
Verheggen, Claudine. 2003. "Wittgenstein's Rule-Following Paradox and the Objectivity of Meaning," *Philosophical Investigations* 26 (4): 285–310.
Verheggen, Claudine. 2006. "How Social Must Language Be?," *Journal for the Theory of Social Behavior* 36 (2): 203–219.
Verheggen, Claudine. 2007. "The Community View Revisited," *Metaphilosophy* 38 (5): 612–631.
Verheggen, Claudine. 2011. "Semantic Normativity and Naturalism," *Logique et Analyse* 54 (216): 553–567.
Verheggen, Claudine. 2015. "Towards a New Kind of Semantic Normativity," *International Journal of Philosophical Studies* 23 (3): 410–424.
Verheggen, Claudine. 2017. "Davidson's Treatment of Wittgenstein's Rule-Following Paradox," in Claudine Verheggen, ed., *Wittgenstein and Davidson on Language, Thought, and Action*. Cambridge University Press: 97–122.

Verheggen, Claudine. 2021. "The Continuity of Davidson's Thought: Non-reductionism without Quietism," in Robert H. Myers and Syraya Chin-Mu Yang, eds., *Donald Davidson on Action, Mind and Value*. Springer: 129–144.

Verheggen, Claudine. 2023. "Linguistic Luck and the Publicness of Language," in Abrol Fairweather and Carlos Montemayor, eds., *Linguistic Luck*. Oxford University Press: 222–240.

Verheggen, Claudine. In Press. "Semantic Non-reductionism," in Ernest Lepore and Una Stojnic, eds., *The Oxford Handbook of Contemporary Philosophy of Language*. Oxford University Press.

Vogelstein, Eric. 2012. "Subjective Reasons," *Ethical Theory and Moral Practice* 15 (2): 239–257.

Von Humboldt, Wilhem. 1836. *Über die Verschiedenheit des Menschlichen Sprachbaues*. 2009 ed., Cambridge University Press.

Wallace, R. Jay. 2006. *Normativity and the Will: Selected Essays on Moral Psychology and Practical Reason*. Oxford University Press.

Warren, Jared. 2020. "Killing Kripkenstein's Monster," *Noûs* 54 (2): 257–289.

Way, Jonathan. 2009. "Two Accounts of the Normativity of Rationality," *Journal of Ethics and Social Philosophy* 4 (1): 1–9.

Way, Jonathan. 2010. "Defending the Wide-Scope Approach to Instrumental Reason," *Philosophical Studies* 147 (2): 213–233.

Weatherson, Brian. 2003. "What Good Are Counterexamples?," *Philosophical Studies* 115 (1): 1–31.

Whiting, Daniel. 2007. "The Normativity of Meaning Defended," *Analysis* 67 (2): 133–140.

Whiting, Daniel. 2009a. "Is Meaning Fraught with Ought?," *Pacific Philosophical Quarterly* 90 (4): 535–555.

Whiting, Daniel. 2009b. "On Epistemic Conceptions of Meaning: Use, Meaning and Normativity," *European Journal of Philosophy* 17 (3): 416–434.

Whiting, Daniel. 2010. "Should I Believe the Truth?," *Dialectica* 64 (2): 213–224.

Whiting, Daniel. 2014. "Keep Things in Perspective: Reasons, Rationality, and the A Priori," *Journal of Ethics and Social Philosophy* 8 (1): 1–22.

Whiting, Daniel. 2015. "Review of Allan Gibbard's *Meaning and Normativity*," *European Journal of Philosophy* 23 (S1): 14–18.

Whiting, Daniel. 2016. "What Is the Normativity of Meaning?," *Inquiry* 59 (3): 219–238.

Whiting, Daniel. 2017. "Against Second-Order Reasons," *Noûs* 51 (2): 398–420.

Whiting, Daniel. 2021. *The Range of Reasons in Ethics and Epistemology*. Oxford University Press.

Wikforss, Åsa. 2001. "Semantic Normativity," *Philosophical Studies* 102 (2): 203–226.

Williams, Bernard. 1973. "A Critique of Utilitarianism," in J. J. C. Smart and Bernard Williams, eds., *Utilitarianism: For and Against*. Cambridge University Press: 77–150.

Williams, Bernard. 1981. "Wittgenstein and Idealism," in Bernard Williams, ed., *Moral Luck*. Cambridge University Press: 144–163.

Williams, J. Robert G. 2007. "Eligibility and Inscrutability," *The Philosophical Review* 116 (3): 361–399.

Williams, J. Robert G. 2019. *The Metaphysics of Representation*. Oxford University Press.
Williams, Meredith. 1999. *Wittgenstein, Mind and Meaning: Toward a Social Conception of Mind*. Routledge.
Williams, Meredith. 2000. "Wittgenstein and Davidson on the Sociality of Language," *Journal for the Theory of Social Behaviour* 30 (3): 299–318.
Williamson, Timothy. 1996. *Vagueness*. Routledge.
Williamson, Timothy. 2000. *Knowledge and Its Limits*. Oxford University Press.
Wilson, George. 1994. "Kripke on Wittgenstein on Normativity," *Midwest Studies in Philosophy* 19: 366–390. Reprinted in Alexander Miller and Crispin Wright, eds., *Rule-Following and Meaning* (2002). Acumen Publishing: 234–259.
Wilson, George. 1998. "Semantic Realism and Kripke's Wittgenstein," *Philosophy and Phenomenological Research* 58 (1): 99–122.
Wilson, N. L. 1959. "Substance without Substrata," *Review of Metaphysics* 12 (4): 521–539.
Wiseman, Rachael. 2016. *The Routledge Philosophy Guidebook to Anscombe's Intention*. Routledge.
Wittgenstein, Ludwig. 1953a. *Philosophical Investigations*. Translated by G. E. M. Anscombe, 3rd ed. Blackwell.
Wittgenstein, Ludwig. 1953b. *Philosophical Investigations*. Edited by P. M. S. Hacker and J. Schulte, translated by G. E. M. Anscombe, P. M. S. Hacker and J. Schulte, revised 4th ed. (2009). Wiley-Blackwell.
Wittgenstein, Ludwig. 1958. *The Blue and Brown Books*. Harper and Row.
Wittgenstein, Ludwig. 1974. *Philosophical Grammar*. Edited by Rush Rhees, translated by Anthony Kenny. University of California Press.
Wittgenstein, Ludwig. 1977. *On Certainty*. Edited by G. E. M. Anscombe and G. H. von Wright, translated by Denis Paul and G. E. M. Anscombe. Wiley Blackwell.
Wittgenstein, Ludwig. 1978. *Remarks on the Foundations of Mathematics*. Edited by G. H. von Wright, Rush Rhees, and G. E. M. Anscombe. MIT Press.
Wodak, Daniel. 2019. "Mere Formalities: Fictional Normativity and Normative Authority," *Canadian Journal of Philosophy* 49 (6): 828–850.
Woods, Jack. 2018. "The Authority of Formality," *Oxford Studies in Metaethics* 13: 207–229.
Wright, Crispin. 1982. "Anti-realist Semantics: The Role of Criteria," *Royal Institute of Philosophy Supplements* 13: 225–248.
Wright, Crispin. 1983. *Frege's Conception of Numbers as Objects*. Aberdeen University Press.
Wright, Crispin. 1984a. "Kripke's Account of the Argument against Private Language," *Journal of Philosophy* 81 (12): 759–778. Reprinted in Crispin Wright, ed., *Rails to Infinity: Essays on Themes from Wittgenstein's Philosophical Investigations* (2001). Harvard University Press: 91–115.
Wright, Crispin. 1984b. "Second Thoughts about Criteria," *Synthese* 58: 383–405.
Wright, Crispin. 1987. "On Making Up One's Mind: Wittgenstein on Intention," in Crispin Wright (ed.), *Rails to Infinity* (2001). Harvard University Press: 116–142.
Wright, Crispin. 1989a. "Critical Notice of Colin McGinn's *Wittgenstein on Meaning*," *Mind* 98 (390): 289–305. Reprinted in Alexander Miller and

Crispin Wright, eds., *Rule-Following and Meaning* (2002). Acumen Publishing: 108–128.
Wright, Crispin. 1989b. "Wittgenstein's Rule-Following Considerations and the Central Project of Theoretical Linguistics," in Crispin Wright, ed., *Rails to Infinity: Essays on Themes from Wittgenstein's Philosophical Investigations* (2001). Harvard University Press: 170–213.
Wright, Crispin. 1992. *Truth and Objectivity*. Harvard University Press.
Wright, Crispin. 2001a. *Rails to Infinity: Essays on Themes from Wittgenstein's Philosophical Investigations*. Harvard University Press.
Wright, Crispin. 2001b. "Rule Following, Meaning and Constructivism," in Crispin Wright, ed., *Rails to Infinity: Essays on Themes from Wittgenstein's Philosophical Investigations*. Harvard University Press: 53–80.
Wright, Crispin. 2001c. "Wittgenstein's Argument as It Struck Kripke," in Crispin Wright, ed., *Rails to Infinity: Essays on Themes from Wittgenstein's Philosophical Investigations*. Harvard University Press: 116–142.
Wright, Crispin. 2001d. "Wittgenstein's Later Philosophy of Mind: Sensation, Privacy and Intention," in Crisping Wright, ed., *Rails to Infinity: Essays on Themes from Wittgenstein's Philosophical Investigations*. Harvard University Press: 291–318.
Wright, Crispin. 2007. "Rule-Following without Reasons: Wittgenstein's Quietism and the Constitutive Question," *Ratio* 20 (4): 481–502.
Wright, Crispin. 2012. "Replies Part I: The Rule-Following Considerations and the Normativity of Meaning," in Annalisa Coliva, ed., *Mind, Meaning, and Knowledge: Themes from the Philosophy of Crispin Wright*. Oxford University Press: 379–401.
Yablo, Stephen. 1993. "Is Conceivability a Guide to Possibility?," *Philosophy and Phenomenological Research* 53 (1): 1–42.
Yuille, Alan and Daniel Kersten. 2006. "Vision as Bayesian Inference: Analysis by Synthesis?," *Trends in Cognitive Sciences* 10 (7): 301–308.
Zalabardo, José L. 1997. "Kripke's Normativity Argument," *Canadian Journal of Philosophy* 27 (4): 467–468. Reprinted in Alexander Miller and Crispin Wright, eds., *Rule-Following and Meaning* (2020). Acumen Publishing: 274–293.
Zalabardo, José L. 2009. "One Strand in the Rule-Following Considerations," *Synthese* 171 (3): 509–519.
Zalabardo, José L. 2019. "Belief, Desire and the Prediction of Behaviour," *Philosophical Issues* 29 (1): 295–310.
Zalabardo, José L. 2023. *Pragmatist Semantics: A Use-Based Account of Linguistic Representation*. Oxford University Press.
Zalabardo, José L. In Press. "What Is Linguistic Interpretation?," in Joshua Gert, ed., *Neopragmatism*. Oxford University Press.
Zhong, Lei. 2017. "Semantic Normativity and Semantic Causality," *Philosophy and Phenomenological Research* 94 (3): 626–645.
Zimmerman, Michael. 2008. *Living with Uncertainty*. Cambridge University Press.

Index

abstract entity, 146, 159
abstraction, 13, 245–253, 257–258
agreement in
    action, 7, 88, 100, 101, 212
    definition, 154–157
    judgments, 100–102, 156–158, 161–162
    meaning, 11, 155, 202, 204
    responses, 73, 88, 121, 156, 161–162, 207, 209–212, 215, 252
Ahmed, Arif, 12, 125, 227
Alston, William, 125
analytic, 114, 115, 184, 185, 187–190, 192, 248
Anscombe, G. E. M., 69, 105, 154
anti-psychologism, 88, 92, 94, 100, 105, 106
Arpaly, Nomy, 135
Ayer, A. J., 221, 244, 249

Bader, Ralf, 185
Baker, Gordon, 69
Blackburn, Simon, 123, 125, 157, 189, 228, 252
Block, Irving, 1
Bloor, David, 201
Boghossian, Paul, 9, 15, 17, 20, 22, 23, 35, 61, 63, 64, 66–68, 107, 109, 116–117, 119, 125, 127, 163, 164, 167–169, 171, 180, 181, 187, 191, 253
Boyd, Daniel, 125
Brandom, Robert, 182, 188, 202, 209
Burge, Tyler, 24, 47–50, 57, 110, 214
Burgess, Alexis, 149
Bykvist, Krister, 191
Byrne, Alexander, 85, 125

Canfield, John, 123
Carnap, Rudolf, 244
Cartesian skepticism, 17–18, 30, 112
Chalmers, David, 182–185, 189, 193
charity, 57, 59, 197, 216, 256

Child, William, 142, 158
Chomsky, Noam, 115, 188
Churchland, Paul, 183
Coates, Paul, 189
communitarianism, 11–12, 36, 89, 98, 101–102, 106, 201–204, 206–210, 212, 214, 216–219, 220, 228, 231, 252
compositionality, 188–189, 197, 198
conceivability, 11, 188, 190, 192–193
conformity of present to past use, 4–5, 28–31, 37, 39, 43–45, 49, 81
correctness
    conditions, 138, 168, 212–215, 254–256
    linguistic, 46–50, 128
    metalinguistic, 5, 31, 36–37, 39, 42–43, 48, 109, 174
    standards of, 49, 146–148, 154–156, 163, 167, 170, 174–178, 227, 254

Davidson, Donald, 5, 11, 24, 48, 49, 57, 59, 149–150, 157, 178–180, 196–199, 201–204, 211–212, 215–219, 256–258
Davies, David, 125
decision theory, 197–199
deflationism, 183, 186, 221
Dennett, Daniel, 183
Descartes, René, 17, 18, 29, 30, 112, 200, 234
deviant
    individual, 205, 208–209
    worlds, 10, 11, 185, 187–188, 190, 192–196, 198
Diamond, Cora, 142
dispositions, 16–17, 19–21, 45, 53, 55–68, 72, 73, 89, 101, 103, 151, 159, 186, 214, 227, 229, 230
Dorr, Cian, 198
Dretske, Fred, 61
Dummett, Michael, 149–151, 204, 221, 239–241

274

Index

Ebbs, Gary, 7–8, 35, 64, 118–120
entitlement, 5, 43, 55, 63, 110, 113–114, 171, 215, 223, 230, 239
essentialism, 146, 148–149, 194
Evans, Gareth, 177, 234
examples, role in learning, 40–41, 43–46, 69, 81

Field, Hartry, 183
Fine, Kit, 193, 194, 245
first-person
　authority, 19–22, 105, 223, 229–230
　epistemology, 4, 19–22, 42–44, 103, 229–230, 233–235
　reference, 130, 134
Fodor, Jerry, 61, 79, 188
Fogelin, Robert, 142, 145
Foot, Philippa, 126
foundational
　inquiry, 6, 70, 161, 180
　theory of meaning, 9, 10, 76, 143, 149–151, 152, 181
Frege, Gottlob, 159, 221, 245–247
Friedman, Milton, 223

game(s), 99, 102–103, 121, 146, 190, 206–207, 226
Gibbard, Allan, 107, 111, 117, 132, 183
Ginsborg, Hannah, 4–5, 15, 17–34, 36, 38, 45, 51–53, 109, 120, 126, 151, 164, 176, 254
Glock, Hans-Johann, 126, 137
Glüer, Kathrin, 124, 126, 127, 149, 191
Goldfarb, Warren, 15, 17, 20, 69, 115–116, 121, 146, 153, 164
Graham, Peter, 132
Green, Derek, 124, 127
Greenspan, Patricia, 140
Guardo, Andrea, 189, 192
guidance, 10, 21, 105, 166, 174, 177

Haase, Matthias, 174
Hacker, P.M.S., 69
Haddock, Adrian, 126
Hale, Bob, 193, 194, 247
harmony, 13, 241, 244, 250, 252, 258
Hattiangadi, Anandi, 10–11, 38, 107, 125–127, 181, 183, 187, 189, 191, 193, 196–199, 254
Haugeland, John, 183
Hawthorne, John, 189, 197, 198
Hlobil, Ulf, 127
holism, 5, 56–60, 62, 65–68, 179, 180
Horgan, Terry, 24
Hornsby, Jennifer, 132

Horwich, Paul, 17, 107, 115, 151, 183, 207, 214, 256
Hume, David, 2, 212, 221, 245
Hurka, Thomas, 131

idealization, cognitive, 14, 23, 38, 60, 188, 190
(in)determinacy, 30, 50, 63–65, 68, 179, 198, 208, 248
individualism, 11–12, 47, 201–204, 210–212, 214–219
instructions, 41, 61–62, 70, 74, 80, 113–114, 158, 165, 197
intentionality, 1, 10–11, 25, 36, 38, 170–172, 181–188, 190–200, 217
interpersonalism, 11, 202–204, 210, 216–217

Jackman, Henry, 5–6, 57, 59, 62, 179
Jackson, Frank, 25, 184
Janssen-Lauret, Frederique, 77
Jones, Matthew, 124

Kant, Immanuel, 135
Kaplan, David, 149
Kearns, Stephen, 181, 184
Keefe, Rosanna, 64
Kersten, Daniel, 199
Körding, Konrad, 199
Kusch, Martin, 125, 232

Lance, Mark, 189
language-game(s), 87–88, 101, 103, 105, 123, 161, 240
Lepore, Ernie, 57
Leuenberger, Stephan, 185
Lewis, David, 6, 11, 17, 53, 57, 59, 74–79, 82, 85, 149, 187, 190, 192, 196–199
Lowe, Edward Johnathan, 193, 194
Lycan, William, 240
Lynch, Michael, 126

MacBride, Fraser, 77, 247
Mackie, J.L., 221
Magidor, Ofra, 181, 184
malapropisms, 47, 48, 50, 211, 213, 215, 217
Mallozzi, Antonella, 193, 194
Mancosu, Paolo, 246, 247
materialism, 10–11, 181–185, 187–188, 193–195, 200
McDowell, John, 22, 52, 69, 89, 92, 119, 125, 142, 152–153, 160, 166, 167, 176, 219

Index

McGinn, Colin, 15, 17, 20, 22, 28, 38, 45, 57, 69, 109, 126, 131, 164, 201
McGinn, Marie, 6–7, 105
McLaughlin, Brian, 57
McPherson, Tristram, 126
meaning, account of
  assertibility conditional, 12, 87–88, 121, 204, 212, 215, 241–245, 247–251, 256–258
  communitarian, 11, 101, 201, 203, 218–219, 231
  compatibilist, 12, 241–245, 247, 250–255, 257
  dispositional, 3, 5–7, 16–17, 56–61, 63, 65–68, 77–78, 114–118, 189–190
  interpretationist, 58, 74, 196–199
  judgement-(in)dependent, 22, 28
  mentalistic, 7, 75, 92, 147
  naturalistic, 3, 92, 99
  non-reductive, 3–4, 8–11, 20, 22, 27, 51, 94, 124–125, 143–144, 149–151, 157, 165–166, 169, 172, 192, 195
  reductive, 3, 38, 43, 53–54, 89, 106, 143–144, 148–149, 151–152, 157, 187, 191–192
  truth-conditional, 204, 213, 215, 221, 240–242, 250, 252, 257
memory, 27, 33, 38, 200
mental
  act, 96–98, 101, 175
  history, 16, 28–29
  representation, 95, 147, 158, 181, 183, 185
  state, 6–8, 38, 73–75, 77, 92, 95, 102, 105, 111, 118–120, 131, 190–192, 197, 234
metasemantic theory, 57–60, 62, 149–152, 161–162, 179
Millar, Alan, 8, 126–130, 138–141
Miller, Alexander, 4, 12, 30, 34, 53, 125–127, 173, 203, 233, 235, 237, 251–252
Millikan, Ruth, 17
minimal physical duplicate, 10, 11, 184–188, 190, 193, 199
modus ponens model, 169–171, 173, 178–179
Montero, Barbara, 185
Moore, G.E., 126
Moran, Alex, 185, 194
Moran, Richard, 231
Moyal-Sharrock, Danièle, 142
Myers, Robert, 48, 53, 159, 179, 214

Nagel, Thomas, 25
naive response, 5–6, 10, 57, 60–61, 74–76, 79–86, 114–115, 169, 178
naturalism, 7, 87–92, 94–95, 99, 96–102, 105–106
normativity, 4, 7–8, 20, 30–34, 37, 45–46, 60, 70, 79, 88–89, 92, 106, 108, 116–118, 124–130, 132–139, 141, 190–192, 195, 214, 232
norms of truth, 8, 125–127, 129, 132–135, 139, 141

Papineau, David, 127
Parfit, Derek, 126, 132
Peano, Giuseppe, 247
Pettit, Philip, 17
physicalism, 25, 38, 185, 194
Plato, 24, 89, 146
Pollock, John, 240, 243
practice, 8, 12, 78, 80, 89, 98–106, 115–116, 119–121, 123, 136, 140, 202–209, 216–219, 221, 224–225, 239
Price, Huw, 183
primitivism, 6, 8–11, 38, 51, 84, 119, 125, 160, 165–166, 171, 181–183, 199, 200
Putnam, Hilary, 24, 68, 198, 249

quietism, 7–9, 22, 89, 106, 142–144, 150, 152–154, 157, 162
Quine, W.V., 25, 30, 57, 59, 217, 219, 226, 227, 237, 243–249, 256

Rabinowicz, Wlodek, 197
radical interpretation, 5, 57, 196–199, 256–258
radical translation, 25, 256
reason-responsiveness, 170, 173, 176
regularity, 6, 69, 71–74, 79–81
Reiland, Indrek, 8, 126–131, 133–138
rigid designators, 188
Robinson Crusoe, 12, 208, 211, 227–231, 233, 237
Rosen, Gideon, 193–195
Ross, David, 135
Russell, Bertrand, 183, 247

sameness, 6, 69, 73, 75, 81, 82
Schiffer, Stephen, 35, 197
Schroeder, Mark, 126, 131, 132, 139
Schwarz, Wolfgang, 75–77
Searle, John, 25, 183
Setiya, Kieran, 140
Shaw, James R. 6, 53, 62, 69

Index

Sherman, Brett, 149
Sider, Theodore, 77
Skyrms, Brian, 226
Soames, Scott, 193
Sorensen, Roy, 64
Sorgiovanni, Ben, 53
Speaks, Jeff, 126, 149
Stalnaker, Robert, 149
Stevenson, Charles L., 221
Stroud, Barry, 125, 142, 164, 172, 178, 179, 254
Sultanescu, Olivia, 9–10, 34, 53, 59, 126, 157, 167, 203
supervenience, 10–11, 58, 67, 184–185, 187, 192, 196, 199
Sylvan, Kurt, 132

tabair, 2, 44, 61, 164–165
Tait, Sylvan, 69
Tenenbaum, Joshua, 199
Thornton, Tim, 125
Timmons, Mark, 24
Tracy, Eric, 127
triangulation, 48, 157, 179, 202, 217–218

uniformity, 6, 53, 69, 73–77, 79–86, 205

vagueness, 64, 85
Vaidya, Anand, 183, 193, 194
Verheggen, Claudine, 8–9, 34, 38, 48, 49, 53, 107, 123, 125, 126, 142, 144, 155, 157–160, 179, 202, 214
verificationism, 4, 22–23

Vogelstein, Eric, 132
von Humboldt, Wilhelm, 188

Wallace, R. Jay, 173
Wallner, Michael, 194
warrant, 7, 35, 104, 105, 108–118, 242
Warren, Jared, 116, 189, 192
Weatherson, Brian, 77
Whiting, Daniel, 8, 125, 126, 127, 131–134, 139
Wikforss, Åsa, 107, 124, 126, 127, 191
Williams, Bernard, 24, 121, 122
Williams, J. Robert G., 182, 197, 198
Williams, Meredith, 203, 209, 217, 219
Williamson, Timothy, 64, 133
Wilson, George, 17, 85, 121, 125, 149, 186
Wilson, N.L., 57
Wiseman, Rachael, 105
Wodak, Daniel, 126
Wolpert, Daniel M., 199
Woods, Jack, 126
Wright, Crispin, 4, 9, 10, 12, 15, 17, 19–24, 26–28, 89, 106, 153, 163, 167–173, 180, 187, 241, 243, 247

Yablo, Stephen, 193
Yuille, Alan, 199

Zalabardo, José L. 12–13, 17, 19–20, 107, 124, 186, 256, 258
Zhong, Lei, 125, 127
Zimmerman, Michael, 132
zombie, 11, 185–188, 192–193, 196, 199

For EU product safety concerns, contact us at Calle de José Abascal, 56–1°,
28003 Madrid, Spain or eugpsr@cambridge.org.

www.ingramcontent.com/pod-product-compliance
Ingram Content Group UK Ltd.
Pitfield, Milton Keynes, MK11 3LW, UK
UKHW040023090825
461685UK00024B/1397